WHAT'S RIGHT WITH FOOTBALL

BY JOHN D. BRIDGERS

EAKIN PRESS ★ Austin, Texas

FIRST EDITION

Copyright © 1995
By John D. Bridgers

Published in the United States of America
By Eakin Press
An Imprint of Sunbelt Media, Inc.
P.O. Drawer 90159   ★   Austin, TX 78709-0159

ISBN 1-57168-016-0

2   3   4   5   6   7   8   9   10

Library of Congress Cataloging-in-Publication Data

Bridgers, John D.
  What's right with football / written by John D. Bridgers.
      p.   cm.
  ISBN 1-57168-016-0
  1. Football — United States — History. I. Title.
GV959.5.U6B74   1995
796.332'0973--dc20   94-23632
                                                        CIP

This book is dedicated to all the football players I coached from the fall of 1945 in Germany through the fall of 1972 at the University of South Carolina. My active coaching covered a period of twenty-eight years with additional stops at Auburn University, University of the South at Sewanee, Tennessee, 1st Cavalry Division Artillery in Japan, Johns Hopkins University in Baltimore, the Baltimore Colts, Baylor University, and the Pittsburgh Steelers. The relationship with the players and the actual coaching were enjoyable in all those places. The players have been an inspiration in the last twenty-two years since I last coached. Ninety-nine percent of those coaching years were rewarding and provided me with satisfaction as well as interesting and fascinating experiences. I learned a lot from the players. I'll always cherish those coaching years, and I believe with very few exceptions the players I knew and coached received the same kind of rewards and satisfaction.

CONTENTS

PREFACE

For several years, and especially since my retirement as athletic director at the University of New Mexico in 1987, I have given serious thought to writing a book about the *good* side of college and professional football. There have been articles in the print media, and particularly in newspapers, for the past fifteen years or so enumerating, almost on a daily basis, the alleged sins, indiscretions, and flagrant violations of rules of conduct and legal regulations by college and professional athletes. An image has been created in the minds of many sports fans that college athletic programs are riddled with corruption and that most participants on college and professional teams are of questionable character and below average mentality.

My intent is not to feed controversy. However, sports reporters in all forms of media exaggerate the pervasiveness and seriousness of violations to such an extreme as to portray a false picture. If it is controversial to challenge such a view, then so be it!

I have a definite advantage over the average sports reporter in that for 37 years intercollegiate athletics has been my consuming interest and has provided a livelihood for my family. I spent an additional three years coaching in professional football, and my friendships with professional coaches and players have continued for the past 35 years.

Many sports reporters enjoy taking exception to the general rule that the great majority of college athletes are sincere and above board. Those exceptions are used to represent the general status of intercollegiate athletics. The media deliberately tries to create controversy, which is what sells to the general public. This is not to say that rules are not broken and ethical standards are not violated. My guess is that college and professional athletes have about the same percentage of violations of ethical standards and rules of conduct as the medical profession, law profession, or any other professional organizations.

Consider the facts as taken from the *Enforcement Summary*, a publication of the National Collegiate Athletic Association, which summarizes all public penalties to member institutions from October 1, 1952 to May 1, 1991. Penalties were not classified as major or minor until 1985, but Dick Schultz, executive director of NCAA, and David Berst, director of enforcement, agree that institutions receiving a penalty of two years or more probation may be the most accurate judgment of separating major violations from other violations in the period 1952 to 1985. Penalties of less than two years probation were for violations not considered as severe or there were mitigating circumstances which lessened the severity of the penalty.

From 1960 until 1992, 34 Division I-A institutions received major penalties or probation of two years or more which included a total of 52 penalties. There were 13 institutions which received more than one major penalty, while 21 had only one major penalty. That averages to only 1.6 violations per year in football and 1.6 institutions per year receiving a penalty for a major violation in the 106 Division I-A colleges and universities. Many of the violations of a less serious nature occurred through ignorance of the rules. I'm sure most coaches do not devote as much time as they should to learning NCAA rules. If all would consider the personal humiliation and embarrassment, as well as the potential embarrassment, to their institutions, I think more of them would take the rules more seriously.

Out of those 34 institutions receiving major penalties over a period of 32 years, I doubt if there were as many as ten players involved in each violation. However, if we consider ten players in the average violation, with an average of 1.6 violations a year, it would add up to an average of 16 players in the sport of football. Far more than 34 colleges or universities in football have made the headlines on the sports pages for alleged violations over a 32-year period, but after the investigations were completed, only a relatively few serious violations were found to be true or could be proven.

Until recently the Division I-A institutions have had a scholarship limit of 95 players. Perhaps the average Division I-A school has 85 players on scholarships due to attrition. For 106 Division I-A institutions there would be approximately 9,000 football players on scholarships. If an average of ten players were involved in each major violation, the percentage would be:

$$\frac{52 \ Violations \ x \ 10 \ Players}{32 \ years} = \frac{16.25 \ Avg. \ Players \ in \ Violations}{9,000 \ Avg. \ on \ Scholarship} \Rightarrow$$

$$0.18\% \ Avg. \ Players \\ w/ \ Violations$$

or slightly less than two per 1,000 players on scholarships involved in major rules violations per year.

Of course, the response might be that there are far more players guilty of major NCAA violations than are proven guilty. Having been a Division I-A athletic director for 24 years at three different institutions and responsible for conformity to NCAA rules at the institutions I served, I don't believe there are far more players guilty of serious violations than are caught. Even if there were more than five times as many, the percentage would still only be one percent of the total on scholarships for one year. There is also a misconception that a few schools are responsible for most of the violations. Actually, 13 different institutions were responsible for 31 violations over the 32-year period.

In this book I deal only with violations in the sport of football, although I feel well qualified to comment on the entire state of intercollegiate athletics.

From 1945 until June of 1987, a total of 42 years, I was a football coach and/or athletic director. My experience includes coaching football at the small college level (University of the South in Sewanee, Tennessee, and Johns Hopkins University in Baltimore, Maryland), at the major college level (Auburn University in Auburn, Alabama, Baylor University in Waco, Texas, and the University of South Carolina in Columbia), and at the professional level (Baltimore Colts in 1957 and 1958, and Pittsburgh Steelers in 1969). In 1958 the Colts won the World Championship against the New York Giants in what has been repeatedly voted by the media as "the greatest game ever played." I have also coached in seven college All-Star games, including the East-West game in San Francisco; the Blue-Gray game in Montgomery; the North-South game in Miami; and the All-American game in Buffalo.

I served 24 years as an athletic director (ten years at Baylor

University, seven years at Florida State University in Tallahassee, and seven and one-half years at the University of New Mexico in Albuquerque). I have been a member of the National Association of Collegiate Athletic Directors, was inducted into its Hall of Fame, and have religiously attended its conventions. I attended almost every NCAA convention from 1958 until 1987 and have participated in numerous coaching clinics where football coaches at every college level were present.

In the past 30 years, I've been acquainted with almost every athletic director at the Division I-A level and have spent a great deal of time with them both in meetings and in social settings. I have had friendships with Walter Byers, former executive director of the NCAA, as well as Dick Schultz, the executive director who held that office until late 1993. I was personally involved in two NCAA investigations, both resulting from incidents of violations prior to my association with the institutions under investigation.

Versatile experiences have given me a good insight, I believe, into the operations of the NCAA and college athletics. There is an added perspective from my pro-football coaching experience.

In this book I attempt to provide an insight into the misconceptions about ethical standards and rules violations. I shall also offer a view on the character and personal traits of well-known and famous athletes, as well as tell of some little-known athletes who showed courage, honesty, and dedication to reach heights far beyond realistic expectations. As a result, they not only achieved success as players but also inspired in teammates, coaches, and many people they came in contact with the will to go beyond themselves. They gained confidence and skills and continued to achieve success that was unrelated to athletic endeavors. Except in the NFL, my experiences have been with athletes who, for the most part, were not recognized as the cream of the crop.

This compilation is not a revelation, particularly, of championship teams, although there were a couple along the way. Rather, it is a reflection of why I believe participation in athletics at all levels can add to a person's confidence, competence, faith, unselfish spirit, and willingness to sacrifice for team goals. These traits are not automatic. As other factors creep in, such as selfishness, discouragement and jealousy, an unbalanced perspective of what is really important and what is not gradually develops.

A sense of humor is very helpful in a person surviving the stress and competitiveness of college and professional football. A great many of the most successful athletes and coaches I've known were able to laugh at themselves and others as they excelled in sports and life. It's important that an athlete, or any person for that matter, not take himself too seriously. You'll find many occasions in this book where a good laugh helped in achieving an important goal.

My secondary purpose in writing this book is to convey coaching philosophy, strategy, relationships between players and coaches, and teaching techniques. Religious faith can be, and is, an important factor in the life of many people. This is certainly true with a great many athletes. Although this is not a book on religion, I have no hesitation in recounting how religious faith and a strong belief in higher powers are important factors in the drive and success of a team or an individual.

A good criterion of whether football participation is good or bad is what happens to the young men who play, and how they judge the effect of their participation on their lives after their playing days are over. The men of whom I write are not much different from those other coaches have known. I could have chosen at least twice as many from those I have coached whose success, attitude, and character would have been comparable to the ones I have written about. I'm not saying that there is a success rate of 100%. There are always those who suffer from discouragement, disappointment, injury, lack of ability or interest, and more. Still, the majority have very positive attitudes toward life which were greatly enhanced by playing experiences.

Many people think football is dangerous, that players go through life suffering from football injuries. In my 28 years of coaching I can't recall a single player who was greatly handicapped by serious injury in the years after playing football. Some have had knee or joint injuries, which were a bother at times, but I know of none who have been prevented from playing golf, tennis, jogging, or participating in other sports.

Some have commented that unless a person has played the game (as Howard Cosell did not), he cannot really understand the impact football has upon the players' lives and memories. Whether their chosen occupations turned out to be as lawyers, dentists, medical doctors, businessmen, college professors or ministers, their fondest and most vivid memories tend to be of their football experiences.

Dr. Ronnie Rogers, now an oral surgeon in Garland, Texas, was an outstanding lineman at Baylor. At 5'7 and 185 pounds, he was a starter and standout on winning teams against LSU in the 1963 Bluebonnet Bowl and against undefeated, 10th-ranked Utah State in the 1961 Gotham Bowl. "There were no negatives about the experience (playing college football) for me," said Dr. Rogers.

The system of college football is certainly not perfect, and never will be. But the comparison of the number of players who do well and who look back on their participation with a great deal of pride and gratitude for the opportunity to have played is far, far greater than the number who look back with regret and wish they had never participated.

A final note: As I discuss football players at Baltimore, Baylor, Johns Hopkins, and Sewanee, I am writing about players who were special people to me and whom I had the privilege of coaching. I believe the game of football helped make the players I write about very special. Yet I have no doubt that there are players at the present time and in recent times who are similar to the players I write about — men who have overcome obstacles, worked very hard to develop their athletic ability, acquired special qualities of leadership, and distinguished themselves in the sport of football and in the hearts and minds of their coaches, their teammates, and all who have known them well. At the same time, depending on the level of their competition, they have served as role models for many young people in their own communities and in some cases for young people throughout the country. They have inspired and challenged youth to develop their own talents and achieve what seemed to be impossible goals.

Football has produced numerous heroes. I don't think anyone can deny that the kind of men I write about and many others coached by other coaches represent the kind of people who have been leaders and achievers in almost every profession. But football by no means has a corner on producing such heroes. There are almost countless ways leaders and achievers in areas other than football can surface. My focus, however, is on those I knew well as a football coach. Today the heroes in professional football may be John Elway, Dan Marino, Reggie White, Steve Young, Emmitt Smith, Joe Montana, Barry Sanders, Jerry Rice, and Art Monk, among many others, but you will find that they have many traits in common with the heroes of 30 years ago in college and professional football.

CHAPTER 1

1945

HOW COACHING ENTERED MY LIFE

My twin brother, Frank, and I were as close as two brothers could be. We both had football scholarships at Auburn University. Frank was a mechanical engineering major and I majored in business administration. We are identical twins, and neither our college nor our high school coach could tell us apart. Our college coach was Jack Meagher, a graduate of Notre Dame, who was a very knowledgeable coach and a real gentleman. Some of the sportswriters called him "Gentleman Jack Meagher."

Frank and I knew football and were very sound fundamentally. Our disadvantage was that we were "small but slow." We were fairly quick, but we didn't look anything like the college linemen you might see at Auburn University today.

Our experience was very limited at the varsity level, but from the fall of 1940 until we both were called to active duty in the army on April 20, 1943, we played freshman football and competed for varsity football positions in the 1941 and 1942 seasons. Frank and I were both honor students at Auburn. I believe it is one of the myths of college football that a player with anywhere near reasonable qualifications cannot study and make passing grades because of the de-

1

mands of practice and team meetings. Frank ended up getting his engineering degree in one-quarter less than the standard four academic years.

Frank served in China working under Gen. Joe Stillwell's Command, and I ended up in Germany when the war came to an end in May of 1945.

I was assigned as athletic officer for the 84th Field Artillery Battalion. We organized softball and volleyball leagues. It was something that the troops seemed to really enjoy, and the competition was very keen.

The 9th Infantry Division announced a division track meet. I organized a track team in our battalion which consisted of about 600 men and represented the 9th Infantry Division Artillery in the meet, competing against regimental teams and special troops consisting of about 3,000 men each. We finished second, which was a good achievement.

When summer came, a division baseball league was organized and I was named as the baseball coach. We had two excellent players. One was a pitcher who had pitched in the Pacific Coast League, whose name I can't remember. The other was a catcher, whose name was Stan Lopata. Stan was 6'4 and 220 pounds and an outstanding athlete. I was a playing coach and the only officer on the team. My most vivid memory was that almost every time I came to bat, the enlisted men attending the game would holler, "Hit the lieutenant in the head!" I don't remember how we finished in the division baseball league. If we had won a championship, I think I would have remembered. I do remember I got through the season without being hit in the head.

As fall approached, I became the head football coach for the 9th Division Artillery team. This was the beginning of my career as a football coach. I went through the personnel records of division artillery, talked to the officers in each battery about their best athletes, and came up with the names of about 45 prospects. I found out which ones wanted to play and got permission from their commanding officers to put them on temporary duty as members of the 9th Division Artillery football team. My best recruiting was to convince Stan Lopata, the catcher on our baseball team, to play football. His family would not let him play in high school because they felt he had a major league career ahead of him in baseball. They were right, as

Stan later was a catcher for the Philadelphia Phillies for about ten years. He was on the team known as the "Whizz Kids," which won the National League pennant in the early fifties. While I enjoyed my job as athletic officer in organizing and supervising athletic leagues and coaching track and baseball teams, I was really in my glory coaching football.

One of the things I had going for me was a great memory for football plays. I remembered all the running and passing plays of Ramsay High School in Birmingham, Alabama. I also remembered the plays and blocking assignments we had at Auburn. At Ramsay we ran the Tennessee single wing and were undefeated in 1939, scoring 234 points to our opponents' 12. The only blemish on our record was a tie (6-6) with our arch-rival, Phillips High School of Birmingham. Our high school coach, Bill "Cannonball" White, demanded that each player be able to diagram every play with assignment of each player. All football players had a gym class the last period of school, and Coach White used that time for a meeting. He would call on a player to diagram a specific play on the blackboard in front of the entire squad. If the player failed to diagram the play correctly, he just didn't play until he learned to diagram the play perfectly. I believe that was one of the real keys to our success — all of our players knew exactly what we were supposed to do on every offensive play and every defensive formation.

I decided that our division artillery team would use the "T" formation plays that Auburn used in 1942. At that time Auburn ran the "T" and the Notre Dame Box, which is a variation of the single wing. Our "T" formation plays were primarily responsible for our shocking upset of the University of Georgia when we beat them 27-13 in 1942. Georgia was undefeated and ranked No. 1 in the nation. They were the only college team in history to have a Heisman Trophy winner and a Pro Football Hall of Famer in the same backfield. Their names were Frankie Sinkwich and Charley Trippi. The loss to Auburn was their only loss of the season, and they won the Rose Bowl against California.

The team showed a good response and practiced with good spirit and enthusiasm. There are a lot of things about football which are sheer drudgery. My approach was to make practice as much fun as possible and to instill as much confidence in the players as possible, particularly in teaching tackling and blocking. We limited the amount of full-speed scrimmage and emphasized technique and confidence.

After about three weeks of practice, I decided we needed a game before we started competition in our division league. I was able to arrange a game with the 3rd Infantry Division at their home base. I became aware that the Air Force would fly an athletic team if planes and pilots were available, and so I arranged transportation with them. The 3rd Infantry Division was located in West Germany, which was about 500 miles from Erding, Germany, where our headquarters was located (about 100 miles east of Munich). A division team draws from approximately 15,000 troops, while division artillery consisted of about 2,500 soldiers. Several of the officers said I was very foolish to schedule the game as we would probably get badly beaten.

We played the 3rd Infantry Division a very good game but were finally beaten by a score of 13-7. Our touchdown was scored on a 50-yard pass and run play by Stan Lopata, the future Phillies catcher. It was the first game Stan ever played, and he was our outstanding player. Even though we lost to a team with superior manpower, we were proud of our performance and were established as favorites to win the 9th Infantry Division Football Championship.

The game taught me that a great athlete is worth a lot of coaching. I remember I worked with Stan Lopata on his blocking technique. About the third or fourth time he tried a shoulder block, he was executing as well or better than anyone on our team. I never coached a tight end at Baylor or the University of South Carolina who had as much ability as Stan Lopata.

About the time we played the 3rd Infantry Division, the 9th Infantry Division had a team practicing to compete in the Third Army Football Conference. When we flew back after the game with the 3rd Infantry, our division team immediately demanded that we send about six or eight of our outstanding players to the division team. The division coaches didn't know a single player on our team existed until we played the 3rd Infantry such a good game. The players whom they wished to draft wanted to play for our division artillery team, and, of course, I wanted them to play for the 9th Division Artillery team also.

I took my case to the division artillery executive officer. I was arguing with a full bird colonel. Guess who won? As a result, several

of our players went to the division team, and the colonel repri-
manded me for not being cooperative and dismissed me as football
coach. It was a mistake to schedule the 3rd Infantry Division team.
If we had not played them, our division coaches would have never
known how good some of our players were. I'm not sure how the
division artillery finished in the division football league, but I seem
to have a faint recollection they finished second.

I spent the rest of the fall on special assignment chasing down
witnesses to war crimes. My first football coaching job had lasted
one game, and I was very disappointed. However, the experience
convinced me that I wanted to be a football coach. I was able to
coach football for the next 27 years, which included eight different
teams.

There was quite a contrast in my personal morale while I was
athletic officer and coach compared to my experience during combat as a replacement officer and being transported to the European
Theater. The kind of exhilaration and confidence I felt as a coach
and athletic officer, compared to the extreme stress and pressure I
felt as a replacement officer and forward observer in one of the truly
elite divisions, had a lot to do with me deciding I wanted to be a
coach.

I went into combat with very little experience at directing artillery fire, which is the primary duty of a forward observer. I received
probably a better rating than I deserved during combat. There were
many times I felt fear, which I know was also true of 90% of the
soldiers who had similar experiences; but despite my fear, I followed
orders and always did my job to the best of my ability. When a replacement officer joins an experienced combat unit during a live
combat situation, there is no time to cultivate friendships. It's a
lonely feeling, and it takes some time to adjust.

A summary of my experiences of being transported to the European Theater and my combat experience might help clarify just
how I felt. After finishing Officer Candidate School, I had brief assignments with the 87th Infantry Division at Ft. Jackson, South
Carolina, and the 71st Infantry Division in Columbus, Georgia. Not
long before Christmas of 1944, I reported to the Boston Port of
Embarkation for shipment to the European Theater of Operations
as a replacement officer.

The following four and one-half to five months were the

toughest of my life. When I arrived in Boston, I had instructions to report to the finance officer. There I was told that I would serve as finance officer for some 5,000 replacement troops on the liberty ship, which was part of a convoy sailing for the European Theater. My instructions were to make a partial payroll payment to troops aboard ship. I told them I didn't know anything about being a finance officer, so they gave me a copy of the army regulations for me to figure it out. Then I was handed a money bag containing $25,000 in $5 bills. When we boarded the ship, I asked the captain if I might leave the $25,000 in the ship's safe. He said that I could, but he could not be responsible for it since there were a number of people who had access to the safe and there was no way he could lock the cash bag separately from the other contents in the safe.

In addition to worrying about whether I was going to spend a good part of my life paying back $25,000 to the U.S. Army, our convoy was being chased by German submarines. Our ship, and others in the convoy, were releasing depth charges to destroy the submarines. It kept us a little on edge hearing the explosion of the depth charges and wondering if a torpedo from a submarine might hit our ship.

To add to our tension, we were in violent storms for most of the trip. The ship was rolling to such a degree that hot meals could not be prepared for several days. Not many aboard wanted to eat, as a large percentage were seasick. You might imagine the stench in the hold of the ship where the seasick enlisted men were throwing up constantly. The few officers aboard had to take turns on duty in the hold. We just needed to remember how lucky we were not to have to stay in the hold for the entire trip.

We finally landed in Le Havre, France. Somehow I had prepared a payroll and given the soldiers aboard a partial payday. It was a great relief to turn in the money bag with the remaining cash and payrolls to army personnel in Le Havre.

The train tracks were only about half a mile from the wharf where we landed. A train had backed up on the tracks with boxcars. That was our transportation. We marched from the ship to the boxcars, carrying our duffle bags. About six inches of snow was on the ground, and the footing was very slippery. A couple of days after we packed into the boxcars like sardines, we arrived at a replacement depot in Belgium.

The artillery officers were told there was a shortage of infantry second lieutenants after the Battle of the Bulge and that the artillery officers would be used as infantry platoon leaders. We were given carbines, which are small automatic rifles, and told we had to zero them in using the snow-covered range. None of us had any training whatsoever as infantry platoon leaders, and we certainly didn't want to gain our first experience with German soldiers shooting at us. For some reason those in command changed their minds. I was assigned to Battery C, 84th Field Artillery Battalion of the 9th Infantry Division, during the latter part of January.

The 9th had fought in Africa, invaded Sicily, and then traveled to England to prepare for the D-Day invasion of France. The battery commander, Capt. Bill Mauser, had been born in Germany, but his family had immigrated to the U.S. and settled in Cleveland. He had a nasty disposition but was an excellent officer. I didn't like him at first, but as time went by, I grew to admire and respect him.

When you prepare for battle, just as you prepare for a football game, you hope to go into the contest well rested, mentally sharp, and confident of your preparation. Such was not the case with me after a stressful trip across the Atlantic, a couple of days in boxcars, and being threatened with a transfer to the infantry. My assignment was as a forward observer. I replaced a lieutenant who suffered combat fatigue (some called it shell-shock). A forward observer normally went with the attack company of the infantry. It was the most dangerous job in the artillery. Another lieutenant, Pete Rice, who now lives in Dallas, and I took turns going forward with the 47th Infantry Regiment and four or five days at a time as a forward observer. When I joined, our division was on the edge of the Hurtgen Forest, where some of the fiercest fighting in World War II took place.

The 9th was constantly on the offensive and ended up on the Elbe River, about 40 miles from Berlin. I had a number of close calls from artillery and mortar shells, and once a German machine gun kicked dirt in my face as we were pinned down in an attack on a German position. I received a Purple Heart from a shell fragment in my shoulder when our battalion became the first artillery unit across the Rhine River at the Remagen Bridge. I had hoped to get a day or two of rest from having been wounded, but the medic sprinkled some sulfa powder, put a bandage on my shoulder, and patted me on the butt as he told me to go back to my outfit. I got back in time to jump off on an attack before dawn as a forward observer. We began to fight our way out of the bridgehead and head deep into Germany. If we had a day off before the Germans surrendered, I don't remember it.

A week or so before the Germans surrendered, the 47th Infantry Regiment at that time was attached to the 3rd Armored Division. We made a combat patrol of about 30 miles and were to advance east, turn north, and then head back to our base. I was in a jeep with my driver, reconnaissance sergeant, and radio operator. Our assignment was to provide artillery support if needed. As we approached a small village, we were being heavily shelled by artillery fire. Shell fragments hit our jeep and injured Daniels, our reconnaissance sergeant. The jeep would barely run and was missing badly. After we had reached the village, I asked Gatewood, our driver, if he could find his way back to our base camp. He assured me he could. The medics took Daniels back for further treatment, although his injury was not life-threatening.

We were able to get another jeep from the 3rd Armored, and Wallace, my radio operator, and I continued on the combat patrol. When we reached the base camp, our jeep driver had not returned. The next morning Wallace and I retraced our route to look for Gatewood and the jeep. We hoped that our combat patrol had flushed all the German troops from the area.

At an intersection where we had made a left turn to the north we saw some German civilians. I asked them if they had seen an American jeep. They told us they had seen a jeep and driver go through the intersection. He had failed to make the right turn which led back to our base camp. Several SS soldiers (the German elite troops) fired on Gatewood as he attempted to flee in the jeep. They shot him in both legs and left him lying in the road. The SS troopers took the jeep, but since it would barely run they took it behind a nearby barn and axed the tires and the engine and left it. It was a good thing the SS troopers had left or they might have had another jeep that ran well. The German civilians said that American medics had picked up Gatewood. We didn't see Sergeant Daniels or Corporal Gatewood again, but we learned that they made it safely back to the States.

In my last three or four months in Germany, I was the only

officer in my battery, which had a normal strength of five officers. We had the responsibility of running and manning outposts on the German-Swiss border. We were also very much understaffed with noncommissioned officers.

There was a significant drop in the morale and efficiency of the noncommissioned officers, and the average soldier as well. The efficiency of the division reached its lowest ebb in April, May, and June of 1946, after almost all of those who had been in combat had rotated back to the States. Their replacements, for the most part, were late draftees who were assigned to be part of the occupation army in Germany or Japan. The 3rd Army headquarters, corps headquarters, division headquarters, and division artillery headquarters had pretty much siphoned off the best soldiers and noncommissioned officers. The leftovers came down to the combat units at the battery level.

I remained in Germany in the occupation army until June of 1946, when my turn to go home for discharge finally came up.

I was head coach of the 9th Division Artillery basketball team in the winter of 1945–46, but it became clear that I was not a basketball coach. My first objective after I returned to the States was to finish the degree I had begun at Auburn in 1940.

CHAPTER 2

1940–47

AUBURN UNIVERSITY: STUDENT, FOOTBALL PLAYER, AND STUDENT COACH

During our high school years at Ramsay, my brother Frank and I always wanted to go to Auburn. In our senior year our high school team was undefeated.

We had visited Auburn once when our high school baseball team played the Auburn freshmen. Also, Vick Costellos, who had been co-captain of our 1937 Ramsay team, was at Auburn on a football scholarship. He was a guard and an outstanding player and leader on our high school team that had won eight straight games after losing the opening game in 1937. He was a player we both admired and looked up to.

In January of 1940 we were invited by Coach Meagher to visit Auburn and have a tryout on a Saturday. Auburn had invited more players than they could handle, so they asked if any of the prospects could stay over until Monday. Frank and I volunteered, as we thought we might have a better chance with a smaller group. During the weekend Frank became sick with a fever, sore throat, and cold. He didn't want to tell the coaches or miss the tryout, being afraid he might not get another opportunity.

The tryouts consisted of running, catching passes, and for linemen, blocking the assistant coaches and what was called 2-on-1, where two offensive linemen blocked a defensive lineman with a back running the ball inside two dummies set about five yards apart.

Since Frank was sick, about every other turn I would take his place on the line of players waiting to block the coaches. I would be Frank one time and John the next. Since we were identical twins, the coaches couldn't tell us apart. After I had blocked once as Frank and the next time as John, one of the coaches said, "Those Bridgers twins block exactly alike."

When we had 2-on-1, I was a defensive lineman against two of the top line prospects in the state. It was a favorite drill for our high school coach and I had probably played 2-on-1 more than all the linemen at the tryout. Success depends a great deal on technique rather than size and athletic ability. I beat the two linemen about three straight times and made the tackle at the line of scrimmage. Later I was Frank on defense and repeated the same performance. It was perhaps my best day as an Auburn lineman! We both were offered four-year scholarships.

During our last two years of grade school and through high school, Frank and I lived with our mother in a one-room efficiency apartment in Birmingham, Alabama. Mom had been single since 1928, when she and our father divorced. He had remarried and had two more children, and died of heart failure in September of 1942. Frank and I slept together in a Murphy bed, which pulled down from a closet, while Mom slept on a couch. When we entered Auburn in September of 1940, we moved up to a one-bedroom apartment. Mom gave us the bedroom, and she still slept on the couch. She supported the three of us as a secretary in the Internal Revenue Department.

In the fall of 1946, after the war, I re-entered Auburn to finish my degree, and Frank went to Purdue University Graduate School in mechanical engineering. When I registered at Auburn for the fall quarter, I went to see Coach Carl Voyles, head football coach at Auburn. Auburn had dropped football in 1943 and 1944 due to the war. Voyles was hired as head coach in 1945 after a successful stay as head coach at William and Mary College in Virginia.

Even though I had eligibility left, I had no desire to play football. I had become a fairly heavy smoker in the army. Not knowing when I might rotate to the States and having been assigned more military duties than I could handle, I had no motivation or time to get myself in top physical condition to play football.

Coach Voyles gave me an opportunity to be assistant coach for the Auburn "B" team. During the war years, freshmen were made eligible for varsity competition. As a result there were over 100 football players on the Auburn squad. Dan McMullen was the head "B" team coach. He was an experienced coach and had played professional football. I worked with the offensive and defensive interior linemen.

Our "B" team was scheduled to play another southeastern university's "B" team on Thanksgiving Day in Talladega, Alabama. For some reason, the other team canceled out on the game. Since the Auburn alumni in Talladega had made comprehensive plans for the game, including a Thanksgiving dinner after the game for players of both teams, it was decided we would play an intrasquad game as a substitute for the canceled game.

Coach Dan McMullen was to coach one team, and I would coach the other team. Since the "B" team had another game on the schedule, Dan McMullen decided it would be better if they kept their first two teams intact, and I would take the third and fourth teams. The Auburn varsity offense was run from an unbalanced line single wing, which was the same offense employed by the "B" team. I decided to use the "T" formation plays Auburn used to beat Georgia in 1942. Our team had everything to win and nothing to lose since the "B" team regulars were heavily favored to win. I convinced our players this was their opportunity to show that the "B" team coaches had underrated them. I told them they were as good, and I thought better, than the players ranked above them. Although the game was important to my scrub players, it was just an "intrasquad scrimmage" to the top ranking players.

Just before the kickoff, my team huddled on the sidelines. I told them an off-color Thanksgiving joke which appealed to a person who considered himself a "leftover." I'm sure the spectators were surprised to see one of the teams in uncontrollable laughter on the sidelines just before the kickoff.

The game was no contest. Our group of leftovers completely dominated the game. We scored early and ended up winning by two or three touchdowns. For our team, winning that game made the season worthwhile and provided a good example of how a sense of humor and some laughter can help a team win. In a real game situation our leftovers had proven they could outplay and win against a team rated much better than themselves by their own head coach.

For me, pulling off that one win gave me more confidence as a coach and convinced me that I wanted to make it my life's work.

Dean Roger Allen, who had been my freshman chemistry professor, had become dean of the School of Arts and Sciences, which included, at that time, the School of Business Administration. He was an outstanding teacher and administrator, a warm and genuinely good person. I had met with him two or three times, and he strongly urged me to go to graduate school.

My grades were better than I had any right to expect them to be. I had a pretty good instinct for figuring out what a professor would ask on an examination. I was awarded the Delta Sigma Pi Scholarship Key for the highest four-year average in business administration. My average was 3.72 in all courses. In business courses I had all A's except one C, when I failed an income tax accounting course final exam. The book was about six inches thick and I did a poor job of anticipating the test questions. The professor asked a couple of questions from the footnotes, which I failed to read.

I told Dean Allen that I wanted to coach football, and he discouraged me. At that time Dean Allen was NCAA faculty representative for Auburn and had a greater knowledge of intercollegiate athletics than most faculty people. He said he didn't know if a coach at that time could be completely honest and succeed. In the postwar years there was probably more cheating in college football than at any other time at the major college level. The National Collegiate Athletic Association wasn't a strong organization, and recruiting rules were not nearly as comprehensive as they are today.

The NCAA is an organization comprising member colleges and universities around the country. The representatives of the colleges and universities make up the legislative body of the NCAA. For the most part, they are on the faculty of the member institutions. There is no question that they pass some bad rules, and some on the knit-picking side, but the member colleges and universities pass the rules — not some power-laden group residing in Mission, Kansas.

I decided then that if I ever did become a college coach I would be 100% honest with my players and that I would not knowingly break an NCAA rule.

Dean Allen offered me a job as a full-time economics instructor in the School of Business for the spring and summer quarters after I graduated in March. I had three classes a day for five days a week teaching Principles of Economics. In the spring quarter I kept a chapter ahead of the students. I was pretty bad in my first class of the first day, a little better the second time I taught the same material that day, and pretty good the third time around. My pay was $200 a month, and I thought I was being well paid. In the summer quarter I did a better job, although I did not receive any awards for teaching economics.

One of my clear memories is a joke one of my teaching colleagues told me. These two economics professors were discussing their classes at lunch. One asked the other, "How did your class go today?" The other replied, "It went pretty good. We were discussing the theory of diminishing utility, and for a minute, I thought I had it myself."

There were a number of football players at Auburn who were excellent football players, good students, who pursued successful careers and lives after their playing days. But there is one particular player, whom I knew well from my high school days, that I will cover in the following chapter. I believe you will find his story inspirational. He is Vick Costellos, a guard who was captain of the 1942 Auburn football team.

CHAPTER 3

VICK COSTELLOS, GUARD: RAMSAY HIGH SCHOOL AND AUBURN UNIVERSITY

At 14, Vick Costellos showed no inclination of wanting an education. He was doing so poorly in school his father sent him off to a Catholic school in Cullman, Alabama, hoping the priests could help him. He stayed there for a couple of years, but somewhere along the way he quit school and ran away to live in New Orleans.

Among other odd jobs, he fought in night clubs where they would match fighters, and the winner would get the total purse of $10 to $15. I'm not sure where he learned to box — maybe in Cullman while he was attending the Catholic school — but he learned well.

After a period of time, Costellos went back to Birmingham. Someone told Coach Bill White, who was head coach at Ramsay, that Vick was a good athlete. Coach White contacted him and convinced him he should return to school and get his high school diploma and play football. I'm not sure whether it was the attraction of getting a high school diploma or the opportunity to play high school football under a great coach, but, at any rate, Vick enrolled at Ramsay in 1936. He became an outstanding player as a guard for the 1936 Ramsay High School Rams.

They called him the "Wild Greek." He was completely fearless and played with an abandon that ignored the welfare of his body. He wasn't big — 5'11 and 170 pounds — but he *played* big.

During that year Frank, my twin brother, and I were freshmen. Vick Costellos was our hero. He not only played well but was the best leader of any player I've ever known. He was always positive with his teammates, encouraging them, telling them how good they were and telling them what they had to do to win. Costellos wasn't a 17-year-old, he was 19 (almost 20) as a junior in high school. Despite his performance and leadership, our team had a very mediocre season. We ended up with a 4-5 record.

In 1937 our team was determined to come back with a good season. Our opening game was with Woodlawn High School in Birmingham, a school with a tradition for excellence in football. Among the standouts from Woodlawn were Harry Gilmer, quarterback, and Holt Rast, end, both of whom were All-Americans at the University of Alabama, and later Bobby Bowden, the highly successful football coach at Florida State University.

Woodlawn beat Ramsay 12-0 in our opening game. Bill White, our coach, was extremely disappointed. Among other mistakes, Coach White felt our linebacker play was inadequate. He called a practice early Saturday morning after our Friday night game and was determined to find a couple of linebackers who could do the job. Coach White had a full-speed tackling drill and made a decision on his inside linebackers. He chose Vick Costellos and Jim Lynch, who was a strong, aggressive player but not a very nifty runner at fullback.

It turned out to be a wise move. Ramsay won their next eight games and finished the regular season 8-1. Vick Costellos was the team leader in tackles.

Ramsay High School was named for a philanthropist who had come from western Pennsylvania to Birmingham. A high school in Mt. Pleasant, Pennsylvania, about 60 miles east of Pittsburgh, was also named for Erskine Ramsay. The Mt. Pleasant Ramsay had gone undefeated, and someone came up with the idea of having the two Ramsay teams play each other. Vick Costellos was ruled ineligible, as the age limit for high school football was 21 at that time, and he had turned 21 after our last regular season game.

The game was played in Birmingham at Legion Field, where Alabama and Auburn played several games during their football season. The Mt. Pleasant Ramsay had some excellent players, but they were no match for the Birmingham Ramsay. Heyward Allen, our tailback, had another of several outstanding days during the season passing the football. Ramsay of Birmingham won easily, 31-7.

Coach White was always coming up with an idea of how to supplement his meager football budget. After football season he planned to have Vick Costellos box the Southern Golden Gloves light-heavyweight champion in a match in the lunchroom at Ramsay and charge the students for admission.

Pete Sarron, who was probably Birmingham's only professional boxing champion, was the retired former Featherweight Champion of the World. He was training Lambert, who was the Southern Golden Gloves Champion. Sarron called Coach White and expressed his concern that Lambert might be too much for one of our football players to box. Coach White told Sarron that he had a football player who could take care of himself and not to worry about him being overmatched.

We had a crowded lunchroom for the boxing match. When the bell rang for the first round, Vick Costellos hit Lambert with about four left jabs that obviously stung Lambert. Then Costellos caught Lambert with a right uppercut, which almost lifted him off his feet. Lambert was out cold, and it took his handler several minutes to revive him.

Of course, all the Ramsay football players were very proud of Vick. It was a shock to Petey Sarron that a Ramsay football player who had no background as a boxer in Birmingham could easily defeat the light heavyweight Southern Golden Gloves champion.

Vick Costellos was named to the Alabama All-State football team, as were Heyward Allen, our tailback, a gifted passer and classy runner, and Charley Sanders, a 6'2, 200-pound tackle, who was also our punter. Allen was also named to the All-Southern team.

The remarkable follow-up story on these three football players is that each became captain of a Southeastern Conference football team. They decided, when they found that a number of major colleges in the South wanted to recruit them, that they would like to attend the same college together. However, neither Georgia Tech nor the University of Georgia were interested in Costellos, who was small for a Southeastern Conference guard.

Heyward Allen went to Georgia and Charley Sanders, who was

a good student, went to Georgia Tech. Auburn offered Costellos a scholarship, and that's where he went.

In 1941, his senior year, Heyward Allen was elected captain by his teammates. Frankie Sinkwich, a junior tailback, was their outstanding player, even though Allen started several games and was the team leader.

In the same year Charley Sanders made the Georgia Tech team and was also their punter. He was elected captain in 1941.

Vick Costellos was a freshman in 1938 and was red-shirted in 1939, leaving him three additional years of eligibility. He played little, if any, in 1940 and was a reserve guard in 1941, but played enough to letter.

Frank, my twin, and I had signed a letter of intent to attend Auburn the following fall. We visited Auburn that spring to watch a spring practice scrimmage. We both studied Vick Costellos in the scrimmage. We thought he played extremely well. He used a forearm lift underneath the shoulders of the opposing blocker to neutralize the blocker and then reacted to the ball. However, Vick played very little that fall.

In 1941, when Coach Jack Meagher, the Auburn head coach, called the lettermen together to select a captain for the 1942 season, Vick Costellos was the surprise choice of the vote by the returning lettermen for the 1942 Auburn team captain. I believe it was a shock to the coaching staff, as there were a number of returning starters from the 1941 team that could have been chosen captain. At any rate, Vick Costellos was a starter at right guard and captain of the 1942 Auburn team. The Auburn Tigers started slowly, which was fairly typical of Jack Meagher-coached teams.

After the first seven games we had three wins, three losses and a tie, but an encouraging factor was that we had limited the opposition to 7.7 points per game, which included four Southeastern Conference teams.

In our eighth game we ran into a buzz saw. We played the Georgia Naval Pre-Flight School in Columbus, Georgia. Their team included many former All-Americans and All-Conference players from universities all over the country. They beat us 41-14 and made it look easy.

The next week we played LSU in Birmingham. Vick Costellos broke through the LSU line and blocked a punt which led to our first touchdown. Monk Gafford, one of the best runners in Auburn history, outplayed Alvin Dark, the LSU tailback, who later gained fame as a big league baseball player and big league manager. We won 25-7 in an upset in Birmingham.

The next week we played Georgia in Columbus. Georgia was undefeated and untied and ranked number-one in the nation. They were a four-touchdown favorite to beat us. At that time we played Georgia every year in Columbus. The previous year Georgia had scored in the final minute on about a 70-yard pass from Frankie Sinkwich to Lamar Davis to edge us 7-0.

One of Coach Jack Meagher's strong points was that he always showed great confidence in his players. I can remember after our last practice he called the team up and said, "All right men, we all know Georgia was very lucky to beat us last year. We had the better team and outplayed them throughout the game until they hit on a lucky pass. We have a better team this year and we are going to beat them in Columbus Saturday."

Vick Costellos was a particularly inspirational leader that week in practice. He kept assuring his teammates we could beat Georgia. His optimism was contagious, and I believe almost every one of our players believed we could win.

We kicked off to Georgia to start the game, and they immediately drove the length of the field to score a touchdown and take a 7-0 lead.

After that the Auburn team took complete control of the game. Monk Gafford ran like an All-American and outgained the combined yardage of Georgia's two great backs, Frank Sinkwich, who made Consensus All-American two consecutive years (in 1941 and 1942), and Charley Trippi, who made Consensus All-American in 1946 after a couple of years in the service.

Vick Costellos and the Auburn line played inspired football as the line opened big holes on offense and held Georgia scoreless until late in the fourth quarter while Gafford and his teammates ran up a 27-7 lead. Georgia scored late to make the score 27-13. The Auburn victory was perhaps the biggest upset in Auburn history. Coach Jack Meagher, Vick Costellos, and others made believers out of the Auburn players that day.

Georgia beat undefeated Georgia Tech the next week, 35-0, and went on to win the Rose Bowl by 9-0 over UCLA. Auburn ended the season with a third consecutive win, as we easily defeated Clemson (41-13) in Auburn.

A 6-4-1 record wasn't that impressive, but we ended the season on a performance level that would have made it difficult for any team to beat us.

Vick Costellos never weighed over 175 to 180 pounds as a player at Auburn, and while I may have some prejudice, I believe he is the finest leader on and off the field of any player I've been associated with as a player and coach. That's quite an achievement for a high school dropout who ran away from home.

Vick died of cancer in November 1980. He worked for over 20 years as a beer distributor in Birmingham.

I talked to his wife recently, and she said, "Vick gave all the credit to Coach Bill White for his being able to turn around his life, play football, get a college scholarship and earn a degree in business administration at Auburn University."

Vick Costellos is another excellent example of the kind of influence that football and a fine coach can have on a young man's life.

CHAPTER 4

1947–51

SEWANEE, THE UNIVERSITY OF THE SOUTH: MY FIRST FULL-TIME COACHING JOB

In July of 1947 I had a phone call from my high school football coach, Bill "Cannonball" White, who was then head football coach at the University of the South in Sewanee, Tennessee. He had a coaching position open and wanted me to apply. I jumped at the opportunity. Sewanee, as it was commonly called, is an outstanding liberal arts school with a graduate program in the School of Theology to prepare graduate students as ministers in the Episcopalian Church.

Sewanee is located atop a ridge in the Cumberland Mountains about halfway between Nashville and Chattanooga, Tennessee. Sewanee has a rich football tradition. At the turn of the century, Sewanee had one of the best teams in the South. The 1899 Sewanee team was one of the most amazing in gridiron history. They won 12 straight games and piled up 322 points to its opponents' 10 to become the undisputed champions of the South.

Sewanee was a charter member of the Southeastern Conference, but it was outgrown by the other universities. In the thirties, Sewanee could not compete with the bigger, wealthier schools and they were forced to drop out of the Southeastern Conference. Up

until the post-World War II years, the Sewanee student body numbered only between 200 to 300 students. Subsequently, Sewanee
dropped football after the 1941 season for the duration of World
War II.

In 1946 Sewanee revived football by fielding a team of non-
scholarship athletes. My high school coach, Bill "Cannonball"
White was named head coach. Coach White had spent three years as
head coach at Howard College in Birmingham, Alabama, now
known as Samford University. He went to Howard in 1940 after
coaching Ramsay High School for ten years. During the three years
he coached at Howard, they played at least three Southeastern Conference teams and in 1942 played five SEC teams. Although they did
not beat an SEC team during those years, the games were very competitive. Coach White served in the Air Force for a couple of years
and then was named as an assistant football coach at the University
of Tennessee in 1945. He was a graduate of Tennessee in about 1924.

Bill White was the perfect coach to start a program from
scratch. He had been the first coach in a couple of high schools,
including my high school, Ramsay High School in Birmingham.
Football was his life, and he was going to coach to win, regardless of
what kind of program he was coaching. Sewanee had an encouraging
season in their first year back in football in 1946 with a 4-3-1 record.

I made a trip to Sewanee and was interviewed by the president
of the university, Dr. Alex Guerry, by the athletic director, Gordon
Clark, and by Coach White. Sewanee has a beautiful campus. The
architecture of the limestone buildings is Gothic. The campus has a
variety of trees, most of them large hardwoods, and looks like one
would imagine Oxford University to look. At that time Sewanee
had the highest percentage of students to qualify for Rhodes Scholarships than any college or university in the nation. It was strictly an
all-male school and very formal. Students were required to wear
coats and ties to class and to all meals. There were approximately
500 undergraduate students.

The entrance requirements were high, and if a young man attended just to play football, he was in the wrong school. At Sewanee
the football team under Coach White had the same kind of discipline, organized practices, meetings and off-the-field training rules
as any major college. In many cases the training rules were even
more demanding. The players had to eat all meals in the university

dining hall and were required to be in bed with lights out at 11:00 P.M. during the season. Even though there was no financial aid for football players, football was important to all who played. Perhaps the only difference was that the practices were not as long and there were no night meetings. We wanted the players to compete in the classroom too.

After I graduated from Auburn in March, I had heard nothing from my applications to Yale and Harvard law schools. One other great event happened in my life. I fell in love. The young lady was Frances Hamilton McMahan. She and I were in the same freshman class at Auburn in 1940. She had married Buddy McMahan, who was a quarterback on the 1940 and 1941 Auburn football team. Buddy was killed in action in France shortly after the D-Day invasion of France. He and Frances had a little girl, Cindy, who was three years old when I met her. Buddy, her father, never saw Cindy as she was born after he went overseas. Frances had come to Auburn to live with her mother and her aunt and uncle. Her father had died of cancer, and her younger brother had been shot down as a tail gunner on a B-17 bomber.

Frances and I were married on November 23, 1946, in Auburn, Alabama. Frances had all the qualities of a charming lady then and still has after almost 45 years of marriage. The first thing that attracted me about Frances was her soft, natural, southern accent. It hasn't changed a bit, although we've lived in such places as Baltimore, Pittsburgh, Waco, and Albuquerque.

Between the spring and summer quarter, Frances, Cindy and I took a trip to Fort Lauderdale, Florida, to visit my aunts, uncle, and maternal grandmother. When we got back from Florida, we had $16 in our checking account. There was a letter from Yale stating that I had been accepted in Yale Law School, but there was one hitch. I had to have $1,000 deposited with the university as a security deposit by the following Monday. I had no way to get that kind of money.

In the meantime, I had been offered the coaching job at Sewanee at a salary of $2,650 a year. That was just too much money to turn down. Incidentally, later I heard from Harvard and I was accepted there also.

I spent five football seasons at Sewanee before being recalled to active duty in December of 1951 during the Korean War. My stay at Sewanee was an enjoyable and rewarding experience. First, I was working with a coach who was as dedicated to his work as any coach anywhere. I had an opportunity to grow as a coach. We worked for an excellent person and athletic director, Gordon Clark. He saw to it that we had very few time-consuming duties other than coaching.

I attended my first coaching clinic at the University of Tennessee. Other than high school coaches, only head college coaches who had attended the University of Tennessee and their assistants were allowed to attend the clinic. Coach Bob Neyland, who is one of the legends of college football, was the head football coach at the University of Tennessee. I still remember many statements Bob Neyland said during his lectures on the zone pass defense. I personally believe Bob Neyland and his staff contributed as much to defensive principles and techniques as any in the history of football. He was conservative and used the kicking game almost to perfection.

Coach Murray Warmath was the Tennessee line coach. Later he had a successful career as head coach at Mississippi State and the University of Minnesota. Murray gave one of the best lectures on defensive line play and team pursuit that I have ever heard. My own coaching was influenced more by the Tennessee system and principles than any other.

At Sewanee we used the Tennessee single wing, which featured a balanced line in contrast to most single wing teams that had four linemen to the strong side of the center (where the wingback was positioned about one yard deep and one yard outside the strong side end). The tailback was directly behind the center about four and a half yards deep and the fullback about three and a half yards deep and about a yard from the tailback on the strong side of the formation. It was the same formation I had played in high school and coached for my first ten years as a full-time college coach.

Considering Sewanee had embarked on a program on which there were no athletic scholarships and an academic program which was very challenging with no easy courses, I believe we had a very successful program. For the five years I was with Sewanee we won 24, lost 13, and tied 3. In 1947 and 1948 we lost one game in each season. Our only losing season was in 1950, when we had a 3-6 record. We lost four games by a margin of six to eight points. As a matter of fact, most of our games during my years at Sewanee were decided by a touchdown or two. We won a few by decisive margin — three touchdowns or more — and lost a fewer number by that margin.

Besides coaching the line, I did most of the scouting of opponents. This was before the exchange of films or videotapes. I made a written scouting report on each team we played and gave a verbal report to the squad. Most of the trips I took were by Greyhound bus. I made trips to places like Clinton, South Carolina, to scout Presbyterian College; Jackson, Mississippi, to scout Millsaps College; Danville, Kentucky, to scout Centre College; and once to Memphis to scout Southwestern University in an afternoon game and then straight on to Jonesboro, Arkansas, to scout Mississippi College against Arkansas State that night.

The games were played in the early fall, and it was cotton picking time in Arkansas. It was a Saturday night and the most crowded bus I've ever ridden. All the seats were taken and the aisles were jammed with people standing from front to rear. Despite the crowded conditions, the bus driver seemed in good humor. Two or three small towns where we stopped along the way to Jonesboro had county fairs. From the highway you could see the ferris wheel, the merry-go-round, and a conglomeration of bright neon lights from rides that make up a fair. At every stop, the bus driver would say, "This is Marked Tree, Arkansas (or Trumann, Arkansas) the biggest little town in Arkansas on Saturday night!" When we arrived at Jonesboro the bus was understandably late, but I hurried to the stadium and had a good look at Mississippi College.

My favorite scouting trip was to St. Louis, where Washington University was located. Washington University is an outstanding private university with one of the best medical schools in the nation. One reason I liked to scout Washington was because I didn't have to ride the bus. I could catch a train in Cowan, Tennessee, which was about seven miles from Sewanee, in the early evening and get a Pullman. The train would arrive in St. Louis the next morning fairly early, and I would have plenty of time to get to the Washington University stadium for their afternoon game.

Washington University had about 10,000 students, compared to about 500 students at Sewanee. Normally they were a better team than we were. In 1948 Weeb Ewbank was head coach at Washington. Both teams were undefeated when we played them in the final game of the season for both teams. We had a tie with Millsaps College, which kept us from a perfect record. The starting right halfback for Washington was Charley Winner, who would be assistant coach with the Colts while I was there, and later head football coach with the St. Louis Cardinals.

Washington beat us 27-6 in Sewanee. It was a close game until the fourth quarter, when they scored a couple of touchdowns late to pull away.

That was the first time I met Weeb Ewbank. Weeb went from Washington to the Cleveland Browns as an assistant to Paul Brown, and who, in my opinion, made the greatest contribution to professional football of any coach in NFL history. His organization, detailed planning, teaching, and astute eye for talent made him a big winner every place he coached, from high school, to Ohio State, and then to professional football with the Cleveland Browns.

One of the most memorable games in my coaching career was our game with Washington University in 1950. Again it was the last game of the season for both teams. An unusual storm system had developed in the middle of November and we had about a foot of snow. At game time the temperature was about two degrees above zero with a strong wind. We didn't have the equipment to clear the snow, but we did clear the snow from the sideline, out-of-bounds marker lines, and the yard-lines at the 10-yard markers from goal line to goal line through the end zone. Naturally, the offense of each team was severely handicapped.

Coach Bill White chose to play a very conservative game. Every time our offense had possession of the ball, whether from a kickoff punt or turnover, we punted it back to Washington on the first down.

In the fourth quarter we were able to get the ball on a fumble. For the first time we ran an offensive play. We made a first down and I urged Coach Bill White to run a throwback pass off our basic running pass with a fake of a sweep to the strong side of the formation. Our blocking back would delay in the backfield while the tailback ran eight to ten yards to his right. When he saw the defensive cornerback move with our end, who ran a deep crossing pattern, the blocking back flared to the weak side and turned down-field. The tailback threw back across the field to our blocking back, who was all alone about ten yards deep from the line of scrimmage. He easily scored, and we kicked the extra point for a 7-0 victory.

That was our first victory over Washington University and a good example of how bad weather can be advantageous to the underdog. It was a game that participants of both teams will never forget.

One other game which had an interesting sidelight was our game with Howard College of Birmingham, Alabama, in 1951. The outstanding player and leader of the Howard team was Bobby Bowden, who is now the outstanding coach of the Florida State University Seminoles. The game was especially important to Coach Bill White since he had been head coach at Howard and had spent more than half of his coaching career in Birmingham.

Everything went our way as we enjoyed an unexpected one-sided victory by the score of 41-0. One of the motivating factors for Sewanee defeating the Bobby Bowden-led Howard team is that one of the Howard players called the Sewanee players "tea sippers" in a newspaper article. While there was a lot of tea sipping at Sewanee, the football team did not want to be known as the "tea sippers."

On November 7, 1951, our son, Dixon, was born. John Dixon Bridgers III has always been a son who has made us very proud. During that weekend Sewanee played Centre College of Danville, Kentucky, in Danville. Sewanee won the game 3-0, and the team gave the game ball to Dixon. Of course, he was only about two days old when he first saw it, but we had a photo taken with Frances and me showing him the ball.

I look back with a great deal of satisfaction on my years at Sewanee. A football player at Sewanee never received a dime for playing football. Our team was made up of players who wanted to play. Their attitudes were excellent. They were as serious about their football as they were about their studies. They learned that there was no conflict in being a tough, aggressive football player and a complete gentleman as well as a good student. Bill Austin, who was an excellent football player and won a graduate scholarship to Harvard, said a study revealed that the football team had a higher grade point average than the university as a whole. As much as anything, Sewanee taught young men to be gentlemen. It was a tradition of the university. Sewanee also taught them to be honorable. The school had an honor system that was the most effective I've experienced at any of the eight universities I've either attended as a student or was employed as a coach or athletic director.

We played single wing football, which is not a finesse system but dependent on sound blocking, good solid defense based on the fundamentals of football. There were few teams we outmanned, but we were almost always well prepared. We had young men who were intelligent, eager, and very responsive to coaching.

My half-brother, Bill, attended Sewanee while I was coaching there. He graduated with honors as a chemistry major, attended graduate school at Duke, and received a medical degree at Washington University in St. Louis. He was on the medical faculty at the University of Miami and the University of Alabama in Birmingham, where he personally founded the School of Public Health and served as dean for many years. He loved Sewanee and is giving serious consideration to spending his retirement there.

On December 1, 1951, I was involuntarily recalled to active duty in the U.S. Army Reserve during the Korean War. My first assignment was at Fort Sill, Oklahoma, where I had received my officer's commission after attending Officer Candidate Class 113. I had been promoted to captain in 1946 after serving three years, four months in World War II.

At Fort Sill I was assigned as athletic officer for the entire army post. My job was to organize and promote athletic activity in a number of sports. I helped organize teams in boxing, basketball, track and field, and baseball.

In April I received orders to go overseas to the Far East Command. I assumed I would go to Korea and be assigned to one of the infantry divisions fighting in Korea. However, I was assigned to the 1st Cavalry Division, which was called back from Korea and stationed in Hokaido, the northern-most island of Japan, to protect against the threat of a North Korean invasion of Japan.

As a captain, I was assigned as liaison officer with the 1st Cavalry Division Artillery. A division artillery liaison officer was assigned to each of the three infantry regiments to help coordinate the field artillery with the infantry regiments. Since we were not in combat, I was given additional duties as athletic and recreation officer. Division artillery had a baseball team in the division baseball league.

In the latter part of the summer a division football league was announced. I was named as the head coach for the 1st Cavalry Division Artillery team. We were able to get a pretty decent squad. Lt. Bob Lunn, who had played in the Rose Bowl at guard with the University of Illinois, and Lt. Joe Kwiatkowski, who was an end at the University of Delaware, were assistant coaches as well as part-time players. I had a great deal of admiration and respect for both of them.

We had a slow start, losing three of our first five games, but we ended up with four straight victories. In our last game we beat the 5th Cavalry Regiment 34-14. The 5th Cavalry had beaten us earlier 18-14 and won the 1st Cavalry Division championship with seven wins and two losses compared to our second-place finish of six wins and three losses. Lieutenants Lunn and Kwiatkowski were the only former college players on our squad. Overall I thought our team improved and appeared to be the best team in the division by the end of the season.

It was a satisfying experience for all our players. We had a tailback in our single wing, Littrell Dogins, who was from Louisiana. He really developed as the season progressed. He had excellent speed and was a strong, slashing runner. He scored three touchdowns in our final victory over 5th Cavalry. One of the writers in the division newspaper had given him the nickname of "Mail Man" Dogins because he carried the mail. Dogins liked that nickname and put a piece of tape on the front of his helmet which read "Mail Man." We had a nice banquet after the season, and General Jark, the division artillery commanding officer, made us all feel good about our season.

Almost immediately after our last game I flew back home for my release from the army. A law was passed that any reserve officer who had been involuntarily recalled could be released from the army by December 1, 1952.

I got back just in time for the birth of our second son, Donald Hamilton Bridgers. Our two sons were only 13 months apart. They have always been very close as brothers and have made Frances and me very proud.

I had resigned from Sewanee when I was recalled to active duty in the army. As a result, I didn't have a job when I returned to Florence, Alabama, which was Frances' hometown and where she stayed with her mother while I was overseas.

Shortly after I returned home, Gordon Clark, who was a very able athletic director at Sewanee, died of a heart attack. Coach Bill White was named athletic director, in addition to retaining his position as head football coach. He offered me a job as assistant athletic director and assistant football coach.

Ernie Williamson had been hired as line coach when I went into the army. I had known him at the University of North Carolina, where I attended graduate school in economics one summer. He had played professional football with the Washington Redskins. Ernie was a very likable person, as was his wife, who was called "Smitty."

I continued at Sewanee until July. At that time I had a call from Marshall Turner, the athletic director at Johns Hopkins University. He wanted to know if I would be interested in the job of head coach at Johns Hopkins. I accepted the job and went on to Baltimore.

I look back on my coaching at Sewanee with very fond memories, and particularly good memories of the players I coached.

In the next chapter, some of the football heroes during my five years at Sewanee talk about their football experience and the university.

CHAPTER 5

SOME SEWANEE HEROES

Reed Bell

The player who was most responsible for Sewanee's early success after renewing football in 1946 was Reed Bell, fullback and linebacker.

A native of Pensacola, Florida, Reed was captain of the football team at Pensacola High School. He was a center on offense and a linebacker on defense. After graduation in 1944, he entered the University of Florida. Freshmen were eligible to play during World War II, and Reed made the team as a defensive halfback. Florida had a fairly successful season, but Reed became disenchanted with college football. According to him, there were disciplinary problems on the team and a lack of unified effort from the coaching staff.

After Reed's freshman year, he entered the military service. Upon his discharge from the military, he entered Sewanee in the fall of 1946. He really didn't plan to play football. His plans were to take pre-med courses and concentrate on his studies. However, Bob Snell, who was a high school teammate of Reed's at Pensacola High School, and a tackle at Sewanee, influenced Reed to join the Sewanee football team.

31

Reed wasn't big — 175 to 180 pounds and about 5'9. He didn't have outstanding speed, but he was well built with particularly strong legs. He also was quick and had natural instincts to find the football as a linebacker. He was a very strong blocker and, with his strength and quick feet, was an effective ball carrier as a fullback in the single wing.

However, Reed's outstanding trait was as a leader. His good looks, self-discipline, positive attitude, effort, and personal attractions instilled confidence in his teammates, coaches, and others.

Reed always has been a person of high principles and great integrity. He has strong convictions about what is right and wrong, and he always tries to do what he thinks is right. To give an example of his leadership, he was captain not only of his high school and college football teams but also his high school and Sewanee basketball teams. He really wasn't an outstanding basketball player, but he was a great leader.

Sewanee returned to football in 1946, after discontinuing football following the 1941 season. In the first three years of playing football (after four years of not fielding a football team), Sewanee had a record of 16 wins, 5 losses, and 2 ties. The standout player during these three years was Reed Bell. Reed didn't make many long runs as a ball carrier, although he did return a kickoff about 75 yards for a touchdown. Very few teams can match Sewanee's record after a four-year layoff. Reed played well, but his leadership and examples were primary factors in Sewanee's success in 1946, 1947, and 1948. He was selected as a Little All-American Fullback by the Associated Press in 1948, his senior season.

Reed was honored as a Phi Beta Kappa at Sewanee. He attended medical school at Duke and trained in pediatrics at Baylor University School of Medicine. His medical practice began in Pensacola. He quickly established a reputation as an outstanding pediatrician and became a legend in Pensacola for his caring concern for the children he treated.

After he had established a thriving practice, he quit his practice to accept the leadership responsibility of building a children's hospital, Sacred Heart Children's Hospital, in Pensacola. One of his responsibilities was to get the support of all pediatricians in Pensacola. He did so, and for the first time Pensacola had a facility which could provide excellent treatment to children. His leadership and ability to get other doctors and key people behind the hospital were the primary factors in making it a reality. Reed was in charge of a training program for pediatric residents at Sacred Heart Children's Hospital for nineteen years.

Reed and his wife, Nell, have six children who are excellent citizens and successful in their vocations. Their sons are Bill, a medical doctor, Kenny, a lawyer and circuit judge, Lance, an x-ray technician, and Brian, a vice-president of a bank. Their two daughters are Mitzi, a nurse, and Terry, a social worker.

Of all his achievements Reed is most proud of his children and their good citizenship and successes. He gives most of the credit to his wife.

One other achievement he feels good about was his year (1987) in Washington, D.C., as national director of the Office of Substance Abuse Prevention. Reed was appointed director by President Ronald Reagan.

Few citizens in Pensacola are more respected or have given more of themselves to the welfare of the community. At age 65 he is still very active and is considering devoting a full year to an organization as a medical adviser focusing on restoring family values.

Some of the positions of leadership Dr. Reed Bell has held are: president of Escambia County Medical Society; chairman, Florida Chapter of the American Academy of Pediatrics; president of the Florida Pediatric Society; Bio Ethics Committee of the American Academy of Pediatrics; Board of Directors, Gulf Power Company; Board of Directors, Barnett Bank; development of Ronald McDonald House; Rotarian; and Physicians Advisory Board to Focus-on-the-Family.

Dr. Reed Bell feels very strongly that coaches are among the very best influences on our youth. He wrote, "I was blessed with wonderful friends, and especially coaches, who helped me more with the living of my life than anyone else I have known. Colleagues in medicine are highly competent but hardly the 'real' human beings I've known in athletics — they are lacking in 'wisdom' compared to my associations in athletics."

Despite some rather serious health problems, Dr. Reed Bell continues to serve the Pensacola community in many ways. He also gives much thought and effort to promoting those values which are so important to young people and to the future of our nation.

Bill Austin, Guard

Bill Austin had more physical ability than any lineman I coached at Sewanee. He was about 5'11 and weighed 190 to 195 pounds. He was very strong and for the most part of his four years at Sewanee was our top weight man — shotput and discus on our track team. He had outstanding speed for a lineman. Bill ran the 100 and 220 on our track team. I was head track coach, as well as line coach in football. Bill's best time in the 100-yard dash was about 10.2 seconds, but it was legitimate. The starters at our own track meets emphasized holding the runners until the starting pistol sounded. There were few track meets we had that he didn't score points in the 100 and 220. Bill had an explosive start and generally led the pack at 30 or 40 yards. There were times when he would get tense and tie up in the last 25 yards, but over the course of his four years of competition, Bill Austin was the all-time leading point scorer in track and field.

In addition to having physical ability, Bill was very intelligent. He graduated magna cum laude from Sewanee and received an academic scholarship for graduate work at Harvard.

Bill had graduated from Sewanee Military Academy before attending Sewanee. He also competed in boxing and was runner-up for two years in the mid-South Prep School conference. My guess is that the boxer who beat him for the championship outboxed him. I don't think he outslugged Bill.

One thing Bill had to overcome as a football player was his temper. He had a tendency to want to challenge his opponent on the other side of the line to a boxing or, more accurately, a slugging match. As Bill became a better football player, he learned to control himself. But it wasn't easy for him.

Since I was Bill's line coach and track coach, every time Bill did something wrong, such as cold-cock one of his teammates in a scrimmage, our head coach, "Cannonball" White, would come up to me and say, "Red, you've got to talk to Austin and get him squared away."

Bill always listened to me and would do better, at least for a while.

Coach White was my high school coach at Ramsay High School in Birmingham, Alabama. My twin brother, Frank, and I were the starting guards for two years on the Ramsay High School team. Coach White could never tell us apart, so he just called both of us "Red." He continued to call me "Red" until he died in the 1980s.

The players at Sewanee called me Coach "Red." At least that's the name they used to my face.

Bill Austin had a great deal of energy and was always in excellent physical condition. Few, if any, players worked harder than Bill in football and track. He was dedicated and wanted very much to improve. I personally liked Bill and wanted to do everything I could to see him reach his potential. I appreciated his effort and spirit.

In 1951 and 1952 Bill was an excellent player. I was recalled to active duty for the Korean War as a captain in the artillery after the 1951 football season, but Sewanee had one of their best years when they went 7-2 in 1952, losing only to Howard College 13-0 (a team we had beaten 41-0 in 1951) and to Wabash College 31-14. Sewanee beat traditional opponents, such as Hampden-Sydney, Millsaps, Mississippi College, Southwestern, and Centre, and upset Washington University in their final game.

Bill has retired from his successful insurance business and lives half the year in Sundance, Wyoming, and half the year in Florida. His two sons are both working for graduate degrees and participate in tennis, track, and wrestling.

Bill expressed extremely well what his participation in football meant to him:

> It is most gratifying to learn that you are preparing to answer the critics in football and other sports. It seems to me the loudest critics, like Howard Cosell, are individuals who never played the game. Certainly, nothing in life is perfect, and the conduct of athletics, like everything else, can be criticized; but it also seems logical that those who never participated can't possibly appreciate the benefits, both material and intrinsic, which accrue to those who actually played the game . . .
>
> *Education* — First of all, football made it possible for me, along with thousands of young Americans, to get an education. Next to my family, my education has been the most important thing in my life. Education has opened, and continues to open, doors for me which would not have been even remotely possible without it. In business, in society, and even in retirement, I con-

tinually call on my education for the knowledge and mental confidence I need to sustain me.

Self-confidence — Nothing teaches one more about himself
— and other people — as does a team sport. Perhaps the best
way to put this is to say that the better one *prepares* and orga-
nizes, the better the chance for success. The way we, as a team,
were prepared for the upcoming opponent made a life-long impression on me. One of the maxims I live by is, "Failing to prepare is preparing to fail." That came from football. Football
made me believe that I could overcome any obstacle, given
enough time.

Associated with Dedicated Men — Whether we, as individuals, admit it or not, all of us are influenced by our coaches. Those
men dedicated themselves single-mindedly every Monday to a
new goal: to prepare the players for success, winning, if you will,
come Saturday afternoon. It was my good fortune to be influenced most positively by the men who coached me. They taught
self-discipline, self-sacrifice, the need for hard work, preparation and the will to succeed; that there is always a price for success *that must be paid* in sweat and in the mind. Those are qualities that are taught in no classroom. These must be *lived* to be
appreciated or even understood. Nonplayers can only read
about it; it's not the same.

Memories — "Backs over there, football players over here."
Remember that? You used to say it at every practice. I'll never
forget it, nor will the rest of "Coach Red's boys." Beating Washington University, stomping hell out of Howard College, who
called us "the tea sippers," bashing Wabash, 140-pound Jim Ed
Mulkin stopping runners in their tracks, losing to Florida State
6-0 in the fog, and my teammates-friendships born of mutual
respect that have lasted for 40 years, stopping Mississippi College on our one-foot-line to win 12-7, gentle John Kennerly
[our trainer], Coach Clark [athletic director] and of course,
"Buckwheat" [players' name for Coach White] . . .

Proud of Things — To have played for a great school and
gotten a good education at the same time. To have been one of
"Coach Red's boys," and certainly this: for three of the four
years I played at Sewanee, the captain of the football team was a
Phi Beta Kappa. They were Reed Bell [fullback and Little All-

American], Jim Ed Mulkin [halfback and Little All-American], and Jim Elam [tackle and Little All-American].

How is Bill Austin's statement as a strong expression of what is right about football?

Jim Elam

Another good football player I coached at Sewanee was Jim Elam from Louisville, Kentucky. In Jim's freshman year, 1949, he played very little. He was about 6'1 and 180 to 185 pounds. Jim matured and grew in strength and know-how. As a junior he was about 190 pounds and much improved offensively and defensively. I particularly remember how he had improved in his offensive blocking techniques.

About three times a week I would scrimmage our linemen with five offensive linemen against three or four defensive linemen. We would run all of our offensive interior plays against the three or four defensive line. We were to play Washington University the following Saturday in St. Louis. It was on a Thursday before leaving for St. Louis on Friday.

The linemen were involved in our 5 on 4 scrimmage just before we came together for team offensive dummy scrimmage. One of the players fell across Jim Elam's leg and hurt his knee. He wasn't able to continue practice. Coach White was really outdone with me getting one of our best linemen hurt the day before our trip to Washington.

I was hoping the injury was not serious, but it swelled up on him and he wasn't able to play against Washington. We had to substitute a player with much less ability than Jim, and Washington beat us 31-13.

That injury taught me a valuable lesson. Don't risk injury with full-speed scrimmage in practice during the season. That full-speed scrimmage will never help you as much as losing one of your top players will hurt you.

In 1952, while I was in Japan during the Korean War, Jim was elected captain of Sewanee's team, and he and Sewanee had an excellent year. They were 7-2, and Jim made the *Look* magazine Little All-American team. Jim was also elected to Phi Beta Kappa.

Jim was a very quiet person. He tended to his own business and was an excellent student. After graduating from Sewanee, having majored in math and minored in English literature, he went into the Air Force and served as a nuclear weapons officer in the Korean theater.

After service he went to Purdue University and got a bachelor's degree in electrical engineering and a master's in industrial management. After graduation from Purdue, Jim became a systems engineer with IBM specializing in computer-aided design and computer-aided manufacturing.

One of Jim's vivid memories was our upsetting Washington University in 1950 on a snow-covered field with a temperature around zero. We won the game on a throwback pass to our blocking back off a fake end sweep to the right. The defensive cornerback went with our crossing left end and left our blocking back, who had delayed and slipped out in the left flat all alone. He caught the pass and scored easily.

His other vivid memory was when he and J.D. "Radar" Rox, who was a strongside end, double-teamed an opposing lineman and drove him across the field and dumped him at the coach's feet in front of an opponent's bench. What an embarrassment for a player!

Jim's father played at Sewanee in the early years, so Jim was a second-generation Sewanee football player.

It wasn't like Jim to make long statements, but he said this about football: "The important thing about football was in experiencing purposefulness, the importance of team effort and closeness to co-players. Knowing that these things existed made it easier to find them later in life."

Jim Ed Mulkin

Jim Ed Mulkin is one of the most inspirational and courageous football players I have ever known. Except for the time he was in college at Sewanee and in the service, Jim Ed has lived in Bessemer, Alabama.

In high school Jim Ed's maximum weight was 115 pounds. Because of his size he did not go out for football until he was a junior. As a high school football player Jim Ed never made the starting lineup at Bessemer High School, which had one of the best football programs and one of the best high school football coaches in Alabama.

The state of Alabama over the past 60 years has had extraordinarily good high school football. Any person who doubts the quality of Alabama high school players need only to look at the number of Alabama high school athletes who have played at Auburn University, the University of Alabama, Georgia Tech, and all the other Southeastern Conference schools. When the population of Alabama is compared with much more populated states, such as Texas, Florida, Pennsylvania, California, Ohio and others, Alabama no doubt ranks very high in the percentage of college football players based on population.

Jim Ed's high school coach was "Snitz" Snider, a highly successful coach for Bessemer High School for many years. He was also a member of the U.S. Olympic Track and Field Team and placed in the hurdles in the 1932 Olympics.

Coach Snider, no doubt, recommended Jim Ed as a potential football player to Coach Bill White, the Sewanee head football coach. Even though Jim Ed did not start at Bessemer High School, he made a letter as a reserve. Coach Snider thought he had potential as a small college football player with added weight and maturity.

The fact is that Jim Ed gained 24 pounds from his high school days until he made the varsity squad in his sophomore year, 1949, at Sewanee. His playing weight was 139 pounds at Sewanee. Despite Jim Ed's lack of size in high school, he played third base on the baseball team and lettered two years. He was an excellent student and leader, a member of the National Honor Society and president of his senior class.

I would guess Jim Ed was about 5'5. You would think of someone his size as being frail, but the opposite was true. Jim Ed was well muscled and very strongly built. He played wingback in our single wing. He was an amazingly effective blocker and ran reverses extremely well. He was fast, but I remember him more for his quickness and his ability to change directions without loss of speed. On defense he was an excellent tackler. He was completely fearless and seldom missed a tackle.

The thing Jim Ed did best was return punts and kickoffs. His quickness and unusual strength for his size made him very difficult to bring down in the open field. Unfortunately, I don't believe any statistics still exist on his runbacks of punts and kickoffs. I do remember his runbacks were a significant part of our offense in 1949, 1950, and 1951.

Jim Ed's all-around ability as a football player gained the respect of every player and coach at Sewanee. He was elected captain of the 1951 Sewanee team and was selected first team Little All-American.

On campus and in the classroom, Jim Ed was as much of a leader and top performer as he was on the football field. As a student he was Phi Beta Kappa and was selected for Blue Key, another honorary fraternity, for leadership. Jim Ed was president of his fraternity, the SAE chapter at Sewanee, and was selected for Who's Who in Colleges and Universities.

His most memorable experience was playing against Florida State University in 1950. Florida State was in the fifth year of intercollegiate football and was dedicating Doak Campbell Stadium before a homecoming capacity crowd of 15,000. With only portable bleachers, Sewanee's capacity was approximately 1,500. Florida State had an undefeated, untied season in 1950, and Sewanee gave them their closest game, losing 14-8. Two years later Florida State was playing a Division I-A schedule. Doak Campbell Stadium now seats 60,519 and Florida State averages over 60,000 fans per game. Florida State was the small-college power in the Southeast in 1949 and 1950, but they had a difficult time defeating a Sewanee team led by a 139-pound halfback — Jim Ed Mulkin.

Immediately after graduation from Sewanee in 1952, Jim Ed went into the Air Force as a lieutenant during the Korean War. After his discharge from the Air Force, he wrote me a letter at Johns Hopkins and inquired about a coaching job there. Perhaps fortunately for Jim Ed, I did not have an opening on my staff.

He used what money he had to buy a junkyard and went into the auto parts business in Bessemer. He was very successful and 35 years later sold his stores to a firm by the name of Alabama Crankshaft. At the present time he manages the stores for the new owners.

Jim Ed said he found it very hard to put into words what college football meant to him. He wrote, "My lasting memories of my coaches, teammates, managers and trainers — coaches who shaped my life as much as my parents, teammates who were like brothers (I was an only child), and John Kennerly [Sewanee trainer], who kept me alive.

"On the playing field and the practice field I learned what discipline, training and teamwork meant in the game. Leadership and heart will win more games than physical ability. It's a feeling that's hard to explain unless you have played the game and experienced the feeling in a locker room at half time."

His older son, James E. Jr., graduated from Sewanee and received a master's degree at Carnegie Mellon in Pittsburgh and now teaches the classics at New York University, City College of New York, and at Brooklyn College. He is finishing his Ph.D. at City College of New York. Jim Ed's second son received a tennis scholarship to the University of Mississippi and went into business in Birmingham after graduating. The youngest son played tennis at Tulane, graduated, and now works for AmSouth in Birmingham.

Jim Ed Mulkin has kept in shape, his weight being 145 compared to his playing weight of 139. Jim Ed and his wife, Jane, have been happily married since 1955. He plays a lot of tennis and thoroughly enjoys it. There are not many 139-pounders who have received the satisfaction, enjoyment, and achievement of playing college football as has Jim Ed Mulkin.

Bob Snell

Bob Snell was another one of our players at Sewanee who had the physical attributes to play football at the major college level. At 6'0 and 200 pounds, he had a relatively long body with very strong and sturdy legs. Except for Bill Austin he probably had the most speed of any lineman we had at Sewanee. Bob was very handsome — dark, curly hair, a square jaw, the look of an athlete.

Bob played football at Pensacola High School and had the opportunity for a football scholarship to the University of Florida, but chose Sewanee due to the influence of Bishop Frank A. Juhan, a former Sewanee All-Southern center, who played on the 1909 Sewanee team (the last Sewanee team to win a Southeastern Conference championship). Bishop Juhan also was the chancellor of Sewanee.

Bob came to Sewanee with the goal of becoming an Episcopal priest. He had played on Pensacola High School's undefeated team of 1944 and wanted to play football at Sewanee when he entered in

1945. He was very disappointed to find that Sewanee did not have a team.

However, in 1946, Gordon Clark, the former athletic director, returned to Sewanee after being discharged from the navy, and immediately set out to revive football at Sewanee in 1946. Dr. Alex Guerry was vice-chancellor at Sewanee at that time and was a great educator with very high ideals. He decided Sewanee would resume football without any athletic scholarships. Dr. Guerry and Gordon Clark agreed to hire Bill White, my former high school coach at Ramsay, as head coach.

Bob said that he was "less than impressed" initially with the selection of Coach White. He said Coach White had a "football-shaped brain," and bordered on the maniacal. However, Bob said, "From Coach White I learned that football required discipline, organization, brains, guts, determination, zeal, and all those good things that people say are the important lessons of life. I came to respect him greatly and to enjoy his craziness."

Make no mistake about it, Coach Bill White was totally involved as a football coach. It was his one consuming interest. On the other hand, Coach White realized how important education was at Sewanee, and he set the parameters of football to allow the players the opportunity to compete in the classroom at Sewanee.

Bob played weakside tackle on our single wing formation and right defensive tackle. His techniques were very good. One of the things he did best was pursue the play. He made a number of tackles with his speed and pursuit when it appeared the opposing ball carrier might go all the way. He was also strong enough to be effective on plays run at him.

After graduating from Sewanee in the spring of 1949 with a major in English literature, he entered St. Luke's School of Theology at Sewanee that fall. Since Sewanee did not have a team his freshman year in 1945 he was eligible for football, even though he had graduated and was in graduate school. Bob was elected captain of the 1949 team. His presence lent leadership and maturity to our team.

He relates his most memorable experiences: "We lost to an excellent Florida State University team 6-0. The only touchdown was scored on a reverse just after Coach Bridgers thought I was hurt and substituted for me. Actually I only had a slight bruise and could have continued. We would have held Florida State to a 0-0 tie if I had been in the game. I think I would have stopped the scoring play. The clouds had come down over the mountain and you couldn't see across the field. On a punt the players had to wait until they heard the thump of the ball hitting the ground to know where it was."

Bob said he met some of his former high school teammates who played for Florida State on Hardee Field, where we played our games after their practice the day before our game.

One of the players asked, "Where is the stadium?" Bob pointed to the portable bleachers and said, "You are standing in the middle of it."

Florida State had a 9-1 season, and won a postseason game at the Cigar Bowl in Tampa. Sewanee lost one other game to Washington University in St. Louis. We had an almost certain victory taken away when Kenyon College canceled our game with them. We had beaten them 47-13 in Kenyon the year before.

Bob was assistant line coach in his last two years in the seminary. He did a good job. He was young enough and good enough to demonstrate effectively.

Another memorable event for Bob was our game with Hampden-Sydney in Sewanee on November 22, 1947. Hampden-Sydney's star player was a 210-pound running back who had played the previous year at the Naval Academy. He had an outstanding game in Navy's victory over Army the year before.

It was the final game of the season for both teams, and Lynn Chewning had been Hampden-Sydney's leading rusher and scorer throughout the season. Early in the game Chewning broke into the clear. Snell ran him down on the 20-yard-line, and we kept Hampden-Sydney from scoring on that drive. We ended up winning the game 32-7, and Chewning did not score.

"The date of the Hampden-Sydney was 'Willie Six Day,' honoring our beloved black trainer in his eighties," remembered Bob. "*Life* magazine wondered why a conservative segregated white men's southern college was honoring a black man. They sent a photographer to cover the event. I had my picture in *Life* magazine carrying Willie Six off the field after the game."

Bob wrote the following on "What College Football Meant to Me":

I loved every minute of it; games and practices alike with the possible exception of spring practice in February . . . From the short, round Coach Clark [athletic director] I learned to chuckle when things are tough and then to dig in and get tough myself . . . He also taught me off the field that my explosive temper that I loved not to control was a luxury that I could not afford. He promised me in 1946 that if I ever had another tantrum, I would be on a bus back to Florida. I believed him. Forty-five years later I haven't had another temper tantrum.

The next year we had a young line coach fresh out of Auburn by way of the U.S. Army. From John Bridgers I learned that line play is not all grunt and muscle. Finesse, precise movements, blocking and tackling skills are more to be desired than bulk and brawn. At 197 pounds I could hold my own against any lineman we played against. Coach Bridgers was a serious student of the game destined for a more prestigious career than Sewanee could offer. He conveyed a pride in performance that was quietly contagious among the team members. He was a good complement to Coach White, the sometimes apparently wild man. . . .

The tradition of the Sewanee Gentleman was as real on the sport field as it was at the spring dance weekend. The gentleman/scholar/athlete was a reality in my life at Sewanee. It wouldn't have been a complete experience without football, the noble contest of will and skill.

Bob Snell retired in January of 1991 after 39 years as an Episcopal priest. He still lives in Tallahassee, where he served his last parish. Bob had quadruple bypass surgery in October of 1989. He is now enjoying life with his wife, children, and grandchildren. I hope he will have many more years to enjoy his family and pleasant memories of his priesthood and his Sewanee experiences.

Charles Lindsay

When I decided to write this book, I sat down and jotted the names of the players from each university and team where I coached who impressed me as football players and individuals. The most difficult decision was to limit the number of players to those I selected. When I considered Sewanee, I thought of Charles Lindsay. I was his line coach for only his freshman and sophomore years, and really didn't realize some of his outstanding achievements in his last two years.

Charles was very bright, eventually earning a Fulbright Scholarship for graduate study in Paris. As a football player he was eager, knowledgeable, and quick to learn. I felt that he always played up to the maximum of his ability. I remember him as about 5'11 and 170 pounds as a sophomore.

His academic achievements are most impressive. He was elected to Phi Beta Kappa as a junior and was later awarded the Danford Graduate Fellowship (for students who show particular promise for graduate study) and a Fulbright Scholarship to the University of Paris. Other achievements include Head Proctor, president of Order of Gownsmen, Blue Key (awarded primarily for good citizenship and leadership qualities), and recipient of the Sullivan Award (determined by the faculty for outstanding graduating senior).

In football he was elected captain in 1953, was a three-year starter, and was named to Tennessee Small College All State Team. Charles' father was his coach in high school at Lincoln County Central High in Fayetteville, Tennessee.

Charles was a true scholar. After attending the University of Paris as a Fulbright scholar, he received a master's degree from the University of Iowa in mathematics and a Ph.D. from Peabody College of Vanderbilt University in mathematics. He is now a professor of mathematics at Coe College in Cedar Rapids, Iowa, where he has taught since 1957.

I was very impressed with the enthusiasm and accuracy of his memory as he described his experiences to me.

Most Memorable Experience in College Football — Several [experiences] come to mind. During my sophomore year at Sewanee I played offensive center and defensive linebacker. I played all 60 minutes in five games that year, and more than 50 minutes in each of the others. One of the games that helped me most, both as a player and as an individual, was the game at Centre [Danville, Kentucky]. I did play the whole game, and we won (3-0). (By the way, that was the first time Centre had been shut out in a quarter of a century.) Their defensive guard who lined

up on "my nose" had been named "Little All-American" the previous year. (Coach Bridgers, you really got me ready for that
game.) Sometime during the game I realized that I was able to
block that "good" player effectively. When it was third and
short, we ran up the middle and made the first down. (I recall
once in that situation "my man" did make the tackle, but he
caught the runner from behind after a gain of about 10 yards.)
When we passed, "my man" was not putting pressure on our
passer. My confidence in my blocking soared. I won't claim that
I beat "my man" every time thereafter (I didn't), but I always
thought I was going to do so before the play began. And this
new confidence also rubbed off in non-football activities.

I also remember the first game I started as a freshman. Our
defensive captain, a linebacker, had severely sprained an ankle in
practice; the number two center and linebacker had quit the
squad a couple of days before this accident. I was number three,
and suddenly Coach White (he must have been planning for the
future) named me as defensive captain. We kicked off against
Hampden-Sydney. We had two basic defenses against the run, a
basic pass defense, a goal line defense, and a few variations. I
called our best run defense (my opinion) on their first play.
They ran and gained seven yards. I called our other run defense
second. They ran and gained 12 yards. I did not expect them to
pass on their third play, but I called our pass defense because it
put me in a position where I thought they would run. They
passed, it was complete, and our safety ran their player out of
bounds on our three-yard-line. I called our goal line defense.
Their back scored standing up. We did not come close to blocking the point after. FRUSTRATION!!! I recall saying to the
defensive unit on the sidelines, quietly so that Coach White
would not hear, that if that was the way we were going to play
defense, then it made no difference who was calling defensive
signals or what defense was called, and that we could do better.
They got only one first down on their next offensive series. The
next time we held them to two yards gained in three plays. I
called for an attempted block of the punt rather than a return,
and we succeeded. We even recovered it in the end zone for a
touchdown. The score was tied (7-7). I was elated, and as proud
of a group of guys as I could be. We lost the game, they were a

bit better than we were that day. But I was a full team member after that blocked punt (no, I did not block it), and not just that little freshman (my weight was 155 that year) who had no "right" to be on the field with the upperclassmen.

That reminded me of my first series of plays for Sewanee a week or so before the Hampden-Sydney game. We played the game in Winchester at night. We won easily, so I got in during the last few minutes on defense. I expected a pass, and I sailed through and was "sacking" the quarterback when I realized that it was a draw play. I even made the real tackle from behind after they had gained 35 yards, but I felt most foolish.

The single most memorable play for me was during the first game of my sophomore year. We were ahead 14-7 in the third quarter, they were driving and had first and goal on our nine. I intercepted a pass on our two, got it back to our 12; and it gave us the momentum. We dominated the rest of the game on defense, and won 14-7. (Note: I haven't looked up any records, so my memory of "exact" scores may be a bit off.)

I also recall the thrill of being a part of the offensive line during my junior year when we were often playing so very well as a unit. I am fondest of the following example of that line play. One game we ran the fullback up the middle eight times in a row for a total gain of 54 yards. On each play after the third time their defensive guard would ask me, "Gonna run it again?", and I replied, "Yes indeed!" Then we ran it again for a gain of seven or eight yards. Fun? You know it was!

There are many such nice memories. A final example shows how an individual can mature during a game. At Wabash we were ahead (big surprise to all) 21-20 at the end of the third quarter. They won 40-21. We had more individuals carried off the field than in any other game that I recall. (One guard had a ruptured spleen.) I realized during the first few minutes of the fourth quarter that I was the only Sewanee lineman who had started the game who was still on the field. I decided that I had to finish the game, and I did. I never was as battered and bruised at the end of a game as I was that day. My staying in the game made no difference in the outcome. But it made a big difference to me. I did not show "them," but I did show "me," that I could finish what I started. They did not have the satisfaction of knowing they had knocked out all of the starters. I could hold my head up the next day; I was not ashamed of myself.

What College Football Meant to Me — The much too lengthy comments above answer this for me. In brief — college football means teamwork, discipline (i.e., self-discipline), friendships, and the many kinds of satisfactions that come from a job well done. There is nothing quite like the elation that comes with some victories. (To win over an outmatched opponent is not what I'm talking about.) But the satisfaction of having played as well as you could, in victory or defeat, lasts even longer.

I have really enjoyed thinking about things past — my days at Sewanee, the football games, the teams, the successes and failures, the GOOD TIMES I had, and the memories I made that have lasted a lifetime (almost). Thanks for giving me a reason to remember them all.

After graduation at Sewanee, I had a year in Paris as a Fulbright scholar. It was great in many ways — living with a French family, falling in love with a girl from Illinois and marrying her in Paris (we've been married since May 7, 1955), and learning a bit about many things from astronomy and mathematics to French literature and history. We have four children, all of whom are on their own and all of whom are college graduates. Yes, I am well and enjoying life. Coe College is similar in size and athletic programs to Sewanee (then and now). It has been a good place for me to be since 1957. I still enjoy teaching. I have served many years, though not at present, on Coe's faculty committee on athletics, and as our faculty representative to our athletic conference....

Thank you again for teaching me so much. I've told many people that I learned some of my most valuable lessons from those I called "Coach" (rather than "Professor"). And I had you in mind, along with my Dad.

Charles Lindsay could have attended college on his academic scholarships without spending a day as a football player if he had desired. His feelings about football are common among men who have played, but few, whether they be players or not, can express it so eloquently.

CHAPTER 6

1953–56

JOHNS HOPKINS UNIVERSITY: MY FIRST COLLEGE HEAD COACHING JOB

After five years at Sewanee I was ready for another challenge. I wanted to be a head coach and the opportunity to be head coach at Johns Hopkins excited me. Marshall Turner, the athletic director at Hopkins, was a Sewanee graduate. Marshall was very much a gentleman, and I appreciated the opportunity he gave me.

Johns Hopkins is probably best known as a medical school, but it also ranks among the top ten universities academically in the United States by knowledgeable educators. Johns Hopkins has outstanding schools in public health, engineering, physics, and a number of other disciplines in the arts and sciences.

Frances, Cindy, and our two sons, Dixon and Don, moved to Baltimore in August of 1953.

The sport of lacrosse, originated by Native Americans, ranked foremost as the sport which Johns Hopkins gave the greatest interest. In the early years of its development, Johns Hopkins ranked among the best lacrosse teams in the country.

There were no athletic scholarships at Johns Hopkins. The university had a large endowment and there were many scholarships available based on academics, leadership, and all-around achievements of student applicants. But even with a scholarship, a student of average means found Johns Hopkins to be expensive.

One of the things I enjoyed very much at Hopkins was eating at the Faculty Club. The Faculty Club had an endowment which kept the cost of meals very reasonable. The meals were very good with excellent service. At one large table faculty members who came to lunch alone could sit and meet with others who didn't have companions. I had a chance to become acquainted with many members of the faculty whom I probably would not have met.

The 1953 Johns Hopkins football squad was the weakest college football squad I have ever coached. There were very few players who had been starters on their high school teams. The majority of players had been reserves on their high school teams and a few had not played high school football at all.

Frank Burns, my predecessor as head coach at Hopkins, was a very good football coach. He later became head football coach at Rutgers University. I think he just became discouraged at Johns Hopkins as head coach — which was easy to do. As a result, he did not make much effort in his final year to recruit any players. Regardless of the level of play, recruiting is a must. Even though football scholarships are not offered, there are a surprising number of young men who want to play football because they like it and want to experience the challenge of a sport which emphasizes strength, physical contact, speed, quickness, technique, skill, and teamwork.

While we didn't get many talented players at Johns Hopkins, I don't believe I've ever coached a group who appreciated the game more. This has been emphasized by the attendance we've had at football reunions in 1985 and 1991.

In my first year at Hopkins, Ed Goldberg, who was an undersized guard but one of our best linemen, said he would not be able to practice the next day as he had a chemistry test coming up on the following day. I said, "Ed, when you decided to play football, you took on the responsibility of budgeting your time so that you could practice football and keep up with your studies. We'll never have a football team here if every time a player has a test he takes a day off from practice. Football is a team game and if key individuals miss practice every time they have an academic examination, we may as well give up on having a competitive team."

Ed said, "Coach, I'll be at practice tomorrow."

Ed traveled all the way from the state of Washington to attend the 1985 reunion in Baltimore. There's no question that he has more fond memories from his football experience than he has from that chemistry course. This is not in any way meant to minimize the importance of academics, as no one can deny that that is the most important reason people attend college. If it is not, it should be.

At Johns Hopkins, the Department of Athletics and Physical Education was treated like any other department at the university. The athletic department generated no revenue and prepared a budget as a request for their financial needs. Marshall Turner was athletic director, and I don't know what pressures were put on him as far as finances were concerned, but our expenses for all sports were very limited.

The policy of expenditures for athletics changed over the years when Bobby Scott became athletic director in 1973. Perhaps the university came to realize that it was important to have a first-class operation in athletics as well as academics, even if competition in athletics other than lacrosse was at a lower level.

Marshall Turner was a very able administrator and a conscientious one. I am indebted to him for recommending me for the head football coaching position. Otherwise I doubt if I would have had the opportunities which developed.

In my first season as head coach, Ross Sachs was offensive and defensive backfield coach. Ross had been an outstanding quarterback at Gettysburg College, where he played under John Yovicsin, who later became head coach at Harvard. Ross was also head basketball coach and had many excellent qualifications as a coach. He was knowledgeable, patient, very loyal to his players, the people with whom he worked, and the institutions he served.

Bill Schwarz, who was in graduate school, working toward a doctorate in chemistry, was our offensive and defensive line coach. He obviously had time limitations with his graduate work requirements, but was cooperative and very intelligent.

Our first game in 1953 was against Franklin and Marshall College in Lancaster, Pennsylvania. We were clearly outclassed. At the half, we trailed 35-0.

I remember walking off the field at halftime and looking at the scoreboard. If they beat us as badly in the second half, the score would be 70-0. However, we played better and I think Franklin and

Marshall played their reserves for a good portion of the second half. The final score was 47-12. The next two weeks we were shut out by Carnegie Tech and Hampden-Sydney, losing 27-0 and 26-0.

We played Susquehanna in Selinsgrove, Pennsylvania, where Alonzo Stagg, Jr., was the head coach. His father, Alonzo Stagg, Sr., was advisory coach. The elder Alonzo had coached longer than any football coach in history. We won 12-6, with Dick Watts, our outstanding player, scoring the winning touchdown. It was our first win after three decisive losses.

Three weeks later we played Dickinson and squeaked out another victory, 13-12. Our final game of the season was against Western Maryland, our traditional rival. We decided to surprise them with a spread formation, with John Steers at tailback. Steers' passing had been our primary offense all year. In fact, John Steers completed more passes in 1953 than Johnny Unitas did at the University of Louisville.

The spread backfired and Western Maryland won 46-0. I've always been slightly prejudiced against the spread formation since that game.

My first year as head coach of a college team we were 2-6 and scored 47 points to our opponents' 209.

In 1954 we had a better team. We lost to Franklin and Marshall in the opening game 41-19. However, we were definitely improved over 1953. Again we could only win two games. We beat Hampden-Sydney 14-13 and Swarthmore 20-19 in the sixth game of the season. John Steers ran for a touchdown against Hampden-Sydney and passed to Barrie Wood for 65 yards and a touchdown. Dick Watts kicked two extra points, which provided the margin of victory.

In the Swarthmore game John Steers ran for 107 yards and Jack Lawrence for 103 yards. Both scored touchdowns, and Dick Watts kicked two extra points to win 20-19. The next week we lost to Dickinson 13-6 and the final game went to Western Maryland 12-7.

After the 1954 season I received a notice from the Alumni Office. It was an announcement of an alumni reception at one of the downtown hotels. President Lowell Reed was scheduled as the main speaker. I had been at Hopkins two football seasons, but I had never met the president of the university.

I called Osmar Steinwald, director of the Johns Hopkins Alumni Association, and asked him if I could attend the reception.

Os said, "Sure, John, just send me a check for $7.50, and I'll send you a ticket."

At the reception I waited for my opportunity to meet President Reed. After he left a group, I introduced myself. He looked at me and said, "Yes, I think I've heard of you. Please excuse me. I have some people I must see."

That was the only time I ever met the president of the university.

In 1957 Dr. Milton Eisenhower, the brother of President Dwight Eisenhower, would accept the presidency of Johns Hopkins University. He had been president of Penn State University. It encouraged me as I felt he had an interest in college athletics. However, I accepted a job with the Baltimore Colts before Dr. Eisenhower took office as president. All the sports programs at Johns Hopkins did improve after he was president, perhaps because Hopkins just had better coaches.

In 1955 we were again improved but not good. We lost our opening game in Lancaster to Franklin and Marshall 14-7. However, we didn't win until our seventh game, when we beat Swarthmore 19-6. We lost to Dickinson 7-6 and played Western Maryland in a snow storm. Ben Civiletti, who later would be attorney general under President Jimmy Carter, blocked a punt and then picked it up and ran it in for a touchdown. With that spark we went on to a 33-0 victory.

It appeared our players enjoyed playing in the snow more than Western Maryland did. In a two-year period we had gone from a 46-0 loss to a 33-0 victory. That win gave us confidence for the 1956 season.

The academic department which showed the most interest in the football program was the physics faculty. Dr. Leon Mandansky, a professor in the Physics Department, and his colleagues developed a keen interest in our football program. I began showing the game films after lunch in 1955. Other faculty members attended, but the physics faculty was most prevalent.

I wanted to be a good football coach more than anything in the world. Yet we had a grand total of six wins against 18 losses in my first three years as head coach in college football.

During the off-season I did everything I could to increase interest among our players. I asked some of the Baltimore Colt players to come out and demonstrate some of their techniques to our players. We had Arthur Donovan, an All-Pro tackle, talk to our linemen and demonstrate his technique of meeting the pressure of the blocker, getting rid of him, and reacting to make the tackle on a running play or rushing the passer on a pass. Bert Rechichar, who had been a great player at the University of Tennessee and a safety for Baltimore, came out and talked about defensive secondary play and place kicking. Jim Mutscheller, the Colts' tight end, demonstrated his blocking technique and his release from the line of scrimmage on a pass play. Mutscheller was a classy gentleman. He had graduated from Notre Dame.

I requested film from the University of Tennessee, where Bowden Wyatt was head coach. Bowden and his Tennessee team, using the single wing, won the national college championship in 1956. We added some of the Tennessee plays to our offense. Bowden Wyatt was also chosen the American Football Coaches Association Coach-of-the-Year in 1956 by his coaching peers.

In 1955 Wilson Fewster, a former great lacrosse player and head lacrosse coach, became our offensive and defensive line coach. Wilson had played football at Poly High School in Baltimore. Although he did not play in college, he had a good mind and good instinct for coaching. He and I worked together well. He was very intense and did an excellent job. Wilson was also an assistant lacrosse coach.

Bobby Scott returned from a tour of duty in the army. He was an officer in the Rangers, the elite combat troop in the army. Bobby was head lacrosse coach and freshman football coach. He ended his coaching career with seven national championships in lacrosse, the second most of any lacrosse coach in history.

Ross Sachs, Wilson Fewster, and Bobby Scott were excellent coaches and even better people. I've never worked with coaches who were more loyal, cooperative team players.

I was determined to do everything possible to have a successful season in 1956. During the summer, I sent a letter to all our players every two weeks. I encouraged them to stay in good condition and do what they could to improve their skills and fundamentals as a football player.

Our squad was the team with the fewest number of players on the squad of any I coached and perhaps the smallest players physically of any Hopkins team since before World War II. We anticipated a 28-man squad and had some good players returning. Our three senior linemen were the best linemen we had during my stay at Johns Hopkins. They were Don Gallagher, a center and linebacker at about 6'2 and 185, Ken McGraw, a tackle at 6'1 and 185, and Sam Wright, a guard at 6'0 and 195. They were very sound fundamentally and had good quickness and enjoyed physical contact. We also had Ben Civiletti returning at strong side end. Ben was a good blocker and an excellent defensive end. He blocked the Western Maryland punt which sparked a big win in 1955.

In the backfield, senior Jerry Carr returned at blocking back. He was a consistent blocker, pass receiver, and excellent defensive back. At our reunions in 1985 and 1991, Jerry mimicked me as head coach. I think he could have well been a stand-up comedian rather than a very successful financial administrator for a very large insurance company. He may also have been a great coach.

We had four excellent junior players, including Cliff Harding, a triple threat tailback. Cliff was the best athlete we had at tailback in my four years. He was a very good runner with quickness and speed, a better than average passer, and an able punter.

Harry Warfield was our fullback. He looked like a football player and was a strong runner and blocker at about 190 pounds.

Bobby Edwards was a bright-eyed, intelligent football player who was a clutch player on offense and who came up with big plays on defense. He played weak side end on offense and defensive right end.

Dowell Schwartz was a very heady football player. He backed up Jerry Carr at blocking back and when Jerry missed two or three games, he filled in with no letdown.

We had three good prospects off the freshman team and an upper classman who joined our squad for the first time. He was Ernie Bates, fullback (and the first black football player at Johns Hopkins). Ernie was the fastest back on our squad and was a strong runner. He was an excellent football player.

Milt Holstein was a 155-pound guard who was about 5'7. It's hard to believe how well he played and how good he was fundamentally.

Frank Frenda was a guard who didn't start, but he was a very capable player. He was strong and quick, and made an excellent back-up guard for Sam Wright and Milt Holstein.

Dick Auffarth was a very good football player in high school in Baltimore at Patterson Park High School. We changed his position from guard to wing back primarily because we wanted a good blocker there to improve our running offense. He was an excellent defensive player. Dick scored the winning touchdown in our game with Hampden-Sydney on a reverse and preserved a tie with Franklin and Marshall with an interception inside our ten-yard-line in the fourth quarter with less than a minute to play.

Don Gallagher and Ken McGraw were our co-captains. They were dedicated to their schoolwork and to football. On the final exam in an atomic physics course, Don and Ken made the two highest grades.

Before official practice began, Ken McGraw called all of our players living in Baltimore and set a time and place where they would meet together. Ken led the workouts almost every afternoon to prepare for the 1956 season. With the number of players we had, it was imperative for our players to be in good condition.

A week before our opening game we traveled to Lexington, Virginia, and had a game-like scrimmage with Washington and Lee University. They had over 60 players in uniform, while we had 27. To my pleasant surprise we dominated the scrimmage both offensively and defensively.

There was only one very sad and disturbing event. Don Gallagher, our senior co-captain and center, suffered a severely injured knee. Don had led our team in tackles for two seasons. He was an outstanding student and leader. He was 6'2, 185 pounds, and had the instinct of finding the football that all good linebackers have.

We only had one other center on the squad. That was Larry Littman, who had attended a high school in Baltimore County that didn't have a football team. Except for freshman football, he had never participated in a game before. Larry's performance in the scrimmage against Washington and Lee was surprisingly good.

Our opening opponent was Franklin and Marshall. We viewed them and Carnegie Tech as the two strongest teams on our schedule.

Franklin and Marshall had a halfback, George Darrow, who weighed about 205 pounds with good speed. He was bigger than anyone on our team.

I met with Ken McGraw, our other co-captain, and told him he would have to learn to snap the ball the coming week and start the game at center and linebacker. I just didn't want Littman to start with his inexperience. We would substitute Littman at center late in the first quarter and Ken McGraw would go back to his regular tackle position.

Franklin and Marshall was heavily favored, but we got the jump on them. In the first half they did not make a first down on the ground as our defense swarmed Darrow. We drove to the one-yard-line but failed to score on fourth down.

On our next possession, Guy Railey, who was a substitute for Cliff Harding at tailback, threw a 38-yard touchdown to Bob Edwards to give us a 7-0 halftime lead.

Franklin and Marshall came back strong in the second half and Darrow scored on an 18-play drive. He kicked the extra point to tie the game at 7-7. Franklin and Marshall had a long pass completion to our 11-yard-line in the fourth quarter, but Dick Auffarth intercepted a pass with a minute left to preserve the tie.

We lost to Carnegie Tech 19-13 in Pittsburgh. We led 13-12 at halftime. Ernie Bates ran 45 yards for a touchdown and Bobby Edwards scored on a 65-yard run back on a pass interception.

We beat Hampden-Sydney in our first Mason-Dixon conference game 14-13. Cliff Harding ran 30 yards on a sweep for a touchdown, and Dick Auffarth scored on a reverse. Harding kicked both extra points. Hampden-Sydney scored in the third quarter to make the score 14-13 but missed the extra point.

We lost two games to probably the weakest teams on our schedule, Haverford and Swarthmore. We lost to Haverford College 14-13. Haverford scored twice on touchdown passes, one after recovering a fumble on our 38 and a 65-yard scoring pass from their 35. We dominated most of the game but weren't able to make the plays to win.

We scored on a 77-yard drive, with Harding throwing to Civiletti in the end zone and a 62-yard drive with Warfield scoring from the one-yard-line, but a missed extra point by Cliff Harding gave Haverford the win.

We played our second conference game in Ashland, Virginia, against Randolph-Macon at their homecoming. We played to a scoreless tie for three quarters, but Cliff Harding scored twice in the fourth quarter. He went in from the one on a 48-yard drive and then scored on a 27-yard sweep around left end to make the score 13-0.

Harding and Warfield gained 250 yards between them on the ground of our 302 yards rushing.

The next game in Baltimore we played Swarthmore on a very muddy field. The only score came after Harding shanked a punt out of bounds on our 26-yard-line. Swarthmore drove in for the only score in a 7-0 victory.

We had our best offensive game of the year when we beat Dickinson 40-0 in Baltimore. Dickinson had beaten Swarthmore earlier in the year.

Our final game of the year was in Westminster, Maryland, against Western Maryland. A win would give us the Mason-Dixon Conference Championship and the first winning football season at Johns Hopkins since 1948. The game was a defensive struggle. We finally scored in the third quarter when Ernie Bates scored from the one on a wedge play. Our defense played extremely well. The final score was 7-0.

In the last four games our defense gave up seven points, the touchdown scored by Swarthmore. Even though we had three losses, we were only 14 points from an undefeated season. Our opponents averaged 7.4 points per game for the season. From 1953, when our opponents averaged 26.1 points per game, we improved defensively each year. In the first three games of the 1953 season our opponents scored 100 points.

When Dowell Schwartz was injured in the fourth quarter of the Western Maryland game, we didn't have a blocking back since Jerry Carr was out with an injury. We played Sam Wright, a guard at blocking back, about five or six minutes in the fourth quarter. Frank Frenda took Wright's place at guard.

It was one-platoon football, and the coach couldn't call plays. Sam said he knew the blocking back on our off-tackle play blocked the end. He called our off-tackle play about five or six straight times and we were able to control the ball until the final whistle. Sam was one of the best offensive blockers on our squad, and he felt his blocking made the play go. It certainly helped.

Ken McGraw awarded the game ball to Don Gallagher, who was unable to play after his knee injury in the Washington and Lee scrimmage. Don Gallagher continued to show leadership throughout the season. McGraw was named to second-team Associated Press Little All-American. He accomplished the unusual feat of playing every second of every game. He played every play on offense, defense, and special teams.

Larry Littman, our sophomore center, who had not played high school football, played 60 minutes in the last seven games. Cliff Harding was our leading ground gainer and passer. One other starter who played up to his potential was Don Macaulay, our strong side tackle. Don was about 6'0 and 190 pounds. The average weight of our starting line was about 180 pounds or less, and the average weight of our team was under 175 pounds. Our starters probably averaged 50 to 55 minutes per game.

We were very fortunate not to have many injuries. The only starters I recall missing games because of injuries were Jerry Carr and Dowell Schwartz at blocking back, and Don Gallagher at center.

With only 26 active players we could not afford injuries. Our practice time was limited to an hour and a half. We continued blocking and tackling drills, but the drills were not at full speed. We emphasized good form and proper technique. On offense we emphasized timing, technique, and all-out hustle. On defense we drilled on stopping the plays our opponents performed best, pursuit, and swarming defense. Perhaps one of the most underemphasized fundamentals is "locate the football and run it down."

My best years as head coach followed the principle of no full-speed contact after preseason and to limit practice to an hour and a half or an hour and forty-five minutes. Even in my worst years, my teams improved and played better the last third of the season. When the emphasis is on scrimmage and full-speed drills, a coach becomes a selector of survivors rather than a coach.

One of the best compliments I ever received from a player came from Micky O'Ferrall, a guard on one of my Hopkins teams. At our 1991 reunion he said, "One of the things I admired most about you, Coach, was that no matter how many disappointments you had, you always came back the next week with enthusiasm. You never gave up. I thought of you often when I had a discouraging event in my law profession. I remember how you kept trying as hard as you could."

The university awarded chenille H letters for a football award. Our players got together and ordered handsome blue and black (Johns Hopkins colors) jackets with the letter "H" and the inscription, "Mason-Dixon Conference Football Champion 1956." The players paid for their own jackets. Some of them wore their jackets to our reunions in 1985 and 1991. The jackets may have fitted a little tighter, but the men could still get in them.

The Hopkins players were every bit as proud of their championship as the Baltimore Colts were of their World Championship in 1958 in the "greatest game ever played" with the New York Giants. I know because I helped coach both teams.

Many people might say that football wasn't really important to anybody at Johns Hopkins. But don't say that to those players who won the 1956 Mason-Dixon Conference Championship.

The university gave me the Gilman Award. It was an award given to a member of the faculty who made outstanding contributions to student life. I was the first coach to receive the award.

My overall won-lost record at Johns Hopkins was not impressive — 10 wins, 21 losses, and one tie. However, as the years go by, my coaching career there becomes more satisfying. That's primarily due to the attitude and effort of the players.

Counting the last three games of each year, our record was 6 wins and 6 losses. The last two years we were 4-2. In each season we were stronger at the end of the season than we were at the beginning. That's an indication of good morale despite some tough early losses.

At the 1991 reunion, I told our players that the Hopkins football teams of 1953 through 1956 produced 18 medical doctors. The teams of those years may have contributed more to the public health of the nation than any football teams over the same length of time in history. I believe those 18 players who became doctors were better doctors than football players. But the important thing is that they gave their best effort to be as good as they could be in football and medicine.

CHAPTER 7

SOME JOHNS HOPKINS HEROES

Milt Holstein, Guard

Milt Holstein is a football player I will never forget. He did as much with his God-given ability as anyone I ever coached.

When Milt was in high school at Calvert Hall, which was a Catholic prep school in Baltimore, I visited him there and encouraged him to attend Johns Hopkins. Calvert Hall almost always performed well in high school football in Baltimore. As was true with many Catholic high schools, they seemed to get a great deal out of their players.

Milt received honorable mention for the Maryland All-State football team.

The McCormick Company, nationally known for producing cooking products, primarily flavoring spices, gave a very fine banquet each year for Baltimore high school football teams. The unsung heroes were honored at this banquet. Each team selected a player as "an unsung hero," and Milt Holstein was the choice at Calvert Hall.

After Milt finished his freshman football season at Johns Hopkins, I saw him one day on the campus. Milt was very quiet, a little on the shy side. You would never suspect he was a good football player. He was only about 5'7, if that tall, and a little on the pudgy side, probably about 170 to 175 pounds.

I said, "Milt, you've got to get some of that baby fat off you if you are going to be able to play next fall."

Milt replied, "Yes, sir." He was the kind of young man who wanted to please and never made any long speeches.

The next time I saw Milt, he weighed about 155 pounds (if that much). I said, "Milt, what's happened to you?"

"Coach, you told me to get that baby fat off and I got it off," he said.

Milt was not particularly fast, and he wasn't unusually strong. However, he had strong, short legs and good quickness. He also had a capacity to visualize what you were talking about when football techniques were explained. He learned fundamentals of body position, good leverage, good foot movement with short quick steps, and perfect balance from a low football position.

Milt graduated with honors from high school and was a good student at Johns Hopkins. His major was business and industrial management. He graduated in four years and then went to graduate school at the University of Illinois.

During my years at Hopkins, I became friends with Dick Harlow, who was living in Westminster, Maryland, where Western Maryland College was located. Dick had been head coach at Harvard and before that at the University of Pennsylvania. He had the title of advisory coach at Western Maryland.

The first year the American Football Coaches Association (AFCA) named a "College Coach of the Year" was 1935. In 1936 the AFCA awarded Dick Harlow of Harvard the title of "Coach of the Year."

I admired Coach Harlow and visited with him during the off-season. After our win over Western Maryland in our final game in 1956, I took our film of the game and showed it to Coach Harlow. We had shutout three of our last four opponents and allowed only seven points in the last four games.

Dick Harlow was amazed at how Milt Holstein could take on blockers who outweighed him by 40 to 50 pounds, neutralize them, react to the ball, and make the tackle. In the two basic defenses we used, Holstein lined up on either the guard or tackle. He was equally adept at shedding the blocks of either the guard or tackle.

Milt had started all eight games in our season, and I don't ever remember him playing a bad game.

After I began coaching with the Colts, my friendship with Dick Harlow continued. The Colts' preseason training camp was held in Westminster at Western Maryland College. Dick Harlow would sometimes watch our practice sessions, and I also visited him at his home in the evenings when our schedule permitted.

When I applied for the head coaching job at Baylor University, I asked Dick Harlow to write me a letter of recommendation. That probably helped me more than anything else I did to get the job. Dick's letter made me appear better than I was, but most letters of recommendation exaggerate somewhat. I really believe that Milt Holstein's vivid impression on Dick Harlow in the film of the Western Maryland game had a lot to do with Dick Harlow's very strong recommendation.

In a very real sense, Milt Holstein helped me get a head coaching job in Division I-A football. There are not many 155-pound guards who help their coaches get better jobs.

A portion of Dick Harlow's letter was printed in the *Waco Times-Herald* in Dave Campbell's column. Campbell wrote, in part, "And then there is the reference in one of the letters of recommendation received by McCall [chairman of Selection Committee and dean of Baylor University Law School]. It came from a retired coach who, in his day, won about all the honors there were to win. He was head coach for 35 years."

He listed four major reasons cited by Harlow for Baylor to consider me, two of which were:

"He has terrific drive and desire. I saw him under very different circumstances at Johns Hopkins where he did a terrific job without one football player. . . .He is one of the best teachers of fundamentals I have ever known anywhere. He will do as fine a job of teaching on the football field as the best professors you have in science or the classics."

A coach becomes a good coach of fundamentals when his players respond and they have the athletic ability to execute the fundamentals which are taught. I believe Dick Harlow's basis for this highly complimentary statement was due to his impression of Milt Holstein.

Milt currently is director of compensation and benefits, Allied-

Signal Automotive Sector in Northville, Michigan. I'm sure he is
still doing a consistent, excellent job in carrying out his responsibilities as he did when he played at Johns Hopkins in 1956. Milt was
elected co-captain of the Johns Hopkins football team in his junior
year, which reflects the confidence his teammates had in him.

Milt attended the Johns Hopkins football reunions of 1985 and
1991 in Baltimore. He was still the same person — quiet, reserved,
and still about 155 pounds.

His most memorable experience in college football was starting
as a sophomore on the Mason-Dixon Conference Championship
team.

When asked what Johns Hopkins and small college football
meant to him, Milt said, "Johns Hopkins and small college football
gave me the opportunity that I would not have experienced otherwise. The team closeness, competition, win and lose are not unique
to football — but are present in everyday living. College football
was an important factor in preparing me for the real world!" Milt
added a P.S.: "Because of my physical stature — nobody believes
that I played football!"

And nobody, from just looking at him now or 33 years ago,
would believe how well he played.

Ernest A. Bates, Fullback

Ernie Bates was the first black player to participate in football
at Johns Hopkins University. He arrived as a freshman in 1954, but
did not play football until the fall of 1956.

In our single wing offense we played him at fullback. Ernie was
about 5'1 and 175 pounds. In 1956 we had a returning letterman,
Harry Warfield, who was built like a fullback, at about 185 to 190
pounds. Warfield was the starter, but Bates was an excellent back-up
man. Ernie was a strong runner and the fastest back on our team.
His best position might have been at tailback, but he wasn't a passer,
and we needed a back who could throw at tailback.

Ernie was a pre-med major. He was quiet but very bright and
well liked by the other players on our squad.

Only 26 players on our squad were able to play. Ernie Bates just
came to Hopkins and joined the football squad. As far as I know, he

wasn't encouraged by anyone on our football staff to attend Johns Hopkins and play football.

He was from Rochester, New York, and had lettered in high school football and track. He set the 100-yard dash record at 9.9 seconds. That record stood for about 20 years.

Our scrimmage with Washington and Lee University was our first competition on the outside. It was also the first indication that we would be a much improved team in 1956. Our defense played well, and Ernie Bates demonstrated he would be a player to reckon with during the 1956 season.

Our team was pleased with their performance as we loaded the bus to head back to Baltimore. We left Lexington late on a Saturday afternoon, and I hoped we could reach Washington, D.C., or Maryland before eating dinner. However, our players kept repeating they were hungry since they had not eaten since their pre-scrimmage meal that morning. I decided we would stop at a restaurant on the Virginia side of Washington. What concerned me was I wasn't sure Ernie Bates would be served in Virginia, since segregation laws were still very much in effect.

While we were in the restaurant, I kept watching Ernie to see if they would serve him. After a while, it became obvious they would not serve him.

I decided my best course of action was to complain to the manager about the slow service. I told him we had to get to Baltimore, and I went to two or three players, including Ernie Bates, and asked them what they wanted. I asked the waiter to bring the orders to me. When he did, I served the players their orders, including Ernie Bates. After I served them, I gave the manager my meanest-looking glare. He didn't say anything. We were soon on our way back to Baltimore.

In our second game of the season Ernie ran 45 yards for a touchdown, but Carnegie Tech edged us 19-13. In our victory over Randolph Macon, Ernie ran 63 yards for an apparent touchdown but was ruled to have stepped out of bounds.

Ernie showed steady improvement throughout the season. In our final game with Western Maryland the score was 0-0 at halftime. In the third quarter, after Warfield intercepted a pass and returned to the Western Maryland 42-yard-line, Cliff Harding swept left end for 13 to the 29-yard-line. On fourth and 11 Harding threw to Bob

Edwards for a first down on the 12. Harding gained five. Bates ran for a first down to the one-yard-line and then took the ball in the end zone for the winning touchdown and a Mason-Dixon Conference Championship. Harding kicked the extra point to make the final score 7-0.

Ernie played two more years of varsity football and continued to improve as a football player. After graduation he was accepted into medical school at the University of Rochester. He received his medical degree in 1962. After further medical study, he became a practicing neurosurgeon and later founded the American Shared Hospital Services, Inc. He is now chief executive officer of the corporation which has been very successful. Ernie is also a trustee of Johns Hopkins University, one of three of my former players who are trustees.

When we had our first reunion of the Hopkins teams I coached, Ernie came from San Francisco to attend the reunion. He told me, "Coach, the main reason I came back to the reunion was because you stuck your neck out to get me something to eat when we stopped for dinner in Virginia when we scrimmaged at Washington and Lee."

He continued, "You could have said, 'Ernie, we will get you something to eat down the road because they don't want to serve you here.'" Ernie said he always appreciated what I did.

Scoring the touchdown in the 1956 Western Maryland game was his most memorable experience in college football. "I made the closest friends in college from that team," he said, "friendships which have continued for the past 33 years."

Ernie Bates was the first of three black players I coached who were the first to play football at their respective universities. As a southerner from Alabama, I am very proud to have coached Dr. Ernie Bates and the other two players, who became outstanding professionals in the Christian ministry.

Dick Watts, Fullback

In 1950 Dick Watts was awarded a football scholarship at High Point College in High Point, North Carolina. After a year he dropped out of school, got married, and went to work. Then he realized he needed an education to realize his dreams of being a coach.

In the fall of 1952 he was admitted to Johns Hopkins. Since he was a transfer, he could only play junior varsity football and was not eligible for the varsity. By this time he had two daughters. His wife worked, but it wasn't enough to support his family. Dick was able to get a part-time job at a service station. He went to classes in the morning and early afternoon, practiced football, wrestling or lacrosse, depending on the season, went to work after practice and closed the station at 1:00 A.M.

I came to Hopkins as head football coach in 1953. Dick was 23 years old and a sophomore. He was one of the few players on the squad who had varsity high school experience. Dick was our fullback, punter, and place kicker. He loved football and was the leader of our 1953 team. His attitude, effort, and spirit set the pace for the other players.

Dick was 5'11, 175 pounds, and strongly built, but he didn't have great speed. However, you could depend on him to give his best effort at all times. He was the oldest player on the team at 23. He not only was the oldest, he looked the oldest. His hairline was beginning to recede.

In our first three games we scored 12 points while our opposition, Franklin and Marshall, Carnegie Tech and Hampden-Sydney, scored 100 points.

Our fourth game was at Susquehanna University in Sellingsgrove, Pennsylvania. Dick led us to our first win, 12-6. He gained almost 100 yards. Coach Alonzo Stagg, Sr., was the advisory coach at Susquehanna. His son Alonzo Stagg, Jr., was the head coach. The senior Stagg was one of the famous names in the early history of college football. He held the record for the most college victories in history until "Bear" Bryant, head football coach at Alabama, broke his record. Since then, Eddie Robinson of Grambling State University has set a new record. Stagg still holds the record for the most years as head football coach of a college or university.

Coach Stagg came over to our bus and asked for Dick Watts. Coach Stagg shook Dick's hand, and said, "I just want to tell you how well you played in today's game!" Dick says that was his most memorable experience in college football. It also illustrates what a fine gentleman Coach Alonzo Stagg, Sr., was.

Randolph Macon and Swarthmore beat us decisively in our next two games. We came back against Dickinson and won 13-12. Dick Watts kicked the winning extra point.

John Steers and Dick Watts were our offensive leaders for 1953. John Steers (now a surgeon in Baltimore County) was a tailback in our single wing and ended up 28th in the nation in passing. Johnny Unitas of the University of Louisville finished 30th. It's true statistics can be misleading.

Dick Watts and Arlyn Marshall, a blocking back, were elected co-captains for the 1954 Johns Hopkins football team. Our 1954 squad was a bit stronger than the 1953 squad, but we were still not good enough. The scores were a little closer.

We played Drexel Tech in the place of Susquehanna, one of our victories in 1953. Drexel may have been the best team we played that season as they shellacked us 27-0, our most one-sided defeat of the season. We defeated Hampden-Sydney 14-13, which was a 27-point turnaround from the previous season, and beat Swarthmore 20-19, a 20-point turnaround from 1953. We lost two close ones in our two final games, 13-6 to Dickinson and 12-7 to Western Maryland. Dick Watts kicked both extra points in the Hampden-Sydney game for the victory margin and two extra points against Swarthmore, which gave us a win.

In our four wins over two seasons, Dick Watts' place kicking was the winning margin in three games, and his running against Susquehanna was the difference in that victory. Dick also averaged 44 yards punting in a losing cause to Carnegie Tech.

Dick Watts was a fine all-around football player but not a real star. The reason I selected him as one of Johns Hopkins' heroes is because he had amazing determination to get an education, support his family, and participate in sports. Dick worked up to seven hours during football, wrestling and lacrosse seasons, and longer hours during the off-season. While taking a full load of academic courses at one of the best universities in the country, on a schedule few people could have endured, he received his bachelor's degree in 1957.

Dick was ruled ineligible for the 1955 football season as NCAA rules require a player to finish his four years of participation in a period of five years. Since his first year was at High Point College in 1950, his five years were up after the 1954 season. In 1955 Dick was assistant coach for the Hopkins freshman team. He competed in lacrosse, which is a spring sport, and was an excellent player in 1954 and All-American in 1955 and 1956. The five-year rule did not apply in lacrosse since he did not play lacrosse at High Point College.

I'm not sure I've ever known anyone who exemplified better than Dick Watts the inspiring quotation of Calvin Coolidge:

> Nothing in the world can take the place of persistence.
> Talent will not; nothing is more common than unsuccessful men with talent. Genius will not; unrewarded genius is almost a proverb.
> Education will not; the world is full of educated derelicts.
> Persistence and determination are omnipotent.

After graduating from Johns Hopkins, Dick Watts coached and taught at Friends School in Baltimore for seven years; coached football, lacrosse and wrestling at Kenyon College in Ohio for three years; was athletic director and department chairman at University of Maryland-Baltimore County from 1967 to 1985; and since then has been head lacrosse coach and assistant professor of physical education at the same university. His lacrosse team completed a 10-5 season in 1992 and was ranked 17th in the nation in Division I. His 1979 and 1980 Division II Teams played for the National Championship and won it in 1980.

During this period, after graduating from Hopkins, he completed courses at Loyola College at Baltimore and received his master's degree.

Dick is one of those blue-collar workers who has made the grade and passed many gifted white collar individuals along the way. He is 64 years old now and has no thoughts of retiring.

Don Gallagher, Center and Linebacker

Don Gallagher came to Johns Hopkins from Johnstown, Pennsylvania. Pennsylvania is known for rugged, aggressive football players. Don Gallagher fit that mold. He was far and away the best linebacker we had in my years at Johns Hopkins. He was a starter as a sophomore and led our team in tackles in 1954. As a junior, he was elected captain and also elected as co-captain as a senior. He also led the team in tackles in 1955.

Don was 6'2 and 185 pounds, built on the lanky side but strong and an excellent tackler. Don was red-headed and played with a lot of fire. In both his sophomore and junior year, he was honorable mention, Little All-American.

In addition, Don was an outstanding student. He was valedictorian of his class in high school. At Hopkins, he majored in civil engineering. At Johns Hopkins he received the Barton Cup, an award to the outstanding man in the senior class, based on scholarship, leadership, and character.

Don was quiet but was well-liked and very well respected by coaches and players. He didn't say much, but when he spoke, it was meaningful.

One of the saddest moments at Johns Hopkins for me was when Don Gallagher suffered a serious knee injury in our scrimmage with Washington and Lee in Lexington, Virginia. Up until his injury, I thought he was the outstanding defensive player in the scrimmage.

We didn't know but we suspected he was through for the season. We found out, after our orthopedist examined him in Baltimore, that our suspicions were well founded. However, Don continued to be a part of the team, even though he was on crutches. He was at all of our games and came out to practice at times.

In 1955, Don's junior year, the scores were closer but we still didn't play to our potential until the last three games. For the first time in three years we were not shut out. Franklin and Marshall had outscored us 88-31 in the first two years but could only squeak out a 14-7 win. Randolph-Macon had beaten us 27-0 in 1954 and beat us by only three points in 1955.

We lost to Dickinson in Carlisle by 7-6, but won from Swarthmore in Baltimore 19-6.

Our final game was played in a snow storm and we defeated Western Maryland 33-0. It was our first shutout in three years. The game gave us confidence for the 1956 season.

We were 2-6 for the third straight year. There was a 2.4-point difference between our average score and the average scores of our opponents. In 1953 there was a 20.0-point difference.

Don Gallagher had never played lacrosse in high school but became a pretty good lacrosse player before he graduated.

After our final game with Western Maryland in 1956, our players showed their respect for Don Gallagher by giving him the game ball. Don wrote that his most memorable experience in college football was being part of the team that won the Mason-Dixon Conference Championship. He commented further, "The total experience of college football brings back a lot of on and off field memories."

Don Gallagher has been a success since he left college. He is now a regional director of Pennsylvania Electric Company.

College football is still important to Don Gallagher. He wrote, "Firstly, college football was an opportunity to play a game I thoroughly enjoyed. Beyond that, and more importantly, it bonded me to a terrific group of guys with a common purpose, and gave me the opportunity to learn about football from people I respected, namely John Bridgers, Wilson Fewster, Bob Scott, and Ross Sachs. As you told an H Club gathering one night, it helped me to develop in many ways from a boy to a man. Many thanks for your considerable part in that."

Larry Littman, Center and Linebacker

When Don Gallagher suffered a serious knee injury in our scrimmage with Washington and Lee University, we only had one other center on our squad. He was Larry Littman, who had never played high school football. His only experience was on the 1955 Hopkins freshman team.

Larry was about 5'11 and 175 pounds. He had performed well in the scrimmage, but he was no Don Gallagher.

Our opening game was with Franklin and Marshall, a team who had beaten us for three straight years. They had a fast halfback, George Darrow, who was bigger than anyone in our starting lineup.

Since we only had 26 players on our squad, and nobody had ever played center, I decided we would have our most experienced defensive player learn the center position. In the single wing the center looks between his legs at the tailback and fullback, who are almost a yard apart and four to five yards deep. He has to make an accurate snap to either the fullback or tailback and then block effectively. The center also must make the deep snap to the punter. In addition, he had to learn the center's blocking assignments on all run plays and passes.

It's hard to learn to do that in a week and also learn a new defensive position. That's what Ken McGraw, our co-captain and offensive and defensive tackle, had to do. He learned it well. It was something that very few players could have done.

McGraw wasn't very pretty with his center snaps. They looked like knuckle balls. I didn't see any tight spirals, but the most important thing is that Ken was accurate with his snaps.

We got the jump on Franklin and Marshall and were able to hold them without a first down rushing in the first half. Ken McGraw played most of the first quarter at center, and the rest of the game at tackle.

Larry Littman came in and played like a veteran the rest of the game at center. Both Larry and Ken's performances were close to miraculous.

We scored in the first half and led 7-0. Franklin and Marshall scored on an 18-play drive in the third quarter. The game ended up in a tie. Even though a tie is not what you strive for, the achievement of tying Franklin and Marshall without Don Gallagher gave us a great deal of satisfaction and confidence.

In our locker room before each game we always said a prayer. We had Protestants, Catholics and Jews on our team. We didn't pray to win but prayed we would play our best and with courage and confidence. Larry Littman told me, "Coach, I feel like God is with me when I go on the field after our prayer in the locker room."

Larry played center and linebacker for every play in our remaining seven games. His performance surpassed what I thought he would be capable of doing. He continued to play well in his junior and senior years, and was honored by being elected co-captain of the 1958 Johns Hopkins team in his senior year.

Larry is president of the Hemingway Company in Waterbury, Connecticut, a manufacturing company which makes folding cartons and boxes. His position fits his major in economics at Johns Hopkins. Here's what Larry said about what college football meant to him, "Learning what a team really is — when I see Frank Frenda (a medical doctor in Chatam, New Jersey, who was a guard on the 1956 team), Milt Holstein (a guard from Baltimore), and Dick Auffarth (a wingback and linebacker for Baltimore), I really care for them. We spent three years next to each other — to this day, we have deep feelings for each other."

Like almost every other player on the 1956 Hopkins team, Larry's most memorable experience in football was starting as a sophomore, playing 60 minutes in seven games, and winning a championship.

Ben Civiletti, End

The most prestigious person to play on the Hopkins football teams of 1953 through 1956 was Ben Civiletti. Ben served as attorney general of the United States for about a year and a half under President Jimmy Carter. Before becoming attorney general, he held the second highest ranking post in the department, deputy attorney general, and for over a year was assistant attorney general in charge of the Criminal Division.

Ben's list of achievements, memberships in prestigious associations, boards and foundations, and honorary awards and degrees would cover at least two pages in small print. Since this book is about football and athletics, I will concentrate on his athletic experiences, except to mention a couple of his public service activities. Since he has returned to private practice, he has continued his commitment to public service. He chaired Maryland Governor Harry Hughes' two-year task force on funding of public education, which resulted in a $600 million legislative increase for public education. He serves as a vice-chairman of the Board of Trustees of Johns Hopkins University.

Ben came to Johns Hopkins from Peekskill, New York. He was very active in sports in high school, at Irving School in Tarrytown, New York, and ranked first in his class academically in 1952 and 1953, the year he graduated. He was a starter for three years in football, captain of the basketball team (which had an undefeated season 22-0), and set a school baseball record when he struck out 18 batters in a seven-inning game.

Ben continued to play three sports at Johns Hopkins, and was named the Johns Hopkins University "H" Club Athlete of the Year in 1956-57.

A starter on the Hopkins football team in 1956, Ben played strongside end in our balanced line single wing formation. He was used primarily as a blocker on offense. He did catch a touchdown pass in the Haverford game to put us in position to tie the game, but the extra point was wide and Haverford edged us 14-13. Ben's forte was defense.

On the night before our final game with Western Maryland in 1955, we had a snow storm. Almost six inches of snow lay on the field when we kicked off. The first time Western Maryland lined up in punt formation on fourth down, Ben blocked the punt and picked it up and ran it in for a touchdown. That play gave us a spark. We went on to a 33-0 victory — the largest victory margin in my four years. In my first year we had lost to Western Maryland 46-0, which was the largest margin of defeat in my 28 years of coaching.

The blocked punt which turned the game in our favor was the most memorable experience for Ben Civiletti. Another highlight was making eleven tackles against Carnegie Tech. Both of his most memorable experiences were on defense.

Ben addressed the question about what college football meant to him: "It opened my eyes to perseverance and leadership. The single wing was not a flashy formation or style of play, but with execution and teamwork even with modest talent could win, 3 or 4 yards at a time. The coaches blended individual attention with team direction and used all the leadership skills I now recognize to lead the effort and get the best from most student-athletes — pride, discipline, flattery, instruction and sympathy when and where needed."

When we had our 1991 reunion of the Hopkins players who played during my four years at Hopkins, our first meeting was at Ben Civiletti's home for a reception and dinner. He lived in North Baltimore, 10-15 miles from the city limits. Jerry Carr, our blocking back, and our best stand-up comedian, described the setting best. He was called on to say a few words since his comments always brought some laughter. He said, "Ben Civiletti lives on a lot which is half the size of Baltimore County. I got lost in the driveway on the way to his house. It's the longest driveway I've ever been on."

As a football coach and athletic director, I have had the opportunity to attend some extraordinary receptions and dinners, but certainly none better than the one at Ben's magnificent home. It was the perfect setting to kick off the weekend for a great reunion of our 1953-56 Hopkins football teams. Ben and his lovely wife, Gaile, served every kind of hors d'oeuvres you could think of, with emphasis on Chesapeake Bay oysters and crabs. The dinner was delicious.

The players enjoyed the reunion so much they decided we would have one every five years. The next one is 1996 and then 2001. I also want to make the one in 2006. All of our players will be much better than they were in the middle fifties.

Ben Civiletti impressed me as having a great deal of self-confidence. He was never satisfied to excel in just one area. Ben was about

6'1 and 185 pounds at Hopkins. He was good looking, blond, with a strong face. I believe his athletic participation in three sports in high school and college gave him a great deal of energy and endurance. The stamina he developed, along with his desire to excel, his competitiveness and his self-confidence, made a real contribution to his success as one of the country's outstanding lawyers.

There is no question in my mind that high school and college football does far more to make a person successful in his adult life than it does to make him a failure, as some writers indicate in their declaration of the corrupting influence of football.

Kenneth McGraw, Tackle

Ken McGraw came to Johns Hopkins unrecruited and unsolicited by the athletic department from Cumberland, Maryland. He was captain of Allegheny High School in Cumberland and was honorable mention on the All-State team his senior year.

Ken was a good football player when he arrived at Johns Hopkins. He improved each year he was at Hopkins as the season progressed.

Ken was about 6'1 and 185 pounds. He was strongly built but not bulky. He played in a period before weight training came into vogue. He had strong legs and good quickness and speed for a tackle. His physical condition was superb. I don't ever remember him looking completely spent or worn out, even after one of his numerous 60-minute games.

If I had to name one person who contributed the most to our Mason-Dixon Championship in 1956, it would be Ken McGraw.

During the summer of 1956 he showed leadership by organizing a voluntary conditioning program for all the Hopkins players who lived in Baltimore. With only 26 players on our squad after we finished our pre-season practice, we had to have a team in excellent physical condition. We couldn't attain the physical condition required during the three weeks of organized pre-season practice. It was a necessity that the players report for practice in good condition.

When Don Gallagher, our other co-captain, was injured and out for the season with a knee injury in the Washington and Lee scrimmage, I didn't believe we had anyone else on the squad who could learn to snap the football in a single wing formation, learn all the offensive blocking assignments at center, and learn a new defensive position he had never played before, linebacker, in a week's time. Ken not only did that, but to my memory he did not make a single mistake. We were able to get a 7-0 lead over the best team on our schedule while he was playing center.

We only had one other center on our squad, a sophomore who had not played high school football. Even if we had started Larry Littman at center, we had to have someone as a back-up center during the season. Ken McGraw, for the remainder of the season, was our starting offensive and defensive tackle and back-up center and linebacker.

McGraw was very durable. I don't ever remember him being hurt. Of course, he had some bruises and perhaps a slight sprain of an ankle or wrist, but he was always ready to play. He may have been one of the last football players in the country to play every second of every game for the entire season.

The rules allowed platoon football (separate teams for offense and defense) after World War II up to the early fifties, when the rules were changed to one-platoon football. The same players had to play offense and defense. Platoon football came back about 1964.

McGraw was a chemistry major in undergraduate school. He later obtained a master's in business administration at Harvard University and a master's in liberal arts at Hopkins. In 1956 he and Don Gallagher were enrolled in the same class in atomic physics. Our co-captains made the highest grades in the class on the final exam.

When I was at Hopkins, I was a member of the University Baptist Church. Ken McGraw was a baritone soloist in the choir. He began singing in the choir in his sophomore year. I knew little about music and frankly wasn't very interested, but I remember thinking then that I didn't know whether he would ever make a football player being a soloist in a church choir.

Later Ken told me that he was a "paid Baptist." In other words the church paid him to sing solos in the choir. From my experience in the Baptist church, there are not many "paid Baptists," but a great many Baptists who pay dearly to belong to the church (although voluntarily, I might add).

Despite being a soloist in the choir and an excellent student, Ken McGraw became a Little All-American football player at Johns

Hopkins. He was selected first team on the Williamson Rating System Little All-American and second team on the Associated Press Little All-American in 1956. He was also on the Chemical All-American team.

Ken is now a senior vice-president of a prominent investment bank on Park Avenue in New York City. He also has a home in McDowell, Virginia, where he lists his occupation as a farmer in addition to investment banker.

As to his most memorable experience in college football, he said, "No single event stands out. Just the opportunity to play a vigorous competitive sport and to play both offense and defense."

He described what college football meant to him: "Character development, lasting friendships and physical conditioning. Without getting into a rambling philosophical discussion as to the relative significance, each was important. We all continue and enjoy the special friendships established during the Hopkins football years.

"I feel the good health and relatively good physical condition I enjoy today emanate from the good habits and exceptional level of conditioning developed during those years.

"It is difficult to be concise or specific when writing about character building, and playing football at Hopkins was for me only part of the process. However, to work extremely hard, to taste victory and defeat, to share both as part of a group effort, to know physical pain, and to always be ready to come back for more, were but a few of the lessons we learned."

I truly believe the experiences of Ken McGraw and the other Hopkins players I've written about make a strong statement about the good in college football. There are many other Hopkins players I could have written about whose experiences and accomplishments have been comparable to these seven Hopkins heroes.

CHAPTER 8

1957–58

Baltimore Colts: Defensive Line and Offensive Tackle Coach

The 1956 football season at Johns Hopkins had been a very satisfying one. Despite the fact that there were only 26 players on the varsity squad, we had won the Mason-Dixon Conference by winning all three of our conference games with Hampden-Sydney, Randolph Macon, and our arch-rival Western Maryland. Our team was very close-knit and, I believe, played to the limit of its abilities as much as any team I ever coached. As a result, the team and I received more recognition than we were accustomed to getting.

On two or three occasions I was asked to speak on the same program with Weeb Ewbank, head coach of the Baltimore Colts. I had visited with Weeb a number of times to learn their offensive and defensive philosophy and had watched their practices in training camp and during the season. Weeb had coached the offensive and defensive tackles as an assistant coach with Cleveland.

When Frank Lauterbur took the job at Army, and the defensive line and offensive tackle coaching position was left open with the Colts, I think Weeb wanted to hire someone who would coach the defensive linemen and offensive tackles in a way that would fit into his thinking and philosophy. The danger of having assistant coaches is that you may have one who has been trained and has experience in an entirely different philosophy than the kind of football you wish to teach. Even though that coach may try to change his way of coaching to fit into the head coach's philosophy, he still may not be totally committed to an unfamiliar method, especially if the team does not achieve immediate success. Most successful coaches take a good part of their staff with them when they make a change.

Carroll Rosenbloom, the owner of the Colts, never said anything to me about it, but I heard he was both surprised and disappointed at Weeb's decision to hire me. The fact is that when a professional team hires an assistant coach, it very seldom looks for that coach at the Division III level, the lowest competitive level of college football.

I was thrilled with the opportunity and determined to learn everything I could about the Colts' system. The playbook was patterned after the one used by Paul Brown with Cleveland. The Colts played a keying defense in that the reaction of the linemen was based on the initial movements of the offensive linemen. I decided I would write down the precise technique and responsibility of the defensive ends and tackles on all possible blocking patterns by offensive linemen. After I wrote it up I would review it with Weeb so he could make any corrections he felt were necessary. Twelve years later, when I took a job with the Pittsburgh Steelers under Chuck Noll, who had been defensive coordinator with the Baltimore Colts, the Pittsburgh playbook had almost exactly the same assignments I had recorded some 12 years before.

Weeb's staff was composed of the following:

Herman Ball coached offensive guards and center in 1957. In 1958 Herman took over coaching all offensive linemen — center, guards, and tackles. He had been head coach of the Washington Redskins and was one of the finest men I've ever worked with as well as an excellent coach. Herman was highly respected.

Bob Shaw coached all receivers. He was an All-American at Ohio State and an outstanding professional football player with the Los Angeles Rams. He set an NFL record by catching five touchdown passes in a single game. He was knowledgeable and had gained the confidence of the receivers. Bob and I roomed together in training camp. As a player, he had been 6'4 and 225 pounds, with excellent speed. He was our only coach who had played professional football.

Charley Winner was defensive coordinator and coached secondary and linebackers. Charley was bright and did a good job with the defensive backs and linebackers. He later became head coach for the St. Louis Cardinals.

Weeb Ewbank, as head coach, coached the running backs and quarterbacks.

Today, teams have at least nine or ten assistant coaches, including a special-teams coach, and they are paid much more. My starting salary with the Colts was $7,200 annually. Weeb's salary after we won the 1958 championships was about $30,000. Now most assistant coaches in the NFL make in the vicinity of $100,000 and the top head coaches draw $500,000 to $1,000,000. The main difference with the players is that they are bigger and faster. All teams have a weight-training program. None that I knew of had weight training in 1957 and 1958.

Weeb is the only head coach to win an NFL Championship in the National Football League (1958 and 1959) and the American Football League (with the New York Jets in the 1969 Super Bowl). Although he is memorialized in the National Football Hall of Fame, he possibly hasn't received all the recognition he deserves. He has an excellent overall knowledge of football and was always capable of doing a good coaching job with any segment of players, offensively or defensively.

Not many coaches in NFL history organized or planned better than Ewbank. He constantly worked on his playbook during the off season and put in many hours on the game plan for each upcoming game. His practice sessions during the season gave continued emphasis on fundamentals. The sessions were limited to no longer than an hour and a half, which kept the players fresh and ready to play their best football during the latter part of a long and tiring season, when victories were critical in qualifying for the championship game. I remember one day during the season, the big clock in Memorial Stadium showed we had been on the field an hour and 35 minutes. Art Donovan, standing with a group in back of our offensive huddle, said, "This is ridiculous! Absolutely ridiculous!" In a couple of minutes, Weeb ended practice. Very few players liked to work overtime in team practice.

Personally, I shall always be indebted to Weeb. He gave me a chance to coach in professional football and enabled me to learn and gain confidence at a coaching level I probably would have never achieved without his willingness to take a chance on a young coach who was a marginal player in college football.

Weeb is a very likable person with a sense of humor. He has told some interesting stories from his background as a coach and his experiences with Paul Brown, the outstanding Cleveland Browns coach.

If I had to name a fault, it would be one that is quite common among professional head coaches and assistant coaches. Weeb did not always show belief and confidence in his players, and sometimes his actions communicated that to the players. When it came to the team, or an individual, following training rules and a high standard of conduct, he often expressed doubt about the players' intentions and their personal behaviors. As a result, some of the players didn't feel that Weeb trusted them (and that might have been true, to a degree). As a result, not all of his players consistently expressed the kind of loyalty to Weeb which he might have hoped for. There is a quote from Goethe, the great German philosopher: "Treat a man as he is and he will remain as he is; treat a man as he ought to be and could be and he will become what he ought to be and could be." The reply by many coaches might be that Goethe wasn't referring to professional football players, but I personally believe there is a great deal of truth in his quote as applied to football.

Of course, every coach has faults. But with the best ones, their good qualities far outweigh their faults, and this was very true with Weeb Ewbank. He worked hard and expected his assistants to work hard. However, he was considerate. For example, when we worked late, he would give the coaches a couple of hours to go home and eat dinner with their families.

Weeb delegated authority to assistants. All felt they had complete responsibility for their segment of players. Other than insisting that offensive linemen spend sufficient time on pass protection, he seldom offered input or suggestions on practice schedules.

When we graded films, usually on Monday after a Sunday game, we did it with all offensive and defensive coaches present. Every coach felt free to offer comments and suggestions on mistakes and breakdowns of players coached by other assistants. Sometimes we would get in heated arguments on which player was responsible for the breakdown on a particular play. Quite often Charley Winner, our defensive backfield and linebacker coach, and I disagreed. Being in charge of the secondary and defensing of the passing game, he wanted the defensive linemen to go all-out rushing the passer with little attention to the running game. In definite passing situations I wanted the linemen to give first emphasis to rushing the passer; however, if the first movement of the offensive linemen indicated a run, I wanted the linemen to react to the run.

Many coaches say that the running game sets up the passing game and that a team must be able to run effectively to make the passing game effective. I definitely believe it is to the advantage of the offense to be able to do both. The effectiveness of the no-huddle offense and the two-minute offense in the latter part of the half or game demonstrates that the passing game can be effective without the run. However, there must be a combination of pass protection, which is where it all starts for the passing game, receivers who can get open and catch the ball, and an accurate passer who believes in himself and his team.

The truth is that the passing game is more difficult to coach than the running game. It literally takes 11 men on every play for a good passing game. But with a great running back, a team can get by with one good block and a barely adequate block for a great runner to make good yardage. Great runners have been known to make good yardage even without a good block.

The technique most difficult to execute consistently for a lineman is drop back pass protection. Most of the time he is trying to block a person with more speed, quickness, and often more strength. The best athletes among linemen are generally placed on defense.

Some coaches talk about hitting the hot receiver when the defense rushes more than the usual four men, but teams are finding that very seldom is a receiver completely uncovered, even on a blitz. Even if a passer can complete a short pass, he often has to take a hard hit by a rusher who is untouched. Taking what amounts to a free hit by a pass rusher helps destroy the quarterback's concentration and confidence, risks injury, and increases the possibility of an interception. A quarterback who is being rushed hard seldom throws the ball with good timing, and the pressure interferes with his accuracy.

Brigham Young University won a national championship in 1984 with a very well-coached passing game. Lavell Edwards, the head coach of BYU, felt he had a better chance of winning against nationally ranked teams with a good passing game. He believed that the linemen he would be able to recruit, as well as the backs and receivers, would be more competitive with an excellent passing game than with an offense that featured the running game. His teams rank among the top winners in college football over the past 15 years.

Our practices with the Colts seldom ran over an hour and a half. We did most of our teaching in meetings before practice. During practice, we attempted to get in as many repetitions as possible.

With the defensive line, we emphasized pass rushing techniques, form tackling, pursuit, reacting to keys, containment of quarterback, linemen getting their hands high when quarterback throws in their direction, and agility drills. Not many of the linemen liked the agility drills, especially Art Donovan.

I remember one time we borrowed a reserve quarterback who would set up and scramble. It was the linemen's job to keep him contained and stay in position to have leverage on him so as to make the tackle or pressure him. There was a lot of running involved. Art Donovan asked, "Who in the hell thought up this drill?" I answered, "I did. Don't you think it's a good one?" "I don't think it's worth a damn," Donovan responded. He just didn't care to overexert himself with all that running except during a game.

Another time, when we were taking a short break, Donovan said, "I've had a lot of things happen to me in professional football, but there's one thing I thought would never happen and that is I would have a coach from Johns Hopkins."

I happen to be a couple of years older than Donovan, but he had lived a harder life and (I thought) looked older than I did. I teased him one time, "Donovan, you were my hero when I was in high school."

We had some fun when we practiced, and I really don't think it hurt our preparation.

Freddie Russell, an outstanding sportswriter with the *Nashville Banner*, spoke at an NCAA convention, and the theme of his talk was that champions almost always have a sense of humor. That's true with most of the champions I have known.

CHAPTER 9

THE 1958 WORLD CHAMPIONSHIP:
"THE GREATEST GAME EVER PLAYED"

In 1958 the Baltimore Colts won the Western Division of the National Football League with two games left to play to qualify for the World Championship Game against the New York Giants. The Colts came from behind on an 86-yard drive to tie the game at 17-17 with only nine seconds left on the clock. It was the first sudden-death playoff game in NFL history. After stopping the Giants, who had won the toss at the end of the regulation game, the Colts, led by Johnny Unitas, drove 80 yards for the winning touchdown by Alan Ameche. He scored from the one-yard-line to give the Colts a 32-17 victory.

The 1958 NFL Championship Game has repeatedly been voted by the media as the "greatest game ever played," and has been written about and recognized by many sportswriters. The game has meant more to me than any other game I ever coached, as I was defensive line coach with the Colts at the time.

Rather than write about the heroics and record-setting performances of Johnny Unitas, the outstanding Colts' quarterback, and Raymond Berry, the great wide receiver, who both set championship game records in pass completions, pass yardage, pass receptions and receptions yardage, I will reveal little known facts which had a distinct bearing on the outcome of the game.

The Giants defeated the Cleveland Browns in the last scheduled game of the regular season to tie the Browns for first place in the Eastern Division of the NFL. The next week the Giants won again in a playoff game for the Eastern Division Championship, 10-0. In a postgame interview with Roosevelt Brown, the outstanding offensive left tackle with the New York Giants, Brown was happy about the victory and said he was looking forward to playing the Colts. A reporter asked Brown about Don Joyce, who was the Colts' defensive right end and the Colts' defensive player that would be Brown's assignment to block on all pass plays and on some running plays. Brown's reply to the question regarding Joyce was: "I'm not worried about Don Joyce. I can handle him."

I saw the quote in the *New York Times* after the Giants' victory. I cut out the article and showed it to Bob Shaw, our receiver coach. He taped it to a white sheet of paper, highlighted the quotes with colored markers, and taped it on Joyce's locker. When the players reported to practice, I watched Joyce walk to his locker, read the article, rip it off the locker, and crumple it in his hand.

When we were reviewing the film of the Giants' game, Don Joyce's eyes had a fierce look. He was gazing off into space, not looking at the film. I knew he was going to be ready to play. Roosevelt Brown had made a mistake with his comments to the reporter.

In our first pre-season game with the Giants in Baltimore, Brown and Joyce had a flare up and exchanged punches. I don't remember all the details, but I know that Joyce was highly motivated when we played the Giants in a second consecutive pre-season game in Louisville. Brown and Joyce really went after each other. I don't recall any penalties being called, but there was justifiable cause for penalties by both players.

After the game, most of the players had showered and dressed and a number of our players and Giant players were standing outside the locker room, waiting to take buses to the airport. Roosevelt Brown approached Don Joyce and said, "Don, let's shake hands and forget what's happened in the past two games. I'm not the kind of player who likes to play like that. I don't think either of us wants to hold a grudge."

Joyce didn't say much, just sort of grunted and shook hands

with Roosevelt Brown. It just happened I was standing close to Joyce and overheard the conversation.

It was just too much for Joyce that Brown had initiated an apology to him and suggested they agree not to engage in illegal tactics as they did in two pre-season games, and then tell a New York reporter that he could handle Don Joyce.

Joyce played the best game in the championship game with the Giants that he had played in the two years I was defensive line coach. There certainly weren't many times in the game that Roosevelt Brown effectively blocked Don Joyce. Late in the second quarter, Joyce recovered a fumble on the Colts' 14-yard-line after our safety had turned the ball over to the Giants at our 10-yard-line by fumbling a punt. The fumble came on a sweep to the right, and Joyce gave hard chase for the fumble recovery. Joyce also made a key tackle when he caught Frank Gifford on a sweep to the right to stop him short of a first down late in the fourth quarter. A first down might have enabled the Giants to run the clock out and thus prevent the Colts' game-tying field goal with nine seconds left.

The Colts' linemen played a defense which keyed the movements of the offensive players on whom they were aligned. The Giants' favorite play was a power sweep, with both guards pulling leading the play.

The counterplays to the power sweep were a reverse to the back, who was normally a blocker for the ball carrier on the sweep, and a bootleg by the quarterback, who would fake a handoff to the halfback on the sweep and then roll out in the opposite direction on an option run or pass. The Giants ran the reverse once and were limited to a four-yard gain.

On the Giants' power sweep, the offside tackle would pull and pick up any penetration in the guard-center gap. If there was no penetration, he would continue down-field and block the offside linebacker. On the reverse or bootleg, the offside tackle would block the defensive end aligned on him to allow the quarterback to bootleg to the outside or allow the ball carrier on the reverse to get outside.

My instructions to our defensive ends were as follows: If the flow is away from you (the backs running a sweep to the opposite side) and the tackle pulls, chase the ball carrier as hard as possible. If the flow is away and the tackle blocks you, then work to the outside to contain the quarterback on the bootleg or make the tackle on the reverse. Our offside defensive end was able to help on the tackle three or four times on the sweep away from him. It took all-out hustle for a 250-pound defensive end to catch a back with a head start, but sometimes a back has to slow down to make his cut.

When we were warming up before the game, the thought came to me that it might help our defense against the sweep if we had one of our defensive tackles lined up on a guard, to shoot the gap left when he pulled on the sweep. By doing so, the tackle would be very vulnerable to a trap from his inside. Normally, our tackles took a pursuit angle in the direction of the sweep to cut the ball carrier off at the pass.

I told Lipscomb, who was our fastest tackle, to call the name of our middle linebacker when he was going to shoot the gap. The middle linebacker would move closer to the line of scrimmage to make the block of the offensive tackle, who had to clear behind the defensive tackle, more difficult. Such a move would strengthen our defense against the trap on the tackle.

We opened the game kicking off to the Giants. Gino Marchetti, the Colts' left defensive end, gave notice he was going to be tough to handle as he knocked down Heinrich's pass as it left his hand on the first scrimmage play. On the Giants' second possession, he tackled Heinrich for a seven-yard loss, forced a fumble, and recovered on the Colts' 45-yard-line.

In the game, our left outside linebacker, Leo Sanford, sustained a knee injury early in the game. Bill Pellington was moved from middle linebacker to left outside linebacker to replace Sanford, and Don Shinnick was moved from outside linebacker to middle linebacker. Steve Myhra, who was also our place kicker, went to right outside linebacker. At halftime, I told Shinnick about Lipscomb blitzing when Lipscomb called his name.

In the fourth quarter, with the Giants leading 17-14, they moved the ball from their 20 to the Colts' 42-yard-line with second down and six yards for a first down. Another first down and the Giants would be within easy field goal range. (The goal posts were on the goal line in 1958 rather than on the end-zone line.) Lipscomb called the blitz to Shinnick. The Giants' play was a sweep to the left. On the snap, Lipscomb came through the gap from where the guard pulled untouched and hit King, the Giant ball carrier, just as he was taking a handoff from Conerly about five yards in the backfield. King fumbled and the ball bounced to our 42-yard-line, where it was recovered by Ray Krouse, a defensive tackle who was subbing for Donovan.

It was unquestionably one of the biggest defensive plays in the game for the Colts that resulted in a 16-yard loss and a turnover when the Giants were within field goal range. From our 42-yard-line the field goal attempt would be 49 yards, as the goal posts were on the goal line. Big Daddy Lipscomb picked the perfect time to decide he was going to blitz.

The Giants made only two first downs in the game rushing. The official game statistics listed three first downs rushing, but there were only two in the official play by play. One was a ten-yard gain by Gifford in the fourth quarter on their power sweep and the other a quick toss to Gifford, who got outside Steve Myhra, our right outside linebacker, when both outside linebackers blitzed on a third and one situation. Gifford gained 38 yards, which was the longest run of the game, and set up their field goal to give the Giants a 3-0 lead in the first quarter. During the season the Giants gained more yardage rushing than passing. Excellent defensive play by the Colts' defensive line and linebackers prevented the Giants from having any consistency with their usually effective running game.

Rather than using their regular drop back passing offense, the Giants featured play passes when Conerly, the Giant quarterback, would fake a handoff to a running back and then drop back and throw. It was good strategy against the Colts' defense. Gino Marchetti was recognized as the best pass rusher in the NFL, and the Giants did not have anyone who could consistently block him. When the Giants' linemen blocked aggressively and faked a running play, our linemen would initially play the run, which slowed their penetration to the passer. Our best strategy would have been to call a blitz. With a back faking a run, the Giants could not have maximum protection. But hindsight doesn't count.

Charley Conerly had three pass completions for 149 yards, one for a touchdown and another for a first down on the Colts' two-yard-line, which resulted in a touchdown and a 17-14 lead in the second half. All three completions came off of play-action passes.

In the end, Johnny Unitas moved the Colts 86 yards in the last two minutes to tie the score on a field goal from the 13-yard-line with nine seconds left. Gino Marchetti had stopped Gifford two feet short of a first down on a third-down play, forcing a Giants' punt. Lipscomb assisted on the tackle but fell across Marchetti's right leg, breaking it in two places. Donovan was in on the tackle before Lipscomb arrived.

The winning 80-yard drive featured passing by Unitas, clutch receiving by Raymond Berry, a 22-yard gain on a trap play up the middle by Alan Ameche, and his touchdown run from the one-yard-line.

Another vivid memory after the game was Giants' quarterback, Charley Conerly, waiting outside our locker room to congratulate the Colts' players and coaches as we came out. I don't ever remember seeing anyone more gracious in defeat in a game which meant so much to both teams. I believe Charley Conerly recognized there was something special about the game even if the Giants lost. The writers had voted Conerly the outstanding player of the game in the fourth quarter, but took another ballot after the overtime period and voted the honor to Johnny Unitas.

In contrast to the Giants' success with play-action passes, the Colts suffered a couple of sacks on Unitas when play-action passes were called. Our bread and butter was straight drop back passes which, in the end, proved enough for one of the greatest football victories of all time.

Defensively, the Colts allowed the fewest yards rushing in both 1957 and 1958 in the NFL. Marchetti led our team by a large margin in passes knocked down and in sacks. He was also second to Big Daddy Lipscomb in tackles for the entire team.

In the championship game our offense was primarily Johnny Unitas, Raymond Berry and Alan Ameche, along with great pass protection by the offensive line, especially in the 86-yard drive for the tying field goal and the 80-yard drive in overtime which provided the winning margin. Lenny Moore and L. G. Dupre also provided some key runs and pass receptions that kept our two long scoring drives alive.

To really boil it down, it was a great overall team effort involving offense, defense, and special teams, which are truly the most important factors in winning.

CHAPTER 10

1957–58

GINO MARCHETTI:

BEST DEFENSIVE END EVER

In Rick Korch's book-length series of stories written for *Pro Football Weekly*, "The Best Ever," Gino Marchetti was selected as the best defensive end ever to play in the NFL. He was also selected as the best defensive end of the NFL's first 50 years. He played in ten Pro Bowl games and was named All-Pro each year from 1956 through 1964.

"He's the best I've ever seen," said Hall of Famer Bob St. Clair. "He was so far ahead of everybody else . . . second place is way down the ladder compared to him."

"Marchetti was relentless," remembered Marion Campbell, the former Atlanta and Philadelphia head coach. "He had obvious talent, but he went way beyond that. He batted down a lot of balls . . . ."

Gino Marchetti combined unusual quickness, speed, and strength to be rated by many coaches and players as the best pass rusher of all time. He was 6'4 and weighed 250 in 1958. He was not only a great football player but, from my observations, also had great character and integrity. He was a team man who recognized the worth of other players on the squad. There was a time when a few of the players on the Colt squad took a racist view of Big Daddy

90

Lipscomb. Marchetti's comment was, "We can't win without Big Daddy playing well." He made this statement in the early part of the 1958 season, before the Colts ever won a championship. Gino was normally very quiet and modest about his own achievements. I doubt if there was anyone on the Colt squad who commanded more respect from the players and the coaches than Gino.

Gino played college football at the University of San Francisco under Coach Joe Kuharich, who later was head coach with the Washington Redskins and Philadelphia Eagles. The University of San Francisco had an undefeated football team in 1951, and that team produced more football players of prominence than any college team in history. In addition to Gino as an NFL Hall of Famer, Bob St. Clair, an offensive tackle with the 49ers, and Ollie Matson, former 400-meter Olympic runner and All-Pro running back with the Chicago Cardinals, were on the 1951 University of San Francisco football team and were selected to the NFL Hall of Fame. At least seven other players on that team were starters for NFL football teams! Marchetti was a returning veteran from World War II and had fought in the Battle of the Bulge as an infantryman.

Gino said, "The first time I reported for fall practice at San Francisco, I rode a motorcycle to the campus and was wearing a black jacket. When Kuharich saw me, he said, 'Where in the hell did this guy come from?'" Gino said he thought that Kuharich was going to run him off before he had a chance to put on a uniform.

Kuharich used to say to the team, "You've got to be more tenacious!" Gino said, "I never did know what that meant." If Gino really didn't know what tenacious meant, he didn't have to know — he was one of the most tenacious men to play the game.

Before any game, while the team waited in the locker room, Gino Marchetti was like a caged lion. Unable to sit still, he stalked back and forth.

One of the greatest games Marchetti ever played was the opening game of the 1958 season against the Detroit Lions. It seemed that he put pressure on Bobby Layne, the outstanding Lion quarterback, every time Layne went back to pass. The Lions started out trying to block Marchetti with their offensive right tackle. After Marchetti had sacked Layne and put a great deal of pressure on him, they left the back on Marchetti's side to double-team Marchetti. He still sacked Layne and put pressure on him. Later in the game, the

Lions let the tight end stay in to help the tackle and the back. Three men were blocking on him, and he still made a sack on the quarter-back. Bobby Layne became so upset and disgusted that he took his helmet off and slammed it to the ground and walked off the field. It was an unexpected, relatively easy win for the Colts, thanks to the greatest exhibition of a pass rush by a defensive lineman I've ever seen.

Of course, Gino was not always as good as he was that day against the Lions. He would not have been human if he had been that good every time he took the field.

Sid Gilman, the head coach of the Los Angeles Rams, made a training film of Marchetti. He cut film of outstanding plays by Marchetti, which included a number of pass rushes from our basic defense and pass rushes on blitzes in which the Colts committed five or six defensive players to rushing the passer. There were also plays where Marchetti batted down a pass as it left the passer's hand, pursuit on end runs to his side of the field, where Marchetti tackled the ball carrier for no gain or minimal gain, and other outstanding plays. The film was spliced together on a 400-foot reel. One of the plays in the film was Marchetti making a sack on Bobby Layne when he was triple-teamed. I doubt if anyone could look at the film and not be convinced that Marchetti was the best.

Those readers who are really devout fans of football and others who played football might be interested in Marchetti's techniques. The Colts' basic defense featured four defensive linemen, a middle linebacker, and two outside linebackers. The outside linebackers lined up on the tight end. If there was a split end to his side the linebacker usually lined up a yard or two outside the defensive end, who was in a down or three-point stance on the outside shoulder of the offensive tackle. The linebacker's position varied depending on the type of defense and pass coverage called.

Marchetti was the defensive left end. In his defensive stance his left foot was staggered about one and a half to two feet in advance of his right foot. His right arm was extended vertically to the ground with some weight on the tips of his five fingers, which were extended and spread. His left arm was bent 90 degrees at the elbow in a relaxed position across his body at about the level of his left knee. His back was fairly level and his head was up. His legs were in a strong position, similar to a sprinter in a starting stance. His stance was cocked to the inside at about a 40-degree angle so that his power was directly at the right shoulder of the offensive tackle. He lined up as close to the ball as possible without being offsides. He keyed on the movement of the right tackle.

On the tackle's initial movement, he stepped forward quickly with his right foot, bringing it approximately parallel to his left foot. If the tackle moved forward with his shoulders low, Marchetti met him with his right shoulder and with his forearm under the blocker's shoulder so as to stop his charge and control him, and at the same time locating the football. Marchetti then released from the blocker by pushing off with his left hand and right forearm, enabling him to react to the football and make the tackle.

If the tackle's shoulder raised, which was an indication of a pass or draw, Marchetti got his hands, as quickly as possible, to the upper chest of the blocker with his elbows locked. He had a great feel for where the blocker was most vulnerable, either to the outside or the inside. By the time he got his hands on the blocker, Marchetti was taking his second step. His feet never stopped moving until he hit the quarterback or the ball was thrown or handed off. Sometimes Marchetti would give the offensive tackle a quick pull to the inside as he took an outside rush or vice versa on an inside rush. At times he might start to the outside, and would come back inside the blocker.

Marchetti's secret was in having extremely quick feet, strong hands and arms, and a feel for when the blocker was the least bit overcommitted to the inside or outside. If the quarterback released the ball before Marchetti could get to him, Marchetti raised his hands as the quarterback's arm started toward him and tried to put one or both hands on the pass after it was released. I doubt if any lineman in the league was close to Marchetti in the number of balls batted down at the line of scrimmage.

In 1958 Marchetti was named the Defensive Player of the Year in the NFL. After the 1957 season, one of our objectives in 1958 was to see how many passes our defensive line could knock down or deflect at the line of scrimmage. Almost every day we drilled on having a quarterback drop back and throw in different directions. If the quarterback threw away from a rusher, he continued to rush without raising his hands, but if he threw toward the rusher, he tried to put one or two hands on the ball. In my first season as head coach at Baylor in 1959, the Colts played the Giants in Dallas in a pre-season game. I drove from Waco to Dallas to attend the game. Marchetti knocked down two or three passes at the line of scrimmage. I visited the locker room after the game and Gino said, "John, every time I knock a pass down at the line of scrimmage, I think of you."

Marchetti's character is further illustrated by his reaction to Carroll Rosenbloom's offer to our team to divide $100,000 between them if we beat the Rams. Rosenbloom's offer was against the league rules, although I wasn't aware of it at that time. In 1957 we were tied for first place. With a victory we would have an opportunity to play for the NFL Championship. In light of today's salaries, that does not seem to be much money, but at that time salaries were only a fraction of what they are now. The Rams beat us handily due to a great passing day by Norm Van Brocklin. He threw the slant pass as well as I've ever seen it thrown and was able to get it off in around two seconds or less. That loss was one of the main reasons we set a goal of seeing how many passes our linemen could knock down or deflect in 1958.

Gino told me that he talked to Rosenbloom after the 1957 season and told him, "Don't ever offer me extra money to win a game. Whether we are playing for first place or last place, I'm going to give you my very best, and it's an insult to me for you to offer me extra money to do my best. If you want to give me a bonus or something extra after we win a game, that's okay, but don't offer me money to do my best before a game."

In 1958 Rosenbloom never made any offer of extra money, and we won the NFL Championship.

An assistant coach who coaches a particular segment, such as the defensive line, really becomes more familiar with each player's style of play, both good and bad, than anyone else connected with the team. First of all, he grades the player on every play in which the player participates in a game. Then he shows the film and points out errors, as well as good plays, to his segment of players after a game. In addition, he reviews the films during the off-season in considering changes in team defense or in individual techniques.

In my intense observation of Gino Marchetti, I don't recall ever seeing him trying to hurt or maim an opponent by using illegal tactics. Once the defensive line was watching the film after a game and Gino said, "John, run that play again. That tackle really gave me a shot." The film clearly showed the offensive right tackle throwing a forearm to the face of Marchetti. Gino added, "I told him if he wanted to play like that, I can play the same way. He didn't throw his forearm to my face again." At that time most defensive linemen had a single bar on their helmet, which left enough room for a forearm to get under the chin or to the mouth or nose.

Two other incidents reveal Marchetti's personality and beliefs. As a rookie coach in 1957, I was designated as the bed checker in training camp and during the season when we were on the road. Shortly after our training camp opened in 1957, I was checking the beds and Marchetti, Don Shula, Carl Taseff and I believe, Bill Pellington, walked in the dormitory about five minutes after the deadline. I told them they were late for bed check. Gino said, "John we had to stop for a red light, or otherwise would have been here on time." I replied, "Why don't you explain that to Weeb? If it's all right with him, it's okay with me." I felt that if I made an exception on the deadline for any players, it would be very difficult for me not to make exceptions for all of them. I didn't want to make the decision that five minutes late was okay, but eight minutes or ten minutes was not acceptable. I could lose the respect of all the players if I did that.

Weeb wouldn't excuse them for being five minutes late, and Gino was mad at me for several days. Whenever I looked at him, he had a scowl on his face and did not say a word.

About this time my twin brother Frank, who had an engineering business in Albuquerque, made a business trip to Washington. He came to visit me at our training camp in Westminster, Maryland, which was just a short drive from Washington. I told him that Gino and the others were late for bed check and that I thought Gino was mad at me.

Frank had to make a trip to the men's room, and he was standing at a urinal when Gino walked in. Gino stopped at the next urinal and looked at Frank with that mean-looking scowl, but he didn't say anything. It made Frank a little nervous. He said "Gino, I'm not John. I'm his twin brother, and I'm just up here visiting." Frank just wasn't sure what Gino might do. Gino didn't answer but just walked out. In two or three days Gino got over his madness and we never discussed the matter again.

About three or four years after I left the Colts, I was in Los Angeles for an NCAA and football coaches' meeting. The Pro Bowl game was to be played that weekend, and the players on the West squad were staying in a nearby hotel. I went there to see if I could find any of the Colt players. The first players I ran into were Gino and Johnny Unitas. We sat down and talked awhile.

Weeb Ewbank had just been fired as head coach of the Colts. I asked, "Why was Weeb fired?" After all, Weeb had won two NFL championships in 1958 and 1959. Gino replied, "Weeb got so he would let players come to meetings late or miss bed check and wouldn't fine them and just failed to maintain the discipline standards that you must have to be champions." I have no idea which coach checked the beds after I left the Colts, but he may not have felt it was as important to stick to a strict deadline as I did.

I didn't remind Marchetti of the time he got mad at me for turning him in for being five minutes late for bed check. I think Gino's statement illustrated that the good football players realize how important discipline is to the success of the team, even though they might not like getting fined themselves for being a little late.

After I had finished writing this chapter on Gino Marchetti, I mailed him a copy and asked him to make corrections of anything that I had gotten wrong. About three weeks later I had a call from Gino, who now lives just outside Philadelphia. He corrected a couple of minor details, and we talked about the years with the Colts and some of the players.

Gino said, "What I really called you about is I want to apologize for getting mad at you when you turned me in for being late for bed check. I've felt bad about that for over 30 years and have thought about apologizing." I told him I understood why he got mad and I really didn't think any less of him. Gino replied, "I was 1,000 percent wrong and you were 100 percent right."

That's another strong indication of Gino's character — that he would make a long distance call to apologize for something that happened 33 years ago.

Gino Marchetti is a man I truly respect as a player and as a person. He and Alan Ameche, the outstanding Baltimore Colts fullback, went into the fast food business after their retirement from active playing. They opened a chain of restaurants called "Gino's" on the East Coast. After building up a profitable business, they reportedly sold it for an eight-figure amount. Gino and Alan Ameche not only knew how to play football; they also knew how to run a successful business.

CHAPTER 11

1957–58

JIM PARKER, OFFENSIVE TACKLE: BEST OFFENSIVE LINEMAN EVER

One of the truly great football players in the history of professional football and college football was Jim Parker, who played linebacker and offensive guard for Ohio State in 1954 through 1956. He was a Consensus All-American at Ohio State and number-one draft choice for the Baltimore Colts in 1957.

Parker was selected in a recent NFL alumni magazine, *The Legends,* as the "best-ever" offensive lineman in professional football. The story entitled "Cavalcade of Stars" was written by Rick Korch, who did considerable research and solicited the opinions of NFL players, coaches, and the media as to whom they thought were the best. Korch wrote, "Football fans will always debate whether Jim Brown or Walter Peyton is the best running back ever, or whether Don Hutson or Jerry Rice is the greatest receiver of all time. But when it comes to offensive linemen, there is no debate."

Why? Jim Parker.

"Parker," Korch continued, "a Hall of Famer who played fourteen years at guard and tackle for the Colts, was the greatest and the consent is nearly unanimous."

Jim Parker was born and raised in Macon, Georgia. During the time of segregation in the South, Jim Parker was among a number of black players who were recruited out of the South by the Big Ten and other top college teams in the East and Midwest. He played for Woody Hayes at Ohio State. Jim has a great respect for Woody and feels a debt of gratitude to him for strongly encouraging Jim to complete his academic work for a degree at Ohio State, as well as for his inspirational leadership and coaching.

Parker was a rookie lineman at Baltimore in 1957 when I was a rookie coach in professional football. I was hired by head coach Weeb Ewbank to coach the offensive tackles and the defensive line. I had come from Johns Hopkins University in Baltimore, a Division III football school, which was much better known for its lacrosse team than its football team.

As a rookie, Jim Parker was 6'3 and weighed 275 pounds. He was the kind of lineman who can lengthen a coach's career.

Consistent pass protection is the most difficult technique for a professional offensive lineman to learn. Jim probably had less experience in college in professional type pass protection than 90% of all rookie linemen. At Ohio State, under Woody Hayes, it was almost an "event" when a pass was thrown. When the Buckeyes did, it was usually a play-action pass where the pass would come off a fake of a running play. Aggressive blocking similar to that on a running play was used by the offensive linemen.

Jim had to learn drop back pass protection from scratch, and he became good at it quicker than anyone I've ever coached or observed. He just seemed to do the things instinctively that it takes to be a good pass protector. He set very quickly and in such a strong position that it was useless for anyone to try and run over him. He had quick feet and could adjust so as to keep good position on the pass rusher. Whatever direction the pass rusher took, he ran into something hard and unyielding — maybe a head, a shoulder, an elbow, or something else that made it difficult to penetrate to the passer and sometimes caused pain to the defender. Jim had made All-American at Ohio State on his run blocking skills and his defense. He needed little coaching on his run blocking.

He was one of the most conscientious players I ever coached. He aimed for perfection. On Mondays the coaches met at Weeb Ewbank's house to grade films of Sundays' games. About 5:30 P.M. Weeb would give the coaches a couple of hours to go home and eat dinner with their families. Every Monday at about 6:00 P.M. I would get a call at home from Jim. He wanted to know how he did in Sunday's game. He was intent on knowing any mistake he had made. The sooner he knew his breakdowns, the sooner he could make mental preparations to eliminate them.

I always told him the good things he did first and then I would tell him his mistakes. Most of the times he remembered his errors and didn't alibi for them.

When Jim called, our daughter Cindy, who was then about fourteen years old, would race to the phone, hoping it was a boyfriend calling. Cindy always recognized Jim's voice and would say in a slightly disappointed tone, "Daddy, it's Jim Parker." Jim would try to disguise his voice, but he couldn't fool her. One day Cindy's friend answered the phone. She called me to the phone. When I answered, Jim said, "I fooled her . . . I fooled her!" I said, "Jim, that was the girl from next door." Jim could only say, "Oh, heck."

In 1957 the Colts went to the West Coast with a one-game lead in the Western Division of the NFL. We lost to the 49ers in the last fifteen seconds and then played the Rams while tied for first place with the Detroit Lions. Norm Van Brocklin, the Ram quarterback, had one of his great days and threw for over 300 yards. About 200 yards came on a slant pass to Elroy Hirsch and others.

In 1958, the year the Colts won their first championship, Weeb Ewbank gave me the responsibility to coach the defensive line only. Herman Ball, who had coached the offensive guards and centers in 1957, took over the offensive tackles. I missed coaching Jim Parker and George Preas, the offensive right tackle, but it made for a more efficient operation.

Jim Parker liked and respected Herman Ball, but I think he may have felt a little more comfortable talking to me since I had coached him in his rookie year. He continued to call on Mondays after we graded the films to talk about his game the day before. The offensive and defensive coaches graded the films together, so I could watch and take notes while the offensive coaches were grading the offense.

Our offensive line did a superb job of protecting Johnny Unitas. Jim Parker made All-Pro his second year in the league, which was unusual. But Jim Parker was an unusually good player.

Our curfew rule during camp was that all players had to be in their dormitory by 10:00 P.M. and in bed with lights out at 11:00 P.M. When we were on the road, I just made one bed check at 11:00 P.M. and the players just had to be in their rooms. In the following years the players stayed in a local hotel the night before a home game, but in 1957 and 1958 they stayed in their own homes.

There were a rather large number of bed check violations in 1957, but the players came to learn that I was going to make a bed check every night I was assigned to do so. When one or more were late, they tried to talk me out of reporting them. My stock reply was, "Talk to Weeb about it, and if it's okay with him, it's okay with me." In 1958 I don't remember a single player missing bed check. There may have been one or two in training camp that I've forgotten, but I'm sure none after the season started.

In 1957 segregation was still very prevalent in the South and Southwest. When we had a pre-season game with the Cardinals in Austin, Texas, the only hotel or motel we could find who would accommodate our black players was a Holiday Inn located near the city limits. When I checked Jim Parker and Sherman Plunkett's room, Jim said, "John, come in and let me talk to you a minute. Sherman and I ordered a sandwich, and I asked the boy who brought the sandwiches, 'What would they do if I jumped in that swimming pool out there?' The bellman replied, 'They wouldn't do nothing except pour kerosene on the pool and light a match to it.'" Jim said, "John, if some people in white sheets came around and started building a fire outside our room, would you speak up for me?" I said, "Jim, you know I would speak up for you." Jim replied, "I'm not sure, you might start tearing up a sheet to make a rope." Jim wrote his wife a postcard which read, "The men in the white sheets got Sherman Plunkett, but I managed to get away. I'm on a freight train headed toward Baltimore."

It's a sad commentary that the segregation laws existed, and I am sure that down deep Jim Parker resented the laws very much. But he grew up in Georgia and understood how things were. At that time Jim personally could do nothing about the laws. The fact that he could address the issue with humor may have made a more convincing statement than anything else he could have done.

Despite hardships and unfairness, college athletics and professional football have been good to Jim Parker. He was able to get his college degree at a prestigious institution and to live life at a higher level than he could have anticipated had he not possessed his ability as an athlete and had the opportunity to participate in football. Jim Parker has been good for college and professional athletics as well. He is a good citizen, a successful businessman and a role model worthy of emulation.

CHAPTER 12

1957–58

EUGENE "BIG DADDY" LIPSCOMB:
DEFENSIVE TACKLE, ALL-PRO

One of the biggest and most colorful players in the history of the NFL was Eugene "Big Daddy" Lipscomb. He was 6'6 and weighed 295 pounds. I know because I weighed him once a week during the 1957 and 1958 seasons.

Big Daddy grew up in Detroit and, after finishing high school, joined the Marines. He played football as a tight-end and basketball in high school. While playing on the Camp Pendleton Marine football team, he was scouted by the Rams and signed by them when he was discharged. He was one of the few players ever to play in the NFL without the benefit of college experience.

At the time Big Daddy was playing with the Rams, I was head coach at Johns Hopkins. The Colts gave me complimentary tickets to their games, so I got to see Lipscomb play with the Rams when they played in Baltimore every year. The Colts and Rams were both in the Western Division of the NFL. I had no particular reason to single out Lipscomb when the Colts or Rams played, but he played so well, I couldn't help but notice him.

In 1956 the Rams put Lipscomb on waivers. I really don't know why. Obviously, there was something the Rams didn't like about

Big Daddy. The Colts immediately claimed Lipscomb off waivers, and he was a starter the week after he was claimed.

Big Daddy became an instant favorite with the Colt fans, and there were a lot of cheers for Big Daddy when he came off the field with his shirttail out (which was normal for him) after the Colts defenders had stopped their opponents. The Colts had some good victories in 1956 but struggled down the stretch. In the final game of the season the word was that the Colts would have to win in order for Ewbank to keep his job as head coach.

The Colts played the Washington Redskins at Baltimore that year. The Redskins were leading in the final seconds of the game when Unitas threw a long pass to Jim Mutscheller. It appeared that Norb Hecker, the Redskin safety, had an interception, but Mutscheller came back to the ball and took it away from Hecker on the five-yard-line. He then drug Hecker in the end zone for a touchdown. It was one of the most exciting plays I've ever seen, and it gave the Colts a victory.

From the beginning I got along real well with Big Daddy. In fact, in the two years I coached Big Daddy I don't believe there was a harsh word exchanged between the two of us. Having been born and spent most of my early years in Alabama, I was sensitive to the problems of prejudice and discrimination that existed for black people, particularly in the fifties.

Big Daddy fit well into the Colt defensive system. Simply put, the defensive linemen took their initial read from the movement of the offensive linemen, delivered a blow with either a forearm lift or a hand shiver to neutralize and control the blocker, located the ball, and made the tackle. Nobody, with the possible exception of Gino Marchetti, played the defense better than Big Daddy. In 1957 Big Daddy led the Colts in tackles. In a 12-game regular season schedule he made 129 tackles, an average of 11 per game. That's unusually good for a down lineman playing head up on the offensive guard for the most part.

In both 1957 and 1958 the Colts allowed the fewest yards rushing of any team in the NFL. The achievement of defending against the run better than any team in the NFL was a source of pride for the defensive line.

In 1958 I left shortly after our championship game with the New York Giants to accept a job as head football coach and athletic director at Baylor University. I never did get the final statistics on the number of tackles Big Daddy made. My impression was he had a better year in 1958 than in 1957. Big Daddy made first team All-Pro in 1958.

Big Daddy was better against the run than he was as a pass rusher. However, he was effective against the passing game. Marchetti was unquestionably the best pass rusher in football when he played, and perhaps the best of all time. Many times when Marchetti rushed the passer and flushed him out of the pocket, Big Daddy made the tackle. Big Daddy was very effective against screens and draws.

When we played the 49ers in Baltimore in 1958, Y. A. Tittle threw a screen pass to Hugh McElhenny, who was one of the best running backs in the league. I was on the sideline with the telephone to the press box. McElhenny caught the ball near our bench on the sideline. As McElhenny turned his head down-field to run, he saw Big Daddy, with his arms spread about ten feet, three yards from him. McElhenny said, "Shoot!" (or something like that). Big Daddy clubbed his arms together as he put a perfect form tackle on McElhenny for no gain.

Referring to the passer, Big Daddy would say, "Make him throw it out of a well." That's the thought that a passer must have if he is to throw a pass over a 6'4 to 6'7 defensive lineman who has penetrated with his hands high in the air as the passer releases the ball.

Big Daddy was the best tackler for a defensive lineman I've ever known. He seldom missed a tackle, and he would make tackles from sideline to sideline. One time when we played the Lions in Detroit, Hopalong Cassidy broke on a 56-yard run. It was Big Daddy who ran him down and tackled him inside our ten. It's true that Cassidy had to do some zigzagging on the run, but how many times have you seen a 295-pounder tackling a halfback 56 yards from the line of scrimmage?

I read a story in which an offensive player for an NFL team told how he had a sore foot and Big Daddy would purposely step on his foot. In two years of grading Lipscomb in game films, I never saw him make a dirty play against an opponent. He would tackle the backs hard but usually helped them up. He wasn't a mean person at all, but he did want to make the tackle on every play.

Since Big Daddy covered such a wide range on the field, the

Colts tried him at middle linebacker in training camp in 1958. He felt more comfortable at defensive tackle and didn't want to play linebacker. When we would have a break in practice, he would come over to where the defensive linemen were and would say, "Don't worry, I'm going to be back with you. Just save me a place."

Before each practice we had team meetings, and each segment would meet with their coaches. Any time we had to go from a meeting room in one dormitory to a meeting room in another, Lipscomb would "march" the defensive linemen to the next meeting place. He drilled the defensive linemen like a marine sergeant would. He would call them to attention and then command, "Forward march! Your left! Your left! You had a good home and you left!"

When he was working with the linebackers, we tried every defensive lineman as a drill master but none were satisfactory. A rookie might have saved his job for a few days if he had been a good drillmaster. As they say, "The more things you can do . . ."

It was a happy day when Big Daddy was told to report back to the defensive line. He immediately took over and drilled the defensive linemen to the team meeting. All the defensive linemen were happy to have someone who could march them properly, and I was happy I was going to have a chance to coach him again.

Big Daddy was always joking and kidding someone. About the time walking shorts became popular, Big Daddy walked up to the dining room in his new pair. He sat down on the steps and was admiring his legs, which were long and big but not very attractive or shapely. The skin on his legs looked a little like elephant skin. I remember he said, "I've got sprinter's legs."

One of the recreations the assistant coaches enjoyed was watching the players take their flu shots when physicals were given. A number of the players dreaded to have a shot, but none dreaded it nearly as much as Big Daddy Lipscomb. I've never seen anyone who dreaded a shot like he did. They did everything but tie him down when the team physician gave him a shot.

We went to the West Coast in 1957 one game ahead of all the teams in the Western Division. We lost to the 49ers in the last seconds and flew down to Los Angeles Monday morning for our game with the Rams the following Saturday. We were to stay in the Huntington Hotel all week. I bed-checked that night and Lipscomb wasn't in his room.

The next morning I called Big Daddy and told him to come up to Weeb's suite. I roomed with Weeb on the road. When Big Daddy arrived, there were just the three of us in the elegant suite. Weeb asked Big Daddy why he wasn't in his room at bed check.

"I just couldn't get a cab in time to get back for bed check. I was in my old hometown and couldn't find a cab. I was late and I deserves to be fined," Big Daddy related.

That was the only time in two years that Big Daddy was late for bed check or late for any meeting or practice. To my memory, he didn't miss a practice in 1957 or 1958.

Lipscomb was a little sensitive to criticism. The fact that he was the only player on the squad who had not attended college may have had something to do with his sensitivity. In the game program his name was listed along with his number 76, but in the place where the college or university was listed, it read "No College." Big Daddy said, "That stands for Northern College."

The Rams beat us that Saturday to knock us out of the championship game. However, Big Daddy had played a terrific game and made 18 tackles. At the end of the game there was a little scuffle on the field between Big Daddy and a couple of Rams players. I ran out on the field and yelled at the Rams players to go on to their locker room. They had won the game and weren't really that upset. Looking back, I'm glad they weren't real mad when I yelled at them.

I remember Billy Ray Smith, defensive tackle for the Rams, walking up and saying, "Don't worry, coach, we're not going to cause any problems." He's the tackle who came to the Colts in a trade when Big Daddy was traded to the Steelers. I was disappointed over our loss and a little angry we had lost a chance for the championship.

Big Daddy and I walked to the locker room together. Tears welled up in his eyes. He said, "John, I hope you don't think that my missing bed check Monday night had anything to do with our losing this game." I told him, "No, I don't think it had a thing to do with our losing. You played a great game, Big Daddy." And he did.

Knowing that Big Daddy was sensitive to criticism, I always reviewed his mistakes in a private conversation. I also told him what he did well and gave him a written list of his breakdowns and highlight plays before the team looked at the films.

The 1957 season was the first winning season in the history of the Colts. We had come close to getting in the championship game, but barely missed. When the All-Pro selections came out in 1957, Lipscomb was not on the first or second teams of any of the All-Pro teams selected. I personally thought he deserved to be All-Pro. Gino Marchetti and Arthur Donovan made All-Pro from our defensive line. I wrote Lipscomb a letter and told him what a good year I thought he had had. I told him that sometimes a person has to do real well over a period of time before he gets the recognition he deserves. It was a fairly long letter and complimented him on his efforts and achievements.

Not long after that, Big Daddy came to the coaches' office and walked over to my desk. He said in a low voice, "John, I got your letter and I really appreciated it. I put it in my scrapbook." It helped make up his mind to do better next year rather than blame the people who made the All-Pro selections as being prejudiced and racist.

Some people might think that Big Daddy Lipscomb wasn't very smart, but he was very intelligent. He seldom busted an assignment. He knew what he was supposed to do and he did it. He was also a very generous person, perhaps generous to a fault. He remembered friends and particularly children at Christmas and bought them very nice presents.

In 1958 the Colts started fast and we won our first six games. With Unitas out with broken ribs (an injury sustained in our win over Green Bay), we lost to the Giants 24-21. The next week we shut out the Bears in Chicago for the second shutout in three games. Unitas came back against the Rams, and we won easily (34-7).

In the Rams game, Duane Putman, Ram offensive left guard, butted Lipscomb under the chin on a field goal attempt. He butted Big Daddy so hard that Lipscomb's helmet flew off. The butt did not slow Lipscomb a step, and he kept coming and blocked the ball with his face. When the ball hit his face, it went straight up in the air about 20 to 25 feet. The Colts recovered and took possession. If the butt or the ball hitting him in the face hurt him, he didn't show it. He was just mad at Putman for butting him. The Colts easily won the game.

The comeback win against the 49ers clinched the Western Division for us since we were three games up with two remaining to play. What a great feeling to know you are going to play for the World Championship regardless of what happens in the next three weeks.

We went to the West Coast a very happy and relaxed group. It was almost impossible to get the players' full attention. They knew they would be in the World Championship game. The Cleveland Browns or New York Giants would be our opponents.

Our first game on the coast would be with the 49ers. As I worked with the defensive line on some drills, it was obvious that the players did not have their minds on what we were trying to do. Ray Krouse, our third defensive tackle who spelled Donovan and Lipscomb and who had played in a couple of championship games with Detroit, said, "John, don't worry about what we are doing now. When the time comes, we will be ready."

We lost to both San Francisco and Los Angeles by close margins. At one time we had Donovan and Krouse playing defensive tackles, with Lipscomb out of the game. The 49ers broke a trap play up the middle for about 15 or 20 yards. Weeb walked over to me and said, "John, keep Lipscomb in the game. You can alternate Krouse and Donovan, but I want Lipscomb in the game." Weeb realized how good Lipscomb was. There was nothing really at stake, and the Colts just didn't play with the usual intensity after we had clinched the Division Championship.

The Giants' 10-0 victory over the Browns in a playoff gave them the Eastern Division Championship. The World Championship was scheduled at Yankee stadium.

I knew the Giant offensive plays better than I knew our own. However, any time you are playing against a team with Jim Lee Howell as head coach, Vince Lombardi as offensive coach, and Tom Landry as defensive coach, you have your hands full. About three days before the game, our defensive line was going over our special keys for the Giants. The keys were based on the movements of their offensive guards, tackles, and center on some of their basic plays. On certain plays the Giants had no counteraction. When they showed such a blocking pattern, our defensive ends and tackles could take more chances and gamble more to stop the play as indicated by the blocking pattern.

Since the Giants had played three crucial games in the past three weeks, I felt sure they would not make any changes in their offense, particularly as far as running plays were concerned. It wasn't Vince Lombardi's style to change many things during the season. Vince depended on execution rather than surprise.

As we were intently working on our special keys for the big

game, Big Daddy stepped forward and asked for attention. He began imitating Weeb Ewbank when Weeb had met with the players while we were on the West Coast to discuss team and individual money shares from the championship game. Big Daddy did sound like Weeb, and some of our linemen were rolling on the ground with laughter. I couldn't help but laugh myself. It was comic relief right in the middle of a very critical practice. Fortunately, neither Weeb nor any of the other coaches heard us laughing or saw some of our defensive linemen rolling around on the ground. I never did mention it to any of our coaches. I wasn't sure they would appreciate it.

Weeb had been a little emotional in going over the sharing of the championship purse. You can almost figure on players imitating you when you get emotional. After the players met and voted on who would get shares and how much, Marchetti came out of the meeting and said, "Congratulations, John, we just voted you a half a share." I hoped he was kidding and was glad to find out he was.

Our victory over the Giants in sudden death overtime for the championship was as big as they come. In John Steadman's unofficial count on tackles made in the championship game, Lipscomb led the Colts with seven tackles. In addition, Lipscomb caused a fumble on the Giants' 20-yard-line as he tackled Gifford after catching a flare pattern to set up the Colts' first touchdown. Ray Krouse recovered the fumble.

In the fourth quarter, with the Giants leading 17-14 on a drive where they had gone from their 20-yard-line to the Colts' 42-yard-line, the Giants ran a power sweep to the left. One more first down and the Giants would be in rather easy field goal range. Lipscomb tackled Phil King just as he took the handoff from Conerly. The ball squirted out and Ray Krouse recovered on the Colts' 42-yard-line for a 16-yard loss and a turnover. It was a preconceived penetration by Lipscomb to shoot the gap left by the pulling guard and gamble on a big play, and it worked.

Big Daddy Lipscomb was a great player before and after I coached him. What I did to help him more than anything else was to let him know that I believed in him. I personally believe that it is an important part of coaching. The game I felt might have been his best game during the two years I coached him was our first game with the Chicago Bears in Baltimore in 1958. I remember just before the kickoff, when we were still in the locker room, I patted him on the back and told him, "Go out there and show them how the best tackle in the league can play." It was important to Big Daddy for someone to believe he was the best.

After the Colts had won their first three games of the 1958 season, Norman Clark, who covered the Colts for the *Baltimore News American*, wrote a story headed "Big Daddy best in league — Gino."

Clark wrote, "Gino Marchetti, one of the more publicized linemen in Pro Football, has set himself up in the press agent business for Colt colleagues. 'You ought to write more about Big Daddy Lipscomb. He's the best defensive lineman in the league,' says the man who is himself considered the best defensive lineman in the league."

In the article Gino went on to praise the Colt offensive line for outstanding pass protection.

Just recently Gino told me, "Big Daddy Lipscomb was a great player. He covered a lot of ground. He could run like a back and tackle like a linebacker. He was a much better tackler than I and most linemen."

It was typical of Marchetti to minimize his own ability and praise his teammates.

Harley Sewell, who played left guard for the Detroit Lions, a team the Colts played twice a year in the Western Division, played in nine Pro Bowl games and was an All-Pro offensive lineman. After his retirement from playing, he scouted for the Los Angeles Rams for years. I asked him one time when he came through Albuquerque if he thought Lipscomb was one of the best he played against. Harley said, "I don't *think*, I *know* he was one of the best. I just couldn't handle him. He was just so big and strong." Harley was one of the great linemen in the history of the University of Texas.

Ordell Brasse, who played eleven years with the Colts as a defensive end and was a teammate of Lipscomb, said, "When Lipscomb played next to me, I didn't even think about running plays. All I did was try to rush the passer. Big Daddy took care of the running plays inside and outside. After he left, the teams we played started ripping off substantial gains running inside and outside me. I thought, 'I'm going to have to start playing run defense or else I'm going to have to find another job.'"

Big Daddy loved to run and may well have been the fastest man of his size to play in the NFL. He may also have been the best football player in the NFL not to be honored in the NFL Hall of Fame.

Big Daddy had two major weaknesses: alcohol and women. One or both would contribute to his tragic death.

In the two years I was with the Colts, I never saw him take a drink. Nor, to my knowledge, did I ever see him after he had been drinking. He told me that he was always going to be ready to play the games, but after the games he did like to have a few drinks to relax with friends. That may have been an understatement. I believe the only reason Lipscomb has not been considered for the Hall of Fame is the fact that Big Daddy died of a drug overdose in the spring of 1962.

The conclusion by the investigating officers was that the overdose was self-inflicted. But all of Big Daddy's close friends felt strongly that Big Daddy had been murdered. Those friends included Buddy Young, a Colt halfback (and probably the fastest player in Colt history); Jim Parker, an All-Pro (and named recently as the best offensive lineman in the history of the NFL); Sherman Plunkett, an excellent offensive tackle for the Colts and New York Jets (whom Lipscomb was living with in Baltimore at the time of his death and who has since died); and Lenny Moore, a great runner and pass receiver for the Colts in the late fifties and sixties. The primary reasons they felt so strongly that Big Daddy had been murdered were: (1) he was so deathly afraid of being shot with a needle and (2) none of them had ever seen any evidence of Big Daddy having taken drugs before he died. These friends were companions on many social occasions, as well as being Colt teammates. Their friendships continued after Lipscomb was traded to the Steelers.

I visited with Buddy Young in New York during the NCAA Convention a few months after Big Daddy died. He said that Lipscomb had been asked to deliver a package at the request of his sister, who had a friend who was a drug peddler. After Big Daddy delivered the package, he came to the conclusion the package contained drugs. Big Daddy told Buddy Young he was going to let them know they could not use him to deliver drugs again. Buddy's belief was that the drug peddlers got Big Daddy drunk and then shot him with an overdose because they were afraid that Big Daddy would turn them in. Buddy was working with the NFL office in New York at that time.

Unfortunately, Buddy died in an automobile accident after representing the NFL at the funeral of an outstanding young running back for the St. Louis Cardinals who had drowned in a swimming accident. Buddy was driving back to Dallas to catch a plane late at night and evidently fell asleep at the wheel.

Another opinion about Big Daddy's death was that he had just returned to Baltimore from one of his professional wrestling tours and had a substantial amount of cash on him. The assumption was that he went to a bar and met a couple of women who turned out to be prostitutes. After drinking with them in the bar, they purportedly invited him to a room and kept encouraging him to drink more liquor. Their purpose was to have him pass out and take his money, which amounted to over $3,000, but every time they tried to get his money from his pocket Big Daddy would wake up. The story goes that the women called a drug-peddler friend and gave Lipscomb a shot of heroin to put him soundly to sleep so they could steal his money. The mixture of alcohol and drugs then killed him. The police report showed that he had consumed a large amount of alcohol.

Evidently, the investigating police officers felt there was no proof that would hold up in court that Big Daddy was murdered. A needle puncture doesn't leave any fingerprints or other information which could serve as evidence.

One of the great players and personalities of professional football came to an end at age 31.

There are many fans and friends who will never forget him and the very good qualities he exhibited as a gifted player and as a conscientious, thoughtful, and generous person. Big Daddy made some big mistakes which led to this death, but I don't think one of them was to give himself a shot of heroin or any other drug.

George Stewart and Bob Ingram wrote a screenplay about Big Daddy's life and hoped to have it produced in order to clear his name. In it the preacher is delivering the final rites on Big Daddy before an overflowing church, and he states, "The good book says, 'There are many houses in my Father's mansion,' and I'm sure there's a big rambling one up there waiting for Daddy Lipscomb. He was truly a gifted man, too, and, although some say he squandered his talents in riotous living amidst the fleshpots of the many cities his profession took him to, I am also told that he never gave less than all of himself when it came to the game that enabled his life to shine, however briefly."

CHAPTER 13

1957–58

RAYMOND BERRY, WIDE RECEIVER: PRO FOOTBALL'S ALL-TIME OVERACHIEVER

Raymond Berry is a very unusual person. When he retired from professional football in 1968, he had caught more passes (631) for more yardage (9,275) than any receiver in the history of the game. However, his most amazing record is not one that is part of the NFL record book.

Raymond caught 631 passes in regular season NFL games and fumbled the football *one* time! As a general rule, no player is hit harder or is in a more vulnerable position than a pass receiver when he is tackled. Many times he is hit when he has to jump, and his body and arms are stretched to the limit in order to make the catch. Other times he may be hit from the rear or blind side while he is concentrating on the ball and does not see the tackler.

It is no accident that Berry set the record.

The determination not to fumble came in his rookie year in 1956, when the Colts played an exhibition game in Hershey, Pennsylvania. Raymond was a receiver on a hook pass, in which a receiver turns quickly after he tries to force the defender to give him a cushion by making the defender think he is running a deeper pattern. Just as the ball came into Raymond's hands, he was hit hard by a defender. The ball was jarred loose by the force of the hit and the pass was ruled incomplete.

As Raymond came back to the bench, he heard a veteran say, "That damn rookie is listening for footsteps." One of the coaches said, "You've got to put the ball away when you catch it."

Raymond said that he couldn't sleep that night. He kept thinking about how he could avoid coughing up the ball when he was tackled. By morning he had a plan that he hoped would keep him from fumbling again. He decided that every time he caught a football, he would see how quickly he could put it away. It didn't matter whether he was playing catch with a teammate, catching a pass in a team practice session or catching a pass in a game; Raymond would put the ball away as quickly as possible every time a ball was thrown to him. Occasionally, a couple of big linemen would play catch and mimic Berry on putting the ball away. That didn't bother Raymond at all. He had a purpose in making it an instinctive move with every pass he caught. The purpose was not to fumble when hit by the defensive players after a catch. He succeeded admirably.

"Putting the ball away," or as Raymond often referred to it as "putting it in the bank," was a precise technique. First, he would strive to put the ball away in the arm away from the nearest tackler. He would put the web of his spread fingers over the point of the ball. Next, he would bring the ball snug to his body and keep the elbow tight against the ball and his body. Raymond would practice running at full speed with the ball held close to his body. How many times have you seen a ball carrier running while the arm in which the ball is held swings away from the body? A tackler usually hits the ball or the ball carrier's arm and the ball pops out and is recovered by the defense. Holding the ball tightly against the body might slow a runner a fraction of a second, but it is much better than giving the ball to the opposition.

There have been write-ups about Raymond's handicaps while he was playing — not fast (although he was faster than his reputation), bad back (had to wear a brace), one leg shorter than the other (it would take careful measurement to prove, as it wasn't noticeable), bad eyes (he wore contact lenses). Despite these handicaps, Raymond Berry was the most effective receiver of his time. He was the receiver that Unitas looked for most of the time when it was third and long. Berry was at his best in critical situations.

In the 1958 sudden death championship game with the Giants,

Raymond caught twelve passes — a record for a championship game. Five of his catches came on the 86-yard drive to tie the score with nine seconds left and in the 80-yard drive in the overtime period to win the game. His five receptions gained a total of 95 yards. His last catch on the 86-yard drive put the ball on the 13-yard-line, where Myhra kicked the tying field goal. His last catch in overtime gave the Colts a first down on the Giants' eight, with Ameche scoring from the one-yard-line. Earlier he had caught three passes in an 86-yard drive, the last one a 15-yard touchdown catch.

Berry was very modest. More than anyone, he realized his own limitations. I once asked him why he didn't get a job making good money during the off-season. "I'm just not good enough to work during the off-season," was his reply. "I have to spend 12 months working to be a better football player to keep my job." He broke down the film of every game in which he played. He studied the defensive backs. He charted their tendencies, their strengths and weaknesses. He made notes on what he might have the best chance of doing against every back he played. He scheduled time for conditioning, for practice running precise patterns, and for catching drills.

Raymond had each of his pass patterns figured to the exact number of steps he would take until he would come to the breaking point, at which time the ball was delivered by the passer. For example, on a quick out, he would take three steps down-field to the outside shoulder of the defensive back, then break to the outside as he turned his head and eyes to see the quarterback, who would deliver the ball on Raymond's break. This is probably the simplest pattern Raymond ran. The ball would be released in 1.5 to 1.7 seconds. Raymond would usually catch the ball at five to six yards from the line of scrimmage, and if he had separated from the defensive back he would make ten yards or more on the play.

For catching drills he had a net made which he would tie to a goal post, and he would practice catching balls approaching a spot in front of the net from either side (from the right of the net and from the left of the net). He asked the passer to throw bad balls — low passes, high passes, and passes behind him. He would take the position facing a quarterback as he would when running a hook or turn-in pattern, and would have the passer throw high, low left, and right of him. Then, in a sideline drill, the ball was thrown slightly outside the sideline and he would practice getting both feet down inside the line while reaching over the sideline to catch the ball. Berry may have mastered this technique as well or better than any receiver who played. There was no doubt that he worked harder in perfecting his technique on the sideline catch more than any receiver.

If he couldn't find a passer to throw to him, he would get his wife, Sally, to throw. She wasn't a great passer, but after all, he wanted to practice difficult catches.

Raymond had big hands and he constantly worked with a malleable plastic substance to exercise his fingers and strengthen his grip. In addition to stronger hands and fingers, he felt that his fingers could recover more quickly from injuries such as sprains or jams, which frequently happen to pass receivers. If he dropped a pass occasionally, he would just say to himself, "I can catch 99 out of 100 passes like that, so I will likely catch the next 99."

When I got a job as head football coach at Baylor University, one of the first things I did was ask Berry if he would come down in the spring, during his off-season, and coach our pass receivers. Raymond consented to come during our spring practice and work with our receivers. In my ten years as head football coach he came down for spring practice nine years. The only year he did not come was a year there was a great deal of racial tension on the eastern shore of Maryland, and the governor of Maryland asked Raymond if he would volunteer his services to help reduce the tension.

Raymond came for what amounted to paying his expenses. He and I had an excellent relationship, and he thoroughly enjoyed teaching our young receivers. I'm certain there was not one receiver who was not greatly influenced by Raymond as a person and as a coach. Some of our receivers' performances reflected Raymond's teaching. Lawrence Elkins was a Consensus All-American in 1963 and 1964. He caught 70 passes during our ten-game regular season in 1963 and then caught seven more in our Bluebonnet Bowl game against LSU. This was an NCAA record for the most pass receptions by a college receiver in a single season. He was a number-one draft choice in the NFL by the Green Bay Packers and in the AFL by the Houston Oilers. He signed with Houston and played about five years. A serious knee injury in his first pre-season game kept him from reaching the heights projected for him.

Our other wide receiver on the 1963 Baylor team, James Ingram, set a record of eleven receptions in the 1963 Bluebonnet Bowl game. That record was still standing when the Bluebonnet

Bowl ceased as a post-season bowl game after the 1989 season. Ingram also caught two touchdown passes in the fourth quarter of the Bluebonnet Bowl game to enable us to win 14 to 7. The game came after the pro season ended, and Raymond and Sally Berry were our guests at the game.

Raymond had five basic principles for a pass receiver:

1. **Release from the line of scrimmage** — Release as quickly as possible. Use early speed to force the defender to give ground. Do not be held up. As a wide receiver you have room to get away from the defender. Use the technique of faking in one direction and going the other way or just flaring around the defender to keep him from making contact. Develop the confidence and attitude that no one can hold you up or delay you on the line of scrimmage. It takes practice to perfect the technique of releasing without being delayed or held up.

2. **Approach** — Approach as fast as you can with control. Either approach to the outside if the pass is to be thrown to the outside or inside if the pass is to be thrown inside, in order to gain position on the defender. You may also use an outside approach and plant your outside foot and break underneath the defender to the inside. If the pattern is to the outside, drive off with three-step fake inside and break underneath the defender to the outside. A receiver should use this approach on a defender who reacts quickly to the receiver's initial move. One of the best fakes a receiver can make is a "look" to the quarterback on a three-step fake. In most man defenses, the defensive back eyes the receiver until the receiver looks for the ball, then the defender looks to the passer. The receiver then makes his final break as the defender looks to the passer.

3. **Explode off the breaking point** — The quicker you can explode off the breaking point, the more separation you can create between you and the defender. Whip your head and eyes to the passer so that you may adjust to the ball quickly.

4. **"Look" the ball into your hands** — The quicker you see the ball, the better chance you have to adjust to the flight. "Look" the ball into your hands and put it away as quickly as possible. Many times you must anticipate being hit the instant you touch the ball. Unless you can put it away quickly, you may be knocked loose from the ball resulting in an incomplete pass or

fumble. Outrun the ball first! Don't slow down until you are sure the ball is within your reach. This is particularly important on a deep pass but is also important on an outside or inside break. The tendency is to slow down when you look. With your head turned you may lose some speed, but run as fast as you can until you're sure you have the ball beat.

5. **Explode after the catch** — Turn down-field as quickly as possible and run with all your speed. In the great majority of cases you'll make more yardage getting down-field as quickly as possible rather than stopping and looking for a place to run. The defense will close on you and the chances are you will end up with little or no additional yardage if you stop to look.

These five principles of pass receiving are simple and logical. When Raymond ended his career he had averaged 14.7 yards per catch. That is not bad for a receiver who specialized in getting open in the two-minute drills, when everybody in the stadium knew the offense was going to pass and on possession downs such as a third down with five yards or more needed for a first down.

The biggest reward Raymond received from his coaching during spring practice at Baylor was meeting his wife, Sally, who was a student at Baylor. One year after spring football practice was completed, Raymond decided to stay on a little longer. One reason was he could use a small office located next to our football meeting room to study the Colts' films from the previous year. Another reason, and perhaps a more important one, was that he could continue seeing Sally. Not long after his extended stay in Waco, Raymond and Sally announced their engagement.

Sally has been a great companion for Raymond. They share the same high principles and ideals. Sally is a wonderful wife and mother.

Raymond Berry is a Christian. His source of strength comes from very strong convictions, faith, and belief in God. I think he is the kind of Christian that God wants people to be. Raymond does not wear his religion on his sleeve by trying to convert everyone he comes into contact with. His own life is a great example to others. He is quiet, reserved, and modest, and there is no way to estimate the number of young people he has influenced for good. The way he played the game of football, along with his dedication and work habits, influenced more ambitious young football players than perhaps any professional player in history. He has also influenced adults and young people alike with his thousands of speaking engagements over the years to high school groups, college players and coaches, and church groups of all denominations. He has been particularly active in the Fellowship of Christian Athletes, and his continuing appearances and talks to their annual summer camps and meetings have had a strong impact on coaches, high school and college players.

During the years since Raymond's retirement as an active player, he has been an assistant football coach with the Dallas Cowboys, Cleveland Browns, New England Patriots, Detroit Lions, and quarterback coach for the Denver Broncos. His coaching has been primarily with pass receivers and quarterbacks. I never heard a player he played with or one that he coached say anything derogatory about him.

He had a winning record as head coach with the New England Patriots. He was fired when his team had an almost unbelievable run of injuries (which can happen to any team). The Patriots had 19 players on the injured reserve, which meant they were out for the season, and they lost at least three games during the last few seconds.

Even though Raymond Berry had the best won/loss record of any New England Patriot coach in history, the general manager, Pat Sullivan, convinced the owner, Victor Kiam, that Berry should be fired. Sullivan was evidently influenced by some of the New England fans who felt that because Raymond didn't holler at the players when they were on the field during the games, or publicly criticize particular players when they came off the field after making a costly mistake during a game, that Berry just wasn't tough enough.

Raymond Berry was plenty tough, but he was tender-tough. He was tough enough to take the best licks defensive backs and linebackers could dish out for fourteen years and never be intimidated in the slightest. He was tough enough when he found there was a drug problem on the Patriot team to face up to it head on and resolve it to a successful conclusion rather than look sideways and pretend it wasn't there. However, he was sensitive enough to the players' feelings not to berate them on the playing field when the mistake was one that all players make at times.

Three years before, in 1986, Raymond Berry and his staff had taken a losing team and turned it into a Super Bowl team against the

Chicago Bears. The Patriots qualified for the Super Bowl by being the only team in Super Bowl history to play three playoff games away from home and win them all. The Patriots lost by a big margin to the Chicago Bears in the Super Bowl. The Bears were a much better team, and the Patriots had run out of gas after their superb effort in getting to the Super Bowl. However, the Patriot achievement of winning three playoff games on the road cannot be done with luck. It takes great effort and overachievement by every segment of the team, plus a strong confidence and belief in what one is doing. Raymond Berry, with his quiet and intent manner, has to be mostly responsible for such an achievement, along with his influence for a loyal and cohesive coaching staff.

Three years later Sullivan told Berry that he had to fire "X" number of coaches on his staff in order to keep his job. Berry, in a manner totally typical of himself, refused to fire any of his assistant coaches. He knew, with the kind of strong convictions he had, that firing an assistant coach was not a solution to the problem. When he felt it was in the best interest and the welfare of the team to make changes in his staff, he made them. But he could not when he felt strongly that the changes were not in the best interest of the Patriots' future.

Raymond left the Patriots without a word of criticism publicly toward anyone and with nothing but kind words for Pat Sullivan and Victor Kiam.

Joe Fitzgerald of the *Boston Globe* wrote on February 27, 1990, the day after Raymond Berry was fired as head coach of the New England Patriots:

"When hard times come and the heat is on, it tends to define things clearer. Heat not only breeds character, it also reveals character . . ."

These words were spoken by Raymond Berry on December 29, 1989, insisting to reporters that he wouldn't shake up his staff to save his job. Make no mistake about it, Raymond Berry's character — not his stubbornness, not his pig-headedness — is what got him fired yesterday, which explains why, if you watched his gracious exit on TV, you might have noticed that he walked away smiling.

There were no tears, no regrets, no recriminations. Indeed it was the executioner, Pat Sullivan, who wore the long puss yesterday, not the man he was called upon to condemn. Berry, appearing very much at peace with himself, even attempted to take Sullivan off the hook, volunteering that the latter was simply doing his job.

. . . Berry would contend he's not unusual at all, nor is he the mysterious figure his critics made him out to be. There, of course, he would be wrong. It is indeed unusual — at least in the money-laden, ego-driven world of pro sports — to find a man whose principles outweigh his instincts to survive. There are people who'd sell their souls to coach in the NFL. Berry isn't one of them. If that was the price, and yesterday it was, he'd walk away first, which he did . . .

Kevin Mannix, also of the *Boston Globe,* after interviewing some of the New England Patriot players wrote:

Of all the Patriots, Stanley Morgan was perhaps the closest to Berry because their relationship went back to 1978. Although Berry didn't become the Pats' head coach until mid-way through 1984 season, he had been receivers coach from 1978 to 1981. Morgan arrived in New England in 1977 as a first-round draft pick who played running back at Tennessee but was projected as a wide receiver by the Patriots.

"Raymond and I go way back," said Morgan, who holds the franchise records in every receiving category and has been voted to the Pro Bowl four times.

"He was much more than a coach to me. He was a father figure. I learned a lot more than football from him. So did everybody else on the team — not just the receivers or the offensive players."

It was that skill that Ronnie Lippett appreciated most.

"The thing that I could never understand about the fans around here was their feeling that the coach should yell at his players," said the veteran cornerback, who is recovering from Achilles' tendon surgery.

"I kept hearing people say that Raymond should get after us more on the sideline, that he should get mad. The point was that he knew that's the worst thing that he could do.

"He was a player himself so he understands the stress. Having a guy yell at you in that situation wouldn't solve anything."

Like Morgan, Lippett cited the injury list as the reason the Patriots slumped to a 5-11 record in 1989.

"We had 19 guys on injured reserve," Lippett said. "No other team in the league came close to that figure. That's an awful lot of people to have to replace, and you can hardly blame the coaches for that.

"That's why I'm surprised he's gone."

Raymond Berry is a strong man, with strong convictions, and as long as he believes he is giving his very best for the interests of all concerned, he will not blame others for the lack of success in a combined team effort.

CHAPTER 14

1957–58

JOHN UNITAS:

BEST QUARTERBACK EVER

If you met John Unitas on the street or in a social situation and didn't know who he was, you would probably not believe that he was the best, or among the best, professional quarterbacks of all time. In street clothes he doesn't look particularly strong, but he is stronger physically than he looks. His height, weight, physical strength, and speed met the minimum requirements at best. While playing, he was 6'1 and weighed 190 pounds. Frankly, I didn't think he looked that tall or heavy, but he recently confirmed that, and I have to believe him.

During his first two really good years at Baltimore in 1957 and 1958, I had the job of weighing in all the Colt players every week during the season. Evidently, Weeb Ewbank, the Colts' head coach, told John Unitas that he did not have to weigh in as I really don't remember ever weighing him — not that I felt it was necessary, as his performance thoroughly proved his capability as a good quarterback.

Off the field, John Unitas was quiet and unassuming. He was never boastful, but he gave the impression that he had a great deal of confidence.

My impression was that in interviews he answered questions as succinctly as possible. He never exaggerated his role as a play caller by emphasizing how difficult it was to determine what pass he would call. He reduced his decision to the simplest terms. His favorite expression in determining the receiver he would throw to was, "Hit the single coverage." In other words, throw to the receiver who had one man covering him. He felt that receivers such as Raymond Berry, Lenny Moore, and Jim Mutscheller could get open if they didn't have but one man to beat on pass coverage. Of course, the defense would try to camouflage the coverage and many times rotate a change in the coverage after the ball was snapped, but Johnny would normally pick that up as he went back to set in the pocket.

In almost every ranking of professional quarterbacks, Unitas is ranked at the top or near the top. Rick Korch, in his article on the all-time best, selected three quarterbacks in a tie for first: Otto Graham, who quarterbacked the Cleveland Browns to a record number of championships; Joe Montana, who led the San Francisco 49ers to four Super Bowl championships; and Johnny Unitas, of the Baltimore Colts. Without question there are many fans who will disagree, but I think it is a very good assessment of the all-time best quarterbacks.

Unitas had a strong and accurate arm. He could throw any type of pass well — the quick out, the slant, the hitch (possession-type passes), the medium depth or deep sideline, the square-in patterns at 12 to 18 yards, the fly or go patterns, and the deep post or deep corner patterns.

Unitas had different depths on his drop back passes: the three-step drop for quick outs, slants, and hitch patterns, and the five-step drop on patterns on which the ball is thrown in about 2.3 seconds to 4 seconds. If the quarterback takes more than four seconds, he is usually in trouble. Jim Parker, the great Baltimore Colts offensive tackle and guard, said recently, "You always knew where Unitas was going to be, in the spot you had to prevent the defensive rusher from reaching."

On the quick pass series, he set up at three yards, and the Colts' numbering system designated that it would be a three-step set up by the quarterback. The pass would be delivered in 1.5 to 2.3 seconds. The Colts' offensive linemen would set as they normally would on other drop back passes, but after setting they would make an aggressive move and strive to stick their head in the area of the crotch of the defensive rusher to encourage him to get his hands down. They would continue to block aggressively until the pass was released, which was normally under 2.5 seconds.

Some coaches teach offensive linemen to block aggressively at the snap of the ball. The problem with such procedure is that if the defensive lineman has read the quarterback and knows it is a quick passing series, he has an opportunity to recover from an aggressive block and get his hands up by the time the passer is ready to throw and deflect the ball. On all the quick passes the ball is delivered on a low trajectory and can be batted down by a defensive lineman whose hands are up in the line of flight.

As soon as Unitas planted his back foot on the last step of his drop, he would slide his back foot forward and then step with his front foot (his left) in the direction of the throw and deliver the ball. John Unitas was not easily flushed out of the pocket. The goal of the offensive linemen was not to allow the defensive rushers to penetrate the area three yards in depth from the line of scrimmage to a depth of ten yards and a width from the outside foot of the left offensive tackle to the outside foot of the right offensive tackle. This area was called "no-man's land" and was the area in which the quarterbacks made the throw that would provide an effective passing game.

It's a generally accepted opinion that Unitas had the best and most consistent pass protection of any of the great quarterbacks. This great advantage was due to the quality of the offensive linemen, the emphasis given pass protection by Weeb Ewbank, and John Unitas' willingness to stay in the pocket and almost always slide forward toward the line of scrimmage when he did move. When Unitas ran, he usually ran between the defensive ends and the defensive tackles or between the defensive tackles rather than retreat and try to run around the defensive line, which many times can result in a much greater loss of yardage.

Until recent years, most of the great quarterbacks were 6'1 or under. Such greats as Unitas, Y. A. Tittle, John Brodie, Otto Graham, Sid Luckman, Fran Tarkenton, Charley Conerly, Joe Namath, Norm Van Brocklin, Sonny Jergenson, and others were in the 6'-6'1½ range in height. Only in recent years have the prototype quarterbacks such as Terry Bradshaw, Dan Marino, John Elway, Vinny Testaverde, and Steve Walsh been 6'3 or taller. Of course, defensive linemen are taller and bigger, but 30 years ago defensive linemen averaged about three to five inches taller than quarterbacks. Some say that quarterbacks must be taller now in order to throw over defensive linemen. I don't believe that quarterbacks ever really throw over defensive linemen except possibly when they are hanging the ball high in the air where the receiver can run under it on a go or streak pattern or except when they have no other choice.

Quarterbacks always have had to find a throwing lane between defensive linemen. I know that was what Unitas tried to do. His initial set was deeper than the depth from which he threw. One of his objectives in sliding forward was to find a throwing lane between the defensive ends and tackles or between the tackles and nose guard so that the defensive linemen could not deflect the pass. For the most part, I believe quarterbacks still strive to find a throwing lane, even though as a rule they are three to five inches taller than the great quarterbacks of 25 to 30 years ago. Montana is an exception to the modern quarterbacks as he is only a little over six feet. However, he definitely tries to throw his short- and medium-length passes in a lane between the defenders.

There may be an advantage to height, but there are other attributes more important. In my opinion the most outstanding attributes Unitas possessed (other than delivering the ball where he wanted it) were three "C's": courage, confidence, and concentration. One can also add toughness, the ability to take punishing hits and to continue performing well in spite of pain and injuries which would sideline most quarterbacks. Dick Szymanski, who played 13 years for the Colts as a linebacker and offensive center, told me recently that he thought Unitas was the toughest player he had ever known. He recalled a conversation with George Allen, who commented that Unitas was often more dangerous after he was hurt than he was before he got hurt.

A good example of Unitas being able to perform as a champion when hurt was the time he suffered two broken ribs and a collapsed lung in our 1958 game with Green Bay. Two weeks later he started at quarterback against the Rams. He was wearing a molded aluminum corset with sponge rubber covering around his chest to below his waist to protect his broken ribs and lung. It weighed nine pounds. On the first offensive play for the Colts, Johnny threw a 50-yard touchdown pass to Lenny Moore. He continued to perform as if he had never been hurt. The Colts won 34-7. "How rusty can you get?" wrote Cameron Snyder of the *Baltimore Sun*.

When Unitas set up in the pocket, he normally stayed there until he delivered the ball. If he was pressured by the rush he would wait until the last instant to release the ball and, no matter how close the rusher was, he would step forward and deliver the ball with perfect balance, as if the rusher were not there at all. In those instances, although Unitas would take a terrific hit, most of the time he would be on target and complete the pass. He demonstrated great courage and concentration. His concentration was so intense on the defensive coverage and on his pass receivers that he would not see the defensive rushers. One reason he could concentrate on the receivers and pass coverage was that his pass protection was so good. But no matter how good a team's pass protection is, there are times when it will break down, as when the defense overloads the protectors with an all-out blitz. And, with great athletes playing defense in the NFL, the best pass protectors will break down on occasion.

John Unitas has great self-confidence. His arm lost a lot of its zip and strength in his later years in the NFL, but he still had confidence in his ability. I doubt if he ever got to the point where he doubted his ability to be an effective NFL quarterback. There have been few quarterbacks in the history of the NFL that had the confidence of his teammates and coaches as did John Unitas. His quiet and unemotional manner impressed his teammates as a person who knew what he was doing. I believe a quarterback who calls his own plays has a better chance to gain the confidence of his teammates than one who has to take a signal from the sidelines. Calling his own plays also influenced Unitas to spend more time studying the film of upcoming games and learning all he could about the pass coverages and individual strengths and weaknesses of the opposing team members.

The story of Unitas playing semipro football in Pittsburgh after being cut by the Pittsburgh Steelers is well known. Colts General Manager Don Kellett made an eighty-cent long distance call to Unitas inviting him to the Colt tryout at Druid Hills Park in Baltimore. Unitas impressed Weeb Ewbank, the Colts' head coach, and was signed to a Colts' contract. John Unitas further impressed Weeb during training camp and was the back-up quarterback behind George Shaw going into the 1956 football season. Shaw had been a number-one draft choice for the year before and had an outstanding rookie year.

Despite playing on a losing team at the University of Louisville and being cut in training camp by the Steelers in 1955, and with no NFL team showing any interest in him, John Unitas retained his confidence and belief that he could play in the NFL. When George Shaw suffered a knee injury early in the season, Unitas took over the starting quarterback assignment. After a shaky start, he began to show his ability as a quarterback who could not only play in the NFL but who could be one of the best to ever play. Unitas remained as starting quarterback until his final year with the Colts in 1972.

Only a player with great personal confidence could overcome the obstacles he faced to go from $6 a game with the Bloomfield Rams to one of the best in the NFL in a two-year period.

Weeb Ewbank was a good friend of Frank Camp, the University of Louisville head football coach. I can't help but think that their friendship had something to do with the Colts giving Unitas a tryout.

Always apparent in Unitas' thoughts was "winning the game." He liked to throw the ball down-field. At the time he retired he held almost every passing record in the NFL. The only record he still holds is the most consecutive games with a touchdown pass — 47 consecutive games. I don't think he ever thought about personal statistics. He wanted the first down or the touchdown.

Unitas was a master in the two-minute offense, which came with two minutes or less in the first half or with two minutes left in the game. He was in full control and usually made the critical completions that made the difference in the outcome of a game.

John Unitas is a legend of the game. He will never be forgotten.

CHAPTER 15

1957–58

ORDELL BRAASE, DEFENSIVE END:

ANOTHER OVERACHIEVER

As the Colts' coaching staff was preparing for training camp for the 1957 season, one of the coaches told me, "Ordell Braase is the first lineman you will cut during training camp. He's not big enough and doesn't have the ability to play professional football."

I had not met Braase, and he was just a football player with a funny name — Ordell. Braase had been in the Colts' training camp in 1954. After only two weeks he was called to active duty as a reserve officer.

Three years later, when we began practice, Braase was 6'4 and weighed about 215 pounds. He really was too small for a defensive end, but he was in excellent physical condition. It was evident he had been working out. He later told me that our trainer, Ed Block, had sent a workout schedule to all the players who were reporting to training camp, and he completed the workout twice a day rather than once a day. He also had returned from Korea in February and had been released from active duty. While he was in the army, he had been through parachute training at Ft. Benning, Georgia. That showed he didn't lack for guts.

Braase was a much better football player than I expected after that appraisal from one of our coaches. He never backed away from anyone. Braase recognized what a great defensive end Gino Marchetti was, and he quickly decided he would learn the fundamentals and techniques that Marchetti demonstrated every day in practice. He also made a smart decision that he would concentrate on learning those techniques as a right defensive end since Marchetti played left defensive end.

When we weren't practicing, Braase spent a great deal of time with game films studying Marchetti. He improved rapidly and performed well in scrimmages and exhibition games. Ordell was very competitive and began to establish the fact that he could play defensive end in professional football. He may have been our only defensive lineman to have worked with weights. As a result he was very strong for his size. Coaches in the fifties had the false impression that weights would slow a lineman down and make him stiff and uncoordinated.

As a tall, raw-boned man from South Dakota who played football and basketball at the University of South Dakota, he had the frame to carry more weight. I believe he gained weight during training camp, and by his second year he weighed about 225 to 230 pounds and later played at 240 pounds, which was big enough in the sixties for a defensive end.

Ordell was born in Mitchell, South Dakota, and grew up there. He was a better basketball player in high school than he was a football player, but at the University of South Dakota he was All-North Central Conference in both football and basketball in his junior and senior years. Braase was not an honors student, but graduated from the University of South Dakota with a major in sociology and physical education.

When we got down to the final cut in 1957, it was a close call whether Braase would survive the cut or not. We had a big tackle by the name of Luke Owens, who was a second-round draft choice. He weighed about 255 at 6'2 and was all muscle. Owens was bigger and stronger than Braase. Owens punished the blocker in front of him more than Braase, but he didn't react to the ball carrier or passer as well. The other thing Owens did well was try to break the bones in a coach's hand when he shook hands with him.

At first, Weeb decided to keep Luke Owens as a reserve defensive end and tackle and was going to cut Braase. I spoke up in our coaches' meeting and said, "Braase is too good a football player to cut." Weeb and the coaching staff went with my recommendation. Braase was kept as a back-up defensive end for Marchetti and Joyce.

He was able to overcome his limitations in size and experience with intelligent effort and hard work. His weight training, film study, and conscientious effort to learn the techniques necessary to play defensive end paid off in a 12-year career in the NFL. That's not bad for a player who was not expected to survive the first cut.

An athlete has to work hard to reach his goals, but hard, blind effort alone won't get the job done. An athlete must play hard and play smart. One is almost as important as the other. Ordell Braase played hard and smart.

In 1957 Braase did not play very much, and in his frustration he often went full speed against Jim Parker, our offensive left tackle. Weeb would have to tell him to slow down as he would disrupt our offensive drills. I remember Braase saying, "I don't get to play much on Sunday, so I have to try and improve myself during the week."

In the 1958 season Joyce continued to start, but Braase got some playing time and always had a good performance when he was in the game. He played well in the 1958 championship game when he substituted for Don Joyce and for Gino Marchetti after Gino broke his leg in the final possession the Giants had before the sudden death overtime period. He was in on several tackles.

After the 1958 season the Colts traded Don Joyce to Minnesota, and Braase was the starting defensive end for the next ten years. He retired after the 1969 Super Bowl game in which the New York Jets upset the Baltimore Colts for the NFL championship.

Braase was selected to play in the Pro Bowl games in 1966 and 1967. Selections to the Pro Bowl games are voted on by players on opposing teams. Many pro players feel that participating in the Pro Bowl is the top honor they can receive. Braase was also a two-term president of the NFL Players' Association, an honor held for players who are leaders and who have the respect of their peers.

The Baltimore Colts had the best won-lost record of any team in the NFL during the sixties, even better than the Green Bay Packers, who were the glamour team of that decade. With a defensive line led by Gino Marchetti at one end and Ordell Braase at the other end, a great deal of pressure was put on opposing quarterbacks. Playing at the same time as Gino Marchetti kept Braase from getting the recognition he deserved.

Braase's strongest attribute was rushing the passer, which is a most important consideration in team defense in professional football.

Ordell Braase is a high-type person and gentleman off the field. He is a good family man, with three boys and a girl and a charming wife, Janice. He said his most memorable experience in professional football was developing lasting friendships with teammates.

Ordell is now district manager for Penske Truck Leasing in Baltimore. He and Arthur Donovan team up for a 30-minute football television show in Baltimore. Braase is the straight man while Donovan is the entertainer with stories which he embellishes to make them even better than when they actually happened.

I feel proud to have coached Ordell Braase. He is one of the players who has demonstrated what is good about professional football.

CHAPTER 16

1959

BAYLOR UNIVERSITY: A HOPEFUL BEGINNING

L. G. Dupre, a Colt halfback whose nickname was "Long Gone," was a graduate of Baylor University in Waco, Texas, and he told me that Baylor was looking for a head coach. I told him I would be interested in the job. He suggested that I write a letter to Judge Abner McCall, who was dean of the Baylor School of Law and faculty athletic representative for Baylor. I wrote Judge McCall a letter and gave him a resumé of my background. My letter was dated somewhere near the middle of December in 1958, before the World Championship Game. I didn't get a reply to my letter, and I just figured they had someone else in mind.

About the first week of January I was attending the NCAA convention in Cincinnati. The night before I was scheduled to return to Baltimore I was in the lobby of the Hotel Gibson, and I decided I would call on the house phone to see if an Abner McCall was registered. He answered the phone. I said, "This is John Bridgers. I wonder if you have filled the head coaching position at Baylor."

"No, we haven't filled the position yet," Judge McCall replied.

"Do you remember getting a letter from me?" I asked.

Judge McCall answered, "Yes, I recall your letter. We had your name in a secondary category."

"I'm very interested in the job," I said, "and I would appreciate the opportunity to talk to you and other Baylor representatives while I'm here in Cincinnati."

He said, "Give me your room number. We have a meeting in the morning with our trustees and if we decide to meet with you, I'll give you a call."

I stayed out late that evening with friends. The next morning the phone woke me up at about 6:30. It was Judge McCall. "We have a meeting with some of our trustees at 7:30 this morning and would like to meet with you," he said. He gave me the room number and I was there for an interview at 7:30. The interview went well, and when I left the room I thought I had a good chance for the Baylor job.

The next couple of weeks in Baltimore the Colts' staff was busy getting ready for the pro draft. I had the job of rating all the defensive linemen in the country. I had them rated 1 through 75.

On January 19, 1958, at about 4:30 P.M., Baltimore time, Colts' staffers were leaving the office when the telephone rang. The call was for me. Abner McCall was on the phone.

"I'm prepared to offer you the head football coaching position at Baylor University," he said.

"I'll accept your offer," I replied.

"Do you have any reservations?" McCall asked.

I answered, "I have none."

After hanging up the phone, I told Weeb Ewbank that Baylor had just offered me the head coaching job. Weeb said, "We've got the NFL draft tomorrow in Philadelphia and we need you up there."

"Weeb, you don't really need me," I said. "I have a list of defensive linemen rated from 1 through 75 with a paragraph appraising qualifications for each of them." We also had five defensive linemen that I doubted any rookie could displace. "Baylor wants me down there as soon as possible," I explained.

Weeb said, "Well, okay. You go on to Baylor then."

It was a real surprise to me to be offered the job without ever having been in Waco, Texas, and knowing very little about Baylor.

I didn't know the job included athletic director until I arrived in Waco and met with Abner McCall. He offered me a salary of $14,000 a year for both jobs, which was a low figure even in those days. That was the first clue I received that Abner McCall really didn't want to spend much money on football or athletics.

After talking to Judge McCall, I went home and told Frances, my wife, and our children that we were going to move to Texas. Cindy, our 15-year-old daughter, wasn't sure she wanted to go since she had a boyfriend. Don, our six-year-old, told Frances to find his cowboy suit. Dixon, our seven-year-old, was excited.

The phone started ringing as soon as I came home. There were calls from coaches who were interested in a job, newspaper writers, radio and television reporters, sportswriters from Baltimore and from many cities in Texas, and friends. In between calls, I phoned my mother in Fort Lauderdale and my twin brother, Frank, in Albuquerque. They were delighted. I made another call for a plane reservation and was able to get one the next afternoon. I also called Abner McCall and told him when I would arrive in Fort Worth. He said someone would meet me at the airport and drive me to Waco.

The phone rang constantly until 12:30 A.M., when I just took it off the hook and went to bed.

When I arrived at Fort Worth, a press conference had been set up at the airport. There must have been 30 to 40 news people and Baylor alumni to meet me and ask questions.

Charley Crenshaw, a Baylor alumnus and father of Ben Crenshaw, the outstanding pro golfer, was there to meet me and drive me to Waco. On the trip to Waco he tried to acquaint me with some of the problems of coaching at Baylor.

Getting the Baylor job was a dream come true. During the previous two years, Baylor finished on the bottom of the Southwest Conference. All of their starting interior linemen had finished their eligibility. A total of eight seniors were drafted by the pros after the 1958 season. Most were linemen who were big and had the qualifications of professional linemen. We had a returning letterman in the backfield, Austin Gonsoulin, who was about 6'2 and about 190 pounds. He was an excellent athlete, but much better defensively than offensively. He ended up playing for about ten years at safety with the Denver Broncos and is in their Hall of Honor with his name on the front edge of the upper deck at Denver's Mile High Stadium.

One encouraging factor was that Baylor had some excellent prospects on the 1958 freshman team, particularly as far as offensive backs: Ronnie Bull, who was from a small town called Bishop in

South Texas; Bobby Ply, a quarterback from Mission, Texas, where Tom Landry played high school football; Tommy Minter, a halfback with excellent speed and an outstanding track man from Gladewater in East Texas; and Ronnie Stanley, a very intelligent and hard-working quarterback from Port Arthur, Texas.

Among the outstanding linemen was Herby Adkins, who had played under Bum Phillips (later the Houston Oiler coach) at Nederland, Texas. He came out of Nederland as a 168-pound center, but was one of the greatest overachievers I've ever coached. Another good prospect was Bill Hicks, an outstanding center, who made All-State in Arkansas. Bill's father was a highly respected Baptist minister in Little Rock.

The athletic offices, the basketball facility, the track, the football practice fields and football dressing rooms were definitely second-class. I decided we would build new offices in the football stadium, a meeting room, a practice field, and use the home team locker room for our football dressing room. We had very little money to work with, but Weaver Jordan, out trainer, had a knack for drawing plans. He became the architect for our athletic offices and our meeting room. The athletic offices as well as the practice facilities did not compare with what you would find at major schools today, but they were a big improvement over what the previous football staff had.

We operated very economically. I was head football coach and athletic director. Bill Henderson, the basketball coach, was appointed assistant athletic director. He retired after the 1960-61 season as basketball coach but continued as assistant athletic director. I named his assistant, Bill Menefee, as head basketball coach. Bill Menefee also served as athletic director at Baylor from 1980 until he retired in 1992. Bertha Acrey, my secretary, was a tremendous help and one of the most efficient, productive secretaries I have ever had.

Athletic departments began competing to see who could have the best facilities and the most appeal to athletes. The University of Texas and the University of Arkansas, under Darrell Royal and Frank Broyles respectively, took the lead and, as a result, dominated Southwest Conference football for the next 15 years.

I was able to put together a good football staff in 1959. Our full-time staff included, as offensive coaches: Chuck Purvis, quarterbacks; Tom Pruett, running backs; and Charley Driver, offensive line (who all were retained from the previous staff). In addition, Cotton Davidson, who had played with the Colts and was a Baylor graduate, was hired as receiver coach while Hayden Fry, a Baylor graduate and successful coach at Odessa High School in West Texas, served as defensive secondary coach. Walt Hackett, from Ceritas Junior College in California, was selected defensive line coach and defensive coordinator, and Catfish Smith, a longtime successful high school coach at Longview and other places, was placed as freshman coach. Bill Newman was a part-time assistant and "B" team coach and in charge of our dormitory, Martin Hall, which housed athletes as well as regular students.

Charles Burton, a veteran columnist for the *Dallas Morning News*, wrote after our spring practice in 1959:

> The Baylor Bears have a new head football coach (John Bridgers), a new set of offensive and defensive tactics (those of the Baltimore Colts), a new lot of fancied-up uniforms, and commendable enthusiasm for the 1959 Southwest Conference Championship.
>
> So . . . the Bears despite all this, loom as number one candidates for the league cellar, a position they have held to stoutly for the last two seasons despite some spectacular offensive bouts.
>
> This will be the most inexperienced and possibly the weakest Baylor team in several years, for as the Bears ended spring training Saturday night, Bridgers thought it quite possible that as many as a dozen sophomores could be starting on Baylor's two top teams next season.

The 1959 Baylor football schedule was rated by Dave Campbell, the sports editor of the *Waco Herald Tribune* and publisher of *Texas Football* (an annual publication which had an estimated readership of over 500,000 people) as the most difficult schedule a Baylor team had ever played.

Louisiana State University, the defending national champions, and the second team on our schedule, was rated number one for the 1959 season in the Associated Press pre-season poll. Southern Methodist University, with Don Meredith at quarterback, was ranked fourth. In addition, during the season Arkansas was ranked ninth the week we played them, Texas was ranked second, Southern California fourth the week of our game.

Baylor was consensus selection to finish last in the Southwest Conference by the sports media. We opened the season with six sophomores in our starting lineup, if you count our two sophomore quarterbacks who shared playing time, Ronnie Stanley and Bobby Ply. Other sophomore starters were Herby Adkins at 185 at right guard on offense and left guard on defense, Bill Hicks at 200 at center and defensive middle linebacker, Ronnie Bull at right halfback and defensive cornerback, and Tommy Minter at offensive left halfback and defensive cornerback and safety.

We had five juniors as starters. Royce West and Buck McLeod, who were back-up tackles in 1958, were our starting offensive and defensive tackles. Both were very consistent and played beyond their ability. Everett Frazier, a junior who was our starting offensive left guard and defensive right guard, was a 190-pound reserve guard in 1958. He and Herby Adkins gave us relatively small but very effective guard play. Sonny Davis, who was 6'2 and 210, played both as wide receiver and tight end on offense and defensive end. He was a very good football player who later played a year with the Dallas Cowboys. Jerry Moore, another junior, shared playing time with Davis and was an excellent receiver and started several games. Jim Evans started at fullback. He was a hard-working and very spirited player.

Albert Witcher was one of two senior starters. He was a tight end on offense and defensive left end. His defensive play was a big factor in our being able to play some highly rated teams almost to a standstill. Austin Gonsoulin was another senior with outstanding defensive ability. He played defensive safety and cornerback and offensive left halfback and wide receiver. Gonsoulin ended up playing safety for the Denver Broncos for 10 years and is in their Hall of Honor.

Our opening game was with the University of Colorado in Boulder, Colorado. Colorado was favored, but the oddsmakers did not know how good Ronnie Bull was. Ronnie in his first varsity college game dominated that game more than any running back I have ever coached. He scored two touchdowns, one a sensational 74-yard run when he should not have gotten to the line of scrimmage, and the other on an 11-yard run in the third quarter. He set up his second touchdown run with 18- and 12-yard runs to the Colorado 11-yard-line. Of our total net rushing yardage of 98 yards, Bull gained 106 on seven carries for an average of 15.1 yards per carry. He also caught three passes for 17 yards. Lost yardage on pass attempts reduced our team rushing total to a net 98 yards. The final score was 15-7.

Sonny Davis at defensive end made a clutch interception in our end zone on a pass from our 15-yard-line late in the fourth quarter to preserve our victory. The game was a confidence builder for us.

LSU beat us 22-0 with all their scoring in the first half. The defending national champions showed us a quick and suffocating defense. Billy Cannon, the Heisman Trophy winner in 1958, ran 50 yards for a touchdown on an intercepted pass. Paul Dietzel was the LSU head coach. He and I became good friends and I coached for him in my last job as a football coach from 1970 through 1972.

Our next game was with Arkansas, the team ranked ninth in the nation that week. They took advantage of opportunities and beat us 23-7. We dominated the statistics, making 22 first downs to Arkansas' 10 and 363 yards total offense to their 177.

In our next three games, we defeated Texas Tech 14-7 and Texas A&M in College Station 13-0, but lost our homecoming game to TCU 14-0. We had two touchdowns called back on penalties.

We played the University of Texas in Austin. They were ranked the second best team in the country in the AP poll. Texas scored first to take a 7-0 lead. We came back in the second quarter and scored on a 23-yard halfback pass off a fake sweep to the left. Ronnie Bull, a left-hander, threw to Austin Gonsoulin in the end zone. We went for the two-pointer but failed, and Texas led 7-6. We scored again on a two-yard sneak by Ronnie Stanley in the third quarter to lead 12-7. We again tried for the two-point conversion and failed. Texas took the lead in the fourth quarter with a touchdown to lead 13–12, which was the final score.

Only about one-third or less two-point conversions are made. We should have gone for the tie after our first-half touchdown. If there is enough time left to gain another possession, sound strategy is not to go for the lead on gambling for a two-point conversion. It is best to go for a tie on a one-point conversion and then on the next possession try to get the lead with a field goal or touchdown. There is not as much pressure when the score is tied as when trailing by a single point.

Our loss to Texas was disappointing, but we gained a lot of respect for the gallant effort by our players. If the head coach had not gone for a two-point conversion early in the game, the result may have been a victory.

Our players were excited about going to Los Angeles and playing the undefeated Southern California Trojans. They were ranked fourth in the nation. Two former Baylor players who lived in the Los

Angeles area, Jim Erwin and R. L. Cooper, made arrangements for our squad to visit Disneyland on Friday before our game. When we got off the bus to enter Disneyland, the Disneyland Band played "That Ole Baylor Line," the Baylor alma mater. Our visit to Disneyland was thoroughly enjoyed by our players and coaches.

Our offense did not play well, but I can't ever recall a defense playing up to their maximum potential any more than ours did against Southern California.

Our offense turned the ball over to Southern California in the first quarter on a fumble on our 27, and the Trojans converted it into a field goal. We then fumbled on our seven and our defense held and took over inside our five. We again fumbled on our 16 and appeared to have stopped Southern California, but a pass interference called on fourth down gave Southern California a first down on our one-yard-line, from where they scored.

Our only offensive threat came when we drove 78 yards for a touchdown early in the fourth quarter. Jim Evans, our fullback, made a great run to score on a two-point conversion. The final score was 17-8.

In the fourth quarter we made another goal line stand. After taking over on downs, we sent in our second team. The coliseum crowd of over 50,000 gave the Baylor players a standing ovation as they left the field. That was the only time I ever experienced that in an away game.

We returned home and possibly played our worst defensive game of the year against Southern Methodist University, as they beat us 30-14. SMU ran from a spread formation and Don Meredith hurt us with his passing in the first half and almost as much with his scrambling in the second half. Ken Hays, our back-up center, intercepted a Meredith pass and returned it for a touchdown in the fourth quarter, but the play was called back on a penalty.

Our final game was against Rice in Houston. We came from behind three times to win. Al Witcher, our tri captain, twice stole the ball from Rice running back Bill Bucek to set the stage for the victory. Bull scored twice on runs of 11 and 6 yards and Ronnie Stanley threw a 26-yard touchdown pass to Sonny Davis, our tight end. Larry Corley kicked a 23-yard field goal in the final seconds. It was our only successful field goal attempt for the year as we edged Rice 23-21.

I was very proud of our team. All six of our losses came from teams which were ranked in the top ten teams in the nation either in the AP pre-season poll or sometimes during the season. Four of the teams, TCU, Texas, LSU and Arkansas, were in the top ten in the final AP poll. Our record of 4-6 earned us a great deal of respect for a team that at the beginning of the season was rated as the worst Baylor team in a number of years (although Baylor had finished last in the Southwest Conference in 1957 and 1958). The play of our defensive line after losing all five interior linemen from the year before was the most surprising performance, but our entire squad played well. We competed with every team on our schedule. Three of our four wins came on the road.

Our 1959 Baylor team gave us hope for the future. We could go into the recruiting wars with something to sell. We would return nine starters in 1960.

I believe the primary contribution to our surprising performances were due to the individual confidence and team confidence our coaching staff was able to instill in our players. The news media, local and statewide, consistently wrote favorably about our performances. Players read the papers, and praise from the press added to their confidence.

We approached the 1960 season with solid confidence that we would be strong contenders for a Southwest Conference Championship.

1959 SEASON RESULTS
Final Record — Won 4, Lost 6

Baylor (A)	15	Colorado	7
Baylor (A)	0	LSU	22
Baylor (H)	7	Arkansas	23
Baylor (H)	14	Texas Tech	7
Baylor (A)	13	Texas A & M	0
Baylor (H)	0	TCU	14
Baylor (A)	12	Texas	13
Baylor (A)	8	Southern Cal	17
Baylor (H)	14	SMU	30
Baylor (A)	23	Rice	21
TOTAL	106		154

A = away   H = home

CHAPTER 17

1960–63

BAYLOR UNIVERSITY:
SOME SUCCESSES AND NEAR MISSES

The 1960 Baylor team was one of the two best teams I coached at Baylor. The only difference between the 1960 team and the 1963 team was that the 1963 team beat LSU in the Bluebonnet Bowl game with one of the best performances offensively and defensively of any team I have ever coached, while the 1960 team lost a heartbreaker to the University of Florida, 13-12, in their final game in the Gator Bowl.

The 1960 team had several outstanding performances, such as the upset of LSU in Baton Rouge as we broke their 16-game winning streak at Tiger Stadium with a 7-3 victory. We had an almost flawless performance against Arkansas in Fayetteville when we went ahead 28-7 in the third quarter and played our reserves the rest of the game. Frank Broyles, the Arkansas coach, told me after the game, "John, I appreciate your calling off the dogs. You could have beaten us by forty points."

The third was our surprising 35-14 win over Southern California. The score was 28-0 before they got on the scoreboard. The fourth outstanding performance was a comeback win over Rice with an 80-yard drive in the last two minutes for a 12-7 victory, which gave us an 8-2 season and an invitation to the Gator Bowl. Despite their loss to Baylor, Rice was invited to play Ole Miss in the Sugar Bowl.

In our loss to the University of Florida in the Gator Bowl, we drove 68 yards with 1:01 left in the game to trail 13-12. Bobby Ply's perfect pass to Ronnie Goodwin was dropped to give Florida the victory. Ronnie Goodwin had set a Baylor record for pass receptions with seven, but he took his eyes off the ball for an instant to see where the sideline was and dropped the ball. He was in bounds by two or three yards. Florida's two touchdowns were scored as a result of two fumbles, one on our goal line (which recovered in the end zone for a touchdown) and one on our 20-yard-line. Florida moved the ball 20 yards for their two touchdowns. We drove 71 yards early in the fourth quarter and then our 68-yard drive with a minute left for a total of 139 yards for our two touchdowns, but two fumbles and a dropped pass were the difference.

Our two conference losses were 14-6 to TCU in Fort Worth and 12-7 to Texas in Waco. Our three losses were by a total of 14 points.

Arkansas won the conference championship. I probably got as much criticism after the 1960 season as I did during any year at Baylor. After looking like a world beater against Arkansas, we lost to TCU and Texas in games we could have won. The high expectations by Baylor fans grew because Baylor had not won a Southwest Conference Championship since 1924, and most of the fans were desperately anxious to win a championship again. Nothing less than a Southwest Conference Championship would satisfy them.

A dropped pass against Florida, a pass to Ronnie Bull which was tipped by a fingertip just enough to deflect the ball above Bull's waiting hands, cost us a touchdown against Texas, and a missed extra point and our only fumble of the game set up TCU's second touchdown to beat us 14-6. On our worst days in 1960 we were just inches away from victories and a Southwest Conference Championship. We knew we were close and had confidence the championship would soon come.

In 1961 we had most of our team returning, including three first-team All Southwest Conference players: Ronnie Bull at halfback, Bobby Lane at end, and Ronnie Stanley at quarterback.

We had a good opening game with Wake Forest, winning 31-0. Then we came from ten points behind against Pittsburgh in Pittsburgh to win 16-13 on a touchdown pass from Ronnie Stanley to James Ingram with less than a minute to play. We then went into a slump and lost four of the next five games. We suffered a number of injuries and our coaching staff got down on our players. We were having longer practices and a different starting lineup every week. During the 1961 season, which was single platoon football but allowed a wild card substitute for the quarterback or a total of 12 starting positions, we had 29 starters during the season.

Injuries were the cause of most of the changes, but we were practicing over two hours a day and our team appeared tired and sluggish. In our four losses we averaged only 182 yards per game total offense, which was a record low for us.

We cut our practice to an hour and a half and won three of our last four games. Our offensive output was improved to 327 yards a game in the games we won. That's not a particularly impressive average, but it was almost twice as much as in our early season losses. With our shorter practices I felt it was important for us to have a little more fun. We already had experienced many sad moments.

The turnaround came after the Texas loss in Austin, 33-7. We had seven turnovers, three interceptions, and four fumbles. The one bright spot was that we played Don Trull at quarterback in the fourth quarter. He showed good leadership and completed a touchdown pass to Ted Plumb. We decided to start Don Trull at quarterback for the first time, and we beat the Air Force Academy 33-7 in our best offensive performance of the season. Trull continued to perform well and seemed to give our entire team a lift as we beat SMU 31-6 to improve our record to 5-4.

We went to Houston to play Rice, hoping for a strong finish, but Rice got the jump on us and led 10-0. We came back and closed the margin to 14-16, but they scored late to win 26-16.

Much to the surprise of everyone, a new bowl game in New York City by the name of the Gotham Bowl called us and wanted to know if we would be interested in playing. Utah State, who finished the season as the tenth ranked team in the nation with a 9-0-1 record, would be our opponent. The bowl operators guaranteed $50,000 to each team. We figured we could make the trip for $20,000 and accepted their invitation after conferring with President Abner McCall and the Athletic Council.

I was curious why the invitation was extended to Baylor with our record of 5-4 before the Rice game. The report I received was that a New York writer had covered our game with the University of Pittsburgh in Pittsburgh, our second game of the season in which we came from ten points behind to win 16-13 in the last minute. It was an exciting game from a Baylor viewpoint. I am glad the writer did not see us play Arkansas, Texas Tech, Texas A&M, and the University of Texas (although the Texas Tech game was exciting as Texas Tech kicked a field goal with 35 seconds left to win 19-17).

The game with Utah State was scheduled for Saturday, December 9, just one week after our last game. The Gotham Bowl management reserved accommodations for both teams in the Hotel New Yorker. I believe it worked to our advantage, as Utah State was much bigger than we were physically and I am sure the Utah State players were not impressed by the physical appearance of "those poor little Baylor players." I believe Utah State felt certain they would beat us in the Gotham Bowl.

There weren't any planned recreational activities, so we just let the players be on their own two nights before the game with an 11:00 P.M. curfew and the night after the game with a midnight curfew. We had a good practice at Columbia University on Thursday before the game. I told our team this was our opportunity to show the nation how good we really were.

On game day the temperature was in the high thirties and overcast. We played at the Polo Grounds, with a disappointing crowd of only a little over 15,000 present. The game was on national television. The network wanted to televise my pre-game or halftime talk to my players. I told them, "No, I don't want to be talking to a national television audience while trying to say something meaningful to our team." John Ralston, the Utah State coach, who later coached the Denver Broncos and Stanford University, agreed to allow his halftime talk to be televised.

We had a couple of 185-pound guards who lined up offensively on their very big tackles, Merlin Olsen and Clark Miller. Herb Adkins, our right guard, faced Merlin Olsen at 6'3 and 265 pounds, while Ronnie Rogers, our left guard, faced Clark Miller at 6'2 and 250 pounds. I felt Rogers and Adkins outplayed Olsen and Miller. Rogers and Adkins were two of the best linemen I coached at Baylor, even if they were very much undersized for major college linemen. I don't recall either of them being outplayed by an opponent except when we played Texas one year and Herb Adkins had an injured shoulder and should not have played.

We scored the first time we got the ball, as Ronnie Bull ran 15 yards for a touchdown up the middle, aided by excellent blocking by Rogers, Adkins and our center, Bill Hicks. Later we kicked a field goal for a 10-0 halftime lead. As we entered our dressing room at halftime, I thought about John Ralston talking to his team before a national television audience while losing by ten points.

We scored twice in the third quarter on a quarterback sneak by Trull and a 38-yard touchdown pass to Ted Plumb for a 24-3 lead. Utah State scored after an intercepted pass in the last minute which was returned inside our five-yard-line. We were very happy with a 24-9 victory.

Ronnie Bull was named the most valuable player by the media. It was a toss-up between him and Don Trull. In the first half, Trull threw a screen pass to Bull off a fake field goal. It appeared Bull would score, but his upper leg hit the ball as he was in the open field headed for a touchdown. It was a good example why it is important to keep the ball tight against the body without allowing the arm action of the arm holding the ball to pump the ball up and down. Bull seldom fumbled, but seeing the goal line within reach, he forgot about an important fundamental. He made up for the error by the way he played the rest of the game.

It was a very satisfying victory and proved to be easier than anyone expected. It was by far our best performance of the year. It turned what started as a very disappointing year into a pretty good one.

Utah State had a number of players who achieved success in professional football. Merlin Olsen won the Outland Trophy as "The Best College Lineman of the Year" and was a nine-year All-Pro with the Los Angeles Rams. Clark Miller, their other tackle, started with the 49ers for five years and played a total of nine years in professional football. Other Utah State players playing professional football from their 1961 team were Buddy Allen, running back with the Denver Broncos; Clyde Brock, offensive tackle at San Francisco; Mel Montalbo, defensive back of Oakland; Jim Turner, quarterback and kicker for the New York Jets and Denver Broncos; Lionel Aldrich, defensive end for Green Bay and San Diego; and Bill Munson, quarterback for the LA Rams, Detroit, San Diego, and

Buffalo. If I had known Utah State had that many players who would turn out well in professional football, I might have recommended we not play them.

The extreme highs and lows of our season illustrate what a difference mental attitude can make in a football game. I am not sure at all that a coach can control that as well as most coaches think they can.

One sad result was the disappointing season by Ronnie Stanley, who was an All Southwest Conference quarterback in 1960. For some reason Ronnie had an unexplainable slump in the middle of the season. He seemed to have lost his confidence. We finally replaced him with Don Trull in the Texas game. In the last couple of minutes he went in the Utah State game and the last pass he threw was intercepted and he broke his leg. I felt like I should have been able to help him but didn't. Ronnie was an "A" student and a great competitor. He received his medical degree and is practicing in East Texas. I still have a sad feeling about the way his football career ended after contributing so much for two and one-third seasons.

In 1962 we lost eight of our eleven starters from the 1961 team, but we had Don Trull returning at quarterback and Ronnie Goodwin, an outstanding receiver and runner, and a nucleus of some good linemen. Again we started slowly with six losses in our first seven games. We lost to the University of Pittsburgh, Arkansas, Texas A&M, TCU, University of Texas, and the University of Houston. We played well against Texas Tech, beating them 28-6.

In perhaps the most exciting game of the season we lost to TCU, 28-26. Lawrence Elkins had his best day of the season as he caught two touchdown passes and returned a punt 92 yards for a touchdown. Each team came from behind three times, but two missed extra points made the difference. Texas beat us 27-12, scoring in the last four minutes to get their insurance score.

We beat Air Force 10-3 after a snow storm at the Air Force Academy. The week before, Air Force had upset UCLA. Trull connected with Elkins on a 20-yard completion for the game's only touchdown. We then went to Dallas and beat SMU 17-13 and closed the season with a 28-15 win over Rice in Waco. Trull passed for 245 yards, and we gained 166 on the ground for 411 yards in total offense.

For the season Don Trull set three Southwest Conference All-Time Records and led the nation in passing. We felt good about our strong finish after losing six of our first seven games.

As is true in every school that does not enjoy winning seasons, there were many critics of my coaching and our team's style of football. There were a great many people, including many football coaches, who felt college teams could not win with a pro-type offense.

Dave Campbell, who was the sports editor of the *Waco Herald Tribune* (and one of the best sportswriters in the country), felt very strongly that Baylor could not win consistently in the Southwest Conference with a primarily drop-back passing attack. With the current dominance of Texas and Arkansas, and the type of offense run by institutions in the Southwest Conference and others in a close proximity who were successful (such as Oklahoma, LSU, and Arizona State), he had some good examples to cite.

As a result of his strong feeling about college offense, Dave and I became somewhat alienated. Looking back, I think it was more my fault than his. I was sensitive to his criticism at times, but instead of clearly explaining the reasons why we felt a pro-style offense was better suited for Baylor than any other offense, I became resentful of his criticism. I felt that his practice of only quoting successful coaches, and others, on the merits of a strong running game and presenting reasons why a passing game would not succeed in college football undermined the confidence of the Baylor supporters, alumni, and even affected the confidence of our own players.

When it comes down to the real truth, systems do not win football games. Good football players, thorough coaching with strong emphasis on the fundamentals of blocking and tackling, speed and quickness, reduction and elimination of costly errors, and superior execution win.

My thoughts were that at Baylor (with limited funds for recruiting, facilities, coaches' salaries, and the kind of eye wash which affects the best football players), we weren't going to be able to compete equally with the state institutions who could offer 50 to 100 percent more scholarships each year than we could. The odds were against our being able to recruit as many of the big, strong, fast linemen and running backs as Arkansas, Texas, Texas A&M, and maybe even Texas Tech.

In the early sixties there was no limit on the number of four-year scholarships a school could offer. Traditionally we held our number to 30–35. We may have gone over 40 a couple of years, but we were also under 30 a couple of years while the state schools such as Texas, Texas A&M, and Arkansas awarded anywhere from 50 to 85 scholarships per year. We gave the fewest football scholarships of any school in the Southwest Conference. We averaged 33 scholarships a year; Rice was next with 35. Arkansas averaged over 48, while Texas, Texas A&M, and Texas Tech averaged over 53. The statistics on average number of scholarships for 1965 through 1968 were compiled by David Caywood, our sports information director and now vice president for public relations with the NCAA. In 1966 a scholarship limit of 50 scholarships was passed by the Southwest Conference. That was still about 17 more scholarships than we averaged.

Even though we gave far fewer scholarships per year, the size of our varsity squads was as large, and in some cases larger, than those in other schools. Our varsity squad numbered from 105 to 115. The reason was that we lost far fewer players to attrition, especially compared to the state schools. Scholarships were granted on a four-year basis. As long as a scholarship player did his class work, came to practice, showed effort, and did what we asked of him, we encouraged him to stay in school and get his degree.

We graduated a number of players who really were not Southwest Conference-caliber players, but we blamed ourselves if we misjudged their ability and offered them a four-year scholarship.

Quite a number of Baylor alumni criticized me because I didn't get rid of the players who didn't have the level of ability required for a winner in the Southwest Conference. I really don't know how the state schools were able to get rid of so many of the players they recruited who did not measure up in ability. Maybe they were very honest with them and told them, "You are never going to be good enough to make our team, and I recommend that you transfer to a school that plays in a lower level of competition. I'll recommend you for a scholarship in a smaller school."

We began the 1963 season with an upset win over Houston in Waco. Bill Yoeman was the Houston coach. I met his plane and we ate lunch together. He told me that we just didn't recruit enough players to win. We only signed 28 players to scholarships, and Houston had signed about 60 or more. Bill didn't know what kind of budget we had.

That night we beat Houston 27-0. All of our touchdowns were

scored on the ground as we gained 220 yards rushing as Don Trull, Tom Davies, Mike Marshall, and Henry Pickett scored. The previous year Houston was able to stop our basic sweep play by shooting a gap between our tight end, who was split out about two and a half yards from our tackle. We expected them to do the same, and thus made an adjustment to correct the flaw from the year before. We made most of our yardage on the sweep, including a 52-yard touchdown run by Henry Pickett, our running back.

The next week we lost to Oregon State in Portland after we had come back from a 15-0 deficit to tie the score 15-15. One of our touchdowns was a 70-yard scoring pass from Trull to Elkins. Oregon State scored in the last 27 seconds on a pass reception which was fumbled inside our 10-yard-line and bounced in the end zone, where Oregon State recovered for a touchdown to beat us 22-15. If we had recovered the fumble, it would have been a touchback and our ball, first and ten on our 20-yard-line.

Our biggest win was against Arkansas, the Southwest Conference favorite, 14-10. Trull connected twice with Lawrence Elkins for touchdowns. The starting guards for Arkansas were Jimmy Johnson, the former Dallas Cowboys' coach, and Jerry Jones, the owner of the Cowboys.

We came from behind to beat Texas Tech 21-17 when we scored two touchdowns in the last six minutes on drives of 65 and 83 yards. Our most decisive victories were over Texas A&M in College Station and TCU in Waco, other than our opening win against Houston. Lawrence Elkins caught 10 passes for 156 yards against A&M, and Trull passed for 244 yards. We beat A&M 34-7 and TCU 32-13.

Our seventh game of the season was against the University of Texas, an undefeated team which had been ranked number one for the previous three weeks in the Associated Press Football Rankings. We were undefeated in the conference and the game was billed as the "game of the year in the Southwest Conference." A reporter from *Sports Illustrated* stayed with us the week before the game.

As I told my players, "We'll motor down to Austin, play the game, and motor back." We leased the bus from a company in Waco who had nothing but old buses, but they generally were able to get us to our destination and back without any trouble.

The game was a complete sell-out, with 64,530 in the University of Texas football stadium. The game received more media attention than any game I had ever coached in except perhaps the 1958 World Championship Game between the Baltimore Colts and the New York Giants.

The game proved to be a defensive battle on a windy and overcast day with occasional showers. A 15-yard penalty set up Texas' only touchdown. Texas dominated on the ground as they rushed for 242 yards, while Trull's 19 completions for 204 yards were our offensive weapon. Lawrence Elkins, our All-American receiver, caught 12 passes for 151 yards but took a lot of punishment from the Texas secondary and linebackers on almost every reception.

We drove inside the Texas 30-yard-line late in the fourth quarter. Trull's pass to what appeared to be wide-open to Elkins in the end zone was literally taken out of the air by Carlisle, the Texas safety, an instant before it hit Elkins' outstretched hands. Carlisle appeared to come out of nowhere to make a great interception in the final minute of the game. The final score was Texas 7, Baylor 0. Texas went on to win the national championship in both polls by defeating Navy and Roger Staubach 28-6 and finished the season undefeated and untied. It was the hardest loss in my 28 years of coaching.

We threatened on two earlier drives, once when Dalton Hoffman fumbled inside the Texas 20 (our only fumble) and again when Trull overthrew a wide-open James Ingram, our other starting wide receiver, in the end zone.

Ronnie Rogers, at 5'7 and 185 pounds, was our outstanding defensive player as he made tackles all over the field playing at defensive left tackle. However, all the Baylor players gave their utmost but came up a little short against a great Texas team.

The next week we played Kentucky before about 12,000 people in Baylor Stadium. Elkins only played briefly due to an injured ankle he received in the Texas game. Kentucky returned an interception for a touchdown and had two touchdown passes as they beat us 19-7. It appeared we were still in mourning over our Texas loss.

We ended up the season with victories over Rice and SMU. We beat Rice 21-12 as Trull ran for three Baylor touchdowns and then defeated SMU 20-6.

We played LSU in the Bluebonnet Bowl and came from behind to beat them 14-7 with two fourth-quarter touchdowns on passes from Trull to James Ingram. Ingram's record of 11 catches for 163 yards was still a Bluebonnet Bowl record when the Bluebonnet Bowl ceased playing in 1990. Elkins caught seven passes for 66 yards. He was double covered on almost every down by LSU.

Don Trull set a Southwest Conference and Baylor all-time record with 26 pass completions against LSU. In 1963, not counting the Bluebonnet Bowl game, Trull broke three NCAA all-time records for the most passes completed, the most yards total offense, and the most number of plays running and passing (406). Trull and Elkins broke 16 Southwest Conference records between them. Elkins set the all-time NCAA record with 70 pass receptions in 1963.

I don't believe I've ever been prouder of a team I coached than I was of the 1963 Baylor team. Our defense held LSU to a total offense of 108 yards. Their only four first downs came in the first 11 minutes, when they scored to take a 7-0 lead. In the last 49 minutes LSU was held to no first downs, no yards passing, and only 40 yards rushing. LSU was the top rushing team in the Southeastern Conference that year.

Coach Charles McClendon was a close friend and an excellent coach. I knew he was conservative, and I felt he would not pass if he was ahead. In effect, we played almost an 11-man line for the last 49 minutes.

After we went ahead late in the fourth quarter, the LSU quarterback threw a pass to their big tight end, Billy Truax. They had returned a kickoff to about our 25-yard-line when Elkins caught Joe La Bruzzo, who was reported to have 9.7 speed in the 100, from behind and made a touchdown saving tackle. Elkins was the safety man on our kickoff team. Our defensive back covering Truax had slipped down, but Truax dropped the ball. Sometimes it takes a mistake by the opposition to make your defense look good. I believe Truax would have scored if he had caught the ball. One of the oldest axioms in football is "the team which makes the fewest critical mistakes most often is the winner."

The 1963 Baylor football team was the best Baylor team I coached. For us to win the most games that a Baylor team had ever won in the Southwest Conference, and to be able to beat a nationally recognized and ranked team like LSU in the Bluebonnet Bowl, along with the national and conference records we were able to set and the kind of defense our team was able to play most of the time, it was a most satisfying year.

We ended the season ranked somewhere between 10th and 15th in the nation by the Associated Press. They only ranked the first ten, but Baylor was one of several teams listed as receiving votes in the top ten. With our win over LSU, after the last ranking we should have been easily ranked in the top 15 teams, perhaps higher. The final AP ranking was on December 9, 1963, before our LSU game. Some writers may have ranked us ahead of Navy after their loss to Texas in the Cotton Bowl by three touchdowns.

Looking back over my coaching career, which lasted 28 years, I believe the best help a coach can give a player and a team is to give them confidence. It must be based on the truth and recognizable facts. If it is just empty words, it won't help a player or a team.

Confidence can come to a player when a coach recognizes the best assets of a player. It can derive from physical assets, such as strength, speed, quickness, efficiency of movement or coordination, good balance, quick reaction and endurance — all necessary to play the game of football. But a player's qualities may be mental or qualities of character, such as determination, persistence, courage, a "never say die spirit," intelligence, a spirit of loyalty, leadership, toughness, an attitude of unselfishness and putting the team goals ahead of his own individual goals. If a player has any of these qualities, it gives his confidence a boost when his coach recognizes them.

It is most often more effective if the coach gives individual compliments in a private conversation. To single a player out before the entire squad may result in embarrassment or give the feeling among teammates that the player is one of the coach's favorites. The kind of compliments that work best before the entire squad are when the player makes an outstanding play in a game or scrimmage. It can be done when the squad is viewing a tape or film of the game, and the players can recognize the excellence of the play. It can be a block, a run from scrimmage, a pass reception, a defensive play resulting in a tackle for a short gain or for a loss, or a short yardage or goal line defense. In fact, any individual performance which results in a positive result as far as the team performance is concerned is worthy of a statement of praise to the player.

Another way a coach can give the players and the team confidence is through the game plan of the week. In reviewing the game plan, the head coach or an offensive or defensive coordinator may point out to the team a weakness or pattern of play by the opposing team that can be taken advantage of.

I will give four specific examples from my own experience:

1. When we were preparing to play Arkansas in 1960, we noticed in their 3-deep zone pass defense the defensive corner backs were deep conscious and gave the offensive receivers a generous cushion. One of our key objectives was to throw an out or sideline pass to our wide receivers. We played perhaps the best game during my career at Baylor as we completed a number of sideline passes to our wide receivers.

The next year we played Arkansas at home and on the first play we threw a sideline pass to a wide receiver for a first down. The Arkansas defensive coordinator was reported as saying, "They just wanted to see if that out pattern was still there."

2. Our opening game in 1966, with Syracuse in Waco, was aired on national television (ABC). Syracuse was known for their great running backs, such as Jim Brown, whom many rate as the best running back in pro football history. In 1966, they had Larry Czonka at fullback and Floyd Little at halfback, both destined for the Pro Football Hall of Fame.

Defensively, they used an eight-man front and stressed an aggressive, forcing defense. They blitzed a lot. Their theory was not to give a quarterback time to pass. In the secondary they used a three-deep man for man on the tight end and two wide receivers. We felt the key was our pass protection plus being able to pick up their blitzes. If we could accomplish that, we felt we could beat their secondary defense. In our pre-season practice we worked very hard on pass protection, including all the blitzes Syracuse had shown the previous year.

The game met our highest expectations as we threw five touchdown passes and beat Syracuse 35-12. Our defense contributed greatly as they limited Syracuse to a single touchdown until we had a four touchdown lead.

3. In 1963 we received an invitation to play LSU in the Bluebonnet Bowl game. Charley McClendon was named head coach when Paul Dietzel left LSU to take over as head coach of the Army football team. Charley had been defensive coordinator. I knew Charley Mac was conservative, as most defensive coaches are since they try to convince their defense that when a ball is thrown that the defense has just as much chance as the

offensive team to catch it. I might add also that Charley was a great football coach.

LSU scored the first time they had the ball and took a 7-0 lead. Our defensive coaches felt as long as they were ahead they would not pass. We moved our three-deep backs up to about five yards from the line of scrimmage. Joe Jones, our safety, was an excellent tackler and played like a linebacker until we went ahead 14-7 late in the fourth quarter. LSU did not make a first down after their opening scoring drive.

4. The University of Arkansas used a slanting five-man defensive line in the sixties. In 1967, the year of our poorest record, we came up with a variation in our blocking scheme on a simple handoff to the fullback who was lined up in a halfback position. For example, with our flanker and tight end to the right, the fullback was lined up behind our right offensive tackle in a halfback position. Our halfback was in a similar position behind our left tackle. With the nose guard (lined up on the nose of our center) slanting either to his left or right, which he did on almost every defensive down, our center would set quickly and then block the middle guard in the direction he slanted. It was an easy block by the center. The tackles would set to the inside quickly to cut off and screen the tackle from penetrating inside. It was a tough block if the defensive tackle was slanting inside, but by anticipating an inside slant, the tackle could get in position to screen off the defensive tackle. Our fullback would take the handoff from the quarterback, look to see which way the nose tackle was slanting, and make his cut away from the slanting nose guard behind the block of the center. Our two guards blocked the inside linebackers, who were three to four yards off the line of scrimmage.

We gained about 130 yards on that one play, including a 32-yard run for a touchdown by our fullback, Charles Wilson. The play averaged over 10 yards per attempt. Only a field goal late in the fourth quarter enabled Arkansas to tie the game 10-10. It was the first time in five games that season that we had outgained our opponent. That was the last year Arkansas used a slanting five-man defensive line. I am not sure whether that play or that game had anything to do with them changing their defense, but I believe it did.

Coaching would be a lot easier if you could always take advantage of perceived weakness. Many times a team is not good enough to take advantage of what the coaches believe is a weakness. There are many other times that the coaching staff can't find a weakness that their team is capable of taking advantage of. However, if the coaching staff can find a weakness in the opposing team or an individual, it can give its players a boost in confidence.

Another factor that can help a team's confidence is setting goals for the season and being able to achieve those goals. Knowing the coaching staff are strong believers in the basic fundamentals, and that they do an excellent job of teaching those fundamentals, can be a source of confidence.

Following is a letter I received from a doctor in Phoenix, Arizona, dated February 23, 1993. I have never met Dr. Anspach or had any communication with him prior to this letter. It's an impressive example of how Baylor football appeared to some.

February 23, 199

Dear Coach:

I had just recently had the pleasure of meeting your granddaughter, Penny Blanchard. I am a family practice physician in Phoenix, Arizona. Penny recently became a patient at my office. In talking with her I found that she grew up in Waco, Texas, which is my hometown, and then as we talked further, I found out that she is your granddaughter.

This was very exciting news to me. I have been a died in the wool, green and gold Baylor fan from the time I was about 11 or 12 years old. Baylor football was the most important thing in my life throughout my junior high and high school years. Those were the years that you were head coach for the Bears. Some of the very best memories of my life still center around some of those epic ball games that your teams played through those years.

The bowl games, the big wins and some of those bitter losses, all now blend into pleasant memories. As I grow older and the burdens of life mount, I sometimes wonder if there ever will be a time when I can be so totally enthralled and so totally involved in a single event as I was on those autumn afternoons when the Bears played football.

I had every radio in the house tuned to the station two hours before the game would start and on Sunday morning, win, lose of draw, I read every line of every report on the Bears. Names like Bull, Goodwin, Trull and Elkins are easier to remember than some of the names of even my best friends in school.

You and your teams created some of the very best memories for a teenage boy those many years ago, and they are memories that I will treasure forever. I just want to take this moment to say thank you, coach, and may God bless you.

Sincerely,
Royal B. Anspach, M.D.

1960 SEASON RESULTS
Final Record — Won 8, Lost 3

Baylor (H)	26	Colorado	0
Baylor (A)	7	LSU	3
Baylor (A)	28	Arkansas	14
Baylor (A)	14	Texas Tech	7
Baylor (H)	14	Texas A&M	0
Baylor (A)	6	TCU	14
Baylor (H)	7	Texas	12
Baylor (H)	35	Southern Cal	14
Baylor (A)	20	SMU	7
Baylor (H)	12	Rice	7
Baylor (H)*	12	Florida	13
TOTAL	**181**		**91**

*Gator Bowl

1961 SEASON RESULTS
Final Record — Won 6, Lost 5

Baylor (H)	31	Wake Forest	0
Baylor (A)	16	Pittsburgh	13
Baylor (H)	13	Arkansas	23
Baylor (A)	17	Texas Tech	19
Baylor (A)	0	Texas A&M	23
Baylor (H)	28	TCU	14
Baylor (A)	7	Texas	33
Baylor (H)	31	Air Force	7
Baylor (H)	31	SMU	6
Baylor (A)	14	Rice	26
Baylor*	24	Utah State	9
TOTAL	212		173

*Gator Bowl

1962 SEASON RESULTS
Final Record — Won 4, Lost 6

Baylor (A)	0	Houston	19
Baylor (H)	14	Pittsburgh	24
Baylor (A)	21	Arkansas	28
Baylor (H)	28	Texas Tech	6
Baylor (H)	3	Texas A&M	6
Baylor (A)	26	TCU	28
Baylor (H)	12	Texas	27
Baylor (A)	10	Air Force	3
Baylor (A)	17	SMU	13
Baylor (H)	28	Rice	15
TOTAL	159		169

1963 SEASON RESULTS
Final Record — Won 8, Lost 3

Baylor (H)	27	Houston	0
Baylor (A)	15	Oregon State	22
Baylor (A)	14	Arkansas	10
Baylor (A)	21	Texas Tech	17
Baylor (A)	34	Texas A&M	7
Baylor (H)	32	TCU	13
Baylor (A)	0	Texas	7
Baylor (H)	7	Kentucky	19
Baylor (A)	21	Rice	12
Baylor (H)	20	SMU	6
Baylor*	14	LSU	7
TOTAL	205		120

Bluebonnet Bowl

CHAPTER 18

1964–66

BAYLOR UNIVERSITY:
HIGH HOPES AND HARD LOSSES

As we began the 1964 season, we had reason to feel some optimism. We were coming off the best season of my five years at Baylor. Even though we lost most of our starters, including Don Trull, who had set more records than any Baylor quarterback in history, we had Lawrence Elkins, Consensus All-American wide receiver returning, and an excellent prospect at quarterback, sophomore Terry Southall. Terry was from the same hometown as Elkins, Brownwood, Texas. Southall had been coached by Gordon Wood, who set a record for the most wins in Texas of any high school coach in history. I later learned he had the most wins among all coaches in the nation, high school or college. Terry's father, Morris Southall, was backfield coach at Brownwood and had been Gordon Wood's assistant for many years.

Two of our best defensive players were Bobby Maples, a two-year starter at linebacker, and James Rust, another two-year starter who played defensive end primarily but was also a fine offensive end as a blocker and pass receiver. Bobby Maples also played quarterback and offensive center. Bobby ended up playing 14 years in professional football with the Houston Oilers and Denver Broncos.

159

Bobby Maples and James Rust were voted co-captains by their team-mates.

We traveled to Seattle, Washington, for our opening game with the University of Washington. Washington had played in the Rose Bowl on January 1, 1964, and lost to the University of Illinois, with Dick Butkus as fullback and linebacker. Washington jumped on us from the opening kickoff and built up a commanding lead of 28-0 before we could score. They won 35-14. Two of our few highlights were Mike Marshall, our starting quarterback, throwing a 74-yard touchdown pass to Lawrence Elkins, and a 55-yard touchdown pass to Ken Hodge, tight end.

Washington was coached by Jim Owens, a former Oklahoma graduate and an excellent coach. His teams were very aggressive and tough, but I doubt if they ever won any sportsmanship awards.

At the University of Washington stadium, the visiting team and home team used the same tunnel entrance beneath the stadium to their respective dressing rooms. While we were standing in the tunnel waiting to take the field, the Washington squad came out of their dressing room. They immediately began yelling obscenities at our players. I was very surprised, as I had never witnessed that type of sportsmanship anywhere during my previous 19 years as a coach. The same thing occurred at halftime. In addition, they banged on the visiting team's dressing room door as they went by on the way to their own locker room and on the way to the playing field prior to the game and at halftime. It was something our team would not forget as we had a game scheduled with them in Waco the next year.

We lost four of our next six games and went into the final three games with a 2-5 record.

One of our victories was against Texas A&M at homecoming after trailing 16-7. We scored twice in the fourth quarter, the last touchdown on an 80-yard drive engineered by Terry Southall to win 20-16. We had taken Terry out of the game earlier, and Mike Marshall, our second team quarterback, had led us to a touchdown in the fourth quarter.

I just had a hunch Southall was ready to go back in and win the game. I asked him if he thought he could take us to a touchdown. His reply was, "I know I can."

We had another disheartening loss to Texas in 1963, when they won the national championship. We were anxious to play them in

1964. The game was in Waco. At the end of the third quarter Texas led 13-0. We forced a Texas punt and began a drive on our nine-yard line. The Texas defense was a 6-2 or a 4-4 with a three-deep zone. In today's football terminology, their defensive ends would be called "outside linebackers."

Texas played them in two different positions. If their team decided to double-cover our wide receivers, they would widen the ends to a position almost head-on with our wide receivers and they would cover our wide receivers to a depth of 10-15 yards. The cornerback would cover the wide receiver deep in their one-third of the field zone. The safety would cover the middle zone and react to the ball when it was thrown.

When they were in their double cover positions, we would check off to our sweep to the side of our tight end and block the defensive end, who was split out 8-12 yards on our wide receiver with our offensive strong-side guard who would kick out the defensive end. Our offside guard would normally turn up outside our tight end's block and seal back to the inside so as to provide a running lane between the guards' blocks as our strong-side wide receiver would block the safety. Most of the game Texas played their ends close to our tight end, as Terry Southall threw for 225 yards in the second half.

If the defensive end stayed in close to our tight end, the quarterback would check off to a quick out to the wide side of the field, which was the side where Lawrence Elkins lined up. Elkins would run a five to six yards out pattern and usually gain 10-15 yards or more. On the sweep we averaged five to eight yards per carry. We mixed in a dive run over the middle to our fullback, but these were the two basic plays we used to drive 91 yards and 44 yards for two touchdowns in the fourth quarter to take a 14-13 lead. Ken Hodge, our tight end, scored our first touchdown on a 15-yard pass from Southall, and Elkins scored the second on a quick out from the eight-yard-line.

There were almost four minutes left when we kicked off to Texas with a 14-13 lead. Texas began a drive from their 25 and got down to our 35-yard-line when, on third and long yardage, they called a sideline pass to George Sauer, Jr. (a son of George Sauer, Baylor head coach in the early and middle fifties). It so happened the pass was called on the left sideline, where the fathers of our players were standing. It was "Dad's Day," an annual event where the fathers of our players were invited to a game as Baylor's guests. The pass was on the mark and appeared to be complete but, as Sauer came down, he lost control of the ball and dropped it in the midst of the dads. Terry Southall's father, Morris, picked the ball off the ground and handed it to an official, but the official's vision was obscured by all the fathers in that area and called it a completed pass, giving Texas a first down on about our 20-yard-line. On the next play, Texas threw a touchdown pass to Sauer in the end zone.

I wanted Lawrence Elkins to play safety on the drive which Texas scored, but he had sprained an ankle earlier in the game and it had begun to swell on him. Our safety man froze as George Sauer ran past him into the zone and caught a perfect pass for a touchdown. The extra point made the score 20-14, with only seconds left to play.

It was our fourth loss to Texas in six years by seven points or less.

Our two touchdown drives engineered by Terry Southall were picture-perfect, and the running of Richard Defee, halfback, and clutch catching and running after the catch by Elkins almost brought a victory. A missed call on the third down reception by an official to give Texas a first down, and the crucial mistake by our safety in not following his coverage rule of "as deep as the deepest man and cover the man to whom the ball is thrown" won the game for Texas. Sauer's pattern was just a "streak" — straight down the middle behind the safety. These were not fancy moves, just good speed and a good throw and catch.

After losing to Texas, our next game was with Kentucky. We were going to play them at Stoll Field in Lexington, and we decided that game would be our "bowl game" since, with five losses, that would be as close as we could come to a bowl game. We named it the "Stoll Bowl."

The Kentucky coach was Charley Bradshaw, who had been an assistant coach to Bear Bryant for several years at Alabama. I was in the same class at Auburn with Jim Bradshaw, Charley's older brother, who was a center on the Auburn squad.

Lexington is a beautiful city and, as was our custom for an "away game" where we had not played before, we took a bus tour of Lexington and of Calumet Farms on Friday. Calumet Farms is one of the famous thoroughbred horse farms near Lexington. We passed a full-size statue of Man of War, the great thoroughbred race horse who retired undefeated. Our trip was an enjoyable one, and we played one of our best games to lead Kentucky 17-7 in the fourth quarter. We ran the ball extremely well, much to the surprise of the Kentucky coaching staff who expected us to feature our passing game. Tom Davies, our fullback, gained 108 yards on 20 carries.

Kentucky scored late to make the score 17-15 after converting a two-point play. They tried an on-side kickoff, but we recovered and ran out the clock for a satisfying victory in the "Stoll Bowl." Southall connected with Elkins on some clutch passes, which kept a couple of drives alive.

One of the highlights I recall was the play of our right tackle, Bill Ferguson, who weighed about 200 (if that much). He played against a big tackle named Sam Ball, who was a first-round draft choice by the Baltimore Colts and played five years for the Colts. Sam was 6'4 and 240 pounds. I thought Ferguson outplayed Ball by a clear margin, even though he was outweighed by 30-40 pounds.

We defeated SMU in Dallas 16-13. We came from behind to beat Rice at home when a Southall pass to Elkins gave us a two-pointer to tie the score 20-20 late in the fourth quarter. We forced a fumble and recovered on the Rice 12. Ken Hodge made an impossible catch on a Southall pass to give us a 27-20 victory and to wind up the season 5-5.

In 1965 we felt we would have a good football team. We lost Lawrence Elkins, who had made Consensus All-American in 1963 and 1964, but we probably had as many good linemen as we ever had during my years at Baylor. Greg Pipes, a 235-pound 6'0 guard who had excellent strength, quickness and speed, was a sophomore. We also had Dwight Hood, a 6'3, 230-pound tackle from Waco who had lots of ability. Other excellent linemen were Bill Ferguson, tackle, 6'1 and 201, and Jerry Haney, tackle at 6'2 and 218. Mike Bourland, a guard from Fort Worth, who came on a one-year scholarship, had developed into an excellent leader. He had our players believing that we *couldn't lose.*

We opened the season at Auburn. The Tigers had not lost an opening game in years. "Shug" Jordan was the head football coach. He had coached Auburn to a national championship in 1958 and had one of the best records of any Auburn coach in history. Coach Jordan was an assistant coach at Auburn in the early forties, when I was on the squad. He coached the centers and linebackers and was known as an outstanding scout. He was a gentleman, and I liked him very much. Shug Jordan was given a great deal of credit for Auburn's great upset victory over Georgia in 1942. His thorough scouting report on Georgia's team gave our defensive linebackers some tips which greatly aided our defense.

We played Auburn on a hot and humid afternoon in September. We really dominated the game offensively and defensively and led 14-0 with five minutes left in the game. Auburn finally scored and then made a two-pointer to make the score 14-8. There was less than a minute left and we ran out the clock to win the game. Terry Southall's passing and the running by Charley Wilson, a 210-pound fullback, made the difference. Paul Becton and George Cheshire, two sophomore wide receivers, also played well. On the negative side, injuries to Becton and Wilson put them out for the remainder of the year. Our defense was superb.

It was a great thrill for me to return to Auburn and win against my alma mater. A group of my former teammates attended the game, and one of the great thrills in my coaching career was greeting them on the field afterwards. I remember that Vick Costellos, who was captain of Auburn's 1942 team and co-captain of our Ramsay High School team in 1937, was there.

On Friday, while the Baylor team was practicing at the stadium, Dean Roger Allen, who was dean of the School of Arts and Sciences at Auburn, came to the practice field and visited with me. While I was a senior at Auburn, he was the one who told me that he didn't know whether a coach could be completely honest and coach a major college football team. I said, "Dean Allen, I've been completely honest with my players and with everyone for that matter. To the best of my knowledge neither my coaches nor I have violated any NCAA rules."

He said, "I believe you, John."

The next game was with the University of Washington in Waco. We had a score to settle with them.

We scored first, but Washington went ahead 14-10 with a couple of minutes left in the half. We started a drive from our 20 with our two-minute offense. We went 80 yards in six plays and only took little over a minute off the clock. We ran what we called an "in and out" pattern where the wide receiver went down-field about eight yards and broke three steps to the inside, looked at the quarterback, and broke to the outside. Southall would hit the receiver on the outside break, and the gain was 12-15 yards. The receiver went out of bounds to stop the clock.

I thought surely Washington defensive backs would do something different, but they took the inside fake every time. On our fifth completion of six attempts we got into the end zone to take a 17-14 lead.

One of the axioms in football is to keep going with what works; make the other team stop what is successful before you change. I can remember several instances during my coaching career when we had something working, and I decided we would change up and fool the defense. However, we ended up only fooling ourselves (and occasionally ended up with a turnover). This time we just kept doing what was working, and it got us in the end zone.

The second half was hard fought, and we controlled the ball for most of the half, but there were no scores. With less than two minutes remaining, we had the ball near midfield. Our regular center, Calvin Kirkham, was hurt and when we came up with fourth and one, I was tempted to go for the first down. While we were trying to make a decision, we were penalized five yards for delay of game.

My worst fears were realized. Our reserve center snapped the ball about ten feet over the punter's head, and Washington took over with a little over a minute to play on our 19-yard-line. A touchdown would win the game, and they were within easy distance for a field goal to tie the game.

We knew we had to gamble. We called four straight blitzes where we blitzed four down linemen and two linebackers. In four plays we threw their quarterback for two losses of 17 yards, stopped a draw play for no gain, and caused the incomplete pass which took them out of field goal range on fourth down. David Anderson, defensive end, Dwight Hood, defensive tackle, Randy Behringer, linebacker, and Jerry Haney, defensive tackle, led an outstanding defensive effort.

It may have been the best defensive series of downs in a critical situation in my coaching experience. We won the game 17-14 and were thrilled we could even the series with the Huskies after their rude treatment of us in Seattle the year before.

We played Florida State the next week in Tallahassee. It had rained all day, humidity was close to 100 percent, and the temperature was in the high eighties. There wasn't a breath of air stirring.

On our third offensive play, Florida State blitzed and tackled Southall for a loss. Another defensive player came in on him late and broke his leg.

Mike Marshall had to take over at quarterback. Mike had receivers open, but he just couldn't make connections often enough. He did connect with George Cheshire on a 21-yard touchdown pass for our only score. Mike just didn't have the poise and confidence to lead us to touchdowns. We ended up losing 9-7, even though we held Florida State to eight first downs.

On our flight back to Waco, our plane resembled an ambulance. In addition to Southall with a broken leg, George Cheshire was suffering from heat exhaustion. The combination of humidity, heat, and lack of any wind affected several of our players, but Cheshire most of all as he did a lot of running as a wide receiver. He gave us all a scare as he passed out while perspiring profusely and shaking like a leaf. We had a couple of other injuries, but not as serious as those suffered by Southall and Cheshire.

Southall's injury ended our chances for a good football season. While we still had hopes that one of our quarterbacks could come to the forefront, that was not to be. We did have two or three excellent games by our quarterbacks, but none of them showed the consistency to be a winner over the course of our last seven games.

The next week against Arkansas we had six interceptions and lost a fumble as Arkansas beat us 38-7. It was the largest margin of defeat in my first nine years at Baylor.

We made a remarkable comeback the following week against Texas A&M at College Station. Gene Stallings was in his first year as head coach at Texas A&M. I had read or heard somewhere while he was a secondary coach at Alabama that he had used a zone defense with two safeties and what amounted to five short defenders. The outside linebackers lined up to about a yard off the line of scrimmage and slightly outside the wide receivers. Their job was to keep the wide receivers from releasing outside so as to cut down the width of zone the two safeties had to cover. Each safety was responsible for his deep one-half of the field and generally lined up about 12 yards deep on the hash marks.

We decided to start Kenny Stockdale at quarterback. Kenny had a good football mind, but really lacked the physical qualities to be an outstanding quarterback. He was not big, he lacked speed, and really wasn't very strong.

Texas A&M, rather than playing fast cornerbacks on our wide receivers, played more linebacker-type defensive players. We told our wide receivers to just flare laterally to the outside and then turn up-field outside the defensive men who were supposed to keep them from releasing to the outside. It worked perfectly in the game. Stockdale would lead the receiver so that he could look over his inside shoulder and catch the ball close to the sideline without the A&M safeties getting there in time. Kenny Stockdale completed 20 of 27 passes for 286 yards which, at that time, was the second highest yardage a Baylor passer had ever thrown in a game. We went on to beat the Aggies 31-0 in College Station, although we were a three-point underdog before the game.

One of the game highlights in our first drive was when we had third and five on the A&M five-yard-line. Tommy Smith, a wide receiver, was dressed out for the game for the first time in the 1965 season. He had suffered a compressed fracture of one of the vertebrae in his back in a car accident. He and three other Baylor players had hit a soft shoulder in a driving rainstorm as they were returning to Texas from the Fellowship of Christian Athletes Conference in Estes Park, Colorado. I sent Tommy in the game with instructions for Stockdale to throw him a quick out pattern. Kenny led him a little too much, but Smith leveled out parallel to the ground and made a diving catch for a touchdown. Tommy was expected to miss the entire season but miraculously rehabilitated himself to the point he could play with a cumbersome brace.

We lost the next three games to TCU, Texas, and Texas Tech, as Stockdale could not work his magic again.

We finished strong again as we beat SMU 20-10 in Dallas. Donnie Lawrence, a defensive end, was responsible for our win over SMU. First he tackled the SMU quarterback for a loss and then tackled him in the end zone, forced a fumble, and recovered the fumble for our go-ahead touchdown. Later he intercepted an SMU pass to set up a field goal by Bob Purvis to give us a 20-10 victory.

We defeated Rice in Waco 17-13. Rice scored first but missed the extra point, and we came back to go ahead 14-6 on two touchdown runs by Richard Defee of 17 and 11 yards. Rice drove 80 yards with a second-half kickoff to narrow the margin to 14-13. Bob Purvis kicked a 35-yard field goal to pad our margin to 17-13 with less than two minutes left in the game. We ended up with a 5-5 season.

In our 1966 spring practice, John Westbrook, the first black player at Baylor, had an impressive 9.6 average with 29 carries. He had come to Baylor as a walk-on, and I had told him that if he performed well in spring practice we would award him a full scholarship for the fall semester. I thought he earned a scholarship on the basis of his showing.

We had an outstanding defensive lineman in Greg Pipes, who was quick, strong, and had excellent instincts as a defensive lineman. Greg was 6'0, and 230 pounds, and was in very good condition.

Other talented linemen were Jerry Haney, defensive tackle, Dwight Hood, defensive tackle, Earl Maxfield, offensive tackle, Calvin Kirkham, center, and Tommy Shaffner, a guard. We had two excellent inside linebackers in Randy Behringer and Raul Ortiz, and two very fine defensive ends in David Anderson and Willie Walker. Jackie Allen, Ridley Gibson, and Steve Lane all had excellent ability and speed at defensive backs.

At wide receiver, George Cheshire, Paul Becton, and Bobby Green were proven performers, while Jack Eisenhart was a steady performer at tight end.

We opened the 1966 season against Syracuse University at home. Syracuse had one of the best winning records in the country under Ben Swartzwalder. Floyd Little and Larry Czonka were All-Americans at halfback and fullback. Both had great professional careers — Little with Denver and Czonka with the Miami Dolphins. In 1966 Little was a senior and Czonka a junior.

The game was selected for national television by ABC, with Chris Schenkel as the announcer and Bud Wilkinson, the former University of Oklahoma coach, doing the color. ABC wanted to spotlight Floyd Little, who was a pre-season All-American choice. The September 10 game was the nation's first college game of the 1966 season.

Syracuse used an eight-man front with lots of blitzing. We felt the key to any hopes we had was pass protection. Our offensive line did an excellent job of picking up the blitzes, and we threw five touchdown passes against the Syracuse man-to-man defense.

Terry Southall had a "hot" day and threw four touchdown passes to Bob Green, Paul Becton, Richard Defee, and Pinky Palmer. The touchdown pass that broke Syracuse's back was on a fake field goal when Kenny Stockdale, the holder, threw to Charles Wilson for a touchdown.

Our defense played equally well and we went into the last five minutes leading 35-6. We tried to get everyone in the game who was dressed out, and Little scored in the last few seconds to make the final score 35-12.

John Westbrook became the first black player to play in a Southwest Conference game. On his first play he gained five yards over left tackle. Jerry Levias of SMU was the first black player to receive a scholarship in the Southwest Conference, but SMU did not open their season until a week later.

Syracuse went on to win the award as the best team in the East and played in the Gator Bowl.

Three weeks later we played Colorado after two open dates. Terry Southall had developed a sore arm. Southall didn't look like the same quarterback against Colorado as he did against Syracuse. With the score tied 7-7 in the fourth quarter, Colorado intercepted a Southall pass and ran it back to the Baylor 27. The Buffalos drove for a touchdown to take a 13-7 lead. Baylor threatened but couldn't score. Our last gasp drive was ended when Hale Irwin, who later won fame with U.S. Open and PGA championships in golf, intercepted a pass in the end zone. Colorado had another great defensive back in Dick Anderson, who was a Pro-Football Hall of Famer with the Miami Dolphins.

We traveled to Washington and played Washington State in Spokane on a rainy day. The winning touchdown was scored by John Westbrook when he went in an off-tackle play from the Washington State 12 as we won 20-14. Richard Defee, our starting halfback, was outstanding with 108 yards rushing and 103 yards on four pass receptions.

Our biggest victory of the season came the following week as we defeated Arkansas 7-0 in Fayetteville. Arkansas was the two-time defending Southwest Conference Champion and winner of 25 straight regular season games. Greg Pipes, playing at defensive left tackle, did a superb job pressuring and containing Arkansas' fine quarterback, Jon Brittenum. He was named *Sports Illustrated*'s

"Lineman of the Week." Baylor was ranked 10th in the nation after our victory over Arkansas in the Associated Press Football Poll.

Jon Brittenum, the excellent Arkansas quarterback, could only complete 10 of 29 passes. Our lone touchdown came on a 21-yard pass from Southall to Bobby Green. Southall was still not up to par, with only 13 completions in 33 attempts.

We played Texas A&M at the Baylor homecoming the next week. We had a horrible start as Texas A&M scored three times in the first half to lead 17-0. In the second half we shut down the Aggie offenses with a blitzing defense and scored twice to make the score 17-13.

With a first down on the three-yard-line, I called a time-out and told Terry Southall to run our goal line offense. We had met at noon for about 45 minutes each day during the week to review our game plan with the quarterbacks. For some reason, Terry went blank on our goal line plays. He called a dive play up the middle on two consecutive downs, a play which was not included in our goal line offense for the Aggie game. We ended up not scoring, and the Aggies held on and beat us 17-13.

I blame Terry for not calling the plays in our goal line offense, but most of all, I blame myself for not telling him what specific plays to call. This was during a time when the coaches did not call every play, and a coach left it up to the quarterback to use his judgment in selecting a play which was included in a group of plays to be used in certain situations.

Our loss to Texas A&M was devastating to the Baylor fans after we beat the two-time defending Southwest Conference Champions in our first conference game. They tell me I was hung in effigy about a half-dozen times in Waco that weekend. It may well have set a new all-time Southwest Conference record for the most times a coach was hung in effigy. We had beaten the Aggies for three straight years, and our fans could not accept a loss when Baylor appeared the team to beat in the Southwest Conference.

In the next two weeks we did nothing to regain the confidence of the Baylor alumni and fans. When we played TCU in Fort Worth. We lost Richard Defee and John Westbrook, our first two offensive halfbacks, and Terry Southall was still handicapped by a sore arm and lack of practice during the week.

After TCU kicked two field goals to take a 6-0 lead, Jackie Allen, our safety, returned a punt 78 yards for an apparent Baylor touchdown, but the play was called back for clipping. It was the third straight year that Bruce Alford, the TCU field goal kicker, beat us with a field goal.

The next week, against Texas, we faced a running back, Chris Gilbert, who was named to the Consensus All-American team in 1966. We could not stop Gilbert, as he gained 245 yards rushing (probably the most yardage a running back had ever gained against a team I coached). An injury kept Raul Ortiz, our right linebacker, out of the game, but I doubt if his presence would have made much difference. Actually, we led 7-6 at the half, but Chris Gilbert had runs of 35, 55, and 65 yards in his 24 carries.

Southall showed signs of regaining his touch as he completed 25 of 36 passes for 188 yards, but Texas still beat us 26-14.

We came back against Texas Tech as a recovered fumble and interception set off two touchdown drives and gave us a 14-0 lead. We went on to win 29-14.

Our game with SMU was truly one of the most exciting games of the year. SMU led 14-0 at halftime and then Jerry Levias, their outstanding wide receiver, returned the second-half kickoff 100 yards to give them a 21-0 lead.

Then we started to play. Five plays later we scored to make it 21-6. Then Southall threw a touchdown pass to Paul Becton to close the margin to 21-12. On our next possession we went 53 yards with a Southall bomb to Tommy Smith for the score, making it 21-19, SMU. We moved ahead 22-21 on Bob Purvis' 44-yard field goal with 2:37 left. We stopped SMU and advanced the ball to midfield. However, on fourth down, we were forced to punt with perhaps a minute left to play. Terry Southall, instead of lining up at a normal 13 yards from the ball, lined up at 11 yards. His punt was blocked and SMU took over at midfield. An SMU lineman stuck his right hand as high as he could reach and the ball struck him on the palm of the hand. If Southall had been set his normal depth, the ball would have easily been over the punt rusher's upraised hand.

We double-covered Levias, but he caught a quick out and avoided two tacklers as he cut back inside but fumbled the ball. His fumble hit the ground and bounced into the hands of an SMU player. Livingston, the SMU quarterback, hit Levias again for a gain and then Livingston ran out of bounds at the three-yard-line to stop the clock with seconds left. SMU kicked a field goal to win 24-22 with 15 seconds left on the clock.

It was another disheartening loss. SMU only completed 4 of 16 passes, but two came on the last drive. Southall set an SWC record with 50 passes and 29 completions for 350 yards. We had 29 first downs and Tommy Smith tied Lawrence Elkins' record for 12 catches in a single game. Hayden Fry, a Baylor graduate who was on our staff, was SMU's head coach. He is now the head coach with the third most victories among active coaches in Division I-A football at the University of Iowa.

Our final game was with Rice in Waco. It was Jess Neely's 40th and final game as head coach, and his 400th game. Jess Neely achieved what I wanted to. If I couldn't be the best coach that ever lived, I wanted to be one of the oldest. Rice had a 14-7 lead at half-time, but we drove 60 yards late in the third quarter to score on a 14-yard pass from Southall to Bobby Green.

On our next possession in the fourth quarter we drove 79 yards with Richard Defee scoring from the one. Rice came back strongly, but Billy Hayes intercepted a pass in the end zone to give us a 21-14 win.

Jess Neely was truly one of the fine gentlemen in the coaching profession. He also had to be a winner to survive forty years as a head coach. I knew him quite well and thought highly of him. After he retired from coaching, Jess became athletic director at Vanderbilt, the university where he had received his undergraduate degree.

The 1966 season was a big disappointment. For the first time during my years at Baylor, I lost confidence in our team and didn't feel they were playing up to their capabilities. It was especially true in games with Texas A&M, TCU, and our defensive play against Texas.

As far as sheer talent, Terry Southall had more than any quarterback I ever coached. He was only 5'10 but was very strong physically and had as strong a throwing arm as any quarterback I've coached. Terry was a knowledgeable football player but had mental lapses which proved to be very costly, such as not remembering the goal line plays when we had the ball on Texas A&M's three-yard-line and a touchdown would win the game. Then in the SMU game, after Terry had led Baylor to one of the great comebacks and passing exhibitions in the history of college football to overcome a 21-point lead to go ahead 22-21, to line up at 11 yards instead of 13 which caused his punt to be blocked.

Southall's broken leg in 1965 not only forced him to miss eight games less three downs in the Florida State game, but the injury seriously affected his play in 1966. Terry had an incredible spring practice as he completed 85.7% of his passes in spring practice scrimmages without being in top notch physical condition (due to his lack of activity while his broken leg was healing). As a result, he developed a sore arm after throwing four touchdown passes in our surprising opening game win over Syracuse. His sore arm handicapped him for the next five games. He really was not effective with his passing until the Texas game, which was our sixth game of the season. Very few quarterbacks in Southwest Conference history could match Southall's statistics in the last four games of the 1966 season. He averaged 24 completions and 275 yards passing during that stretch. Our opponents were University of Texas, SMU, Texas Tech, and Rice. Each game was competitive as the final scores were decided by differences of two to 15 points. We weren't good enough that Southall could throw just to pad his passing yardage. We lost to Texas 26-14, beat Texas Tech 29-14, lost to SMU 24-22 after overcoming a 21-point lead to go ahead 22-21 but lost 24-22 as the result of a blocked punt, and won from Rice 21-14. In the process, Terry set six all-time SWC records.

One of the most difficult skills for college players to become highly adept in is drop back pass protection. I believe it was something we did particularly well at Baylor, even in the later years when victories were hard to come by. Our scheme and coaching points for pass protection is something I would like to share with high school and college coaches, as well as the devout football fan whose interest goes beyond the strategy of the game to the skills and techniques of one of football's most difficult offensive blocks.

Other than a quarterback who has a good arm and is an accurate passer, the most important element in a successful passing game is pass protection. It's my belief a good pass offense must have the ability to protect against an eight-man rush, although a defense will very seldom commit eight players to a pass rush. What the defense does, however, is threaten eight rushers but rush from three to six and drop eight to five in the pass coverage. What makes it difficult for the offense is they are not sure which six players are going to rush the passer, so they must be prepared to block all eight.

If a team is able to protect against eight rushers, they must commit eight offensive players to pass protection. Since the primary rushers are normally down linemen, inside linebackers and outside linebackers, I advocate assigning the five offensive linemen to down linemen and two inside linebackers. If an inside linebacker drops back in pass coverage, the linemen assigned to block an inside linebacker have a secondary responsibility — either block an outside rusher or be a back-up blocker for the center's block or back-up blocker for a teammate. The back-up responsibility may be changed from week to week to counter the pass rushing strength of the opponent. On the snap count, the blocker sets about a yard deep, so that if his linebacker drops, he can instantly turn to the outside and get in position to block an outside linebacker. A method that is difficult but possible is that if the guards are covered by down linemen and the center is on the middle linebacker, the center sets a yard deep and turns out on the outside rusher if the middle linebacker does not blitz. Whether it's a guard or center blocking and outside linebacker, it is a difficult block, and it takes a number of repetitions to execute successfully.

Normally, we would like for the five offensive linemen to block down linemen, but most defensive schemes only have three or four down linemen. The other assigned blockers are the tight end, or if no tight end, a slot back and two offensive backs. If the offensive formation has three wide receivers, there can be only seven blockers. The two in addition to the linemen are the remaining back and a slot receiver. With four wide receivers an offense can only have six blockers, and they are the five linemen and one running back. If more than six defensive men are in position to blitz, the quarterback should check to see if there is an uncovered wide receiver and throw a quick pass to the uncovered receiver. The quarterback would call an automatic at the line of scrimmage. If there are seven potential rushers, the pass coverage is in all likelihood man-to-man coverage on the four wide receivers. Quarterbacks must call quick route to a wide receiver because if seven men rush, the blockers are outnumbered so the pass must be thrown quickly. The priority is to block the interior rushers first and if there is a free rusher, he is outside our offensive tackles and it will take him a little longer to get to the passer. My preference would be to have three wide receivers and a slot back where the seventh rusher will have an assigned blocker (the slot back or running back).

Most professional teams block an inside linebacker blitz with a back. I believe a lineman has a much better chance to prevent penetration on a hard rush than a back who is four yards off the line of scrimmage and is frequently lined up in an offensive halfback position.

I don't favor the "hot receiver" philosophy where the quarterback tries to throw to a receiver who is uncovered and a defensive rusher is free to rush the passer. A quarterback can just take so many free hits by blitzing linemen and linebackers before he starts to look for the rushers instead of concentrating on the receivers.

I advocate assigning the tight end (or slot) and backs to a rusher who is an outside linebacker or defensive back. If their assigned defensive player does not rush and drops back in pass coverage, then the assigned blocker (tight end, slot or back) is free to release on a pass pattern which is a complementary pattern run by the wide receiver and is the pattern the passer calls in the huddle (or in a no-huddle offense the play called at the line of scrimmage).

Below is a diagram which shows the objective of drop back pass protection.

Objective of Pass Protection

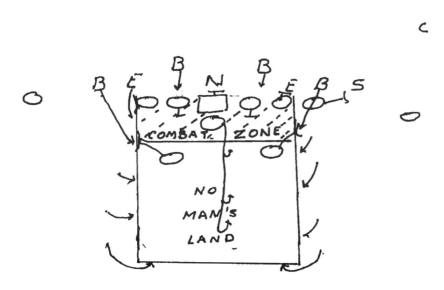

The objective is not to allow defensive rusher to penetrate an area between offensive tackles and seven yards deep from combat zone.

Blocking Assignments for Drop Back Passing

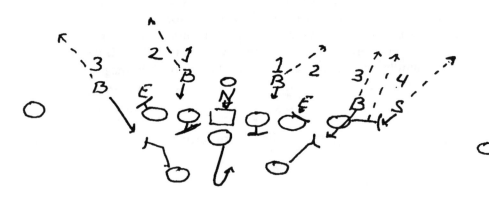

The side of tight end is designated as strongside. The side of the split end is designated as weakside. If formation is called where there is no tight end or two tight ends, quarterback's call designates strongside.

Center — #0 — If nose tackle moves to either gap he is still zero.
Strongside Guard — #1 if blitzes — If linebacker drops in pass coverage will provide back-up block on outside strongside linebacker.
Strongside Tackle — #2
Tight End — #4 if blitzes — If drops back in coverage run assigned pattern.
Strongside Back — #3 if blitzes — If drops in coverage, run assigned pattern.

Weakside Guard — #1 if blitzes — If drops in coverage, back-up block for center or any rusher who penetrates middle.
Weakside Tackle — #2 on line of scrimmage.
Weakside Back — #3 or outside linebacker (tackle blocks down lineman whether he is inside or outside the outside linebacker).

Tackles responsible for making call to their side of the ball with strongside tackle making first call. In above diagram, the strongside tackle would call "4" or code word meaning "4." The weakside tackle would call "3" or code word meaning "3."

4-3 Defense — Weakside Safety Blitz

If there is a "4" call by weakside tackle with either a nose tackle or middle linebacker on the center, the quarterback will automatic to pattern where both backs block weakside as below. (Advantage for strongside back to shift to fullback position.)

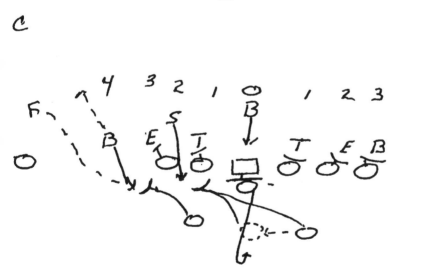

When both backs go weakside, the tight end blocks #3.

4-4 Defense — Middle Blitz

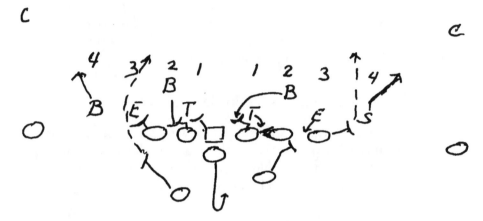

SS Guard — Works with SS tackle blocks #1 or takes inside blitzer.

SS Tackle — Works with SS guard — #2 or outside blitzer. If linebacker drops in coverage, backs up block on #3.

Tight End — #4 if blitzes. If #4 drops in coverage, run assigned pattern. If there is a "3" call, tight end releases and runs pattern without checking blitz.

SS Back — #3.

Center — Works with WS guard. Blocks #1 weakside or takes inside blitzer.

WS Guard — Works with center, if #2 blitzes, blocks outside blitzer.

WS Tackle — #2 on line.

WS Back — #4 — If drops in coverage, run assigned pattern.

There are other defensive alignments. As you can see, pass protection gets a little complicated with varied defensive alignments and a variety of blitzes. These assignments should be taught beginning the first week of practice and reviewed every week during the season. It is highly unlikely for one team to run all the defenses diagramed, but scouting will determine the defensive blitzes a particular team likes. In the week of the game blitz protection is emphasized against those defenses. If the offense knows their assignments, they will be prepared to pick up blitzes the team hasn't shown before.

The technique of pass protection for the linemen and backs is very important. The two basic techniques which are taught are:

1. Where the goal is to maintain a **nose-on** position on the center of the pass rusher throughout his pass protection assignment.

2. The blocker sets as quickly as strongly as possible in a position to take the inside away from his assigned man, and his objective is to work the defender to the outside. A key is to have the blocker's inside foot slightly inside the inside foot of the rusher. The blocker is in position to slide inside farther if rusher goes inside. Depending on the position of the rusher, the pass protector is cocked to the outside at about a 40-degree angle. The wider the defensive end, the greater the angle the offensive blocker must cock up to a 90-degree angle from the line of scrimmage. If the rusher goes upfield, the blocker's position may be up to 180 degrees from the line of scrimmage as he continues to strive to prevent the rusher to cross the vertical plane from the original position of the offensive tackle up to depth of seven yards from the combat zone.

If the rusher charges directly over the blocker, he should be in such a strong position that he will not give ground and work from inside to the outside to keep the defensive rusher from penetrating the pocket.

If the rusher charges inside, the blocker's first movement will be to slide his inside foot so as to keep his inside foot inside the rusher's inside foot. Blocker should not turn inside but maintain the cocked to the outside position so that he is in position to take on the rusher if he quickly changes his direction to the outside. In effect, by a strongly braced position blocker is taking away an inside charge and a "bull rush" directly over him. He is inviting the rusher outside but maintains his body position so that he may take him to the outside and aggressively pressure him to the outside so that he cannot penetrate no man's land. It's generally easier for a guard to maintain a good position than an offensive tackle as the defensive tackles do not try to get up-field as fast since they must protect the middle against a draw play by a running back or by the quarterback.

One maneuver a defensive end will try is to first commit up-field to the outside and get the blocker overcommitted where he can come back inside the blocker. The important fundamental is to maintain the inside position by being able to stop quickly and slide to the position where the defender is cut off to the inside.

Defensive ends are among the biggest, strongest and quickest players on defense so offensive tackles cannot make any wasted moves and must maintain their balance and body position to keep pressure on the defensive rushers.

Defensive linemen will run twists where one lineman will loop around an adjacent defensive lineman. The blocker assigned to the looping lineman should immediately call, "Switch," and be ready to take on a lineman slanting in his direction. It is most important to be able to attain an inside position. Only as a last resort should the blocker turn his body inside, as you want the same inside-out position to block the rusher most effectively.

It's most important the **back** set strongly and quickly in a slightly inside out position at the imaginary vertical line which designates no man's land. He then makes an adjustment to pressure the rusher as strongly as possible. In effect, the blocker is using the rusher's momentum to block him: if rusher tries to bull over him, he works him to the outside; if rusher goes inside, he takes him inside; and if he goes outside, he uses his momentum to take him outside. Another big advantage in using this type of technique is a throwing lane is opened up for the quarterback or a running lane is opened up for the ball carrier on a draw play.

The third advantage is that it's easier to maintain an inside-out position than to maintain a head-on centered position on the defensive rusher. There is only one very small point as the absolute center on a defensive rusher, whereas an inside-out position may cover a radius of from two to three feet. In a center's block when a man is lined up head-on, center can set so that he invites rusher to his outside (either left or right), then close quickly to take him the way he goes.

On a draw play the assignments are exactly the same as a pass protection except the tight end blocks #3 instead of #4. There should be even more emphasis for the tackles to set inside so that a running lane is opened inside the offensive tackles. The back who blocks leads the ball carrier through the hole inside of the block on #3 to his side. The draw can be a very effective play in a drop back passing game. I wish I had placed more emphasis than I did on the draw when I was coaching. Trap blocking can be used as a variation.

There is no easy way to pass protect, and if a coach is looking for a simple method he is doomed to disappointment. The defensive coaches will come up with a blitz that will defeat a simple one-rule type of protection.

Axioms of Pass Protection

1. Set quickly, set on the line of scrimmage (if you are a lineman), set inside (inside foot slightly inside foot of assigned defensive man).

2. If your assignment is a linebacker off the line of scrimmage, set back three feet from line of scrimmage. (You can better adjust to linebacker if he stunts around adjacent lineman.) If linebacker drops back in pass coverage, know your secondary responsibility.

3. Always take an inside fake — slide inside — never take an outside fake. (May adjust body and feet position but don't commit.)

4. Stay with your man until ball is thrown.

5. Overanxiousness and committing yourself before rusher does can get you in trouble.

6. Learn to slide to adjust position. Keep one foot on the ground. Do not pass protect on your tiptoes.

7. Make your stand on the line of scrimmage if rusher tries to bull over you.

I have chosen to go into pass protection in detail since I believe it's a phase of football not widely known and fully understood by many college and high school coaches. Even in professional football, I believe some coaches put the quarterback at risk by sending out too many receivers and not having enough blockers to keep the quarterback from getting a big hit. I don't have available statistics, but my impression is there have been more quarterbacks on the injured list and more games missed by quarterbacks than any other single position in football. I also believe a lot of those injuries are caused by a hit taken by a quarterback when the defensive man was untouched by a blocker. The system I have described allows the tight end and both backs to run their assigned pattern if their assigned defensive man, either linebacker or defensive back, does not rush the passer, so it's possible to have five receivers in the pass pattern (which is as many as you can get in a pass pattern).

The passing game is difficult to coach, for you must have good protection, timing, accurate throwing, and good patterns run by receivers. I haven't gone into the fundamentals of pass receiving or some important quarterback fundamentals, but some basic fundamentals in those areas are covered in Chapter 13 and Chapter 14.

When I was coaching at Baltimore in 1957 and 1958, I believe Baltimore had the best pass protection in professional football. There is no question in my mind that a great deal of the success John Unitas had was due to a higher level of pass protection than what most quarterbacks had. As is true with all quarterbacks, Unitas suffered some very hard hits, but I think he took fewer than any of the truly great quarterbacks. Unitas was able to play for 18 years in professional football and may have played longer if his arm had not gone dead.

Most of the principles I've written about came from the Colts' pass protection, but there are some other coaching points and techniques I've learned during my years with Baylor, the Pittsburgh Steelers, and the University of South Carolina. There are a few college teams that have good pass protection but not many. The University of Miami, Florida State, and Brigham Young have had good protection most of the time and there are some more college teams that have good pass protection, but there are far more that have real problems with protecting their quarterbacks.

I hope that high school coaches and college coaches who might read this book will profit from what I have written about the passing game.

One little known fact that made a big difference in our downfall in the 1967 and 1968 seasons was that Terry Bradshaw, who led the Pittsburgh Steelers to four Super Bowl championships, made a verbal commitment to attend Baylor as a freshman in the fall of 1966.

Terry was probably the best high school quarterback in the nation. He not only led his high school team to a great season, but he broke the National Scholastic Record in throwing the javelin well over 200 feet, which is evidence of a particularly strong arm. With Terry Bradshaw as a Baylor quarterback in 1967 and 1968, I might still be coaching the Bears. But for reasons known only to Terry, he withdrew his commitment to attend Baylor. I always liked Terry. I recall when coaching with the Pittsburgh Steelers, Chuck Noll and I went to Miami to scout Terry in the North-South College All-Star game. Bradshaw was almost apologetic to me for not attending Baylor. The Steelers made him the number-one pick in the college draft that year. He proved that to be a great decision.

We lost three conference games to Texas A&M, TCU, and SMU by a total of 12 points. If those games had been turned into victories, we would have won the SWC championship. We were good enough to win, but just didn't get it done. SMU won the Southwest Conference in 1966. They finished 10th in the final Associated Press football rankings. Two other teams we defeated, Arkansas and Syracuse, finished in the top 20. The AP Poll rated only the top 10 but listed 11 other teams which received top 10 votes with records of 9-1 to 7-3. Arkansas and Syracuse, with 8-2 records, had the same record as four other teams.

The 1966 season really cost me my job. We went into the 1967 season on the last year of my contract. It made recruiting very difficult, and there was a great deal of speculation about my being fired. Herb Zimmerman took a job at SMU; Ken Casner, our scout team coach, was awarded the job of defensive line coach; and Ben Nicholson was hired as scout team coach. With Herb Zimmerman's departure, we had lost every defensive coach on our staff from our 1963 Bluebonnet Bowl team.

1964 SEASON RESULTS
Final Record — Won 5, Lost 5

Baylor (A)	14	Univ. of Washington	35
Baylor (H)	6	Oregon State	13
Baylor (A)	6	Arkansas	17
Baylor (H)	28	Texas Tech	10
Baylor (H)	20	Texas A&M	16
Baylor (A)	14	TCU	17
Baylor (H)	14	Texas	20
Baylor (A)	17	Kentucky	15
Baylor (A)	16	SMU	13
Baylor (H)	27	Rice	20
TOTAL	**162**		**176**

1965 SEASON RESULTS
Final Record — Won 5, Lost 5

Baylor (A)	14	Auburn	8
Baylor (H)	17	Univ. of Washington	14
Baylor (A)	7	Florida State	9
Baylor (H)	7	Arkansas	38
Baylor (A)	31	Texas A & M	0
Baylor (H)	7	TCU	10
Baylor (A)	14	Texas	35
Baylor (A)	22	Texas Tech	34
Baylor (H)	20	SMU	10
Baylor (A)	17	Rice	13
TOTAL	**156**		**171**

1966 SEASON RESULTS
Final Record — Won 5, Lost 5

Baylor (H)	35	Syracuse	12
Baylor (H)	7	Colorado	13
Baylor (A)	20	Washington State	14
Baylor (A)	7	Arkansas	0
Baylor (H)	13	Texas A&M	17
Baylor (A)	0	TCU	6
Baylor (H)	14	Texas	26
Baylor (A)	29	Texas Tech	14
Baylor (A)	22	SMU	24
Baylor (H)	21	Rice	14
TOTAL	**168**		**140**

CHAPTER 19

1967

BAYLOR UNIVERSITY:

THE YEAR OF DECLINE

Baylor's last Southwest Conference championship was in 1924. I kept telling the Baylor alumni, "Patience is a Christian virtue." I reminded them that it took Moses 40 years to lead the children of Israel out of the wilderness, but there was no way they were going to wait that long for me.

In my ten years at Baylor we played one of the toughest schedules in the nation. The Southwest Conference teams in the sixties were ranked higher than in recent years. Texas won two national championships in the sixties and Arkansas one. TCU and SMU finished in the top 10 in other years. Baylor was ranked 12th in 1960 in the Associated Press Poll. In 1963 the AP only ranked 10 teams at that time but listed 10 to 12 other teams along with their won-lost record as having received the most votes of all other teams in the nation for a top 10-ranking. Based on the scores of the teams listed for votes in 1963, Baylor finished from 13th to 15th as there were four other teams tied with the same won-lost record, including LSU, which we defeated in the Bluebonnet Bowl.

Our normal schedule was seven conference games and three non-conference games. However, over the ten-year period our non-conference games (including the bowl games) included 34 games, many of which consistently ranked in the top 20. Our intersectional (non-conference) record was 18 wins and 16 losses. Among those top-ranked teams were University of Washington, Syracuse, Southern California, LSU, Pittsburgh, University of Houston, University of Florida, Auburn University, Florida State, Michigan State, University of Colorado, Utah State (1961 ranked 10th), Indiana University (1968 played in Rose Bowl following an AP ranking of 4th and 13th when we played them), and Oregon State University (played in Rose Bowl January 1, 1965, after being ranked 8th the year we played them).

Most of the games were very close. In a total of 34 non-conference games we won three games by three touchdowns or more and lost three by three touchdowns or more.

In the 1960 and 1961 regular seasons we won six straight non-conference games against Colorado, LSU, Southern California, Pittsburgh, Wake Forest, and Air Force. Counting bowl games, we won seven of eight non-conference games, losing to Florida 13-12 in 1960 and beating Utah State 24-9 in 1961. In the four seasons from 1960 through 1963, we won 26 and lost 17. We played in three bowl games (winning two and losing one by a single point). Incidentally, in none of the bowl games did I nor any of our coaches receive a bonus of any kind.

During the 10-year period I was football coach at Baylor, I doubt if there were more than half a dozen teams in the nation that matched the strength of our non-conference schedule or of our full schedule including conference games.

One of the necessities of winning football in Division I-A competition is good teamwork and cooperation between the athletic director, the president of the university, and key administrators.

A few years back, when University of New Mexico played Baylor in Waco, I asked Marie Abel, who was the business manager at Baylor, to give me a copy of one of our football budgets when I was coaching at Baylor. She gave me a copy of the 1963 budget, which was the year we played Texas down to the wire and beat LSU in the Bluebonnet Bowl. Rather than include our entire budget (which would be meaningless to most readers), I'll just give a few comments on specific items in the budget.

We had seven coaches whose salaries totaled $68,600 (or an

average salary of $9,800). Three or four years ago, Florida State University gave Coach Bobby Bowden a lifetime contract at $600,000, which is almost three times the *entire* Baylor football budget in 1963.

One expenditure I did not understand was $10,000 that our athletic department was required to pay the university for complimentary tickets. Included were complimentary tickets for players, coaches, and special friends of the athletic department. I know of no other institution where the athletic department had to *pay* for complimentary tickets.

Another exceptionally low expense was $15,000 allotted for recruiting. Even five years later, the recruiting budget was only $19,000. The increase may not have equaled the five-year increase in inflation.

Of course, there has been a great amount of inflation since the sixties, but still, it was not the kind of budget you would expect for a team playing at least five or six opponents each year that ranked among the top 20 teams in the country.

Another $40,500 was labeled as stadium rent, which was the annual payment to retire the university's debt on the stadium.

Many of the top teams in Division I-A football are now spending from $4–6 million (or more) annually on football alone.

I certainly don't think having the biggest budget is the most important thing, but it *is* important that the budget be large enough to pay competitive coaches' salaries and allow the athletic department to stay up to par with institutions in their own geographical area in its provision of football practice facilities, weight rooms, meeting rooms, athletic offices, and football stadium. The only facility we had that was either even with or ahead of other Southwest Conference schools was our stadium.

As we approached the 1967 football season our prospects for a successful season were very questionable. Our strength appeared to be with our defense. Our top defensive player was Greg Pipes, a 235-pound defensive tackle who was quick, strong, and had all the qualities you look for in a defensive lineman. Randy Behringer at 225 and Raul Ortiz at 210 were the best pair of linebackers we had at Baylor in my years as Baylor football coach. David Anderson at defensive end or outside linebacker had been a two-year starter. He was an excellent player.

Jackie Allen, Billy Hayes, Ridley Gibson, and Steve Lane gave us adequate size, good speed, and experience in the secondary. We were short on defensive linemen with experience, but Don Ellisor, Roy McDearman, Earl Maxfield, Walter Groth, and Ronnie Woodward had shown promise. Except for David Anderson, we lacked experience at defensive end.

Offensively, we had lack of experience and unproven prospects at quarterback. Terry Southall had graduated. Kenny Stockdale was a senior who had had some high moments in his sophomore year but had played little as a junior when Southall was our quarterback. Alvin Flynn had been held out as a sophomore. I felt he had the tools and ability to be a good one, but he never really distinguished himself as a varsity quarterback. He did show flashes of ability. Joe Reed was a good-looking, eager young man with excellent speed and a good arm. I don't think I did a good job in bringing out the best in him. He was never able to develop confidence in his ability to throw the ball. As a result, he sometimes made the decision to run when he had receivers open.

We had two fine fullbacks in Charles Wilson and Pinky Palmer. Both were strong runners and good blockers. At halfback we had John Westbrook and Brian Blessing, who was really more of a fullback type, as he lacked breakaway speed. We later shifted him to fullback and then to defense as a linebacker in 1968.

We had some proven wide receivers in Bobby Green, George Cheshire and promising newcomers in Jerry Smith and Mark Lewis. Ted Gillum, a sophomore, was an excellent prospect at tight end. In the line we had several fine prospects but very little experience. Richard Stevens at 6'5 and 235 pounds was the finest offensive tackle I had at Baylor. John Kelley, Calvin Hunt, Bob Stephenson, and Richard Denard were excellent prospects as offensive linemen.

We opened the season with Colorado in Boulder. Our performance was one of the most disappointing in my years at Baylor. Colorado led 20-0 at the end of the third quarter. We finally got on the scoreboard on a 29-yard touchdown pass from Alvin Flynn to Bobby Green. Bob Anderson, an outstanding quarterback at Colorado, scored his third touchdown to make the score 27-7. I remembered that Bud Wilkinson, the great Oklahoma coach, said, "If you don't have a good football team at the time you play your first game, the chances are you will not have a good team." We did not have a good football team in that first game. Our offense showed no consistency running or passing. We lost our second game 7-0 to Syracuse. I believe our offense was as inept as any game I coached at Baylor. Our defense improved, but Syracuse controlled the ball most of the game.

We improved the next two games as we beat Washington State 10-7 in Waco. Alvin Flynn threw a 21-yard touchdown pass to Bobby Green, and Terry Cozby kicked a field goal to provide the victory margin of 10-7.

We really outplayed Arkansas and it appeared we had them beat 10-7. Arkansas slanted their five-man defensive line on almost every play. In our game plan we decided to feature a quick handoff to the fullback from a split backfield over our center. Our center would hesitate and take the nose tackle the way he slanted. Our offensive tackles would step quickly to inside and turn back on the defensive tackles to wall them off from penetrating outside. Our guards blocked straight ahead on the inside linebackers. The play which we called Dive 20 or Dive 21 from a strong left formation averaged over 10 yards per try and Charles Wilson, our fullback, ran 32 yards for a touchdown on the play. We gained 181 yards rushing against Arkansas, which lacked only about 100 yards of matching our total rushing yardage in our first three games.

We tied Arkansas 10-10 but really outplayed them. We led 10-7 after Terry Cozby kicked a field goal. Late in the fourth quarter Arkansas drove to our 12-yard-line but with long yardage tried a field goal. There was a poor snap from center and the holder could not control the ball. In desperation he put his finger on the ball with it lying flat and sideways. We had a couple of rushers in perfect position to block it. The kicker took a swipe at the ball and kicked what looked like a knuckle ball underneath the outstretched arms of the defensive rushers. The ball barely floated over the cross bar for the tying points.

Frank Broyles always was a lucky coach (and a good one, I might add). I'll bet his kicker could take ten more tries with the ball flat and sideways and not get one through the goal posts.

I could foresee we were headed for a long season. I called President McCall, either just before or just after our game with Arkansas, and arranged a meeting with him. I told him I realized I was in the last year of my contract and wanted to know where I stood.

Judge McCall said, "John, don't worry. Everything will be all right."

I heard Judge McCall say more than one time at alumni meetings that I would be the Baylor coach as long as he was president. However, that statement was forgotten as time went by.

Our fortunes got worse before getting better. Our defense, which had played reasonably well on the first three games, became ineffective as we lost to Texas A&M at College Station 21-3, to TCU at our homecoming 29-7, and to Texas in Austin 24-0.

In our first seven games our offense had scored only 37 points or an average of 5.3 points per game. We were fortunate to get a win and a tie with that average.

In our last three games our offense showed great improvement, but our defense continued to slide as we lost to Texas Tech 31-29, SMU 16-10, and Rice 27-25. Joe Reed had his best game of the year as he threw three touchdown passes against Texas Tech. He had a fourth-quarter lead against Tech and a tie with SMU, but our defense could not prevent late scores to give us an opportunity for a victory.

Against Rice, Billy Hayes returned an interception 39 yards for a touchdown in the third quarter to narrow Rice's lead to 21-17, but Rice scored again to gain a 27-25 win. We scored late to cut the margin. Kenny Stockdale threw two touchdown passes to Pinky Palmer and George Cheshire. We averaged 23 first downs in the last three games but couldn't get a victory. We ended up alternating our quarterbacks and sending in the play with the incoming quarterback. I don't personally think that's the best system, but it worked pretty well with unproven quarterbacks.

Only Greg Pipes was able to play consistently well in our interior defensive line in 1967, although he didn't play up to his normal standard in the latter part of the season. However, Greg was selected as first team defensive tackle on the American Football Coaches All-American Team. It was an honor he well deserved based on his three years as a starter. Jackie Allen and Randy Gibson had five interceptions each and David Anderson had four. However, our defense allowed well over 200 yards passing by Texas, Texas Tech, and SMU. TCU gained 404 yards rushing against us. We finished last in the conference in total defense and had more points scored against us than in any previous year.

The year 1967 was the first in my nine years at Baylor that we won less than four games. When I look back, I don't think there was any one reason that stood out for our poor performance. I believe it was a combination of a number of factors.

We really didn't have a defensive coordinator in 1967, as Herb Zimmerman took the job with SMU late in the year. I don't believe it was the fault of any single individual coach, but the defensive staff as a whole was not effective as a group. Our players did not play with the spirit, confidence, and enthusiasm which had characterized our defense in previous years. Except for a couple of positions, we had defensive personnel who favorably compared to our best defensive players in the early years. Injuries were a factor, but you have to expect some injuries during a season.

There was a great deal of negative publicity, and the confidence of our fans continued to diminish after the midseason disappointments of our 1966 team. I'm sure that had some effect on our players. When alumni and writers continually ask players what is wrong, and suggest that the players may not be receiving competent coaching, it's certain to have some effect.

Offensively, we shuffled three quarterbacks and didn't really get a good performance out of any of them until the last three games. Our pass protection was well above average, but we did not have breakaway speed in our backfield. John Westbrook spent most of the year on the injured list. As a team we only completed 43.7% of our passes to finish sixth in the conference in passing yardage and seventh in percentage of passes completed. In the previous seven years we had led the conference in passing yardage for six of seven years and second in the only year we did not lead the conference.

As a head football coach I felt I knew more football than I had ever known offensively and defensively. However, I did have some distractions and added burdens. President McCall had been critical of our lack of revenue and questioned whether we should continue funding sports other than football at the level we had the past eight years. He wrote an article for the *Baptist Standard,* which questioned whether Baylor could continue to support its athletic program at the level we did at that time. If the truth be known, President McCall really did not like football.

We had won two Southwest Conference championships in track and field and were competitive in baseball, basketball, golf, and tennis with part-time coaches in all but basketball and track and field. Several of our top players in football were participants in other sports, such as Ronnie Bull in track, Ronnie Goodwin, All-Conference in baseball, Tommy Minter in track, and others. There were a number of others we recruited who had planned to participate in other sports but decided to limit their participation to football after they enrolled at Baylor.

I spent a larger amount of time in private fundraising in all parts of Texas and in northern Louisiana. We were able to raise far more funds from private sources than ever in Baylor's previous athletic history, but it never seemed to be enough.

One policy I followed from my first year was to answer all correspondence which was signed and addressed to me personally. The volume continued to increase in the latter years as we were struggling. My work day lasted from early morning (about 5:30 to 6:00 A.M.) to late at night seven days a week. Recruiting was very time consuming. I was expected to visit personally, correspond with, and talk long distance to each prospect. For about half of my years recruiting did not end until after spring sports season ended in May as the Southwest Conference would not allow a recruit to sign a financial aid agreement until he had finished competition in all sports.

The only time of the year I had any free time was late spring and summer, but even then meetings with staff, conference and NCAA meetings, and normal administrative duties such as hiring assistant coaches and coaches for other sports and being available for conferences with players and coaches in all sports gave me a full day most of the time.

The 1967 record of one win, one tie, and eight losses was the worst I ever experienced as a head coach. I really wasn't worried because I remembered what Judge McCall had told me when I visited him at the time we played Arkansas. When the season ended, there were stories in all major newspapers in Texas speculating whether I would be fired or not.

One of my good friends from Dallas called me and I told him what Judge McCall had told me when I visited him. My friend in turn told Carr P. Collins, who was a trustee at Baylor and the president and founder of the Fidelity Union Life Insurance Company in Dallas.

The message was relayed back to me that Carr P. Collins called Judge McCall and said, "Mr. McCall, is it true you told John Bridgers about the time Baylor played Arkansas that everything would be all right for him after this season? Please answer me yes or no."

Abner McCall replied, "Yes."

A couple of days after the season the Athletic Council, which was the committee that determined athletic policy, came to my office and spent more than an hour trying to convince me I should resign.

I told them I would not.

It was reported in the newspaper that President McCall would announce the week following the season whether I would return as coach in 1968. I was present at the announcement and felt I knew what President McCall's decision would be.

Sure enough, President McCall announced that I would return as head coach in 1968 but with no contract. In other words, I would be coaching on a day-to-day or week-to-week basis.

1967 SEASON RESULTS
Final Record — Won 1, Lost 8, Tied 1

Baylor (A)	7	Colorado	27
Baylor (A)	0	Syracuse	7
Baylor (H)	10	Washington State	7
Baylor (H)	10	Arkansas	10
Baylor (A)	3	Texas A&M	21
Baylor (H)	7	TCU	29
Baylor (A)	0	Texas	24
Baylor (A)	29	Texas Tech	31
Baylor (H)	10	SMU	16
Baylor (A)	25	Rice	27
TOTAL	101		199

CHAPTER 20

1968

BAYLOR UNIVERSITY:
THE FINAL YEAR BUT WITHOUT SHAME

With no contract I began my last year at Baylor. While attending the American Football Coaches Convention, Jack Green, who had been head football coach at Vanderbilt, approached me. He had a job at the University of Kansas as a defensive coach, but he said he would like to coach with me.

I said, "Jack, do you know what my situation is at Baylor?"

"Yes, I'm aware of it," he said, "but I would still like to come down there and work with you."

Jack had been a Consensus All-American guard on one of the Army's great teams in 1948. He had coached with some outstanding coaches and was highly thought of by everyone who knew him. We had lost our defensive coordinator, Herb Zimmerman, who had taken a job at SMU with Hayden Fry in 1967. I appointed Jack Green our defensive coordinator in 1968.

Our best defensive players from the 1967 squad had graduated: Greg Pipes, All-American tackle; Randy Behringer and Raul Ortiz, two excellent linebackers; David Anderson, defensive end; and our two starting defensive cornerbacks, Billy Hayes and Ridley Gibson.

We had some good offensive players returning, but there was

only one player among our offensive personnel who I thought could help the defense — Richard Stevens. He was a sophomore tackle from Dublin, Texas, at 6'5, 240 pounds. I really thought he had better potential as an offensive tackle since he didn't have the outstanding speed desired for a defensive player. Richard made All-Conference as offensive tackle in 1958 and later played five years as offensive tackle with the Philadelphia Eagles.

As we began practice for the 1968 football season, I told our team we were in the same position as the 101st Airborne Division when they were completely surrounded by the Germans during the Battle of the Bulge. The Germans began a desperate counteroffensive which caught the Allied troops off-guard. The commanding general of the 101st, General McAuliffe, gathered his top commanders around him and is reported saying, "This can be the greatest moment in the great and glorious history of the 101st. We are completely surrounded. For the first time we can attack in every direction!"

The 101st, with help, fought their way out of the predicament.

In 1968 we faced the toughest schedule in my ten years at Baylor. We opened the season with four "away" games.

Our opening game was with Indiana, a team that played in the 1968 Rose Bowl. Most of their starters were returning, including Harry Gonso, an excellent quarterback, and Jay Butcher, a fine receiver.

The game with Indiana turned out to be a wild offensive game. We had scoring drives of 69, 78, 80, 93, and 70 yards to take a 36-34 lead on a field goal by Terry Cozby with a minute and fifteen seconds left in the game. But Gonso completed a 50-yard pass to Butcher and then scored from the three on an option run or pass play with 28 seconds left to win the game for Indiana 40-36.

Our second game was with Michigan State. We took a 3-0 lead on a field goal by Terry Cozby, but Michigan State came back and scored on an 83-yard pass to take a 7-3 halftime lead. Michigan State overpowered us in the second half and won 28-10.

We lost to LSU in Baton Rouge. We had won two straight from LSU, but Coach Charley McClendon had them ready for us. It was 14-14 after the first quarter, but LSU dominated the remainder of the game to win decisively 48-16.

Our next game was in Fayetteville against Arkansas. Arkansas took a 21-7 lead, but we came back in the fourth quarter to score to make the score 21-19 but missed connections on a two-point play. Arkansas then drove 80 yards in 17 plays to lead 28-19 with less than three minutes to play. We started a drive and advanced to midfield, but fumbled, and Arkansas recovered. Arkansas scored on a pass play with 11 seconds left to make the score 35-19.

I really didn't appreciate Frank Broyles going for the final touchdown on a pass play with seconds left after they had the game won. But the Arkansas coaches were much more concerned about their national ranking than rubbing salt into the wounds of an opposing team and coach on his way out.

We played our first home game against Texas A&M. We surprised the Aggies and Coach Gene Stallings as we won 10-9. We took a 7-3 lead with two minutes left in the first half and then kicked a field goal on an 82-yard drive in the third quarter to lead 10-3. The Aggies were defending Southwest Conference champions. We outplayed them and played our best defensive game of the season. They scored early in the fourth quarter but missed the extra point, and we managed to hold on to a 10-9 victory.

We lost to TCU 47-14 after the score was tied 14-14 in the second quarter.

Our game with Texas was exciting and competitive as we led 13-12 at the half. The score was 34-26 with Texas leading in the fourth quarter, but their power began to tell in the fourth quarter when they drove 80 and 77 yards for touchdowns to win 47-26. The Longhorns were in their first season of over a 30-game win streak. The last team to defeat Texas before their streak began was Texas Tech early in 1968.

Tech was our next opponent, and they were tied for first place in the Southwest Conference. They led 28-13 when we scored with 54 seconds left in the third quarter and made a two-point play to make the score 28-21. We had our best offensive quarter of the season to score 21 points in the fourth quarter to defeat Texas Tech 42-28. We had scored 29 points in the last 15 minutes and 55 seconds on scoring drives of 75, 80, 46 and 20 yards.

It was a great win for us. J. T. King was the Texas Tech coach, and we usually had a long visit the night before we played. I read where he felt his friendship with me kept him from getting his team ready to play.

The next week we led SMU 17-14 at the half, but the Mustangs scored three times in the second half to beat us 33-17. That was the final nail in my coffin as football coach at Baylor.

We had one game left, with Rice, the following Saturday, on Thanksgiving weekend.

The Athletic Council recommended to Abner McCall that I be fired following the SMU game. My firing was announced on Friday, the day before we played Rice.

The first person in the coaching profession to call me and express his personal feeling and regrets over my being fired was Bud Wilkinson, the great Oklahoma coach.

At this point I want to make a few comments on the head coaches in the Southwest Conference during my ten years at Baylor.

Darrell Royal and Frank Broyles were head coaches at Texas and Arkansas, respectively, during those 10 years. It is superfluous for me to say that both were great coaches. Each has been named "College-Coach-of-the-Year," and each won national championships.

I believe their genius was in the way they organized their programs and in the coaching staff they hired. Another great quality each one had was the ability to sell what they were doing to their fans, alumni, players, and to the media in Texas and Arkansas.

I personally believe both ran honest programs. I'm sure each had alumni and fans who were guilty of "hanky-panky" and near or definite rule violations. But I think each did all he could to see that his program was run on an above board basis. I had more personal contact with Darrell Royal as he was only 100 miles down Interstate 35 from Waco. Among the head coaches I knew during 43 years in athletics, Darrell Royal impressed me as being as honest and sincere as any.

At SMU I coached against Bill Meeks, who was head coach from 1959 through 1961. Bill was from my hometown, Birmingham, Alabama. We played high school football against each other. He attended the University of Tennessee and was an excellent player there. Bill was a very good coach. His downfall may have been allowing injuries and bad breaks to affect him in his later years at SMU.

Hayden Fry was head coach at SMU the next seven years. Hayden worked for me two years at Baylor. He was a very knowledgeable coach, an excellent recruiter, and another excellent salesman of his school and football program. At this writing Hayden is still at the University of Iowa as head coach.

At TCU, Abe Martin was coach until he retired after the season in 1966. Fred Taylor, one of his assistants, took over. Abe was liked by everyone. He could really get the "Horned Frogs" up for the Texas Longhorns. Abe was down-to-earth, with a homespun sense of humor and the ability to simplify football fundamentals. He died shortly after he retired. TCU and Texas were our jinx teams. We had a winning record against every other team in the Southwest Conference except Arkansas, which we played to the hilt even when we lost to them. Fred Taylor was a sound coach, but a little on the quiet side, and I didn't know him as well personally as I did others.

At Texas A&M, Jim Meyers, Hank Folberg, and Gene Stallings were head coaches. I had known Jim Meyers as line coach at the University of Tennessee. He later became Tom Landry's offensive line coach with the Dallas Cowboys, where he remained for many years. Hank Folberg was a great football player at Army and Ole Miss, and Gene Stallings was a high school teammate of Raymond Berry and was coached by Raymond's father in Paris, Texas. Stallings is now head coach at the University of Alabama, where he served as assistant to Bear Bryant for a number of years. His national championship for the 1992 season demonstrated his ability as a coach.

Jess Neely was head coach at Rice for my first eight years at Baylor. He was a true gentleman, had very high standards, and was greatly respected. He retired after the 1966 season and took a job at Vanderbilt as athletic director. Bo Hagan replaced Jess Neely. He was a very bright coach, but the program at Rice had slipped in Jess Neely's later years.

J. T. King was head coach at Texas Tech after Dewitt Weaver was fired. Weaver was head coach in 1959-60 and was an excellent coach. He had a Tennessee background, as did many head coaches in that era. J. T. King was also an excellent coach. He did a particularly good job of getting his players ready to play Texas.

Overall, there was a good spirit of friendship and comradeship among the head coaches. Certainly, to the best of my knowledge, there were minimal rules violations in the Southwest Conference during my years at Baylor.

The alumni at SMU and Texas A&M were the most difficult to

control. The loyalty and zeal of Aggie alumni are well known, and some were willing to compromise on the rules to get good football players for the Aggies. The Aggies were on probation when Bear Bryant was head coach and later under Jackie Sherrill. SMU was on probation when Homer Smith was head coach and later received the "Death Penalty" for penalties during Ron Meyer's and Bobby Collins' regimes as head coaches. In order to put SMU on top, there were alumni in Dallas who were willing to give big dollars toward players' benefits. I do not know to what extent the coaches influenced the alumni actions, or if at all, but it may very well be that those alumni who were guilty were influenced by assistant coaches or head coaches. In order to prevent alumni and friends from violating NCAA rules, a head coach and his coaching staff must be very positive and firm with friends and alumni by discouraging the giving of any kind of benefits to prospective student-athletes without checking with the athletic director.

Winning the Rice game still meant a great deal to me. The day we played turned out to be the worst weather of any game in which I coached. There was a driving rainstorm with the temperature in the mid-thirties. The field was a quagmire, and it was impossible to effectively throw the ball.

Rice led 7-0 at halftime. John Lerner, a halfback from Rio Grande City, gave us a great boost when he returned the second-half kickoff to the Rice 18-yard-line. Gene Rogers, our starting tailback, scored from the three-yard-line and Cozby kicked the extra point to tie the game at 7-7. Later in the third quarter a Rice fumble was recovered by Ed Marsh, a very fine punter and defensive halfback. We drove to their 21, where Stan Cozby kicked a field goal to give us a 10-7 lead.

Rice drove for a first down inside our 10 but we took over on downs on our four. Gene Rogers broke on a counterplay for a 70-yard run to the Rice 26. It was the decisive play in our winning the game. We substituted John Westbrook for Gene Rogers, and John scored in four plays to make the score 16-7.

Gene Rogers set an all-time Baylor record for yards rushing in one game with 145 yards. John Westbrook, the first black player in Baylor history and the first to play in a Southwest Conference game, ended his career by scoring the final touchdown in my 10-year tenure as head football coach at Baylor.

It was an emotional experience for me in the dressing room following the game. I couldn't prevent tears from coming as I met with my Baylor team for the last time. I felt they had given an outstanding effort all year. I went to each player and thanked him for his effort and spirit during a very difficult season.

After my firing was announced, I had refused to make any comments. The most important thing to me was to give my best effort to win our last game.

We had a press conference in the Baylor press box after the Rice game. I shared my thoughts with the writers in the press box. We had continued to be competitive. In the Southwest Conference, over a 10-year period, Baylor ranked behind Texas and Arkansas for the best won-lost record in conference games as well as non-conference games.

RECORD OF SWC TEAMS 1959 – 1968 (Including Bowl Games)			
	Won	**Lost**	**Tie**
Texas	83	21	3
Arkansas	81	24	1
Baylor	49	53	1
Texas Tech	46	52	4
Texas Christian	44	53	5
Southern Methodist	36	62	4
Rice	34	62	6
Texas A&M	31	64	6

Of our 22 starters on offense and defense, 20 were undergraduates who would return in 1969. On offense, the 1968 Baylor team had set an all-time Baylor record for first downs and for total offense with a total offense of 356 yards per game. Our defense needed strengthening, but with the experience gained, we felt our defense could improve in 1969.

A 1968 rule change in college football caused a significant change in college football offense that very few people are aware of. The college rules were changed to stop the clock after each first down and allow the chain crews to move the chains. The clock was restarted on a signal from the referee after the chainmen had moved the first-down chains. As a result, if you compare the total offensive plays (run and pass) for each SWC team prior to 1968 to total plays in 1968, the number of offensive plays increases significantly. For example, for 1963 compared to 1968, the number of total offensive plays increased by 92 plays at Baylor and by 254 plays at SMU. The two factors which influenced the higher number of offensive plays were the total first downs (clock stopped when chains moved) by a team and increased number of pass plays (clocks stopped on incomplete pass) by a team. The average number of offensive plays within the conference in 1968 was increased by 149 (or 24.4%) over 1963. That's an average of 15 offensive plays per game.

There is no question that when a coach loses the majority of games, he is likely to be fired. Yet there were a number of things I was very proud of and feel good about during my years at Baylor.

There were very few games in which we were not competitive. In 1967 we lost four games by seven points or less and the last three by a *total* of 10 points. The only team we played that scored over 30 points was Texas Tech, and they beat us 31-29. Our biggest loss was by three touchdowns.

In 1968 we were very competitive with every team we played, at least through the first half. Only LSU led us by more than one touchdown before the third quarter, as LSU led 27-14 at the half. We were tied with TCU until there was 3:49 to play in the third quarter. We trailed Texas by eight points with under three minutes left in the third quarter. We were behind Michigan State 7-3 with 10-minutes left in the third quarter. SMU went ahead 20-17 in the third quarter, and that score stood until the fourth quarter. We lost to Indiana in the last 18 seconds, 40-36.

Our biggest problem was that we just didn't have the defensive personnel to compete with most of the teams on our schedule. We had a few good defensive players, but not enough. The only year we gave up 200 points or more was in 1968, when we gave up 322.

Offensively, Gene Rogers, a starting halfback, and Pinky Palmer, a fullback, were our leading ground gainers and played consistently well all year in 1968.

In the offensive line, Richard Stevens at tackle was outstanding as a run and pass blocker. As mentioned earlier, Stevens made first team All-Southwest Conference and played offensive tackle for the Philadelphia Eagles for five years. Richard was an outstanding person as well as an excellent player.

Calvin Hunt at 6'3 and 220 pounds was an excellent center and played a couple of years with the Houston Oilers. Calvin was All-Conference in 1968. Ted Gillum at tight end and John Kelley at offensive tackle also played well throughout the season.

Steve Stuart, a sophomore quarterback from Nederland, Texas (who ended up as our starting quarterback in 1968), showed a great deal of improvement as the season went along. I thought he had the throwing arm, leadership, and intelligence to make an excellent quarterback for a pro-type offense, but with the coaching changes, he was not given much consideration for a sprint-out pass offense.

A surprising performer at wide receiver was Don Huggins, a 5'10, 165-pound walk-on wide receiver from Oklahoma City, who was very quick and ran excellent patterns. Derek Davis, a sophomore from Dallas, and Mark Lewis, a junior from McAllen, Texas, caught the ball well too.

Three of our four losing seasons (1962, 1967 and 1968) came when I had one year on my contract, in my last year of my contract, and the year I didn't have a contract (1968). There is no question that having two or more years on a contract is most helpful in Division I-A football.

With the exception of my first year, when we lost two of our last three games to Southern California, ranked fourth in the nation, and to a Don Meredith-led SMU team, we finished strong in eight of my last nine years. We won two of three, three of four or three of three of our last three or four games in eight of those years. The only other year we didn't win most of our last three or four games was in 1967, when we lost all three games by a total of 10 points. Our record after the Texas game for the last nine years was 21 wins and 9 losses. If we could have avoided our midseason slump, I might still be at Baylor.

As stated previously, Baylor signed fewer players to football scholarships than any other Southwest Conference school (an average of 33 per year). Our coaching staff at Baylor started out as a very strong staff offensively and defensively. As the year went by, and salary increases at Baylor failed to be competitive, many of our strongest coaches went on to better opportunities.

After the 1967 season, which was the low point of all my years at Baylor, I met Jack Green and hired him as defensive coordinator. Jack changed our defense from a 4-4 or 6-2 with a three-deep zone to a slanting five-man line. One of the defensive backs was designated as monster man. He was a strong safety with responsibility for run support and the strong side flat as far as passing was concerned. Our pass defense was a three-deep zone.

Without question, in 1968 we had the weakest defensive personnel during my tenure at Baylor, so our defensive performance was not impressive. However, I never blamed Jack Green for the team's performance. He was a top-class person and continued to work very hard to improve the defense until we played our last game. He never made any excuses; just did the very best he could.

I believe every coach we had gave his best effort and tried his utmost to give Baylor a winning team. As the years went by, we did lose some valuable experience among coaches who left and, for the most part, could not match their experience with the incoming replacement coaches. After Cotton Davidson left, I decided Coach Chuck Purvis and I would work with the receivers during the season, and Raymond Berry would be our receiver coach during spring practice.

After the 1966 season, Abner McCall scheduled an appointment with me. When I arrived at his office, a couple of members of the Athletic Council were present. Finally, it became evident that the group wanted me to make staff changes. They urged me to fire three or four coaches. I just told them that our assistant coaches weren't our primary problem and that I did not want to fire any of them.

With the low salaries we had to offer, I did not understand how they could expect me to bring in better coaches than we had. The lack of job security, with only one year remaining on my contract, would scare top-flight assistants away even if we had the money to hire them.

Looking back on my 10 years at Baylor, plus observations and convictions I have acquired over 40-plus years, I have come up with some changes in strategy and policy that I would follow if I had the opportunity to relive my life as a football coach and athletic director.

Some Lessons Learned

The Scoreboard — The scoreboard can be a coach's biggest ally. If the scoreboard shows a victory, it will overcome other shortcomings. If it shows a loss, it can be his worst enemy and there are few alternatives which will make a great deal of difference.

Scheduling — I was partly responsible for my own demise by scheduling the toughest intersectional games away from home to enable us to have a balanced athletic budget. In my last two years we played eight home games and 12 road games. At home we were four wins, three losses, and one tie. On the road we were 0-12. The fact is, a team usually has to be better than the other team to win on the road. In 1967 and 1968 we faced Colorado, Syracuse, Indiana, Michigan State, and LSU on the road and lost them all. In earlier years we had some great victories on the road against Colorado, Auburn, Pittsburgh, LSU, Air Force, and some conference games, including two against Arkansas. The fact is our teams were better in those early years. Marv Levy, the successful coach with the Buffalo Bills, is quoted as saying, "Adolf Hitler assembled the greatest army history has ever known, but he had one fault. He couldn't win on the road!" A coach can't win on the road if he consistently plays against better teams on the road. I decided I would never schedule myself out of a job again. I've never had another opportunity as head coach, but I've tried to follow that axiom as athletic director at Florida State and the University of New Mexico.

Spending Time with Decision Makers — An athletic director must have good relations with the president and administrative staff of the university, especially the financial administrators, if he expects to have a long tenure. A head football coach should make time to spend with the athletic director (and the athletic director should meet with the president of the university) on a regular basis, such as weekly or biweekly. The reason is that there are many fans who just don't think a coach should ever lose a game. Every time a game is lost and if the fans have access to the president or athletic director, they will belittle and criticize the coach for losing. Believe me, the coach takes the blame for not winning a game.

When a coach meets with the athletic director or athletic director with the president, he should give as accurate an appraisal as possible about the status of the team. In high school the coach should establish a good relationship with the principal and meet with him on a weekly basis. If he feels he made a mistake, he should admit it and be careful not to alibi. The coach or athletic director has to be more believable than the critics, and he should be, for the critics are usually amateurs. A university president, particularly at private schools, has control over funds that can be steered wherever he can be convinced there is a need, such as intercollegiate athletics.

There are only a very few athletic departments which can support an intercollegiate program including, at most, two sports (men's football and men's basketball), which are moneymakers, and then anywhere from 12 to 24 men's and women's sports, which are just expenses as far as the budget is concerned. Since a very small percentage of schools earn enough television and other revenues to support the entire athletic program, they are the exceptions rather than the rule. It is of extreme importance that a president do what he can to keep the overall athletic program from suffering a large deficit. A deficit, next to losing, is the most negative thing that can happen to an athletic director or football coach. I've always been in favor of a university having a comprehensive athletic program, but I feel non-revenue sports should be supported by funds provided by the university, such as student fees, state appropriations, or by private designated contributions. I also believe football and basketball should be self-supporting at the Division I-A level. Sufficient reserves should be accumulated to balance the budget in lean years.

Recruiting — In recruiting, one coach who is knowledgeable and experienced should be appointed as recruiting coordinator. The coordinator should not be assigned an area in which to recruit but have the task of evaluating and helping the other coaches recruit their areas when called upon to do so. All prospective recruits should be given approval by the position coach and the recruiting coordinator for a scholarship to be offered. If either one rejects the recruit, he should not be offered a scholarship. Only the head coach should have the privilege of overruling the recruiting coordinator and the position coach.

There are times when a football player has the courage, character, confidence, intensity and desire to become an overachiever. A head coach probably has a better opportunity to recognize a potential overachiever than do the assistant coaches. We had a number of those at Baylor: Ronnie Rogers, a guard from Garland, Texas; Herby Adkins, a guard from Nederland, Texas; Mike Bourland, a guard from Fort Worth; Tommy Smith, a receiver from Corpus Christi, Texas; Don Trull, a quarterback from Oklahoma City; Albert Witcher, an end from Lampasas, Texas; James Ingram, a receiver from Odessa, Texas; Joe Jones, a defensive safety from Marlin, Texas; David Anderson, a defensive end from Haskell, Texas; and Donnie Lawrence, a linebacker from Rockdale, Texas. There were probably others, but the above players performed exceptionally well even though they lacked at least one or more physical requirements such as size, speed, agility or height. And, in almost every case, Baylor was the only school to offer them a scholarship.

I believe we recruited too many players who really did not have the talent to play Southwest Conference football. Even though all teams make recruiting mistakes, avoiding as many of those mistakes as possible is one of the best assurances of a coach keeping his job. I don't regret our policy of allowing all the players who "lacked ability but showed effort and good attitude" to continue as members of our squad and obtain their college degree.

Relations with the Media — A good relationship with the media, especially the hometown media, is of extreme importance. What they write or say can have a strong influence on the attitude and public confidence in the coach or athletic director by the fans of a community. I probably disagreed with a sportswriter about 100 times during my career of 43 years as coach and athletic director, and my won-lost record for those encounters is 0-100.

Team Defense — Another change I would make if I were a head coach (based on what we did in my years at Baylor) would be to change my defensive strategy.

We played a very conservative defense at least 90% or more of the time. With the advent of more emphasis on passing, with four wide receivers and one running back, along with the run and shoot philosophy (which also has four wide receivers), I would blitz five or six linemen and linebackers 25 to 50% of the time.

I would show an eight-man front most of the time and blitz six, and I would try to outnumber the blockers to the outside, in the middle, or to one side or the other. I liked to really test the offenses' ability to pick up a blitzer when they were outnumbered.

I put great emphasis on the pass rusher to get his hands up to deflect or knock down a pass that was thrown in his direction. The run and shoot employs a three-step drop by the quarterback, and except for deep patterns, the passes are susceptible to being knocked down or deflected. The defensive calls indicate which linebackers will blitz. The blitzers and pass rushers should particularly strive to protect the open short zones from which linebackers blitz by getting their hands up when the pass is thrown to the open zones. I would use a zone pass defense and give the offense a short zone, but have three backs playing deep zone pass defense. The cornerbacks should have a dual responsibility — deep and outside. The way General Neyland expressed it, "Deep as the deepest man in his zone and as wide as the widest man when the ball gets there." The safety man (or if two deep safeties) should be as deep as the deepest man. The only man you cover is the man to whom the ball is thrown. Good safeties cover a lot of ground when the ball is in the air.

I would take away the long patterns on a blitz and have two of the four linebackers cover the two inside receivers with a match-up zone. We might get hurt at times on short passes, but we would always have three defensive backs converging on the ball when it is thrown. About 25 to 50% of the time when we did not blitz, we would threaten a blitz with an eight-man front. It has a tendency to make the quarterback hurry when he reads blitz. Sometimes quarterbacks in their rush will throw to a defensive player.

A blitz is generally an effective defense against the run as it turns out to be a gap defense and can be very effective against the draw, which the run and shoot features. Much emphasis would be put on the blitzers locating the ball as quickly as possible and on defending the corners with emphasis on pursuit by those defenders away from the point of attack who do not have contain responsibility.

There is a contrast between a basic defense in which the defense takes on the blocker and neutralizes his block then reacts to make the tackle and the blitz in which the defense lines up in the same position but penetrates the gap. It forces the offense to use two entirely different techniques to block the defensive down linemen and the blitzing linebackers. It takes a very well-coached offensive lineman to handle both effectively. Such a defense may very well result in interceptions, fumbles, and sacks.

It would be fun to coach as well as fun to play. Our goal would be to *make the big play without giving up the big play.*

An eight-man front with two blitzes (diagrams on pages 211–212) will be effective against the blocking rules of just about every pro team or major college team. The reason is that unless a team commits eight men to pass protection assignment, there will be a free blitzer to sack or pressure the passer. The blitzes are equally effective against the run as every gap is covered, which is what a team normally does on a short yardage or goal line defense.

These defenses were used by the Baltimore Colts in 1957 and 1958, the first year Baltimore won an NFL Championship. We called one an *outside blitz,* where the two outside players on the strongside of the formation and the two defensive players on the weakside of the formation blitzed. The other was a *middle blitz,* where the defensive tackles and two inside linebackers blitzed. The inside blitzers penetrated their gap, found the football, and ran to it as hard as they could.

On the outside blitz, the end man penetrated from the outside at approximately a 45-degree angle to the inside so as to close the hole between him and the adjacent blitzer just inside him. His goal was to force the play deep and keep leverage on the quarterback or ball carrier trying to get outside and make the tackle or pressure the quarterback.

We used the same blitzes at Baylor for nine years. At Baltimore and Baylor these blitzes were very effective and had the fewest yards gained against them of any defense or blitz we used.

I was responsible at Baltimore for keeping the statistical record on all basic defenses and blitzes we used. Our biggest mistake was not calling the defenses and particularly the blitzes more frequently.

Sid Gilman, former head coach of the Los Angeles Rams, quizzed me about those two blitzes and the basic defense. He said they never did figure out how to block them. Sid may have lost sight of the fact that the basic defense and the blitzes were eight-man fronts, and a team has to commit eight players to pass protection in order to block all three defenses.

It has come down through the years that a well-played zone is just as effective as man coverage and there is much less chance of giving up the long gainer or big play. On man coverage a player is responsible for covering his man from sideline to sideline and from where the ball is located through the end zone. If the talent and speed are anywhere near equal, a receiver has the advantage over the defender. One of Weeb Ewbank's favorite expressions, adopted by John Unitas, was "Hit the single coverage!"

One variation which I think can be effective is using a three-deep zone but covering the two inside receivers on middle blitz man-to-man (tight end and the offensive weakside back) by the strong safety and weakside linebacker. If offensive formation has four wide receivers, the two inside wide receivers would be covered man-to-man by the strong safety and weakside linebacker, or in the outside blitz by the two inside linebackers. The cover men might have to cheat a little to their coverage just before the ball is snapped. It gives the possibility of getting tight coverage on the short receivers, and if the blitz works as planned, the quarterback would not have time to throw a pass (which takes as much as 2.7 to 3.0 seconds to get off).

I believe strongly that a team using a three-deep zone must put strong emphasis on the fairly simple rules of the three deep backs. The cornerbacks line up six to eight yards deep and from head up to outside the wide receiver to his side. I don't think it's possible to play inside the wide receiver and be able to see the quarterback or passer and the receivers in his zone from the time the ball is snapped until it is thrown by the passer. It's very important for the cornerback to be able to see the passer and the receivers in his zone and cover as much ground as possible while the ball is in the air. The more ground the cornerbacks and the safety can cover when the ball is released by the passer, the more effective the zone defense will be. The safety and cornerbacks may make adjustments on receivers, but should not commit until the passer releases the ball.

There have been many great safety men, and some of the best have not necessarily been the fastest. They are able to move to the ball as soon as it is released and to accurately judge the flight of the ball so that they have efficient movement to the ball.

In the first year I coached in professional football (1957) there were many professional coaches who felt a professional team could not use a zone pass defense due to the skill and accuracy of pro quarterbacks. Zone pass coverage is now by far the dominant pass coverage in professional football.

At Baltimore in 1957, after winning our first three games, we lost three games in a row. The losses in the last two came in the final minute of each game on long scoring passes. Our coaches lost confidence in one of our defensive backs, so we went to a three-deep zone pass defense where the back in question played as a rover or strong safety to the strong side of offensive formation and did not have responsibility on deep coverage. To the best of my memory, we used the three-deep zone for the next four games and won four straight games. The only time we used man coverage was on blitzes. (At Baylor we used a three-deep zone on the blitzes.) In our last two games we started mixing other coverages in our pass defense and lost both games.

The experience convinced me that it wasn't necessary to have a lot of variation in pass coverages to be effective and win in professional football.

EIGHT-MAN FRONT — BASIC DEFENSE

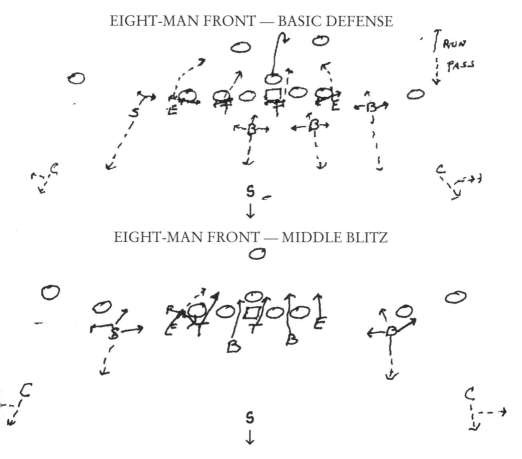

EIGHT-MAN FRONT — MIDDLE BLITZ

EIGHT-MAN FRONT — OUTSIDE BLITZ

One of my greatest satisfactions while at Baylor was gaining the respect of many sportswriters across the state of Texas. When I was fired, at least 15 to 20 Texas writers in the major cities wrote complimentary columns about my stay at Baylor. I'll close my chapter on Baylor University with articles written by two of the best sportswriters in the nation, Blackie Sherrod, now with the *Dallas Morning News* but formerly with the *Dallas Times-Herald*, and Mickey Herskowitz, with the *Houston Post*.

Different Polls of Popularity
by Blackie Sherrod, *Dallas Times-Herald*

That is one brand of popularity. John Bridgers had another among the Southwest coaches. He beat four conference schools more than they beat him and usually played the Tom Fool out of the others. Nobody ever considered Baylor a patsy under Bridgers. In fact, the Baptists were generally the most dreaded opponent of the year because of their offense. You had to work harder in preparation for them. Darrell Royal used to break out with the hives the week of the Baylor game. The Bears had this foreign type attack, you see, where they threw the ball and the Texas fellers were unaccustomed to this angle and they were apt to lose it in the sun. In truth, a Bridgers team never once beat a Royal team, but that fact never impressed the Longhorn staff. When Baylor had a quarterback operator, the Bears were perhaps the most feared foes in the league. They were much like a boa constrictor. You know there are ways it can be handled, but you'd much rather not.

Bridgers had a rather unique reputation among the coaches. You might hear a few cutting remarks or innuendoes around the family ranks, but none about Bridgers. His compatriots all seem to regard him as a completely honest man to deal with, sincere and dedicated. His sense of humor about his own fortunes or lack of it was a big part of his personal attraction.

Mind you, this popularity wasn't a wild flood, sweeping through the land, overwhelming all it touched. Bridgers had some bitter opponents among the Baylor alumni. Not that they disliked the man personally but they didn't like that 44-year respite from the championship. They claimed his team passed too much, that it wasn't solid defensively and the defensive teams were the winning ones. They claimed his staff was too loosely organized, that the ship wasn't run tightly enough.

In turn, John held that he was strapped by a small budget. That the alumnus wanted champagne fare on beer prices. He was openly defensive about his coaching record and the style of football he favored.

"We try to show that a passing game is a sound part of football," he said. "There is this tendency in college football to passing when all hope is lost, a desperation maneuver not sound in principle."

Familiar words now. Bridgers said them years ago.

Whatever Bridgers' aptitude for a major head coaching job is not to be judged by this amateur. But for his popularity among his rivals, any pressboxer can attest.

Sports Column in *Houston Post*
by Mickey Herskowitz

In his ten years as the Baylor drillmaster, John Bridgers always enjoyed a good joke, even at his own expense, as they frequently were.

Frank Bridgers would be sitting there in the stands high above the chalk-marked meadow, and in due time he would be aware that the fans around him were doing double-takes and buzzing to themselves.

"Good heavens," the whispers would go. "How can he? What

nerve. Right while the game is in the balance. And his boys playing their hearts out."

It tickled Frank Bridgers to be mistaken for his brother John. He would turn and wave and smile and say hi.

"I might as well be sitting up here," he'd say, with a shrug. "They never pay any attention to me anyway. Won't do a thing I tell 'em."

With that he would return his gaze to the field, where John Bridgers would be tugging at his wispy red hair and rushing substitutes into the fray.

On another occasion, Frank subbed for his brother when the Baylor coach was unable to attend a preseason function in Fort Worth. This was one of those public confessionals, where each coach stands up and declares that with a little luck, and by scraping and scratching, he will field a team that fall. For good measure he may add that any team in the conference, on any given day, or night, depending on the schedule, can beat any other team.

The audience was in its customary emotional state — that is yawning — when John Bridgers took his turn. Or rather, Frank took John's turn, neglecting to inform the audience that a substitution had been make.

He wowed them. Boy, did he wow them. "Modesty has got me nowhere," he roared, as heads snapped. "You want to know how Baylor will come out in the Southwest Conference? Baylor will win the championship."

He went on in that vein at some length, observing that it was indeed a marvelous happenstance that brought so much talent, as Baylor had, under the direction of so qualified a coach.

It wasn't until much later that the crowd, and the other coaches, were permitted to share the gag. But it had to be one terrific act, to fool anybody who really knew John Bridgers.

If in his ten years at Waco, the cheerful redhead ever uttered an unkind, indiscreet or boastful word, it went unrecorded. Even in that moment of wrenching hurt and discomposure, at that moment when Baylor told him his services were no longer needed, Bridgers conducted himself with restraint.

He said that he was disappointed, a mild choice of words, no doubt. He added that he regarded the action as unjustified. And he concluded, with more pride than bitterness, that ten years from now

Baylor might be pleased with a coach who suffered four losing seasons.

That was his record. In three other years the Bears broke even, and three times they appeared in bowl games. Win, lose and tie, it was a decade of exciting football and towering heroes named Ronnie Bull, Don Trull, Lawrence Elkins and Terry Southall.

But John Bridgers was never able to give Baylor what it wanted most, what the school and its long-suffering flock have not had in over 40 years. He could not give them a championship.

One would scarcely size up John Bridgers as a failure, not in the areas that count. No coach seemed to be more lavishly admired by his competitors.

No Baylor–Texas game could commence until Darrell Royal had delivered a speech, saying how much he respected the man on the other side of the field. When the Bruins upset the Texas Aggies this season, a grimacing Gene Stallings decided: "Well, one good thing about it, maybe this will take some of the heat off Bridgers."

It didn't. And one is forced to conclude that John Bridgers was ahead of his time. When he entered the league, he brought with him a style of play that included pro sets and gave a priority to the forward pass. It was immediately labeled "spectator football," and many scoffed and said it couldn't win and wouldn't last.

Now all the colleges are playing spectator football. And John Bridgers is out of a job.

But he refused to indulge in fantasy. For security, coaching is no longer in a class with migrant fruit picking, but you don't see many collecting a pension either. "A football coach had better get himself a philosophy," Bridgers said, then, with a grin, "and it had better be a deep one. I haven't got one yet, but I'm working on it hard."

I never remembered, in the years since then, to ask if he had come up with one.

But the new coach must be prepared to work a few miracles. He will need to bring the plant at Baylor up to the level of its opposition. He will almost surely require a larger budget. And, above all, he must take an attitude of supreme confidence that the task can be done.

Maybe Baylor should hire John's brother.

1968 SEASON RESULTS
Final Record 3-7-0

Baylor (A)	36	Indiana	40
Baylor (A)	10	Michigan State	28
Baylor (A)	16	LSU	48
Baylor (A)	19	Arkansas	35
Baylor (H)	10	Texas A&M	9
Baylor (H)	14	TCU	47
Baylor (H)	26	Texas	47
Baylor (H)	42	Texas Tech	28
Baylor (A)	17	SMU	33
Baylor (H)	16	Rice	7
TOTAL	206		322

CHAPTER 21

1960–67

FOUR BAYLOR

ALL-AMERICANS

Don Trull, Quarterback

When Don Trull came to Baylor, the coaching staff didn't know much about him. He was an All-State high school quarterback from Southeast High School in Oklahoma City. He was an excellent passer, but in 1959 there were few colleges recruiting passing quarterbacks. Another notable achievement was that Don was valedictorian of his high school class. He also was All-Conference or All-City in basketball and baseball.

Don Trull did not play in his sophomore year since we had two junior quarterbacks returning who shared playing time in 1959. However, as a sophomore red shirt in 1961, he became the starter over the two experienced seniors in the eighth game of the season and led us to a bowl victory over Utah State.

I remember in the spring of 1961, Don began to make himself known. Coach Chuck Purvis, our quarterback coach, had given him some passing drills to work on, and he took them seriously. Don began developing the technique and fundamentals which would make him an outstanding college quarterback.

At Baylor, Don majored in math and continued to do well academically. He was on the Dean's List in 1962, 1963, and 1964.

The first half of our 1961 season was very disappointing. We got off to a decent start with wins over Wake Forest and Pittsburgh, but then we slumped badly and lost four of the next five games. Our senior quarterback, Ronnie Stanley, wasn't playing well, and Bobby Ply was hurt. In our Texas game we were trailing 33-0 after giving up four fumbles and three interceptions, so we decided to go with Don Trull. He threw a touchdown pass to Ted Plumb and showed good leadership. We decided to start him in our next game with Air Force Academy. We won the game 31-7 and then beat SMU 31-6 to improve our record to 5-4. We lost our final regular season game to Rice 26-14 in Houston. Surprisingly, we were invited to play Utah State in the Gotham Bowl in New York. Utah State was undefeated and ranked 10th in the nation.

Utah State players were very big and a number of them would have prominent careers in the NFL, including Merlin Olsen, who was All-Pro for nine seasons with the Rams; Clark Miller, a tackle who started his first five years with the 49ers; Jim Turner, a quarterback who played 15 years as a place kicker with Denver; Lionel Aldrich, a defensive end with Green Bay for ten years and two years with San Diego; Bill Munson, quarterback with the Rams one year and with other AFL teams; and Clyde Brock, offensive tackle for the 49ers and others.

We played by far our best game of the season as we shocked Utah State with a 24-9 victory. Don Trull threw a touchdown pass to Ted Plumb, our wide receiver, who has had a long career as assistant coach in the NFL with the Bears, Eagles, and Cardinals. Trull also scored from the one-yard-line on a quarterback sneak. Ronnie Bull and Trull were outstanding and our defense held Utah State to 194 yards total offense. Their only touchdown was scored as a result of a pass interception in the last minute of the game.

Ronnie Bull was voted the outstanding player, but it was a toss-up between him and Don Trull.

In 1962 Don Trull led the nation in passing with 125 completions and 229 attempts for 1,627 yards. Again we started badly with five losses in our first six games, but we came back to win our last three as we defeated Air Force 10-3, SMU 17-13, and Rice 28-15.

In 1963 the substitution rule for college football was liberal-

SUMMARY ON DON TRULL
1961–63 NCAA & SOUTHWEST CONFERENCE RECORDS AND SOUTHWEST CONFERENCE & NCAA LEADER

NCAA Records

1.	Pass Completions 1962	125
2.	Pass Completions 1963	174

NOTE: First passer to lead nation two consecutive years since Davey O'Brien in 1937–38.

NCAA Leader

1.	Touchdown Production (Run & Pass) 1963 (Run 10 — Pass 12)	22

Southwest Conference Records — 1963

1.	Pass Completions Season	174
2.	Most Pass Attempts Season	308
3.	Most Pass Yards Gained Season	2,157
4.	Total Offense (Run & Pass) Season	2,276
5.	Most Total Plays Season	406
6.	Pass Completions (Career)	325
7.	Most Pass Attempts (Career)	593
8.	Most Pass Completions Game (Baylor/LSU)	26
9.	Most Pass Yardage (Career)	4,143
10.	Most Total Yards Gained, Runs & Passes (Career)	4,505

Southwest Conference Leader — 1963

1.	Scoring — TD/10	60 Pts.
2.	Touchdown Production (Run 10 — Pass 12)	22
3.	Pass Completions & Yardage (Conference Only) (Attempts 230 — Completions 127)	1,519
4.	Total Offense (Conference Only 1963) Net Rush 96 — Net Pass 1,519	1,615

ized. We took full advantage of it at Baylor and had what amounted to an offensive and defensive team, although our offense had to play some defense and the defense had to play some offense.

We had an outstanding opening game in 1963 in Waco as we beat a favored Houston team 27-0. The year before, Houston had beaten us 19-0 in Houston. At that time Houston was not a member of the Southwest Conference.

Our next game was with Oregon State in Portland. Oregon's head coach was Tommy Prothro, one of the most intelligent coaches in college football. Oregon State jumped to a 15-0 lead, but Don Trull scored on a short yardage play and threw a 70-yard touchdown pass to Lawrence Elkins, along with a field goal by Tom Davis, which tied the score at 15-15. Oregon State scored with 27 seconds left when a completed pass was fumbled in the end zone and was recovered for a touchdown.

The next week we began our conference schedule and upset Arkansas, the team that had been picked to win the conference, 14-10. Don Trull threw two touchdown passes to Lawrence Elkins for the Baylor scores. We then beat Texas Tech 21-17 as we scored two touchdowns in the last six minutes on drives of 65 and 83 yards with two touchdown passes from Trull to James Ingram.

We beat Texas A&M 34-7 and TCU 32-13.

The next week we played Texas at Austin before a sell-out crowd of 64,530. It was a rainy and windy day. It was the game that would determine the Southwest Conference championship. We threatened twice but fumbled inside the Texas 20-yard-line and then Trull overthrew on fourth down to a wide-open Ingram in the end zone.

Texas scored after a 15-yard penalty gave them a first down inside our 20. In the final moments we drove inside the Texas 30, but a pass which appeared to be a certain touchdown from Trull to Elkins was intercepted on a great play by Duke Carlisle, the Texas quarterback and safety, in a three-deep zone pass defense.

Texas became national champions and finished the season undefeated and untied.

We were 6-1 in the conference and played LSU in the Bluebonnet Bowl in Houston. Don Trull had one of his best days ever, completing 26 passes of 35 attempts for 255 yards. That was the most passes ever completed in a single game by a Baylor quarterback up until that time, and the most in a single game by a Southwest Conference player. LSU scored on their first possession and led until the fourth quarter, when Trull found Ingram twice for touchdowns to win 14-7.

Don Trull again led the nation in passing as he completed 174 of 308 attempts for 2,157 yards in 1963. He was the first passer to lead the nation for two consecutive years since David O'Brien of TCU in 1936 and 1937. The number of completions and his total plays, 406, were all new NCAA records. The effort of Trull and Elkins set 16 Southwest Conference records in 1963.

Don Trull was not only a great passer for Baylor, he was an outstanding leader. His teammates liked him and had great confidence in him. He used our check-off system better than any college quarterback I've ever coached. (A check-off is when a quarterback changes a play at the line of scrimmage to take advantage of the defense.) Tommy Prothro of Oregon State, and later head coach of UCLA and the San Diego Chargers, was very impressed with the way Don Trull hurt his Oregon State team when they blitzed with check-offs at the line of scrimmage.

Trull was an excellent runner. He was not fast but was very shifty and had quick feet. Not counting yards lost attempting to pass, Trull gained 776 yards rushing in his two and one-half seasons as a quarterback. The only running play we had for the quarterback was a quarterback sneak, which we used on short yardage or on the goal line. The remainder of his yards gained was on pass plays when he couldn't find a receiver and ran.

Don Trull also led the Southwest Conference in scoring in 1963 with 10 touchdowns. When we beat Rice 21-12 in 1963, Trull scored all three of Baylor's touchdowns. Don Trull led the nation in touchdown production in 1963. He ran for 10 and threw for 12.

For a number of years the passing game in college football had become dormant, something a team used when they were behind, a play action pass as a surprise, or rollout or sprintout type patterns which were option runs or passes.

Baylor was one of the first college teams to go to a 100 percent pro-type offense in 1959. Trull led Baylor to two winning seasons and two bowl victories: the Gotham Bowl against Utah State in 1961 and the Bluebonnet Bowl against LSU in 1963.

Don Trull was an All-American in 1963. He also made Academic All-American in 1962 and 1963. Roger Staubach, quarterback for the Naval Academy, made Consensus All-American in 1963, but he trailed Trull in total completions, passing yardage, rushing touchdowns, and touchdown passes. I can't imagine Staubach being any more valuable to the Navy team than Trull was to Baylor. In career total offense, Trull had 801 plays for 4,501 yards while Staubach had 808 plays for 4,253 yards. In career pass completions, Trull had 325 completions for 4,143 yards and Staubach had 292 completions for 3,571 yards.

Trull was awarded the Earl Blaik Fellowship, a graduate scholarship award by the NCAA. He was the number-one draft choice of the Houston Oilers in the American Football League, and had been drafted as a junior by the Baltimore Colts in the NFL. Trull played for six years, first with the Oilers, then with the Boston Patriots, and came back to the Oilers in 1969. He played in Canada in 1970 and 1971. He really never had the kind of success he enjoyed in college.

There are so many things that determine a quarterback's success in professional football, one of which is the chemistry between the quarterback and the coaching staff, and with the team. The confidence of the head coach in the quarterback, the quality of the receivers and the pass protection of the offensive line, and the quarterback's own self-confidence (which can ebb and flow, much like a golfer's confidence) are other factors in a quarterback's success. I personally don't believe Don was able to get his confidence level up to what he had at Baylor.

Don Trull said, "My most memorable experience in college football was being a member of a Baylor squad to go to three bowl games, the Gator Bowl in 1960, the Gotham Bowl in 1961, and the Bluebonnet Bowl in 1963. The most memorable of all was the 14-7 victory over LSU in the Bluebonnet Bowl in 1963."

In reply to what college football meant to him, Trull said, "College football and my receiving a scholarship enabled me to receive a degree from a major university which otherwise I could not have afforded.

"College football taught me how to experience winning and losing. The same elements that go into preparing yourself for life are never more evident than preparation for college football. Hard work, desire, discipline and dedication are just a few things I learned in college football that have helped me throughout life.

"Without college football I do not think I would be the person

I am today. College football teaches a boy to become a man and deal with adversities and triumphs of life. It also teaches you to depend on others and for others to depend on you. 'Teamwork' is what makes America a great country. I thank God I had the opportunity and skills to participate in college football."

Trull is now a partner in a long distance telephone company after being an assistant coach at the University of Arkansas from 1972 to 1974. He has been active in Houston in community and charitable causes. Among the charities and organizations he has been involved in are Special Olympics, Alzheimer's Association, Epilepsy Association, Fellowship of Christian Athletes, the National Football Foundation (as a member of the board of directors), and the National Football League Alumni.

Don Trull represents many of the good things about college football. He has had an exciting career and a high sense of responsibility that keeps him giving his best efforts in a number of different areas, including his responsibility as a family man, helping charitable organizations and community projects, as well as his business.

NCAA and Southwest Conference records established by Don Trull are listed on page 219. Trull set NCAA records for completions in 1962 and 1963. He also set 10 Southwest Conference records in 1963. Trull's record for pass attempts in 1963 broke Davey O'Brien's (of TCU) record of 237 attempts in 1937. His record for career attempts broke Sam Baugh's record of 577 from 1934 to 1936.

The average length of the 10 records Trull broke was 20.3 years in length and ranged from 1936 to 1958. Again Don Trull broke barriers and showed that a team could win with a passing game.

Lawrence Elkins, Wide Receiver

Not long after I decided to write this book, I called Don Trull, our quarterback at Baylor who led the nation in passing during the 1962 and 1963 seasons, to ask him a question. After we talked I asked him if he had heard from Lawrence Elkins. Elkins was his battery mate at Baylor. Elkins caught 70 passes in 1963 to set a new NCAA college record for passes caught in a single season.

Trull replied, "Lawrence sent me a picture from Saudi Arabia. He was on a camel, and he had written underneath the picture,

'Lawrence of Arabia.' It was typical of Elkins. He has a good sense of humor and is normally a happy person. Elkins was in Saudi Arabia during the Desert Storm War working with a large contracting company which was involved in converting salt water to fresh water.

Elkins made Consensus All-American in 1963 and 1964, which means he made the majority of all the All-American teams which are selected for each of those two years. There are normally about 10 or 12 All-American teams selected.

Lawrence Elkins was not only a great football player but certainly one of the players who ranked among the best I coached and among those I enjoyed coaching the most. He wanted to do what the coaches wanted him to do, and he did it all with his best effort. Elkins was 6'1 and 182 pounds. He was one of the best conditioned athletes I've ever coached. In high school he set a state record in the Division 3-A competition in the 880-yard run. He was really too big to run the 880 (at 175 to 180 pounds) and he really didn't have world-class sprinter's speed, but he used every bit of speed he had. The uniform slowed him down very little.

When we played LSU in the 1963 Bluebonnet Bowl, he was our kickoff man and safety. The LSU kickoff returner, Joe La Bruzzo, broke free on a kickoff return after we had gone ahead 14-7 in the fourth quarter. La Bruzzo was reported to have 9.7 speed in the 100-yard dash, but Elkins caught him from behind and tackled him on about the 25-yard-line. Our defense held and we won the game 14-7.

Lawrence liked to come by my office and visit. He didn't have any pressing reason. He just wanted to talk about the last game, about his schoolwork, or the upcoming game. He would tell me what he thought and ask me how I felt about the same subject. He wasn't necessarily seeking advice, but was a very likable person who enjoyed visiting with friends. I appreciate that he considered me a friend as well as his coach.

Raymond Berry, the Hall of Fame receiver from the Baltimore Colts, coached our receivers during spring practice. Raymond thought highly of Lawrence and foresaw a great professional career for him. One of the fundamentals that Elkins exemplified and that Raymond Berry stressed was "exploding off the breaking point."

Elkins ran the "quick out," which was five to six yards down-field and a break to the outside. There were many times on this pattern that he would break so quickly and separate from the defender

SUMMARY — LAWRENCE ELKINS
1962–64 NCAA & SOUTHWEST CONFERENCE
RECORDS AND
SOUTHWEST CONFERENCE LEADER

NCAA Records

  1. Passes Caught 1963   70

Southwest Conference Records

1.	Passes Caught 1963 Season	70
2.	Yardage Gained Pass Receiving 1963 Season	873
3.	Passes Caught (Career 1962–64)	144
4.	Most Yards Gained Career	2,093
5.	Most TD Passes Caught (Season)	8
6.	Most TD Passes Caught (Career)	20

Southwest Conference Leader — 1964

1.	Scoring — TD — 7 PAT — 8	50 Pts.
2.	Pass Receiving (Conference Only) 38	612 Yds.
3.	Scoring (Conference Only)	38 Pts.

to the degree that he cut up-field before the cornerback could catch him and end up gaining 20 to 25 yards more on the reception.

Lawrence also ran the "slant" pattern well, where he would take about three steps down-field and then break at a 45-degree angle to the inside. Against Air Force in 1962, the year the Air Force football stadium was completed, Elkins caught a slant pattern on a snow-covered field and just exploded past the safety and defensive corner for a 20-yard touchdown reception for the only touchdown scored in the game.

We ran a slant in and out where he would break inside on the slant, take a quick look at the passer, and then on his third step break back to the outside at a sharp angle. Of the 19 pass receiving touchdowns and five two-pointers on extra points he scored during his three years of eligibility, I would guess that at least half a dozen scoring plays came on the "slant in and out" pattern. We had run this pattern so much on the goal line that I remember we were playing Rice in the final game of the season in 1964 with Rice leading 20-12. We scored to make it 20-18. We called the "slant in and out" pattern to Elkins for the two-pointer. Rice put one defender three yards inside Elkins and another about three yards outside him —the perfect defense for a "slant in and out." Elkins ran the slant, and when he broke back to the outside he saw the defender waiting for him. So he just hooked up and Terry Southall, our quarterback, threw the pass for the two-pointer between the two defenders. After we recovered a fumble on the Rice 12, Ken Hodge, who was the best offensive tight end in my years at Baylor, made an impossible catch for a touchdown. We beat Rice 27-20.

Lawrence ran all his patterns well, but his next most productive pattern was the "go" or the streak in which he faked the out with a look and then tried to beat the corner deep and outside. He also ran the "go" with an inside fake, a "look" and then faded outside and deep. As you would expect, Elkins had excellent hands and could make difficult catches look easy.

In 1959 we were one of the first college teams to go 100% to a pro-type offense. Actually, the 1958 Baylor team ran a version of a pro offense and did well offensively. However, their defense left something to be desired, and the Bears finished last in the Southwest Conference. Almost every college coach at that time believed that a team could not primarily depend on a passing attack and win. As

Darrell Royal of the University of Texas said, "When you throw the ball, three things can happen and two of them are bad." I really didn't prove Darrell wrong, as Texas beat us 10 straight years. Four of our defeats were by one point, five points, six points, and by seven points in 1963, when Texas won the national championship. Still, most of our other six games were very competitive, and our biggest loss was by four touchdowns in 1962.

In the last minute of our game with Texas in 1963, with Texas leading 7-0, Elkins ran a "go" pattern and beat the defensive cornerback. Trull's pass looked perfect, but Carlisle, the Texas quarterback and safety, made one of the best defensive plays I have ever seen as he came flying over and literally picked the ball out of Elkins' hand in the end zone for an interception which prevented us from having an opportunity to beat them. We would have gone for two on the extra point, so there would have been no tie — just a win or a loss.

Elkins caught 12 passes that day against Texas, but took a terrific beating as the Texas defense tried to punish him on every catch. Baylor was 6-1 in the conference and Texas was 7-0.

Our intention was not of setting records with our pass offense but to balance our running game with our pass. In 1963 we gained 1,191 yards running and 2,159 passing in our 10-game schedule, but Don Trull, our quarterback, lost 202 yards attempting to pass which, if added to our rushing total, would have given us 1,393 yards rushing or an average of 139.3 yards per game. In college football, yards lost passing come off the rushing total while in professional football they come off the passing total. In 1991, the highest average rushing of any team in professional football was 146 yards per game.

Our game in 1963 with SMU was postponed because it had been scheduled during the week President John Kennedy was assassinated. There was a very deep feeling of grief by our players and coaches over the president's assassination.

We beat Rice in what would have been the last game on our schedule, but due to the president's death, we played SMU the following week. For the first time we became aware that Don Trull and Lawrence Elkins had opportunities to set NCAA records in passing and receiving. Elkins ended up with 70 receptions for a new record on pass receptions, and Trull passed for 2,157 yards with 174 completions and 406 total plays, the latter two NCAA records. In all, the pair broke 16 all-time Southwest Conference records. In the SMU game, which we won 20-6, we ran for 164 yards and passed for only 110 yards.

We wound up the season by coming from behind to beat LSU 14-7 in the Bluebonnet Bowl game. It was a very satisfying victory, as we played the best defensive game any Baylor team had played during my tenure at Baylor. We held LSU to 108 yards total offense and four first downs. Elkins caught his season average per game of seven passes, even though he was double-teamed on every play.

Perhaps most Southwest Conference football fans remember Lawrence Elkins as just an outstanding pass receiver. The fact is that he was an excellent all-around football player. In clutch situations, he played safety for pass defense purposes. Against Texas Christian he intercepted a pass and returned it 69 yards to the two-yard-line. He was also an excellent punt returner. He returned a punt against Texas Christian in another game for 92 yards and a touchdown, which is the second longest punt return in Baylor history. As mentioned earlier, Elkins kicked off and was safety for opponents' kickoff returns. In 1962 he averaged 22 yards per punt return, which is the second highest average for Baylor in the modern era behind Ronnie Bull, who averaged 24 yards per return in 1960.

In three years Elkins scored 20 touchdowns, which ranked him third behind Del Schofner and Ronnie Bull with 22 each, both of whom were primarily running backs while at Baylor. Lawrence Elkins and Mike Singletary, the great Chicago Bears linebacker, are the only Baylor players to be chosen as Consensus All-American for two consecutive years. Elkins was selected in 1963 and 1964.

Elkins caught 50 passes in 1964 and averaged over 17 yards per catch. Terry Southall, a sophomore from Brownwood, Texas (as was Elkins), was at quarterback. Almost every time Elkins lined up he was double-teamed. Opponents would put a short man on him, usually an end (or what would be an outside linebacker in today's terminology), and a defensive corner to cover him deep. Southall improved as the season progressed and we won our last three games to end up with a 5-5 record. Key receptions by Elkins made a difference in those three wins.

In late January of 1965 Lawrence came to my office and said he had missed so many classes from playing the East–West game in San Francisco and Hula Bowl in Hawaii, plus making personal appearances on television and out-of-town banquets honoring All-American selectees, that he didn't think it was possible for him to pass the courses in which he was enrolled. He wanted to drop out of school for the fall semester before exams. I told him he couldn't drop out of school and that he could pass the courses if he really put his mind to it. I called a couple of his professors and told them the kind of pressure he had been under to attend so many out-of-town functions related to the honors he had received, and asked them to encourage him and give him an opportunity to make up the assignments he had missed. Lawrence stayed in school and passed all his courses. He received his degree in June.

When the pro draft was held, Elkins was number-one draft choice for Green Bay in the NFL and number-one draft choice by Houston in the AFL. He signed with Houston and in his first pre-season game he caught a touchdown pass (back when the goal posts were on the goal line). In attempting to avoid a head-on collision with a goal post, Elkins suffered a serious injury to his left knee. It was an injury from which he would never fully recover.

One other factor which I think hurt his chances was that his coaches kept urging him to gain weight. His natural playing weight was between 180 and 185, and when he gained to 195 it cost him a step in speed, which was much more important to him than the 10 to 15 extra pounds.

When I went to the Steelers as assistant coach in 1969, the Steelers signed Elkins as a free agent. In the pre-season games he was the leading receiver for the Steelers, but in the final exhibition game against Green Bay in Montreal, he was sandwiched between two tacklers as he caught a pass in the middle and his collar bone was shattered. During training camp, we had a shortage of wide receivers due to the fact that few receivers were drafted and some of our receivers had suffered minor injuries. This resulted in few receivers to alternate with him and he literally ran until he was completely leg-weary and his legs lost their spring which contributed to his injury. He was paid for that season by the Steelers, but the next year he was cut by the Steelers before training camp began.

A couple of times while living in New Mexico, Lawrence Elkins came to visit me without prior notice. Once I was playing golf and was on about the 12th hole and looked up and saw Elkins walking down the fairway. We went to dinner together and had a good visit. He just wanted to reminisce.

I would not be a bit surprised if he shows up any day for another visit. At present, Lawrence is an environmental consultant. In reply to a question of what college football meant to him, he replied, "My four years at Baylor as a football player was the greatest four-year experience in my life! I would not trade it for anything; I wish I could do it again to strive to be better athletically and academically."

Lawrence gave me a great compliment, but I'm not sure there is much truth in it. In commenting on his most memorable experience he said, "Being coached by the most honest, courageous, and smartest college football coach in America who never gave up on me!"

The national and conference records set by Elkins are listed on page 225. The six conference records he broke were an average of 23 years in existence and ranged from 13 to 34 years old.

Ronnie Bull, Halfback and Fullback

My first game as head football coach at Baylor University was against the University of Colorado at Boulder in September of 1959. The head coach at Colorado was Sonny Grandelius, in his first year as head coach after serving as an assistant to Duffy Daughtery of Michigan State.

Colorado was the favorite. Baylor had lost five starting interior linemen. All of our linemen were first-year starters. All of our backs were first-year starters except Austin Gonsoulin. We had a sophomore running back, Ronnie Bull, who was a great prospect, and he showed me how good he was that day.

The first game of my career as a head coach in Division I-A football meant a great deal to me. We had an extremely difficult schedule. Our non-conference schedule included Colorado, a very good Big Eight team, LSU, ranked number one in the nation in the pre-season Associated Press poll, and Southern California, ranked number four in the country (at least through our game with them in November).

Ronnie Bull's father and mother attended the game. Just before the kickoff, Ronnie's father happened to see my wife and my twin brother, Frank, sitting near him in the stands. He nudged his wife and pointed at Frank and said, "What kind of coach has Baylor hired now?"

Mr. Bull didn't know I had a twin brother. It was the first of many times that Frank was mistaken for me. There were fans who came up to him at the Baylor home games and said, "Coach, you sure play it cool!" They really thought it was me sitting in the stands with my wife while my team was playing on the field.

We had very hot weather in Waco during our pre-season practice. Ronnie Bull's normal weight was right at 190 pounds, but he weighed about 180 when we played Colorado. Ronnie was 6'0 and had well-developed, powerful legs. He had excellent speed and balance. In addition, he was a very good-looking young man.

Colorado scored first after recovering a fumble deep in our territory. In the second quarter Ronnie made one of the greatest runs I've ever seen without a single block. The play was "flow 45 wham." It was run from a split backfield with the left end split as a wide receiver and with Bull lined up at the right halfback position. Against Colorado's 6-1 defense the left tackle's assignment was to block the defensive end to the outside. The left guard was assigned to take the tackle to the inside. The left halfback would lead through the hole and block the outside linebacker.

Neither our tackle nor our guard made a good block, and there wasn't enough daylight for a peephole much less for a back to run through. Ronnie started for where the hole should have been but, seeing nothing but bodies, veered to the outside. The outside linebacker had blitzed across the line of scrimmage and had penetrated too deep to make a play on Bull. Ronnie turned upfield between the linebacker and defensive end. He cut upfield inside the defensive corner and then headed diagonally toward the sideline toward our bench with the safety in good position to make the tackle and the cornerback chasing him.

I thought I would give him some help, so I hollered, "Outrun them, Ronnie!"

Ronnie cut back toward the middle of the field and the safety lost leverage. From that point he just outran all the Colorado Buffalos to the goal line. It was a 74-yard touchdown run.

What a great individual effort on Ronnie Bull's part! Obviously, there were defensive errors by the Colorado players; otherwise, the game would be too easy for outstanding running backs.

The year 1959 was the first year for the two-point rule for the extra point. We didn't realize what a low percentage there would be on a two-point conversion, and we went for the two. Tommy Minter caught a pass in the end zone. I'm really not sure whether Bobby Ply or Ronnie Stanley threw the pass. Anyway, it gave us an 8-7 lead.

Late in the third quarter we moved the ball to the Colorado 11. Ronnie Stanley pitched to Bull on an option play, and Ronnie made another great run for a touchdown. Larry Corley kicked the extra point to give us a 15-7 lead.

Ronnie Bull gained over half our total yardage on six carries from scrimmage for over 100 yards. Colorado played excellent defense except on the two touchdown runs by Bull.

The 1959 season ended up better than most of the experts predicted. We had four wins and six losses in a very difficult schedule. Bull led the team in rushing, pass receiving, punt returns, scoring, and tied for the lead in pass interceptions.

Ronnie had another excellent season in 1960. Again he led Baylor in scoring, rushing, punt returns, and was second in pass receiving. Ronnie had particularly good games against Colorado, Texas Tech, Texas, and Southern California. We had an 8-2 season but lost a heartbreaker to the University of Florida in the Gator Bowl 13-12.

Two of Ronnie's best talents did not show up in statistics, and those were his blocking ability and defensive ability. He was actually a number-one draft choice by the Chicago Bears as a defensive back but switched to offense after the season began, when two running backs were injured, including Willie Galimore. Ronnie Bull was switched to offense and ended up as "Rookie of the Year" in 1962 in the National Football League.

In Ronnie's senior year he led Baylor again in rushing, receiving, and scoring. He was named the Gotham Bowl game's "Most Outstanding Player." Ronnie had minor injuries in 1961, particularly with his back, that weren't bad enough to keep him from playing but kept him from playing up to his full potential.

He still made a couple of All-American teams including the Pro Football Scouts All-American team. The professional scouts looked beyond just statistics to select the best players.

Ronnie Bull was the best running back I ever coached in college. Besides his talent and all-around ability, Ronnie had a great attitude. If he ever complained about anything, I never knew about it. Whether he was called upon to block on run plays, pass protect, play defense, or return punts, he gave his best efforts.

Some of his greatest runs were made on screen passes. In 1960 Ronnie ran 50 yards for a touchdown on a screen pass against Texas Tech. At least seven or eight Tech players had a shot at tackling him, but he kept his feet and scored the winning touchdown. He also made a great run on a screen pass to score against Texas in our 12-7 loss to them in 1960.

Ronnie was an excellent citizen during his college days at Baylor. He was selected for the Academic All-Southwest Conference and Academic All-American teams, was elected captain of the West squad in the East-West All-Star game, and played in the Senior Bowl game. He graduated in four years in business administration with a B average. He also competed for Baylor in track and scored points in the 220-yard low hurdles in 1961, when Baylor won the Southwest Conference track and field championships.

Ronnie was a starter and leading ground gainer for the Bears in the 1963 Chicago Bears World Championship Game victory over the New York Giants 14-10.

Bull played 10 years in the NFL, nine years with the Bears, and one year with the Eagles. He was cut by the Bears after he suffered a serious knee injury. In 1971 he played with the Eagles and was their leading ground gainer.

Ronnie made his home in Chicago after he retired from professional football. He is president of Ronnie Bull Sports Sales.

After having an opportunity to think about it for 31 years, I would use Ronnie Bull a little differently than we did. I would not use him as a wide receiver but would feature him more as a running back with more emphasis on draw plays, quick traps, quick hitters, power sweeps, and screen passes. With his blocking ability, I would use him as a pass protector and blocker on running plays when he was not a ball carrier or pass receiver. With his variety of talents we probably did not specialize in his ball-carrying ability enough. I followed the pattern used by the Baltimore Colts in 1957 and 1958 of using their halfbacks as running backs and wide receivers.

Ronnie Bull was a very unselfish player, and whatever he was asked to do, he gave his very best efforts. There have been few players in Texas who were more highly recruited than Ronnie Bull as a Texas All-State and high school All-American from a small town, Bishop, Texas. He was always a perfect gentleman, a model citizen, conscientious student, and team player.

If I could have had a couple more backs at Baylor with the ability of Ronnie Bull, I believe from what I learned coaching him that we might have won a Southwest Conference championship.

Ronnie was an underrated player in professional football, even though he was named Rookie of the Year in 1962. Ronnie probably never weighed over 200 pounds as a professional player. Most of his years he was used as a fullback, and the Bears were always looking for someone bigger to take his place.

The fact is that he was one of the best blockers in the NFL. If the truth were known, Ronnie Bull probably made more key blocks on the many sensational runs made by Gayle Sayers than any other player on the Bears team.

I remember seeing a game on TV when Ronnie played with the Eagles in 1971. The thing that impressed me more than anything was his blocking. There were few, if any, backs in the league who could match him as a consistent and effective blocker on runs and passes.

My personal contact with Ronnie Bull has been very sparse in the past 31 years, but I know he is a model citizen and real credit to college and professional football.

Greg Pipes, Defensive Tackle and Guard

Perhaps the lineman with the best overall credentials for a college lineman during my 10 years at Baylor was Greg Pipes, who played at the same high school as Mike Bourland, Paschal High School in Fort Worth. Whereas there were few college recruiters who felt Mike Bourland was a good college prospect, Greg Pipes was one of the most sought after linemen in Texas during my years at Baylor.

Greg weighed about 235, was very strong, quick, and explosive, had good speed, and was in excellent physical condition. The only thing that kept him from being a top pro prospect was he was only about 6'0. To be a great college lineman, it's not necessary to be 6'4 or more, as most professional scouts believe a great pro lineman must be.

We started practice with the squad taking a lap around our two practice fields, which were parallel to each other and about 25 to 30 yards apart. A lap was about 500 to 600 yards. Greg Pipes took it as a personal challenge to lead all players in the warm-up lap. There were few players who would challenge him since most players wanted to conserve their energy for practice. Regardless of whether he was challenged or not, he set a fast pace.

Normally, you don't expect a 235-pound heavily muscled lineman to set the pace in a 500- to 600-yard run. Greg prided himself in his physical condition and speed.

When Greg was a freshman he was a marginally average student, but he gradually improved his academic standing and was a solid B student by the time he reached his senior year.

In order to raise contributions, we asked our alumni and fans to contribute to academic-athletic scholarships. Each scholarship was $1,000, and we assigned our best student athletes in all sports to those scholarships. Every fall before our final scrimmage prior to our first game, we invited our contributors to a barbecue at the stadium and introduced the students who were assigned to our student-athletic scholarships. We asked the players to dress neatly and try to look more academic than athletic. Those invited ate barbecue with the contributors.

One day after one of our academic-athletic scholarship barbecues, Greg and I were walking together toward the locker room after practice. He asked me, "Coach, what do I have to do to get a chance to eat barbecue with those contributors?" I told him, "Greg, you have to make good grades. The minimum average to be assigned to a scholarship is B minus or a 2.5 average or better."

Within a year Greg Pipes had improved his grade point average to qualify for an academic-athletic scholarship. He continued on an academic-athletic scholarship through his senior year.

I recall Greg playing extremely well in a number of games. When we opened the season in 1965 against Auburn and shut them out for 58 minutes, Greg was one of the leading tacklers in the game. Greg was even better when we played Syracuse with Floyd Little and Larry Czonka in the same backfield. Baylor led 35-0 until Syracuse scored late to make the score 35-12.

Against Arkansas in Fayetteville with the Razorbacks on a 25-game regular season winning streak, Pipes was probably most responsible for our shutting out the Razorbacks as we beat them 7-0.

We played Pipes on the strongside of Arkansas' formation. On the strongside Arkansas played Harry Jones, a great runner with exceptional speed at slot back, and had Jon Brittenum at quarterback, who had led Arkansas to a Southwest Conference championship in 1965.

Arkansas' favorite pass play was to run the split end on the strong side on a 12- to 15-yard curl pattern to the inside and Harry Jones on a quick-out pattern to the outside. Brittenum sprinted out to the side, where Jones lined up and generally threw to Jones, who could turn a short pattern into a long gainer with his speed and running ability. However, if the defense put a short defender on the split end, the end would run an out pattern and Jones would turn upfield between the safety and defensive halfback.

Brittenum did not throw this pattern nearly as well, and the safety had a good chance of covering Jones on the deep pattern up the seam. We depended on Pipes to contain and rush Brittenum. He did an outstanding job as he pressured Brittenum all day and sacked him a couple of times. Brittenum could only complete 10 of 29 passes for 112 yards.

Greg Pipes was selected as *Sports Illustrated*'s "Lineman of the Week." I don't believe there were many interior linemen in the country who could have done the job Pipes did. Our defensive end on Pipes' side of the line played pass defense and forced Arkansas to run a pattern they really didn't like to run. Pipes also did an outstanding job helping to contain the Arkansas running game.

We won the game 7-0 when Terry Southall threw a 21-yard touchdown pass to Bobby Green.

Greg was named All-Southwest Conference for three years and made All-American his senior year. In his senior year he played in the Blue-Gray game, the Senior Bowl, and the All-American game in June of 1968.

Greg was signed by Edmonton in the Canadian Football League. He played with them for five years. He was selected to the Canadian League All Pro team in 1970 and played in the Canadian League All-Star game in 1971.

In 1967 we lost our last seven games and our defense seemed to lose confidence and did not play up to their potential, especially in our final three games.

One thing about football is when a team goes into a slump, it can affect the play of great players even though they continue to try the best they can. Greg is and was a person of high standards and great loyalties. He realized his performances in some of those late games weren't up to his best potential.

He wrote me the following note after the season ended in 1967:

Nov. 30, 1967

Dear Coach Bridgers,

I want to thank you for all you have done for me. I know that I haven't always played my best but you have always done your best to get me the honor [Greg was selected as All-American.] Coach, I know this year hasn't gone our way but you have made it a memorable year for me. I know that right now you are having probably the toughest time in your life. Yet, with all your troubles, you are the kind of person who does nice things for others when others are not being nearly as kind to you. Coach, you are one of the greatest Christians I know to be able to take the kind of pressure that has been exerted. You truly live up to the poem "If" because you have kept your head, heart and sense of humor when all about you . . . . You are truly a great Christian man.

Greg Pipes

When a team loses seven straight games, there are few players who will say anything very nice about their coach. It's human nature to place blame on the person in charge. I believe Greg Pipes' note to me tells a lot about the kind of person he is.

Greg went to Baylor Law School in the winter and spring quarters while he was playing professional football. The year he obtained his law degree he retired from professional football. He graduated from Baylor Law School in the spring of 1972 and passed the Texas State Bar exam in the fall of 1972.

Greg has been assistant criminal district attorney for Tarrant County, Texas, for 18 years.

Here is what Greg Pipes writes on "What College Football Meant to Me":

The greatest opportunities of my life all stem from the educational benefits afforded me because of college football. My family's finances would not have provided me the opportunity to attend college. Without college football I would not have had a summer job that brought me in touch with my bride of 24 years and without college football leading to professional football I would not have been able to enter law school, much less pay my own way . . . .

College football taught me the value of teamwork and the necessity of picking one's self up and getting ready for the next play, case or event that life throws us.

College football was presented to me as a way to get an education and do something I loved to do. That is the way it was administered under John Bridgers. I remember looking at team rosters when we played the University of Texas my senior year. We still had 28 of our original 32 scholarship players from my freshman class. I thought then and I think now that the promise of a college education was being kept, not only for me, but also those others who came as a result of that same promise.

College football brings together people from all walks of life from all parts of the state and the country, and they form one of the most respected groups on the campus. Your teammates are friends you will keep up with and remember the rest of your life.

Does Greg Pipes appear to meet the stigma of a highly recruited athlete being corrupted by major college football and the recruiting process as pictured by some of the critics in the media? The answer, of course, is a resounding *no!*

CHAPTER 22

SOME OVERACHIEVING
BAYLOR HEROES

Herb Adkins, Guard

Herb Adkins came to Baylor as a freshman center in 1958. He had played on a state high school championship team, Nederland High School, in Nederland, Texas, which is in the southeastern part of Texas. Nederland High School was coached by "Bum" Phillips. Coach Phillips was later a successful head coach with the Houston Oilers. His long and successful career took him to many places in high school, college, and professional football.

Few players I've ever been around had the intensity and energy of Herb Adkins. He weighed 168 pounds when he began at Baylor and probably never went over 190 during his four years. His average weight as a guard was 180 to 185 in his three varsity years as a starter.

Herb was born in Opelousas, Louisiana, which is Cajun country, and he speaks with a definite Cajun accent. He is a bright person, but he had never really taken academic pursuits very seriously. As a result, he was borderline as far as having the background and preparation for college work.

He may have had a slight inferiority complex about his academic ability, but he made up for that and any other deficiencies he may have had with his willingness to study as many hours as was necessary to make his grades. To my knowledge he never failed a course and finished college with his degree in the allotted eight semesters without ever having to go to summer school to make up any deficiency.

Mrs. Edna Sorrell, who was assistant registrar of Baylor, told me after I came to Baylor in January of 1959, "John, you had better keep an eye on Herb Adkins. He scored in the lowest two percentile on the entrance examinations." I don't doubt the truth of Mrs. Sorrell's statement, but I believe that Herb didn't really give his best efforts on the test. It was a part of the orientation schedule which all freshmen had to go through before classes began. There are always some students who don't take the orientation process very seriously.

Herb was a starter on the freshman team, and started every varsity game played at Baylor for three years, which included two bowl games.

He played head up against some great football players in the schedule we played. In 1960 Herb played head up in the TCU game against Bob Lily, who was an All-American tackle at TCU and later Hall of Fame tackle with the Dallas Cowboys. Lily was one of the best ever to play in the NFL. Herb admitted Lily gave him problems, as TCU defeated us 14-6 after we had won our first five games.

The only time I recall a player getting the best of Adkins was in 1961, after he hurt his shoulder in the TCU game the week before we played Texas. Herb was lined head up on Diron Talbert, who later played four years for the Rams and ten years with the Redskins.

In effect, Adkins was playing with one arm and one shoulder, but did not want to come out of the game although he probably should have.

When Adkins was a sophomore, we played Southern California at Los Angeles. The Trojans were undefeated and untied through seven games, and were ranked fourth in the nation. We held Southern California to a field goal for the first quarter. The field goal came after Southern Cal recovered a Baylor fumble on the Baylor 27. Another Baylor fumble gave the ball to Southern Cal on Baylor's seven-yard-line. The Bears held, but Southern Cal recovered another fumble on the Baylor 16. The Trojans scored to make the score 10-0. Then Baylor was called on pass interference in the end zone to give the Trojans a first down on the one. They scored to make the score 17-0.

We answered and drove 78 yards and made a two-pointer on a great effort by Jim Evans, our fullback, to make the score 17-8.

When our first team left the field after a great defensive stand in the fourth quarter, the crowd of 44,000 gave the Baylor team a standing ovation. That was the first time I ever experienced that in an away game.

Southern Cal had the McKeaver twins, a couple of 225-pound guards. Mike McKeaver was a much publicized All-American candidate. He said, "That Baylor line is the quickest and toughest I've ever played against. Those boys react like a bunch of panthers, and they really hit. Everett Frazier gave me all kinds of trouble and that little 66 (Herb Adkins) never gives up. They're a great pair of guards."

Dan Ficca, a Trojan tackle from Pennsylvania, said, "I'm convinced the Southwest Conference is just as strong as the Big Ten. Baylor's a lot better than Ohio State . . . You just can't block those Baylor linemen. They're little, but they show more hustle and desire than any lineman I've faced."

Our problem that day was that we couldn't pass protect against the big mobile linemen of Southern Cal. We lost 53 yards on sacks while attempting to pass. Even at that we were the first intersectional team in four games to score on the Trojans.

In 1960 Baylor had a good season. We came from behind in the last couple of minutes to score on a long drive to beat Rice 12-7 (they would play in the Sugar Bowl).

We received an invitation to play the University of Florida in the Gator Bowl. We were trailing 13-0 in the fourth quarter but put two long drives together to narrow the margin to 13-12. We went for two points, but Ronnie Goodwin, our best receiver, dropped the pass in the end zone. There was only a minute left to play.

I had cautioned our team not to retaliate if one of the Florida players committed a flagrant foul. On the kickoff following our last touchdown, a Florida tackle committed a flagrant foul on Herby Adkins. The officials didn't see the foul, but Herb didn't strike back. I thought Herby showed great self-control by not retaliating. Later Herb told me that not retaliating was the toughest thing he had ever done. After the disappointment of not converting our attempted two points, which would have given us a victory, he took an uncalled for foul from the University of Florida tackle.

Self-control is a quality of a champion, and Herb Adkins demonstrated that quality under very trying circumstances. We nominated him for the Southwest Conference Sportsmanship Award, and he was selected for the honor.

In 1961 we really thought we would have a great team, but after winning two games against Wake Forest and Pittsburgh, we went into a terrible slump and lost four of the next five games.

We made Don Trull our starting quarterback after our Texas game, and we won two good victories over Air and SMU. We lost to Rice, but surprisingly were invited to play Utah State in the Gotham Bowl. Utah State was undefeated and was ranked 10th in the nation.

Utah State had two great tackles in Merlin Olsen, who was Consensus All-American and winner of the Outland Trophy as the best college lineman of the year. He was 6'4 and weighed 265 pounds. Their other tackle was Clark Miller, at 6'4 and 250 pounds. He was a high draft choice of the 49ers and played nine years in the NFL.

Their defensive scheme was a five-man line with the nose guard on the center, and their two big tackles played on the outside shoulder of our two undersized guards, Herb Adkins and Ronnie Rogers. In coaches' terminology it was known as an "Eagle defense," since the Philadelphia Eagles had popularized the defense. Herb Adkins, our right offensive guard, had Olsen playing on him, and Ronnie Rogers had Miller playing on him. Our guards were both at about 185 pounds. Adkins and Rogers were two of the best competitors I've ever coached. Herb was a senior while Rogers was a sophomore who had been redshirted a year.

We stayed at the same hotel with Utah State. Herb thought that Olsen and Miller had ignored and snubbed him and Ronnie on a couple of occasions. He may have just used that excuse to help himself get ready for the game. Both of them seemed as ready to play as they had ever been. Herb talked a little more than Ronnie and showed a little more emotion.

When Herb lined up on the first play of the game facing Merlin Olsen, Herb said, "It's an honor and privilege to play against the best lineman in America, but, Mr. All-American, we are fixing to trap your butt!"

Adkins set Olsen up for Ronnie Rogers' trap block, and Ronnie Bull made 10 to 12 yards up the middle as Rogers got a good trap block on Olsen. On the next play Herb said to Olsen, "You should be ashamed and embarrassed to let us trap you like that. This time we are going to run right at you."

Don Trull, our quarterback, checked off to a sweep around the end. On the next play, Herb said to Olsen, "I lied to you on that last play. Now you don't know what the hell we are going to do."

Later Ronnie Bull scored on a trap play up the middle and we kicked a field goal for a 10-0 halftime lead.

We played our best game of the season. In the second half we scored on a 38-yard touchdown pass from Trull to Ted Plumb, and Trull scored from the one-yard-line on a quarterback sneak to give us a 24-3 lead.

Our team played a great defense as we held Utah State to under 200 yards total offense. Utah State scored their lone touchdown in the last few seconds of the game after intercepting a pass deep in our territory. The final score was 24-9.

I felt Herb Adkins and Ronnie Rogers had outplayed Merlin Olsen, the Outland Trophy winner, and Clark Miller. Herb Adkins was consensus choice for All-Southwest Conference team. Ronnie Bull was named the game's outstanding player. Don Trull played extremely well also.

Two or three days after the game, my twin brother, Frank, caught a plane out of Denver to Salt Lake City. A huge man saw Frank and said, "Coach Bridgers, what are you doing out here?" Frank said, "I'm not Coach Bridgers, I'm his twin brother." Merlin Olsen introduced himself and they visited during the plane ride to Salt Lake City. Merlin said that Herby talked more than any player he had ever played against. He really wasn't upset with Herby's talk but seemed more amused.

As a coach, I have never encouraged our players to talk to opponents during a game. However, I really don't think Herby's comments were degrading or insulting. It was mainly good-natured kidding by a very good undersized lineman who was facing a lineman honored as the best in America — one who outweighed him 75 to 80 pounds.

I remember on a trip to Chicago I had a visit with Ronnie Bull. Herby's name came up in our conversation. Ronnie Bull said, "I've never seen anyone like Herby in college or pro football. He had more energy and endurance. I remember when we came dragging off the field during our two-a-day practices in September, with the temperature at 100 degrees and 90 percent humidity. Herby would come off the field doing back flips."

When Herb graduated from college, he went to work for a year. He came back to Baylor and said he wanted to go to law school. I tried to discourage him, as I remembered what Mrs. Sorrell had said about his entrance examination score. However, he was determined. I gave him a graduate assistantship as a coach for our freshman team.

He later told me that the first law school course he took was torts. He said, "I read the first page and the only words I understood were *the, and,* and *of.* I said to myself, 'This is going to be a long, hard road.'"

I never knew any player who was willing to spend more hours studying than Herb did. I had a nice couch in my office and a conference table. He asked if he could use my office at night to study. I believe that many times he studied all night, and if he got sleepy he would take a nap on the couch.

Herb ended up graduating from law school in the allotted three years and passed the bar exam the first time he took it. He took a job with Joe Allbritton, a Baylor graduate who had done very well in business and had vast real estate holdings in Texas, California, and other places. One of Herby's jobs was to look after some of the large buildings Joe owned in California.

Herb Adkins is one of the most loyal people I've ever known. When our daughter, Cindy, died suddenly after an operation for kidney stones in April of 1966, Herby flew back to Waco from California to attend the funeral.

After I was fired from Baylor after the 1968 season, he felt so strongly that Baylor did not treat me right that he has never been back. I tried to get him to go back for a reunion of our 1961 Gotham Bowl team and 1960 Gator Bowl teams, but he would not go.

Herby has strong convictions. Sometimes he is not very tolerant or tactful with those who disagree with his beliefs. His firm beliefs and strong loyalties have not always made friends with all the people he has known through the years. But those same qualities have made him successful in everything he has undertaken.

After he worked a number of years with Joe Allbritton, he bought an oil-drilling business. It prospered and he sold it for a neat profit. He then bought a ranch and raised cattle and cutter horses. He's been successful at both. Herb is still in excellent condition and could probably play a half of good football.

Tommy Smith, Wide Receiver

This is the truly inspirational story of a young man who overcame poverty as the result of divorced parents, recovered from a serious injury, and developed into a good student and an excellent football player.

Tommy Smith was fortunate to finish high school. His sole support came from his mother, who had a difficult time making ends meet after her divorce from Tommy's father. For a period, Tommy lived with an uncle and aunt, Jack and Vanita Baird. However, he was able to complete high school and was a good enough football player that three or four Southwest Conference football teams were interested in him, including Texas A&M and Rice.

Tommy was a quarterback on offense and defensive cornerback on defense in high school. Cotton Ashton, Tommy's high school coach, encouraged Tommy to try for an athletic scholarship in order to attend college. Tommy said no one in his family had ever attended college, nor was there a family member who tried to influence him to attend college.

Coach Vernon Glass, our offensive backfield coach, recruited Tommy. Upon the recommendation of Coach Ashton and after evaluating his performance in game films, Baylor offered Tommy a scholarship.

Tommy Smith was not an instant success. We changed his position to wide receiver. In spring practice he was coached by Raymond Berry, who had a great influence on Tommy. Raymond taught Tommy the fundamentals to get the utmost out of his abilities. Tommy did not have great speed, but he learned to accelerate on the break and he soaked up all the fundamentals which Berry could teach so well.

We held Tommy out in his sophomore year, 1963. We had some good receivers, and we felt he needed a little more seasoning.

Every year, from about 1960 through 1968, we encouraged players who wanted to attend the summer conference of the Fellowship of Christian Athletes conference in Estes Park, Colorado, to do so. Most of our coaches attended one or more years during that period. Tommy Smith was one of our players who attended in 1965. I was there and could tell that the conference had a real impact on him. It was a camp which emphasized the combination of worship, recreation, inspirational meetings with talks by well-known coaches and athletes, singing, and small group discussions. There were several years at the Estes Park FCA Conference when the Baylor players demonstrated some of the fundamentals and intricacies of the passing game. Tommy Smith, who had developed a Raymond Berry-ability to catch the ball, was a part of the Baylor demonstration of the passing game in the summer of 1965.

Tommy Smith left to drive back to Texas the night the conference ended. He and three other Baylor players were riding in a Volkswagen which had a rollback canvas top. They ran into a severe thunderstorm and the Volkswagen hit a soft shoulder, throwing the car out of control. Tommy Smith was thrown out of the roof and suffered a compressed fracture of one of the vertebrae in his back.

I asked a friend who owned an airplane to fly Tommy back to Waco. Since the accident occurred in late August, the doctors thought it was highly unlikely he would be able to play during the 1965 football season.

Tommy had to stay in the hospital for a week to ten days. When I visited him there, I saw he had a Bible on his bedside table. He said, "Coach, don't count me out. I might be able to play yet."

Tommy attended our team meeting just before our first practice in 1965. When practice began, he started walking around the practice field. He walked around the field during our entire practice. He was wearing a very cumbersome back brace.

After a week or so, he had a football and was tossing it in the air and catching it as he walked around the practice field. Later he began to jog around the field. The intensity of his workout increased as the days and weeks went by.

In our fourth game of the season we had suffered a humiliating loss to Arkansas, 38-7. We had six interceptions and lost one fumble. It was our most decisive defeat since I had been at Baylor. Terry Southall had broken his leg in the Florida State game the week before we played Arkansas. He was out for the season. Our reserve quarterbacks just weren't ready to play.

The following Monday on the practice field, Tommy Smith came running up to me, obviously very excited. He said, "Coach, I've just been to the doctor, and he says I can play this week if I wear my brace!"

I could hardly believe him, as I thought surely he was out for the season. Tommy had exercised the muscles in his back to the point where they could support the fractured vertebrae without danger of injuring it again. However, he did have to wear his brace, which was cumbersome and inhibited some movements.

We were playing Texas A&M at College Station, and after our loss to Arkansas, the Aggies were a three-point favorite. Tommy practiced with us in pads Tuesday, Wednesday, and Thursday. We weren't going to start him, but he was definitely going to play.

We thought we had a good game plan for Texas A&M, especially our offensive game plan. Early in the first quarter we moved the ball to the Aggie five-yard-line. It was third and five for a touchdown, and I called for Tommy Smith. I gave him the call for a quick out pass to the split end on the weak side of the formation. That was Tommy's position. I watched Tommy from the sidelines. He made a good cut on his out move and separated from the defensive cornerback. It appeared at first that Kenny Stockdale, our quarterback, had led him too much on his pass, but Tommy leveled out parallel to the ground and made a sensational catch with his fingertips and quickly pulled the ball into his body.

That was Tommy's first catch in a game situation since the 1964 season, and that play was responsible for a 7-0 lead. It gave our team a terrific lift. Kenny Stockdale had the game of his life, as we beat the Aggies 31-0. He completed 20 of 27 passes for 286 yards, the second highest passing yardage in Baylor's history up to that time.

In 1966 Tommy Smith became our regular starter at split end for the first time. He finished the season with 41 catches and made the *Waco Herald Tribune* All-Southwest Conference team.

In our game with SMU, Tommy tied Lawrence Elkins' record of 12 catches in a game. That was the game in which we overcame a 21-point lead to go ahead 22-21, only to lose the game with a blocked punt in the last minute which led to a SMU goal with only a few seconds left in the game.

Tommy was named Baylor's "Most Valuable Offensive Lineman for 1966." He also was awarded the 1966 Sportsmanship Award by Kappa Upsilon Tau, a service fraternity on the Baylor campus. Tommy Smith graduated at midterm in 1967. His major was mathematics.

Tommy married a young woman, Nancy, who earned a Ph.D. in physical chemistry. After graduation he attended Texas A&M and received a master's degree in computer science.

One of our football players, Dwight Hood, a fine tackle, told this story about Tommy Smith: "I was complaining about being poor and my family not having much. Tommy told me, 'Dwight, you don't know what it means to be hungry. I've been so hungry that I would scrape the frosting off the freezer on our refrigerator and eat it.'"

Tommy now lives in San Antonio, where he has his own business as a property tax consultant. His wife is on the faculty at the University of Texas Medical School in San Antonio. They have a son and daughter who are college students and will soon have their degrees.

His story is one of a young man who never thought he would have the opportunity for a college education. Tommy not only earned his way to a college education through a football scholarship but improved each year as a football player and as a student.

His most memorable experience was catching the touchdown pass against Texas A&M after suffering a broken back in August. And his reply to "what college football meant to me" was: "Coach, it meant I could go to college! Without the college football scholarship, I would not have had the financial means to attend college. My mother was divorced and was just making ends meet. No one in my family had a college education, so no one was pushing me. Thanks to you I had an opportunity to play football and get a college degree. Yes, you gave me a chance to better my life, and I shall always be grateful. Words are not adequate at this time, but all I know to say is 'Thanks, Coach!'"

I was selected to coach in the Blue-Gray College All-Star Game in Montgomery, Alabama. I was able to take Tommy Smith, Terry Southall, quarterback, Paul Becton, a wide receiver, and Dwight Hood, a defensive tackle, as players on the Gray team. Tommy Smith had an outstanding game. He was the leading receiver in the game and was selected as the outstanding offensive lineman for the Gray team. We lost the game by a touchdown, but I was particularly proud of Tommy as well as our other Baylor players.

Tommy Smith is one of the majority of scholarship football players who were economically deprived and yet took advantage of his opportunity to greatly enhance his standard of living and make a very worthwhile contribution to society.

Ronnie Rogers, Guard and Defensive Tackle

Shortly after I had accepted the head coaching job at Baylor, I went on a recruiting trip with Catfish Smith, our freshman coach. One of the first players we visited was Ronnie Rogers, a defensive linebacker and offensive fullback in Garland, Texas, a small residential community about 20 miles east of Dallas.

We looked at film of him first, and he was particularly impressive on defense. He ended up being on almost every play where the football was. His nickname in high school was "Radar" because he had a nose for the football and located it like a radar screen would locate an enemy plane during wartime.

The only thing that bothered me when I saw him was that he appeared to be a couple of inches shorter than I am (at 5'9). I doubt if he was over 5'7. However, I had already made up my mind to offer him a scholarship on the basis of the way he played.

We visited his family, who lived in a modest but neat home. His mother and father were obviously excellent parents. Ronnie had a very strong build and while he did not have great straight-a-way speed, he was extremely quick. He had a strong face, and his eyes showed a look of determination and competitiveness.

At the time, college football was one-platoon and a player played both offense and defense. We changed his position to guard. He didn't have the straight-a-way speed we wanted in a fullback and we thought his lack of height would also be a handicap on pass defense as a linebacker.

Ronnie was a part-time starter as a freshman, but we had our two starting guards, Herby Adkins and Everett Frazier, returning from our 1959 team and decided to red-shirt Ronnie Rogers in 1960. While Ronnie was playing on our "scout team," which ran offensive and defensive plays of the upcoming weeks' opponents, Ronnie caught my eye one day. He was playing right defensive guard on an even defense on the nose of our offensive left guard. We were trying to run a play over his position, and after trying to run it a number of times without success, I realized we didn't have anyone on the left side of the line who could block him. Ronnie was just too quick for our offensive linemen to block. Blocking Ronnie Rogers was like trying to put your finger on a minnow in a bucket. Ronnie moved almost too quickly for anyone to touch him, much less effectively block him.

We continued to hold Ronnie out for the remainder of the season, but Ronnie was a starter for the next three seasons as an offensive guard and defensive guard or defensive tackle.

I've tried to remember if he ever played a bad game, and I can't think of one. Some of the outstanding performances I remember were against Utah State in the Gotham Bowl game in 1961, when Ronnie and Herby Adkins outplayed the two big tackles with Utah State, Merlin Olsen and Clark Miller, both of whom had long pro careers, and the Bluebonnet Bowl game against LSU, when the Tigers were held to a total offense of 108 yards running and passing and without a first down in the last 49 minutes of the game. Ronnie was our outstanding defensive player in 1963, when Texas beat us 7–0 and went on to become national college champions. He made tackles all over the field from his defensive tackle position.

I asked Ronnie not long ago if he ever felt that he played against a lineman in college who really got the best of him. He replied quietly, "No, Coach, I don't ever remember playing against an opponent who I felt got the best of me."

In 1963 Ronnie played defensive right tackle. That was the year the substitution rule was liberalized, but it still wasn't supposed to allow offensive and defensive platoons. We came up with a plan where our top defensive players could be on defense 90 percent of the time and about 10 percent on offense. The defensive team would be on offense about 90 percent of the time and on defense about 10 percent of the time.

Ronnie's nickname with his Baylor teammates was "Stump," which was descriptive of his physique and of his resistance to being eliminated from a ball carrier's path.

I've known few players who were more appreciative of the opportunity for a scholarship and to play football at the major college level than Ronnie.

Upon the event of my retirement from intercollegiate athletics from the University of New Mexico, Ronnie Rogers wrote me a letter which I shall always remember. Ronnie is now a doctor of dental surgery in Garland. Here is an excerpt of what he wrote:

> . . . The environment you created was one of stability and trust. I never had a doubt about your sincerity and never questioned your motives and integrity. I felt comfortable you were as con-

cerned about me as a person as you were about me as an athlete, and that you were concerned about my academic progress as you were about my gains on the field.... I also pleasantly recall your unwavering willingness to fill the athletic department's obligations to honor its commitment to educate those men brought in on athletic scholarship; particularly those who could not achieve the level of performance on the field that had been expected of them. I do not recall a single incident of harassment of any person in an attempt to "run him off." Indeed, I recall many who graduated having never played a meaningful role in a game, but who were still part of the team because of your attitude and sense of fairness. Many of those men have achieved high levels of success, and had you been otherwise disposed they might have never received what they originally entered Baylor for — an education. I know those men are grateful to you.

On the more personal note, I would say that I realize how fortunate I was to be exposed to a man who would be willing to take a chance that he could convert a 5'7 high school fullback into a college lineman. This gamble, plus your willingness to give me a chance to work up the ladder to playing status, taught me that achievement through effort is possible for virtually everyone who is willing to capitalize on opportunity. Opportunity is the key that opens the door, and you provided it for me when no one else would. For that I am most grateful.

Recently, in answer to a question of "what college football meant to him," Ronnie said: ". . . It was also an activity [football] that I thoroughly enjoyed and loved to do, and through the team experience opened avenues of lasting friendships and memories that endure the passage of time. There were no negatives about the experience for me!"

Ronnie's most memorable experience was "Comeback victory by Baylor against Texas Tech in 1963. [Baylor trailing 17-9 with six minutes left, scored on drives of 65 and 83 yards to pull the game out, 21-17.] A game that truly proved, 'It ain't over 'til it's over.'"

That comeback represented Dr. Ronnie Rogers' competitiveness and persistence. Ronnie attended Baylor Dental School and was elected to Omicron Kappa Upsilon, the National Dental Honor Society. Ronnie was also named to the All-Southwest Conference Academic Team in his senior year.

Big-time football was good for Ronnie Rogers, and Ronnie Rogers was good for football.

John Westbrook, Halfback

Early in the summer of 1965, Coach Jack Thomas introduced me to a young black man, John Westbrook, who was interested in attending Baylor University. John was 6'1 and weighed about 180 pounds when he visited Baylor. We had completed our recruiting for the year and were experiencing financial difficulties in our athletic program.

Despite the fact that we were raising far more funds from private sources for intercollegiate athletics than ever before, we were still not raising enough money to support our non-revenue sports such as baseball, tennis, golf, track and field, and administrative expenses along with basketball and football. At that time basketball did not support itself, and the only sport making a profit was football.

I encouraged John to attend Baylor. I told him if he should show promise in spring practice in his freshman year, we would put him on scholarship. He had played football at Elgin High School, a small high school near Austin, Texas, in a segregated community. His father was a Baptist minister, and John wished to study for the ministry at Baylor.

I was born in Birmingham, Alabama, and attended college at Auburn University. I knew what racial prejudice was. After coaching football in Japan, where over half of the players were black, my years at Johns Hopkins when I coached Ernie Bates (the first black player at Johns Hopkins who later became a brain surgeon) and my experience coaching Jim Parker (the great offensive lineman) and Big Daddy Lipscomb (the extraordinary defensive lineman with the Baltimore Colts), I had overcome my racial prejudice. From the first time I met John Westbrook, I wanted him to be the first black player at Baylor. However, the state of Texas was very much like the southeastern states of Alabama, Georgia, Mississippi, Tennessee, Louisiana, and others when it came to racial prejudice. All of our coaches were either from the southeast or Texas. Some, but not all of them, had racial prejudices.

John Westbrook was a fine young man, intelligent and sensitive. I'm not sure I have ever known a young man who was a better public speaker. He instinctively knew which players and coaches were prejudiced against him. It takes personal interracial experiences to overcome racial prejudice, and I believe athletic competition has done more than anything else to reduce and eliminate racial prejudice.

John had a remarkable spring practice. During the spring practice of 1966 I kept careful statistics on the performances of our offensive backs and receivers. John Westbrook carried the football 29 times in full team scrimmages and gained 268 yards for an unusual average of 9.6 yards per carry. He had good speed, but not great speed. He had high knee action and ran with good power. He was more of a slashing-type runner than a real speedster. John Westbrook gained the most yardage and had the highest average of any of our backs in the 1966 spring practice.

I told John he would have a full scholarship beginning in the fall semester of 1966. There was no question but that he had earned a scholarship.

Our opening game against Syracuse was one of the most outstanding victories in Baylor's history. Syracuse had Floyd Little and Larry Czonka in the same backfield, two backs that were outstanding for many years in professional football (Little at Denver and Czonka with Miami). In the second quarter we sent John Westbrook in the game. He ran a play inside left tackle and gained five yards. It was the first time a black running back ever carried the football in the Southwest Conference. With Baylor leading 35-6 late in the fourth quarter, I cleared the bench and let every Baylor player who was dressed out for the game play. Floyd Little, a great Syracuse back, scored a touchdown from the one-yard-line to make the score 35-12 with only seconds left in the game.

After the promise John Westbrook showed in spring practice, his football career at Baylor was disappointing. Early in the 1966 season he injured a knee, and that would plague him throughout his career at Baylor. After the 1966 season he had a knee operation, but as sometimes happens, the operation was not successful. Perhaps his best performance may have come in the Washington State game in 1966, when John ran 12 yards for a touchdown (which proved to be the winning points in our 20-14 victory).

During John's junior year his mother developed cancer. She died after a long illness.

Despite the disappointments and the trials of being the first black player at Baylor, John did well in school. He was also in demand as a speaker. He attended the Fellowship of Christian Athletes conference in the summer of 1968 and made one of the finest talks I ever heard by a student athlete at the FCA conference.

After the 1968 season started, John was still having trouble with his knee. He came to see me one day and said he wanted to quit football.

I told him, "John, you can't quit now after you've gone this far. If you do, you will be remembered as a quitter, and I know you are not a quitter."

He agreed to keep playing. The Friday before we played Rice in our final game, I was fired as football coach and athletic director. The Rice game was played in the worst weather I've experienced during my 42 years as a coach and athletic director. It was a driving rainstorm with the temperature just above freezing.

We made a goal line stand in the fourth quarter and took the ball over on our four-yard-line with a 10-7 lead. Gene Rogers, our halfback, ran for 67 yards inside the right tackle on a counterplay. With the ball on Rice's 24-yard-line, we sent John Westbrook in to replace Gene Rogers. John ran four straight times and ended up scoring from the four-yard-line to make the score 16-7.

It was a very satisfying victory. Rogers' run was the play which cinched the victory for us, but I was glad to see John Westbrook score the last touchdown of my 10-year career at Baylor.

John had a total of only 59 carries in his three years of varsity football. He gained 281 yards but lost 30 yards, which brought his average down to 4.2 yards per carry. John only caught two passes but for a total of 74 yards. It appears we should have thrown to him more often.

John Westbrook was a pioneer. He and Jerry Levias, a black player at SMU in 1968, suffered the stress, name calling, ridicule, hardships, and criticisms which pioneers in any area of life usually suffer. In addition, John had an injury which constantly handicapped his performance, and his mother for a long period was dying of cancer. He became terribly discouraged at times, even to the point of trying to take his own life. He took an overdose of sleeping pills, but it didn't have any lasting effect.

John graduated in four years without the benefit of summer school. He entered the Southwest Baptist Seminary in Fort Worth, Texas and received his diploma there.

At one time he worked for me for about a year as academic counselor to the athletes at Florida State University. That really wasn't the niche he was born to fulfill. He was a preacher and became an outstanding one, as he pastored the largest black Baptist church in Houston until his death in the middle eighties from a heart attack (he was in his early forties). John had become very much overweight. One reason may have been that his bad knee prevented him from exercising as he should and his weight continued to increase.

At one time John entered politics and ran for lieutenant governor of Texas. He received a surprisingly large number of votes but not nearly enough to be elected. He really wasn't a politician. He was a great preacher. I doubt if there were few better than he in the great state of Texas, a state long known for great preachers.

His father was a preacher before him. One of the letters I cherished most was from Reverend R. Westbrook shortly after our Rice game in 1968. It read in part:

> I take this method of expressing my appreciation to you and all who are concerned for the courtesy and support that you have given my son, John Westbrook.
>
> I think you are a great coach and a Christian man. I have been impressed very much each time I have heard you speak on Dad's Day. One thing in particular that I noticed is that you were deeply concerned about molding the character of the boys as well as winning football games. I know the character will outlive any football plays if they have the true principle of brotherhood and Christianity within them.
>
> I cannot forget the letter that my wife received from Mrs. Bridgers consoling her and me in our very deepest despondency [Mrs. Westbrook's bout with cancer and subsequent death]. Please give Mrs. Bridgers our best wishes. Of course, you know, I am speaking for one who cannot speak for herself, but had deep regard and respect for Mrs. Bridgers.
>
> Yes, some days must be dark and dreary, but when I think of the poet saying, "Be still sad heart and quit repining; Behind each dark cloud, the sun is still shining." But remember as the curtain closes, we turn and fix our gaze for a goal that is much higher and everlasting . . . .
>
> God be with you until we meet again. Writing as a father to one of your friends, I am sincerely yours, Rev. R. A. Westbrook.

Mike Bourland, Guard

Mike Bourland was another guard. I guess one of the reasons I took a liking to guards was because that was the position I played in high school and college. Overall, a guard can be effective with less size, strength, speed, and overall athletic ability than any position on the football team. As a college and high school player I had short-comings in all of those attributes. Of course, it helps to have all of the above, and most of the great ones have several of those at-tributes. I'm not sure this is as true today since it appears most col-lege guards now weigh in at 250 to 300 pounds. Linemen of the size you see now really didn't start coming in vogue until the seventies, and it seems the requirement for size has increased since then.

Mike Bourland, as a high school player at Paschal High School in Fort Worth, weighed about 175 to 180 pounds. He was about 5'11 without outstanding speed, strength, or athletic ability. I really didn't think he had a chance to play for Baylor. However, there were two things in his favor. He wanted very much to be a Baylor football player, and he had a great deal of character as a person. His mother had attended Baylor. I had met her at a couple of alumni meetings in Fort Worth. She was enthusiastic for Baylor and a classy person.

After much discussion in our staff meetings and with Herb Zimmerman, our defensive coach, who recruited the Fort Worth area, we decided to offer Mike a one-year scholarship. At that time, four-year scholarships were offered to about 98 percent of the play-ers who were offered scholarships. We felt Mike might improve and perhaps gain weight and strength and then become a prospect.

Mike was a freshman in 1961 and was red-shirted in 1962. He showed a great deal of progress in our 1963 spring practice. His technique and fundamentals, particularly as far as pass protection was concerned, improved a great deal. Mike had an excellent teacher in Coach Jack Little, who had been an All-American tackle at Texas A&M and an outstanding offensive tackle for the Baltimore Colts. A bad back had shortened his career, but he turned into an outstand-ing offensive line coach.

In addition, Mike became one of our first players to work hard at weight training. He became stronger and gained about 20 pounds. His strength had increased proportionately.

Mike ended up being a starter at offensive left guard. Mike was very consistent and did a particularly good job in pass protection.

The one game I recall most vividly was our game with the University of Texas in 1963. Texas and Baylor came into the game undefeated in conference play. Mike was paired against Scott Appleton, an All-American tackle at Texas who had won the Outland Trophy as the Outstanding College Lineman of 1963. Mike did an outstanding job of pass protecting against Appleton. To my recollection, Appleton never got close to our passer all day. However, Texas beat us 7-0 in a game that went down to the last minute before they could be sure of a victory.

In 1964 the college rules were changed to allow full-fledged platoon football with offensive *and* defensive teams. Mike continued to be a starter at offensive left guard. Our season started slowly, but we finished strong. As time went on Mike developed as a leader.

Mike became acquainted with a company which emphasized positive thinking and a positive approach to problems. He was able to get some literature from the company and he mailed copies of it to our players. He convinced our players, with the help of Success Motivation, Inc., that Baylor could not lose.

We started the season by defeating two teams which had enjoyed outstanding success in recent years. We beat Auburn at Auburn 14-8. Then we defeated University of Washington, which had beaten us the year before 35-14. The difference was an 80-yard drive with less than two minutes in the half to take a 17-14 lead. In the second half we controlled the game but did not score, but with less than two minutes to play, with our starting center injured, a bad snap on a punt was recovered by Washington on our 19. Our defense threw the Washington quarterback for losses to our 41-yard-line in three plays. Washington was out of field goal range, and we then took over when a fourth down draw play was stopped for no gain. We held on to win 17-14.

Our next game was with Florida State at Tallahassee. On our third offensive play, Terry Southall, our quarterback, was sacked and broke his leg on a late hit. Our defense played a great game and held Florida to two first downs rushing, but their wide receiver, Weatherall, made a fine run on a pass play with the help of an official unintentionally shielding our safety to score the winning touchdown and edge us 9-7.

One of our players told me that Greg Pipes went to Mike Bourland after the game and said, "Mike, you said we couldn't lose."

Of course, the thing Mike could not anticipate was Terry Southall breaking his leg. Unfortunately, our back-up quarterback, Mike Marshall, just could not make the plays to move our offense with any consistency.

Our game with Arkansas the next week in Waco was a disaster. We had six interceptions and lost a fumble and were beaten 38-7.

Our bubble had burst. The only thing we could do was to re-group and try again. We made a great comeback the following week, as Kenny Stockdale at quarterback had the game of his life, and we defeated the Aggies at College Station 31-0. But then we lost to TCU, Texas, and Texas Tech. We ended the season with wins over SMU and Rice for a 5-5 season.

Mike Bourland had our team believing we could win a championship. We may have without the best quarterback in the Southwest Conference breaking a leg The unfortunate thing is that we only had one quarterback with the ability to be a consistent winner.

Mike Bourland was a Consensus All-Southwest Conference guard. He played well all year and was one of the best leaders I ever coached. Mike never missed a game or practice with an injury. He started 31 straight games for Baylor.

Mike attended Baylor Law School and is now a successful lawyer in Fort Worth. Football meant a lot to Mike and still does. He wrote, "College football's meaning is not past tense to me. It still means very much to me. College football is an activity in which very few are privileged to participate. I have encouraged my children to participate in organized athletics at whatever level they have the ability because it is an experience unlike any other experiences with which they will be involved. I have effectively competed in academic life, in military environment, and now in professional life. The emotional rewards of effectively competing in intercollegiate athletics are dissimilar from any other experience with which I have been involved."

Mike Bourland continues to be an active leader in his church and in the Fellowship of Christian Athletes. His attendance at an FCA conference in Estes Park had a lasting effect on his life.

Mickey Kennedy, Guard

During my 43-year career, I had the opportunity to coach or represent as athletic director an impressive number of athletes who were excellent students. Probably the one with the highest academic average was Mickey Kennedy, who had a 3.91 average of a possible 4.0 average in his four years as a scholarship athlete at Baylor. He graduated with the highest grade point average of all male students in his graduating class and was salutatorian of his class.

Mickey was a history major. For the last five semesters at Baylor, Mickey had a straight-A (or 4.0 average). He was awarded a $1,000 NCAA scholarship for graduate study, and of all the athletes in each NCAA district awarded such a scholarship Mickey had the highest grade point average. He also received a Woodrow Wilson Graduate Fellowship, a scholarship awarded to students with unusual promise for graduate study. The Woodrow Wilson Fellowship was open to all college graduates rather than only NCAA student athletes.

Mickey played football at Waco High School in Waco, where Baylor is located. He was an excellent high school football player. He was a 6'0, 195-pound guard in high school and was selected on the Wigwam High School All-American Team in 1960. Mickey was elected mayor of Waco High School and was an honor graduate.

He wasn't very impressive as a freshman in 1961. He was not a starting guard on the freshman team. Mickey said he became disillusioned with football and buried himself in his books. He was redshirted as a sophomore in 1962 and was used sparingly as a reserve guard in 1963.

Mickey became a starter as an offensive guard in 1964. Instead of getting bigger and stronger, he lost weight in college. As senior, he weighed between 180 and 185 pounds. I have no vivid recollections of how he played on offense, but our record for our first six games was two wins and four losses. I don't think Mickey should get any particular blame, as the record was the result of a team effort.

After our sixth game with TCU, we made some changes in our starting lineup. One of the changes was to start Mickey Kennedy at defensive left guard. He lined up on the opponent offensive right guard.

Mickey had one great asset as a defensive player. He ended up where the football was and made the tackle. In the last four games as defensive guard (in today's terminology, Mickey's position would be defensive tackle) he averaged at least 12 tackles per game. Believe me, that's a lot of tackles for a down lineman to make in a game.

Mickey's technique was different from any lineman I've ever coached. Somehow or other he would slip the block of the offensive guard without making hard contact and go directly to the football. He didn't have good speed, but he was quick, and it seemed to be very difficult for the offensive lineman to make solid contact with him. I don't know, as a defensive player, if he ever overpowered anyone, but his style was very effective. I suspect Mickey would make a bit of a lateral movement so that the blocker's power directed at Mickey's original position would be lost. Mickey would then react to the ball with very little contact with the blocker. I've seen defensive linemen who were so intent on their personal battle with the blocker they didn't seem to be able to separate from the blocker and react to the ball carrier.

We played Texas in Waco in 1964. It was the game where we had two long touchdown drives in the fourth quarter to take a 14-13 lead. Then Texas received a questionable call when George Sauer, Jr., was tackled on a third and long situation at the sidelines, where the fathers of our players were standing for "Dad's Day." As Sauer appeared to catch the ball, he dropped it as the ball fell among our players' fathers. The official did not have a good view of the play and called it a completed pass for a first down inside of our 30-yard-line. On the next play, Sauer scored on a "go" pattern behind our safety to give the Longhorns a 20-14 victory.

I remember watching the film of the Texas game and admiring the play of Mickey Kennedy. He made tackles on plays at him, plays to his inside, and plays to his outside. On one play the blocker did make solid contact and knocked Mickey flat. Mickey recovered quickly, got up, and made the tackle. Mickey played only four games as a defensive player. He was credited with 14 tackles in the SMU game, which we won, and with 16 tackles in the Rice game, another we won. I'm not sure how many tackles he was credited with against Texas or in our victory over Kentucky, although, from my impression of the Texas game, he made at least a dozen tackles.

Our record with Mickey on defense was three victories and one loss (as the result of a questionable call by an official). If Mickey had played ten games on defense as he played in the last four games, he would have been selected on the All-Conference team. And, if we had won the same percentage of games as we did with Mickey on defense, we could have been playing in a bowl game and Mickey might have made All-American.

Mickey had another year of eligibility, but he elected to go ahead and graduate and get on with his graduate study at Tulane University.

Mickey was selected as "Baylor's Outstanding Lineman for 1964" and, to the surprise of no one, was chosen Academic All-Southwest Conference. Mickey says his most memorable experience was his final game against Rice. He made a tackle on a punt and caused a fumble. Robert Christian, who was on our punt cover team, recovered the fumble. We overcame a Rice lead of 20-12 to win 27-20.

Mickey earned a Ph.D. at Tulane University and since then has taught history at a small liberal arts college, Winthrop University, in South Carolina. He has been chairman of the History Department for three years. His areas of expertise are the French Revolution, early modern Europe, and ancient and medieval Europe. Mickey has authored three books on the Jacobin Clubs in the French Revolution and is currently working on a fourth. *Choice Magazine* selected the *Jacobin Clubs in the French Revolution: The Middle Years* (Princeton University Press, 1988) for its list of "Outstanding Academic Books for 1988." Mickey has written a couple of dozen other publications and/or articles.

Mickey has received the Phi Kappa Phi Excellence in Teaching Award three times and was named Winthrop University Distinguished Professor in 1981.

In a recent letter Mickey wrote:

> Football meant a great deal to me. I shall never forget the excitement of the games. The great comeback victory against Texas Tech in 1963 and the controversial loss to Texas in 1964 stand out as vividly in my mind as though they happened last year.
>
> Football also helped me further my education. My family had very little money and I would have had a difficult time making it through Baylor University without a scholarship.
>
> Whether football "built character," as the old cliche goes, I will not venture to say. I do know this, it did not hurt. The envi-

ronment at Baylor was very good. My teammates were a remark-
ably fine aggregation of young men. I do not believe there was a
bad person among them; and as you will recall, we had a higher
grade point average than the student body at large. One of my
roommates [Robert Mangum] became a dentist, another [Ron-
nie Wilson] a lawyer. Joe Gerald, my best friend, became a doctor. I shall always cherish the years I spent with them.

My coaches were good role models for me. Two, above all,
stand out in my memory as models of honor and integrity. I
cannot imagine either one doing anything underhanded, or
bending the rules, to win. I am speaking of you, of course, and of
Carl Price, the head football coach at Waco High and former
athletic director of the Waco Public Schools.

Mickey Kennedy was more than a good student — he has become a distinguished teacher and scholar. Mickey used his smarts
also to become a very good and effective football player with a very
positive feeling about his football experiences.

James Ingram, Wide Receiver

James Ingram was an excellent high school athlete in Odessa,
Texas. He played baseball and football, as a quarterback and one of
the best high school baseball pitchers in Texas.

Hayden Fry, who was Ingram's high school football coach
through his junior year, became our defensive secondary coach at
Baylor and recruited James Ingram. Texas had the best baseball program in the Southwest Conference, and they were very interested in
Ingram as a pitcher. Odessa went to the state high school playoffs in
baseball on the strength of Ingram's pitching. However, James
threw his arm out in the 1960 high school baseball tournament.

Hayden Fry signed him to a football scholarship at Baylor.
Even though we felt he might not be able to play quarterback due to
his arm injury, we felt he was a good athlete and we could find a
place for him to play.

When James Ingram came to Baylor, he planned to major in
religion and study for the ministry. He continued to pursue this goal
until his senior year.

With the arm problems Ingram had experienced in baseball, we changed him to a wide receiver. James Ingram did not have good speed for a wide receiver, but he was an excellent athlete and an outstanding competitor, especially in clutch situations. Ingram ran very precise patterns. He knew how to explode off the breaking point and separate from the defender. He had excellent hands and very seldom dropped a pass.

James was 6'0 and 185 pounds. There were three games in his career where he made the winning catch in the last few minutes of the game. The first was against the University of Pittsburgh at Pittsburgh in 1961. We fell behind 13-3 at halftime. Ronnie Stanley threw a touchdown pass to Bobby Lane to narrow the margin to 13-9. The Bears were able to get the ball back and drove to the 12-yard-line, where it was fourth and 12 with only a couple of minutes left. The fourth-down play meant a win or loss.

Stanley rolled out to the right and had to scramble away from two tacklers and then threw to Ingram, who was a wide receiver on the left side. James had crossed the end zone to the right sideline. Ingram came back toward the goal line and made a Raymond Berry-type catch as he kept both feet in-bounds and reached outside the boundary line to make the catch. It gave us a 16-13 victory.

The second game was against Texas Tech in 1963. Tech led 17-9 with six minutes left in the game. We drove 65 yards for a touchdown, with Trull passing to Ingram to close the margin 17-15. The Baylor defense held and began a drive from our 17. The drive ended with Trull passing to Ingram in the end zone in the final minute for a 21-17 victory.

The third game was against LSU in the Bluebonnet Bowl. LSU led 7-0 as the fourth quarter began. Baylor had two long drives that ended with touchdowns on Trull-to-Ingram passes to give Baylor a 14-7 victory. James Ingram caught 11 passes that day for 163 yards, a Bluebonnet Bowl record which still stood when the Bluebonnet Bowl went out of business in 1990.

Lawrence Elkins had set a new NCAA record for passes caught in a single season with 70 catches. LSU concentrated on double covering Elkins, who still managed to catch seven passes for 66 yards.

In addition, James Ingram made many other critical catches on third down and long yardage during his career to keep our offensive drives alive.

James told me that he knew Trull was going to look for Elkins first and that he understood why. Elkins had more speed than Ingram and had proven himself as a great receiver in his career at Baylor. Both Ingram and Elkins were seniors. Ingram said, "I'm going to concentrate on getting open in the event Elkins is covered, so that Don will have another receiver to look for."

That's what happened in two of our greatest victories in 1963. Ingram was open when Trull looked his way and when there was a desperate need to complete a pass. James Ingram ended the season with 51 catches, counting his 11 catches in the Bluebonnet Bowl game. His six touchdown catches made a great contribution to an outstanding season for Baylor.

One other asset James Ingram had was that he was probably our best down-field blocker from his wide receiver position. Ingram was without fear as a football player.

James Ingram was another very handsome young man who continued to improve every year he was in school. He was signed as a free agent by the Houston Oilers. Despite his lack of speed, Ingram impressed the Oiler coaches. They did not have him on the active roster but did keep him on the scout squad during the season.

At one point after his graduation, James went to Japan on a religious mission. He came back with a serious disease which almost cost him his life. He lost from 185 pounds down to about 125. He finally recovered and began to enjoy good health again.

James Ingram decided he would not go into the ministry. Instead, he attended Baylor Law School and is now a successful, hard-working attorney in San Antonio, Texas.

Since writing this piece on James Ingram, the illness he had when he came back from Japan has reoccurred. His condition is serious, but his wife and family are optimistic about his recovery.

CHAPTER 23

1969–73

PITTSBURGH STEELERS AND THE UNIVERSITY OF SOUTH CAROLINA GAMECOCKS

It was a strange feeling for me after working night and day for 10 years as an athletic director and head football coach not to have a job. I was still a relatively young man at 46 years old. Coaching was in my blood and I wanted to continue as a football coach.

Gil Brandt, who was the head of talent scouting for the Dallas Cowboys, offered me a temporary job scouting for the Cowboys. I worked at it for a little over a month in late December and January.

At that time the pro draft was held in January of 1969. After the draft each scout was assigned a couple of free agents to sign. On the night of the draft I flew to Houston and rented a car and drove northeast about 50 miles to Prairie View College, which was a predominantly black small college located in the countryside about 10 miles from Hempstead, Texas. I was given the job of signing a 250-pound tight end to a Dallas contract. I had a difficult time finding him. I finally convinced some of his friends that I wanted to sign him to a contract to play for the Cowboys, and I was able to locate him.

He really wasn't sure about me. He told me he had already been drafted. I told him he was wrong. He had not been drafted and I was giving him an opportunity to play with the Dallas Cowboys. I couldn't convince him so I called the *Houston Chronicle* sports de-

265

partment, and one of the sportswriters checked the list of all the players who had been drafted and told him he wasn't on the list. He still wasn't sure he wanted to sign. By that time it was around midnight. I told him I was going to spend the night at a motel in Hempstead, but I would be back at 7:00 A.M. the next morning. If he wasn't ready to sign then, I would have to return to Dallas. I told him it might be his last opportunity to sign a contract with a professional football team.

I came back at 7:00 A.M. and signed him to a Dallas contract. The Cowboys gave him a small bonus for signing. He was a fine-looking athlete, but he didn't make the squad.

I also went to Norman, Oklahoma, and signed a free agent who played for Oklahoma. I visited a number of colleges and universities, primarily in the Southeast and West. I spent several days in Tampa, where Bear Bryant was coaching an all-star football team. We became good friends.

When Gil Brandt offered me a permanent job, I thanked him but told him I still wanted to coach. I became friends with Tom Landry and his assistant coaches. There was no question but that Tom Landry was the boss and called the shots. He was and still is a man of high quality.

Along about the first of February I had a call from Walt Hackett, who had coached with me at Baylor. He had taken a job as defensive line coach with Chuck Noll, who had just been hired as head coach of the Pittsburgh Steelers. Chuck called me and offered me a job as offensive backfield coach with the Steelers, which I accepted.

The Steeler office was in the Roosevelt Hotel in downtown Pittsburgh. It was only a couple of blocks from where the Allegheny and the Monongahela rivers joined to form the Ohio River.

Art Rooney, Sr., was president and chief executive officer of the Steelers. His son, Dan, was the executive vice-president and ran the business end of the Steelers. Art Rooney, Jr., headed up the talent scouting department. The Steeler football office was on the fifth floor of the Roosevelt Hotel. Bob Frye, who had played with the Los Angeles Rams for several years, was the offensive line coach. Bob had played at Kentucky under Bear Bryant. Max Coley coached the receivers and quarterbacks. Charley Sumner, who was an outstanding defensive back for the Chicago Bears, was the defensive secondary coach. Charley had previously coached with the Oakland Raiders. There was a feeling of friendship and mutual respect among the assistant coaches.

The year was 1969, Chuck Noll's first year as a head football coach. Chuck was a bright person and a very knowledgeable football coach. However, in that first year he wanted to coach every player and position on the team. Except for Walt Hackett, who had coached with Chuck with the San Diego Chargers, he delegated little responsibility to other assistant coaches. As a first-year head coach, Chuck had not matured to the point where doubtful intelligence replaced cocksure ignorance. We won our first game of the season in Pittsburgh but then lost 13 games in succession.

There is no question about Chuck Noll being an excellent coach. A coach doesn't win four Super Bowl championships without being a good coach.

Looking back, I don't think I did a very good job coaching with the Steelers. I was coaching the running backs, which is a position segment that appeals to me the least. I'm not sure that the other assistant coaches did an unusually good job either. It was partly due to the fact that none of them were ever given much responsibility. As a result all of them either voluntarily left or were fired by Chuck within two years after I left, except Walt Hackett, who died of a ruptured aorta while on a scouting trip in the off-season. Walt Hackett was a great friend, as well as an excellent coach.

I'm sure Chuck Noll delegated more responsibility to his assistants in the years after I left. I'm not sure he ever reached the point of doubtful intelligence, as he had supreme confidence in his own judgments. Players who were Noll's teammates with the Cleveland Browns gave him the nickname of "Pope" because he was never wrong.

One of the brightest highlights of our 1969 season was the play of Joe Greene at defensive tackle. He was the Steelers' number-one draft choice for 1969, and was destined to become one of the best to ever play the game.

Football is never any fun when you are losing, but the year was kind of like a refresher course for me. I had an opportunity to watch a lot of football film of every team in professional football and get a close look at what they were doing offensively and defensively. I was surprised how little difference there was from the 1957 and 1958 season when I coached with the Colts. We also looked at a lot of college films in evaluating college players we were considering for the draft.

Since the Steelers had the worst record in professional football, we had the number-one pick in the pro football draft. After we played our final game in New Orleans, Chuck Noll and I flew to Miami to scout the quarterbacks in the North South All-Star Shrine game in Miami. Terry Bradshaw was the quarterback for the South team.

It had been my responsibility to rate the college quarterbacks who were eligible for the NFL draft. I had Bradshaw rated number one by a wide margin. For some reason Chuck was not impressed with Bradshaw. However, when about half the teams in the NFL wanted to trade for our number-one draft choice so they could draft Bradshaw, Chuck began to reevaluate Terry. He and Art Rooney, Jr., decided to make Bradshaw the number-one draft choice. It was a wise choice. All Bradshaw did was lead the Steelers to four Super Bowl championships.

One evening Frances and I were in our family room on a cold winter night. There was about 10 inches of snow on the ground. The telephone rang, and it was a long distance call from Paul Dietzel, who was head football coach and athletic director at the University of South Carolina. He called to offer me a job as offensive coordinator for the University of South Carolina. I told him I would consider it and asked when he needed an answer. Paul replied, "How about tomorrow?"

While I was talking to Paul Dietzel, Frances could tell by my conversation that Paul Dietzel was offering me a job. She kept saying, "Take it, take it!" She didn't like Pittsburgh — the cold weather with almost constantly overcast skies in the winter, the hilly terrain, and the narrow roads. She was a southerner born and bred, and that's where she wanted to live.

One of our sons, Don, was a senior in Upper St. Clair High School and our other son, John Dixon III, was a freshman at Washington and Jefferson College in Washington, Pennsylvania. On one occasion, Dixon was due to come home from Washington and Jefferson for a visit. Frances decided to try and call Dixon when he didn't arrive as expected. We didn't have Dixon's phone number, so she called the long distance operator and said, "I want to call Dixon Bridgers at Washington and Jefferson College in Washington,

Pennsylvania." The operator could not understand her southern accent and told her to repeat her request about three times. Finally, with a sigh of relief, the operator said, "Oh, you wish to call Richard Nixon in Washington, D.C. on Pennsylvania Avenue."

Frances replied with resignation, "That's all right, operator, just cancel the call."

Roy Edwards, a sports columnist for the *Dallas Morning News,* was a good friend. Once when he called, I told him about Frances' experience of trying to call Dixon. He wrote a column with the heading, "The Magnolia Blossom Blooms Again."

The morning after Paul Dietzel's call, I went to Chuck Noll's office and told him about it. From his actions and response, I could tell Chuck didn't care whether I took the job in South Carolina or not. He didn't encourage me to take it nor did he encourage me to turn it down.

I walked from Chuck's office to the elevator to the first floor and asked to see Art Rooney, Sr. I told Mr. Rooney about the job offer, and told him I had decided to accept it. He said, "John, we certainly hate to see you leave. We are giving a 10 percent bonus to all the coaches, and we want you to share in the bonus also."

That's the first time I ever heard of a coach receiving a bonus ($2,000) when he told the boss he was quitting. Actually, it was the only bonus I ever received as a coach or athletic director, except when the Colts won the World Championship.

Art Rooney, Sr., was a prince of a person. I don't ever remember anyone saying anything bad about him. Almost every day he would come up to the coaches' office. He would chat and visit a few minutes and his parting words as he left our office were almost always, "I want to wish youse the best of luck."

For the most part, the South Carolina football teams struggled during the postwar years, although Warren Giese had a couple of 7-3 seasons and a 6-4 record in the late fifties. The state of South Carolina and particularly their alumni were eager to have a football program which could compete with the best in college football. In 1966 the university brought Paul Dietzel in as head football coach.

Dietzel had been very successful at LSU, where he had led them to a perfect 11-0 record in 1958. The LSU team was voted as national champions, and Paul Dietzel was selected as "Coach of the Year." He continued to have successful teams through 1966 with a

10-1 season, but decided to take the head coaching job with the Army football team at West Point. After four years at Army with limited success, South Carolina hired him as head coach and athletic director. South Carolina had high expectations of Paul Dietzel repeating his success at LSU. Paul had coached with some of the nation's outstanding coaches, such as Colonel Earl "Red" Blaik at Army, Sid Gilman at the University of Cincinnati and who later was head coach of the San Diego Chargers and Los Angeles Rams, and Paul "Bear" Bryant at the University of Kentucky in 1951 and 1952.

While South Carolina was unable to have the caliber of teams expected by their fans, Paul Dietzel made a great contribution to University of South Carolina football. Under his leadership South Carolina began to sell out their stadium for almost every game beginning in 1969, when they were undefeated in conference games and champions of the Atlantic Coast Conference with a 7-4 record. The success in fundraising by the Gamecock Club was surpassed by less than half a dozen universities in the country.

During his tenure as athletic director, the athletic facility for every sport was significantly improved. The basketball arena, completed in 1968, was one of the best in the nation at that time, with a beautiful coliseum that seated 12,401. Facilities for baseball, track and field, swimming, and tennis were greatly improved. Paul Dietzel was responsible for raising the money for the present football stadium, which ranks among the nation's best and seats 72,400. Dietzel was able to solicit a $3.5 million contribution from the estate of Mrs. Martha Williams Brice. The stadium is named the Williams-Brice Football Stadium.

South Carolina has had several excellent teams since Paul Dietzel left after the 1974 season, and each of the coaches who experienced success certainly owes a debt of gratitude to Paul Dietzel for the extraordinary facilities he either built, initiated, or had completed during his tenure.

Paul had a great deal of artistic talent. He was innovative and creative. He was very much involved in most of the facilities which were built. It no doubt took some of his concentration away from the football program. However, he continued to call the offensive plays during the games and without question was the man in charge.

Paul devoted a lot of time to coaching football, but I believe when he was not in staff or squad meetings or on the practice field, a lot of his thoughts were directed toward the stadium construction or other projects. As a result of other responsibilities other than football, I don't believe he was as effective with his play calling as he might otherwise have been.

I believe sometime in the near future South Carolina will come up with the big winner in football. The coach who accomplishes that goal should send a note of thanks to Paul Dietzel for the facilities which have been a decided plus when it comes to recruiting the kind of football players required for a highly successful football program. Also, a quality stadium can produce the revenue for a first-class athletic program.

In my first season at South Carolina in 1970, we set an all-time scoring record with 285 points and averaged 354 yards per game in total offense, another all-time record. Other all-time records were most yards passing (2,440 yards), most passes attempted (332), most passes completed (167), and most touchdown passes (17). The player most responsible for such impressive offensive numbers was Tommy Suggs, our quarterback. He threw for 2,030 yards and had 14 touchdown passes. He was able to produce those kinds of numbers with pass protection which was less than adequate. Suggs was sacked 22 times for a loss of 165 yards. He was a good scrambler and was able to avoid rushers and get his pass off for a completion. There were 10 times when forced to run he gained a total of 52 yards or average gain of 5.2 yards. He took a lot of hits after he released the ball, but he was tough and didn't allow a hard rush to interfere with his concentration.

Even though our scoring average of 26 points per game was impressive, we finished the season with a 4-6-1 record. We lost by two points to Tennessee, three points to Georgia Tech, four points to Duke, and six points to Maryland. Florida State and Georgia won by bigger margins. The schedule may have been the most difficult South Carolina ever played up to that time. The combined record of South Carolina teams of the past against nine of their eleven opponents (all except University of North Carolina and Virginia Tech) was 89 wins and 145 losses, or a winning percentage of 38%. Against the six teams to which they lost the record was 24 wins and 75 losses, or 24.2%.

Paul Dietzel was really never able to fully commit himself to a pro-type offense. Actually, I doubt if there was a coach on the staff except me who really believed you could win with a pro offense. It was still a few years before college teams began to win and contend for national championships with a pro offense, such as Brigham Young, University of Miami, and Florida State. His best years of coaching had been with the "Wing T," which featured the running game and play action passes. He also had experienced some success with the shotgun or spread offense. After Suggs graduated, we had a difficult time coming up with a consistent passing game. Paul continued to vacillate between a running game and play action passes: a drop back passing game with some play-action passes and running game with one or two wide receivers or a shotgun formation which was almost exclusive passing. All of these formations had moments of success and failure.

After I left after the 1972 season, Paul went to the "Veer Offense," which was a triple option running attack in which the quarterback handed off to a diving halfback, ran himself or pitched to a halfback running to the outside. With two wide receivers it was also a good passing formation. The reason for the change was mostly due to the presence of Jeff Grantz at quarterback. He was an excellent runner and ball handler, as well as a very good passer. The Gamecocks had a 7-4 record in 1973 but dropped to a 4-7 in 1974, which was Dietzel's final year at South Carolina.

I might add we had two very fine receivers at South Carolina in 1970. Jimmy Mitchell, a junior, who was about 5'10 and 152 pounds, caught 41 passes for 842 yards, seven touchdowns, and a two-point reception against Tennessee, which gave us a one-point lead with about four minutes left in the game. Unfortunately for us, Tennessee kicked a field goal in the last minute to win by two points. Jimmy was quick but not real fast. However, he had an amazing average of 20.5 yards per catch. When he learned how to release from the line of scrimmage and not be jammed or held up by the defenders, he became an excellent receiver and was a clutch player.

We had a tight end named Doug Hamrick. He had below average speed, but he had a knack for getting open and catching the football. Doug caught 38 passes for 418 yards and five touchdowns. He could make the tough catch when you had to have it.

In 1971 the Gamecocks had a 6-5 record. We won five of our first six games highlighted by a 24-7 win over Georgia Tech. The season ended with four losses in the last five games. Decisive losses were to Georgia, Tennessee, and Florida State, and then we lost to Clemson in the season final. Jimmy Mitchell had another excellent year with 47 receptions for 618 yards.

In 1972 the Gamecocks fell to 4-7. We lost the first three games to Virginia, Georgia Tech, and Mississippi. Our most satisfying win was over Florida State, after losing six years in a row to the Seminoles. Dobby Grossman had his best game of the year against Florida State. He completed 10 consecutive passes along with a couple of touchdown completions. However, a 7-6 loss to Clemson ended the season on a sour note. Bill Troup threw a 67-yard touchdown pass to Eddie Muldrow for our only score.

Bill Troup started in our opening game with Virginia in 1972. He completed 20 of 47 passes for 318 yards. Troup had a great arm and was about 6'4. In order to take advantage of his ability we had to have excellent pass protection, as Bill was not a good scrambler. Troup ended up being a starting quarterback for the Baltimore Colts one year, but his lack of mobility hurt him in professional football also. Mike Haggard, a wide receiver, had a good year with 46 catches for 639 yards and eight touchdowns, which ranks him second all-time for most touchdown catches in a season at South Carolina.

The primary reason Paul Dietzel was not any more successful as far as his won-lost record at South Carolina was due to the fact that recruiting of football players was not up to as high a standard as it needed to be. The evaluation of talent recruited by the assistant coaches left something to be desired. There were too many recruits who lacked real ability, speed, quickness, and the athletic talent for South Carolina to be a big winner.

I was the oldest assistant coach on the staff, and I'm pretty certain I spent more days on the road recruiting than any coach on the staff. I recruited a few players who could not play, but when Jim Carlin was in his first year as head coach, he took South Carolina to what is now the Citrus Bowl in Orlando. I went to the game. There were about 15 players still on the squad who I recruited. At least a dozen players had been starters at one time or another during the season. Their best player was Jeff Grantz, a quarterback who made second team Associated Press All-American. Bill Currier, a defensive back, was also outstanding. He played nine years as a defensive safety with the Houston Oilers, New England Patriots, and the New York Giants. I recruited both out of Maryland. Both were very bright and good students. Jeff was an outstanding ball handler and ran the triple option particularly well. He was an excellent passer too.

When I was athletic director at Florida State, I wanted to schedule home games with South Carolina. I made a special trip to Columbia to try to convince Jim Carlin, who succeeded Paul Dietzel as head coach and athletic director. Jim Carlin agreed to a home and home series. He said the main reason he agreed to play us was because I recruited more football players on his Citrus Bowl team than any recruiter.

Paul Dietzel paid me the best compliment I ever received as a football recruiter. He said I was the best recruiter with whom he has ever been associated. I'm not sure I was that good, but I worked hard at it and I never made an illegal offer.

At LSU, Paul and his staff could recruit the best players in Louisiana plus three or four from Texas and Arkansas and compete with anyone. It was a different story in South Carolina. The best players were divided between South Carolina and Clemson, and there just weren't enough good players to make both teams big winners. The integration of blacks and other minorities may well have changed this assessment. There was only one black player in 1970. South Carolina lacked the football tradition to recruit well in the neighboring states, although they could get some good ones from Florida and every now and then from a neighboring state. In building a football program South Carolina had to recruit well in Maryland, New York, New Jersey, and other large population areas where there were not many universities with great traditions in football.

I had the same problem when I was at Baylor of not doing a good job of evaluating the players we recruited. If I had to do it over again, I would have each recruit evaluated by the recruiting coordinator and the position coach and they would have to approve a scholarship offer. The coach who recruited the area, the position coach, and the recruiting coordinator would have the responsibility of recruiting the player. The recruiting coordinator would not have an assigned area but would have the responsibility of approving every player we offered a scholarship and helping to recruit all of those approved for scholarships.

Back in January of 1972, I told Paul that the fall of 1972 would be my final year as a coach on his staff. I turned 50 in January and I thought that was too old to be an assistant coach. I told him I was going to get a head football coaching job, an athletic director's job, and if I weren't successful locating either of those two positions, I would just have to go to work. I talked to one of the largest real estate developers in South Carolina, and he said that I could have a job with him. However, I was fortunate to get the job as athletic director at Florida State, so I didn't have to go to work.

Paul Dietzel's last job was as athletic director at LSU, but unfortunately he had a president who did not appreciate his talents and dismissed him for some exaggerated charges. I strongly believe Paul Dietzel is and was an honest man and would not intentionally violate any institutional or NCAA rules. It was Paul Dietzel who achieved more success than any coach in LSU history and who won a national championship, two Southeastern Conference championships, and his teams participated in two Sugar Bowls and one Orange Bowl game.

At South Carolina Paul Dietzel did a lot of great things, but his downfall as far as won-lost record was overall recruiting and the failure to delegate more responsibilities to assistant coaches. Of course, he may have had good reasons not to delegate more responsibilities, but I think he took too much on himself when he had a heavy burden. Another contribution to a mediocre record was perhaps the toughest schedules a South Carolina coach ever faced during Paul Dietzel's nine years as head coach.

As is generally true in all jobs a person has had, I made some mistakes that I would do differently if I had a chance to do it over again. I'm sure the same is true for Paul Dietzel. Paul had a great career and served LSU and the University of South Carolina very well. He left his mark in a big and good way on both institutions.

Tommy Suggs — A Remarkable Quarterback

Tommy Suggs looked less like a quarterback than any college quarterback I can remember. He was listed in the program at 5'9, but I believe he would have to stretch to reach 5'8. His weight was listed at 186. He really looked more like a pulling guard on a high school football team.

All he did was perform, and he did that throughout his high school career and as a three-year starter at quarterback at South Carolina in 1968, 1969, and 1970. (Freshmen were not eligible when he was a freshman.)

My first contact with him was at South Carolina in 1970, when I joined the University of South Carolina football staff and installed a pro-style drop back passing game. South Carolina had been using almost exclusively a play-action passing attack. We retained the play action passes but added the drop back series to give more diversity. Those who believe that a quarterback must be 6'0 or more to perform adequately at quarterback in a drop back passing offense should have seen Tommy Suggs in action. It's always been my conviction that quarterbacks do not throw over the big 6'4 or more linemen, they throw between them. The only type pass a short quarterback can throw over them is the deep pattern where the quarterback hangs the ball high and allows the receiver to run under it.

Tommy had been a very successful passer in his sophomore and junior years. As a junior, he led the Gamecocks to their only Atlantic Coast Conference championship as they finished the season undefeated in conference games. Tommy set a South Carolina record for passing accuracy in 1969, when he completed 109 of 196 passes for a completion percentage of 55.6%.

A coach couldn't ask for a quarterback to have a better mental attitude than Tommy Suggs; he was calm, confident, and always under control. He could take a hard rush and many times scramble to good yardage running or until he found an open receiver. He was tough and was seldom hurt. If he did suffer a sprained joint or bad bruise, he recovered quickly.

Tommy had quick feet and good balance. In high school he played four sports — football, basketball, baseball, and ran track on the relay teams. As a senior he was All-State in football and basketball and All-Conference in baseball. He ran on the state championship 880 relay and medley relay teams. In addition, he had the highest scholastic average in his senior class, with a 96.7 average.

When a coach talked to Tommy, he gave his full attention and listened intently. He made you feel that what you said was important, and he would do his very best to prove it.

His greatest attribute as a passer was his uncanny accuracy on deep passes.

We had three long or deep passes in our offense:

1. *The Go Pattern* — The receiver would fake an outside or inside break with a four-step break to the outside plus a look at the

quarterback or a three-step break to the inside with a look to the quarterback and then break down-field with a slight fade to outside of the defender. The passer's rule was if the receiver got even with the defender or behind him, he should hang the ball high where the receiver could run under it.

2. *The Post Pattern* — The receiver would run at the defender with a three-step weave in which he would fade outside the first three steps, fade inside the next three steps, and then toward the deep defender the next three steps, which put him about 12 yards deep, then break at approximately a 45-degree angle to the inside looking for the ball over his inside shoulder. The weave was done at about 90% full speed. We also used a three-step weave as an approach on the go pattern and all the patterns in our offense. The two big advantages were that it helped the receiver get inside position on an inside pattern and outside position on a pattern to the outside. On the weave the quarterback knows exactly when the receiver will break deep. On the post pattern if the receiver breaks past the defender, passer hangs ball and lets him run under it. If there is a deep safety who is deeper than receiver, the receiver flattens his pattern and runs underneath the safety. On the underneath break, the quarterback will drill the ball to the receiver and only throw if he can get the ball to the receiver before the defender can reach it.

3. *The Corner Pattern* — Receiver should not split too wide where he will not be out of bounds on his corner break. He runs the same approach as the post, but as he breaks inside on the post pattern he looks and then breaks outside to the corner of the end zone. Normally, the quarterback will drill the ball on the corner pattern as the receiver will not usually break clean deep behind the outside defender. If the receiver is wide open, the quarterback will arch the ball more, which gives the receiver the opportunity to adjust to the ball. The closer the coverage, the more the passer will drill the ball.

In 1970 Tommy Suggs completed 48.2% of the three patterns described above. During the season we featured the deep patterns and the quick passes — slant, quick out, and the slant and out.

Contrary to what most people believe, the deep passes take less time to throw than the 12- to 15-yard possession passes, such as the comeback, square in, and inside curl patterns. The reason is the quarterback must delay to make sure he has a throwing lane between the short defenders. One of the jobs I had with the Steelers was to time the quarterbacks during passing drills from the time they received the snap from center to the time they released the ball.

The amount of time for deep patterns is 2.5- 3.0 seconds, while the curl and comeback patterns take 3.2 to 3.6 seconds. Jimmy Mitchell was Sugg's primary receiver on deep patterns, which resulted in Mitchell's average of 20.5 yards per catch.

When we called the "go" patterns, the tight end ran a post while both wide receivers ran the go. Just before the snap and while he was dropping back, the passer determined which wide receiver he would throw the "go" pattern to. The outlet receiver was the tight end. We normally saw a three-deep zone or two-deep safeties with cornerbacks playing a couple of yards off and outside the wide receivers. If it was a three-deep, we would hit the tight end between the safety and the cornerback or the wide receiver away from a safety. With two-deep safeties the quarterback would key the two safeties and throw to the receiver not covered by a safety, such as the tight end if both safeties went deep. The safety's rule is deep as the deepest receiver, and if they followed that rule, there was a lot of room underneath the safety. I kept a record of each pattern we ran and the result, but in over 20 years and five moves a lot of my papers were lost. I did remember Sugg's completion percentage on deep passes as the best I've ever experienced.

Tommy Suggs received many honors. He was awarded the Steve Wadiak Trophy as the most valuable player in 1970. He played in the Blue-Gray All-Star game, leading the South team to victory, and was voted the most valuable player in the game. When Tommy graduated, he held 15 South Carolina football seasonal, individual, and game records.

Tommy was inducted into the State of South Carolina Hall of Fame in 1983 and the University of South Carolina Hall of Fame in 1989. He was in numerous charitable and community organizations after his graduation from college, such as leadership positions in United Way, American Cancer Society, University of South Carolina Alumni Association, Multiple Sclerosis, president of Chamber of Commerce, and others.

Tommy graduated with a degree in business administration. He also graduated from the Banking School of the South at Louisiana

State University and the National Commercial Lending Graduate School at the University of Oklahoma.

He is presently executive vice-president and chief banking officer for South Carolina Federal Corporation in Columbia, South Carolina.

There were times when Tommy's teammates didn't give him the pass protection or his defensive teammates weren't able to keep a lead after he had led the offense to a score, but I never heard him make a critical remark about a teammate. He had a positive frame of mind and was always ready to come back and help produce touchdowns if he could possibly do so.

Tommy Suggs was and is a truly outstanding person who continues to amaze people with his accomplishments.

Jackie Brown, Wide Receiver

Jackie Brown was the first black football player to play football at the University of South Carolina. He came to the university as a freshman in the fall in 1969 on a partial baseball scholarship, and lettered in the spring of 1970 as an infielder and outfielder. I never saw him play baseball, but the scouting report I received was that he had trouble hitting the curve ball.

Bobby Richardson, who was an outstanding second baseman for the New York Yankees, was the South Carolina baseball coach. Bobby was a great baseball player and an outstanding human being.

Evidently, Jackie Brown did not have much confidence in his baseball future at South Carolina as he joined our football squad during the last two weeks of spring football practice. He was a quarterback in high school, but we changed him to a wide receiver. We had two good wide receivers in Jimmy Mitchell and Mike Haggard, but used them as flankers while we used our split end sometimes as a tight end opposite the tight end on the strong side of the formation. Neither Haggard nor Mitchell had the physical requirements to play as a tight end. We used them exclusively as wide receivers.

Jackie Brown was about 5'11 and 175 to 180 pounds. He was an excellent athlete with good speed but not great speed. He had excellent quickness and was built strongly. He did a good job as a blocker when we called our two tight end formation.

With only two weeks of practice in the spring, at a position he had never played before, he became our starting split end for the 1970 season. Jackie was very bright and gave his best effort in whatever he was asked to do. He ran excellent patterns, but he didn't have the confidence in his catching ability as I hoped he would. He was just a little tense and felt the pressure of being a starter with only two weeks of practice in the spring and about three weeks before the first game in the fall.

Here was a young player who was not recruited as a football player and with only a little over four weeks of practice since high school was scheduled to start against one of the best football teams in the South. Georgia Tech went to a bowl game and had a 9-3 record during the 1970 season, which was the season that Jackie Brown played his first year of football at South Carolina. Truthfully, we probably expected more from Jackie than we should have.

Jackie caught 12 passes in 1970 for 185 yards and one touchdown. His biggest catch was against Tennessee. We were driving the ball with our running game. We sent in a pass play where we faked a running play we had been using on the drive and had Jackie fake an inside pattern and run a "go" pattern. He got behind the defensive back, and Suggs hit him perfectly. Jackie was finally run down inside the Georgia Tech 10-yard-line.

We scored a couple of plays later to narrow Tennessee's lead to one point. We went for the two-point conversion, and Suggs completed a pass to Mitchell to give us an 11-10 lead. Tennessee came back and scored, but Suggs then hit Mitchell for a 61-yard touchdown pass. However, we could not hold the lead. Tennessee kicked a field goal with 15 seconds left to win 20-18.

Jackie showed steady improvement in 1971 and 1972. He caught 25 passes in 1971 for 350 yards and 32 passes in 1972 for 436 yards. Through the 1971 football season Jackie Brown ranked 14th in all-time passing receiving in career receptions with 69 receptions for 971 yards and two touchdowns. In our 1972 game against Virginia he had a career high of nine catches for 140 yards.

Jackie Brown was a very fine young man by any standard you might wish to measure him. He was well liked by his teammates. He was elected president of the Carolina Fellowship of Christian Athletes Chapter. Jackie majored in history and was studying to be a minister. He was a good student and graduated with a BA degree in 1973. His father was a minister in Jonesville, North Carolina.

Jackie realized his goal of becoming a minister and pastored a large church in North Carolina. Jackie unfortunately became ill with cancer and died in his early forties.

Jackie Brown set an excellent example for the many black athletes who followed him as Gamecock football players. He was our only black player in 1970, but black players participated in football in increasing numbers. At the present nearly 70% of the South Carolina football squad is made up of black players.

It was my privilege to coach the first black player at three different universities. Dr. Ernie Bates, who is now a brain surgeon in San Francisco, was the first black player at Johns Hopkins University in 1956. John Westbrook was the first black player at Baylor University when I was head coach there in 1966. He was also the first black player to participate in a Southwest Conference game, against Syracuse in 1966.

I have nothing but good memories of Jackie Brown. I was very interested in him being a successful football player and student at the University of South Carolina. He fulfilled my hopes and expectations of him in every way that really counted. He showed class as a person, and I'm sure he was an excellent servant of God as a minister.

CHAPTER 24

1973–80

FLORIDA STATE UNIVERSITY:
THE BUILDING OF A DYNASTY

I had turned 50 in January of 1972, while working as an assistant coach at the University of South Carolina. I told Paul Dietzel, who was head coach and athletic director, that the 1972 season would be my last season as an assistant coach and that I would try to find a job as a head football coach or as an athletic director. If I failed to find one of those two positions, I was prepared to go to work as a real estate salesman for Tom Jenkins Realty in Columbia, South Carolina.

When December, January, and February passed by, I had about given up hope of getting a head football coaching job. Coaches are usually fired in November or December and hired in December or January, but sometimes as late as February.

Along about March 1 the athletic director's job at Florida State opened up. Clay Stapleton, who was athletic director, took a job as athletic director at Vanderbilt University. I had known Clay for several years, and for some reason he was never happy at Florida State.

I also knew Larry Jones, the football coach at Florida State. Larry had coached a number of years with Paul Dietzel, first at LSU, then at Army, and at South Carolina before getting the Florida State head football job. He was an excellent football coach and a real gentleman. His Florida State team had lost their final game to South Carolina 21-17 with a Peach Bowl bid at stake. He ended up with a 7-4 season after going 8-3 in 1971.

I was invited to interview for the Florida State athletic director's position. It was my last opportunity to continue in intercollegiate athletics. I really wanted the job. Back in the early sixties, Vaughn Mancha was the athletic director at Florida State and called me at Baylor. He offered me the head football coaching position. Since I had about three or four years left on my contract at Baylor, I turned it down. I felt a loyalty to stay at Baylor. I'm not sure it was a good decision, as Florida State has proven to be a great place to coach football or any sport for that matter. Vaughn and I were teammates in high school. Vaughn was a Consensus All-American center and linebacker at the University of Alabama in 1945.

During my visit to Florida State, my last appointment was an interview with President Stan Marshall. I thought it went pretty well, but when we finished, Dr. Marshall said there was another candidate he wanted to interview and that he would be in touch with me later. When I got back to the motel, I was a little discouraged. I had a feeling if I left Tallahassee without a job offer that I would not be offered the job.

I decided to take a risk. I called Dr. Marshall and told him I would like to come by his office for a few minutes before I left town. Dr. Marshall agreed to see me.

I don't remember my exact words, but I said something like this, "Dr. Marshall, I'm the best qualified person you can hire as athletic director at Florida State. I've had ten years experience as an athletic director at the major college level. A young and growing athletic program like Florida State needs someone who can raise money, and I can raise money. I know most of the athletic directors and football coaches at the major colleges in the country. I can get the kind of home and home schedule you need to finance a major college athletic program. More college football games are scheduled on the basis of friendship than for any other reason. I know because I scheduled games for Baylor that have been or will be played up to ten years after I left Baylor. Dr. Marshall, I really want to be the athletic director at Florida State."

Dr. Marshall said, "You've got the job, John."

Believe it or not, I did all the things I told Dr. Marshall I could do — but there were a lot of ups and downs along the way.

I went to work in April of 1973 at Florida State. Our athletic offices may have been among the most rundown and shabbiest offices among major colleges in the country. However, the state of our offices was not a major concern. We needed to get an attractive home and home football schedule and not just depend on road games with major teams in big stadiums to finance our athletic program. We also needed to raise money and find a way to get people to buy tickets for our home football games.

Our full-time administrative staff was very streamlined, to say the least. Counting my secretary, Dee Frye, as an administrator, we had six full-time employees including myself, and a secretarial staff. They included a business manager and budget director, Claude Thigpen, an assistant athletic director, Bill Rowe, a ticket manager, Marian Lee, and a sports information director, Lonnie Burt. Later we hired a full-time academic adviser and a full-time bookkeeper, Patty Marker. In a recent Florida State football brochure, I counted 21 full-time administrators (not counting the athletic director or any secretaries). Dee Frye, my secretary, had served almost every athletic director since Florida State became coed in 1947. She was enormously efficient and tough-minded. She could give orders with the authority and efficiency of a first sergeant in the Marines. Dee knew more people in Tallahassee and more about the coaches and Athletic Department employees than anyone in Tallahassee. She was very helpful. In addition she was an outstanding secretary. She could almost play Beethoven's "Moonlight Sonata" on her typewriter.

I brought Bill Rowe, who was defensive coordinator at University of South Carolina and a West Point graduate, to South Carolina as my assistant athletic director. He stayed a couple of years, but decided to return to his home in Pennsylvania and go into the antique business. Not many good things happened while Bill was at Florida State, but none of it was Bill's fault. I really didn't blame him when he resigned and moved back to Pennsylvania. Bill Rowe was a good man and did the best he could under very trying circumstances. Since we were having financial difficulties, we didn't replace him.

Claude Thigpen was the oldest employee in the Florida State Athletic Department. Claude was conscientious, loyal, hard working and the "salt of the earth" kind of person. What he lacked in educational background, he made up with hard work and a strong desire to please.

One other person I wish to mention as a special contributor was Charley Durbin, who filmed Florida State football practices and games. In addition, the Athletic Department owned a bus. I'm not sure of the capacity — perhaps 40 to 50. Charley was the bus driver and may have been one of the best anywhere. For example, he would leave with a full busload of the men's track team on Thursday afternoon and drive 14 hours to Champagne, Illinois, stopping only to service the bus or for the track team to eat a meal. The track team would compete on Friday and Saturday and Charley would leave after the track meet on Saturday and drive all night back to Tallahassee. He would arrive in Tallahassee early Sunday morning.

I remember asking him if he ever got sleepy on one of those long trips. He replied, "I know I have a job to do and going to sleep never occurs to me."

There's no telling how many dollars he saved the Athletic Department on travel and meal expenses. When you're operating on a shoestring budget, it means a lot.

There were two primary reasons which caused such a large deficit in 1973-74. First, Clay Stapleton, the previous athletic director, scheduled all home games in the afternoon. If you have ever been in Tallahassee about 2:00 P.M. in early September, you realize how hot it can get. There is no breeze, the temperature is in the nineties, and the humidity about as high. Sitting in those steel stands which radiate heat, you actually feel as if you will suffocate.

The second reason was a series of articles that came out in the *St. Petersburg Times* which were extremely disparaging to Coach Larry Jones and his staff. The articles were instigated by a few reactionary student writers with the school paper, *The Florida Flambeau*. It labeled the off-season conditioning program as inhumane in the demands and treatment of athletes. I investigated thoroughly the claims of the investigative reporter from St. Petersburg. The truth is the series of articles were a complete distortion of the truth. One example, the *St. Petersburg Times* claimed chicken wire was used to form a cage in which the athletes were forced to perform exhaustive drills. Actually, chicken wire was suspended by strings to a height of about four and a half feet, and the football players did agility drills by running under the chicken wire. It was designed to keep the athlete in a low, wide-based position (the same as a good lineman in football) as he performed the agility and conditioning drills. If his head touched the wire it would bounce up, but in no way did it provide harm or injury to those performing the drills.

There were few if any truthful statements in the series of articles, but they received nationwide attention.

President Stan Marshall asked the NCAA to investigate to determine if there were any violations of the NCAA rules. The NCAA report named two players who had voluntarily quit the squad, one about three or four years previously, and stated that the university had not followed the proper procedure in removing their names from the athletic scholarship list. The only other violation was that the coaches ran the players extra laps when they missed a conditioning session, which indicated the conditioning sessions were not voluntary.

As a result, Florida State was given one year's probation without sanctions. The probation penalty really hurt Larry Jones, head football coach. He felt the probation indicated to the media and to Florida State fans that Florida State was guilty of the charges made in the *St. Petersburg Times*. Larry Jones is one of the most honest and sincere persons I have ever known. I cannot imagine him having anything to do with a conditioning program which might endanger or hurt the participants in any way.

I'm not sure I have ever seen a coach more depressed than Larry Jones, and his depression lasted throughout the 1973 season. As a result of Larry's mental frame of mind and the fact that Florida State had about run out of good football players, the Seminoles were 0-11 for the 1973 season. The Florida State fans put a lot of pressure on President Marshall, and so Larry Jones was fired after winning 15 games his first two years.

Larry was hired as defensive coordinator at the University of Tennessee the next year and helped Tennessee to a great season and a Sugar Bowl victory. Larry Jones' defense was outstanding.

President Marshall appointed a committee of about 12 members, representing many constituents of the university, to select a new head football coach. Darrell Mudra was chosen. I had met Darrell when I was at Baylor. He was really a different kind of football coach. He had a Ph.D. in education with a major in psychology, which appealed to some of the faculty members on the committee.

Darrell hired his staff with great care. He believed in totally delegating coaching responsibilities to the assistant coaches. He was very intelligent, but he really wasn't very interested in the details of coaching football. He wanted his coaching staff to be dedicated to coaching their particular responsibilities. An area he greatly stressed was recruiting. He wasn't very interested in the academic standing of the recruits. By far his most important consideration was the athletic and football playing ability of the recruit. Darrell felt that academic counseling and advisement could assist and encourage even the poorest student-athlete so that he could maintain his eligibility. He had some good students, but almost half were very marginal.

Another area where he did a good job was the off-season conditioning program for football players. He made certain the players maintained a high level of conditioning during the off-season.

There's no question but that Florida State was short of good football players when Darrell took the job. When he left, there were many more good players than when he came.

After an 0-11 season, our average attendance dropped to 20,000 per game. When all the financial results were tabulated, we ended up with a deficit of between $800,000 and $900,000.

There is nothing that frightens administrators more than a large Athletic Department deficit. We were determined that we would do everything possible to increase our income and at the same time to maintain our level of competitiveness in all sports.

I remember one weekend we spent about 12 hours each on Saturday and Sunday going over every possible expenditure and potential revenue in our budget. We made cuts in all areas but were careful not to cripple any of our team sports. We had suggestions to drop non-revenue sports such as baseball, track and field, swimming, tennis and golf, but Florida State had a tradition of excellence in these sports and we didn't want to eliminate them if we could possibly keep from doing so.

The chairman of the Athletic Council, Dr. Dick Baker, who was a professor in the School of Business, worked with Claude Thigpen and me to reduce our expenditures to as low as possible. Dr. Baker's attitude was to try and help rather than sit back and criticize. His help was indispensable.

We also rescheduled all of our home games to night games. We really had a battle getting the University of Florida to agree to a night game in Tallahassee, but they finally agreed to do so.

With zero home victories in the year before, we decided that we would do everything possible to add entertainment to our home games. We added pre-game parachute jumps in the stadium, circus acts, lucky ticket drawings, and everything we could think of. Night games, ticket promotions, and Bill McGrotha's knowledgeable football columns served to give our fans hope and increased our attendance to an average of better than 28,000 per game. Our lone victory was against the University of Miami in Miami. The increase in attendance was an average of over 8,000 per game.

In addition, we increased our efforts at fundraising and more than doubled the amount of contributions of the previous year. We ended up with a $50,000 profit for the fiscal year, which I felt was a small miracle considering football was the only sport which operated at a profit and we had one win in the last 22 games.

In 1975 we ended up with a 3-8 record, but only one win was a home game. We again increased the average attendance to over 31,000 per game with all home games at night. That's more than you would expect out of one victory in the past eleven home games.

One thing that helped was we were able to eliminate a $370,000 debt on the stadium. Someone suggested the secretary of administration for the State of Florida might be able to help. I had met him once before, when I stood before his desk and asked a favor. He gave me about five minutes and turned me down flat. I decided I would try a different approach. I found out he liked to play golf, and I invited him to play with me. He accepted my invitation. After we finished we went to the 19th hole and sat down for a refreshing drink. I told him about the $370,000 debt which we were repaying at about $50,000 per year. I asked if he could think of a way we might retire the debt. I remember very clearly he said, "John, I believe that was an illegal loan in the first place and I believe we can get that retired through a very simple process."

That's just what I wanted to hear. He wrote a bill which included a lot of legalese verbiage (but never mentioned the Florida State football stadium) and attached it to the appropriations bill that the legislature would vote on at the end of the legislative session. The legislature passed the bill, canceling the entire debt. I'm not sure that as many three or four legislators realized what they were voting on when it was passed.

At that time a $50,000 a year savings was a big item for Florida State's athletic budget.

Darrell Mudra did finish strong in 1975, compared to previous years. He defeated Clemson 43-7 at Clemson and Houston 33-22 at Houston while losing to Auburn 17-14, Memphis State 17-14, and the University of Miami 24-22. Nevertheless, Darrell was fired shortly after the season ended.

To give you an idea how unconventional Darrell was, he bought a house which the university was removing from the campus to make room for another building. He rented a truck and hauled the lumber and all the parts of the house to Wakulla Springs, which was a beautiful area about 25 miles from Tallahassee. Darrell was going to put the house back together on a lot he had obtained in the area.

It was late one Saturday night after a long meeting with representatives of all the constituents of Florida State University that President Marshall, his staff, and I came to a decision to fire Darrell. Dr. Marshall said, "John, you've got to tell Darrell as we are releasing our decision to the newspapers Sunday night."

Early Sunday morning I drove to Darrell's house. I knocked on the door loudly and rang the doorbell but there was no answer. I could hear the dog barking. Finally, his daughter said, without opening the door, "Who is it?"

I told her I had to see her dad. She said that he and her mother weren't there and she didn't have any idea where they might be. I told her it was very important that I see him, but she didn't offer a clue as to where I might find him.

Since it was right in the middle of football recruiting season, I felt he would not be far away. The idea came to me that he might be in Wakulla Springs putting that house together. Darrell and I had driven to Wakulla Springs and he had shown me where he was going to build his house. I drove there and noticed several people working on a house where Darrell's lot was located. The first person I saw was Jean, Darrell's wife.

She said, "Oh, John, you came down to see our house!" I felt bad. I asked where Darrell was. He was in the house working on an electrical fuse box.

He had a screwdriver in his hand and kept working with it as he looked toward me.

"Darrell, I've got to talk to you for a few minutes," I said.

He said, "What do you want?"

"Let's go sit in the car where we can talk privately," I said, and then told him he was fired as football coach at Florida State. He didn't act too surprised, but I could tell it was totally unexpected news for him. He had three years left on his contract, and I believe he was paid in full for the next three years.

He asked me about the remaining years on his contract, and I told him that would have to be worked out with the administration.

Dr. Stan Marshall, the Florida State president, and I decided that he and I would select the next football coach. We decided to interview all candidates off campus to prevent publicity and speculation by the media. Many coaches have withdrawn from consideration when the press began to publicize their interest in another job.

From the beginning I favored Bobby Bowden. He was the first coach we considered. We also interviewed Pat Dye, who was head coach at East Carolina at that time; Bill Peterson, a successful head coach at Florida State in the sixties; and Gene Cox, a highly successful high school coach at Leon High School in Tallahassee.

Of course, Bobby Bowden was our choice. He has now finished his 18th season as head football coach at Florida State, but Bobby was initially signed to a five-year contract at $37,500. He may now be the highest paid college football coach in the country, having signed a lifetime contract at $600,000 per year several years ago.

Bowden's only losing season came in his first year, when he was 5-6. He finished strong with three last-minute victories over Southern Mississippi, North Texas State, and Virginia Tech. The winning margin in each game came as a result of a 90-plus-yard scoring play from scrimmage.

In that first year I decided he was not only a very good football coach, but a lucky one as well.

Bobby Bowden seems to get better with age. He's now 64. In his last seven seasons, from 1987 through 1993, he has won 10 games or more, which is an all-time record for college football, and in 1993 his team was voted national champion by the AP Poll and the Coaches/USA Today Poll. Bowden is not only one of the greatest coaches of all time but one of the best-liked coaches to ever coach the game of football.

One other achievement I felt good about was being able to schedule major football teams to home and home games. Clay Stapleton felt that Florida State could not draw well enough to attract the best college teams for home games in Tallahassee. With a couple of additions to our stadium, we increased the capacity to 48,000 in the middle 1970s. The capacity is now 72,000.

My approach was to offer to swap flat guarantees of $100,000 or more on a home game and away game contract with major teams in the Southeast and throughout the country. A team with a large stadium of 70,000 or more would get more revenue when the game was played in their stadium with a sold-out stadium and a $100,000 guarantee to the visiting team than if the contract was on a 50-50 basis after expenses, which is also a common contract between major universities. We were able to schedule home and home games with such teams as LSU, University of South Carolina, Auburn University, University of Washington, Georgia Tech, and the University of Texas. All had large stadiums and sell-outs, or near sell-outs, at home games. Up until then the only top teams we had been able to schedule at home were University of Florida, University of Miami, and University of South Carolina.

Unfortunately, my successor canceled games with the University of Texas and University of Washington because of high travel expenses. In my mind, that was short-sighted as the guarantees were several times greater than the travel expenses, and when the games were returned to Tallahassee we were almost guaranteed a sell-out with a high quality and reputable opponent. The home and home series with Georgia Tech had also been canceled. I do not know why.

With the prominence which Florida State has attained in the past few years, Florida State is able to schedule home and home games with almost any team in the country. They have played or will play future home games with Notre Dame, Michigan State, Nebraska, and others.

The toughest schedule Florida State ever played was scheduled by Clay Stapleton. In 1981 Florida State played five consecutive games *on the road* against Nebraska, Ohio State, Notre Dame, Pittsburgh, and Louisiana State. They were able to beat Ohio State 36-27, Notre Dame 19-13, and LSU 38-14, but lost to Nebraska 34-14, Pittsburgh 42-14, and finished the season with three home games. The Seminoles lost to Miami 29-19, to Southern Mississippi 58-14, and to Florida 35-3. By the time Florida State reached the final three games, the team was so exhausted it was a shell of the team which began the five consecutive road games against some of the best teams in the country. Three early home game victories gave Florida

State a 6-5 record. My last year at Florida State was 1979. We finished the regular season 11-0 and got a bid to the Orange Bowl.

My twin brother, Frank, was living in Albuquerque, New Mexico. When the athletic director's job opened up at the University of New Mexico, Frank encouraged me to consider the job. The president at New Mexico was Dr. Bud Davis, who was a very personable and able president.

The president of Florida State was Dr. Sliger. He had been a high school football coach at one time and knew football and what it meant to Florida State. The thing that really bothered me was Dr. Sliger had made a commitment to the Golden Chiefs (the top category of Seminole Boosters, who gave $5,000 or more each year) that they could have control of the expenditures of their unrestricted contributions. After the way we had struggled to overcome our deficit of the 1973 season of almost $800,000 and finally got to the point where we were in the black, I didn't think it was right to allow an outside group of contributors to decide how contributions would be spent unless the contributions were designated for a particular purpose. A primary emphasis of the NCAA is institutional control, and I felt Dr. Sliger's decision violated that principle.

Dr. Sliger offered to renew my contract for five years and match the salary offered by New Mexico. I asked him if he would allow the Athletic Department and university to control the Seminole Booster contributions. He replied, "No, John, I can't do that."

"Well, I'm going to take the job at New Mexico," I told him.

I had hired every coach at Florida State. In 1979-80, the football team was 11-0 before losing to Oklahoma in the Orange Bowl. The track and field team finished third in the outdoor NCAA championship which is still their highest finish ever. Dick Roberts was the coach I had hired when Mike Long retired. The basketball team was invited to the NCAA basketball championships. They won a couple of games but lost to the University of Oklahoma in the third round in the 1979-80 championships. The coach was Joe Williams, whom I hired after Hugh Durham took the Georgia job.

The baseball team won the Metro Conference championship and played in the College World Series in Omaha. Mike Martin was the baseball coach and the last coach I hired at Florida State. The golf team won the Metro Conference championship and qualified for the NCAA championships. Paul Azinger, Jeff Sluman and

Kenny Knox, who have all won tournaments in professional golf, were on the golf team. Don Veller was the golf coach whom I hired. He was Florida State's first winning football coach. He was head football coach for five years, with a 31-12-1 record in the late forties and early fifties.

I had hired Dick Howser as baseball coach. Dick was offered the job as manager of the Yankees by George Steinbrenner while Dick was baseball coach at Florida State. Even though the Yankees won more games than any team in the major leagues, they were beaten in the American League playoffs and Steinbrenner fired Dick Howser. Dick was made manager of the Kansas City Athletics and won the American League pennant and the World Series. A year or two later Dick was diagnosed with a malignant brain tumor and died in the prime of his managing career. Dick Howser was one of the all-time nice persons in professional sports.

Our swimming team won the Metro Conference championship, and our tennis team finished second. The 1979-80 season was the most successful year in all sports in the history of Florida State.

In addition, I had hired Barbara Palmer as women's athletic director. She was not only highly efficient and a beautiful lady, but a great fundraiser in her own right. She realized what a hard time we were having financially, so she decided to lobby the legislature for additional financial support for women's athletics. She was able to get the legislature to grant almost $700,000 for women's athletics. The Florida State women's program was one of the best in the South in 1979-80. Barbara resigned a couple of years later, when she was unable to see eye to eye with the athletic director at that time.

I feel obligated to add that Barbara Palmer was the best woman administrator I have ever worked with. She was hard working, had good judgment, was a good fundraiser, and appreciated the problems of not crippling the men's athletic program in order to promote women's athletics. When we met at Florida State's Athletic Hall of Fame meeting in the spring of 1990, when both of us were inducted into the FSU Hall of Fame, we agreed that we were a very good team and both wished we could have worked together for more years. There were many times I wished she could have joined me at the University of New Mexico as the women's athletic director.

We had made a couple of expansions of the football stadium and averaged 48,000 attendance in 1979. Now the Doak Campbell football stadium has been expanded to 72,000, and virtually sold it out for the 1993 season. Florida State football has come a long way since averaging 20,000 fans in 1973.

The most valued friend I had at Florida State was Bill McGrotha, the sports editor and number-one columnist for the *Tallahassee Democrat.* I doubt if I would have survived my first three years, when the football record was 4-29, if it had not been for the friendship and support of Bill McGrotha.

Bill died on January 27, 1993, after his second by-pass operation. Florida State and all the coaches lost an irreplaceable friend. McGrotha had the utmost respect of every coach and athletic director who worked at Florida State. I have never read the kind of tributes to a sportswriter as were given him after his death.

Bobby Bowden and I spoke at his funeral. Bobby emphasized his personal friendship with Bill and how often he sought Bill's wise advice. Bill had the qualities you seek in a great friend. He sought the truth and wrote the truth as skillfully as any sportswriter I've known. He never betrayed a confidence. Florida State coaches knew that, and they confided in Bill about many issues which were very controversial and confidential. They trusted Bill, and he never tried to discredit a coach. Fans would ask him, "Why don't you get after Coach so and so in your column?" Bill would say, "That's not my style."

Perhaps the most important service Bill provided for coaches and athletic directors was to keep hope alive among the fans. Regardless how discouraging things might be, Bill could find reason for realistic hope without overdoing it or being a phony in any way. That's the main reason attendance increased from 1973 to 1975 by 47.5%, in the midst of the most discouraging period in Florida State athletics. Without some hope that would have never happened.

Overall the spirit of the student body and longtime fans has been remarkable. It's one of the few places where I have attended games in the stands and the fans knew the school fight song and the cheers led by the cheerleader and joined in with great enthusiasm. The attitudes of students and faculty and the positive support by alumni and longtime fans make Tallahassee and Florida State a great place for unusual success in college athletics. Bill McGrotha made a great contribution in developing that atmosphere.

From a professional viewpoint, I made a great mistake when I left Florida State to take the job as athletic director at the University of New Mexico. The biggest contrast was in the attitude of the local newspapers. While the *Tallahassee Democrat* was supportive, encouraging, enthusiastic and trusting, the *Albuquerque Journal* and *Albuquerque Tribune* were cynical, critical, sarcastic, and very pessimistic about almost every effort that was made to improve the athletic program at the University of New Mexico.

In April of 1990, when I was inducted into the Florida State Athletic Hall of Fame, Bill wrote the following column about my contributions to Florida State. I believe it illustrates why it was possible to be successful as a coach or athletic director at Florida State University.

Bridgers Over Troubled Waters
From 0 and 11 to 11 and 0

He came at the worst of times, left during the best, and perhaps not so many tied that together.

But only heaven knows where Florida State's program would be today but for John Bridgers, who returned over the weekend for induction into the school's Athletic Hall of Fame.

In 1973, just as the sky started falling, he became athletic director. Bridgers was greeted by a major scandal almost immediately, an all-losing football season soon after, and then an alarming deficit that threatened the survival of football and two or three other sports as well.

He left in late 1979, not only declining an invitation to stay through FSU's first big-bowl appearance — the Orange — but a raise and 5-year contract as well.

"He comes as close to turning water into wine with what he's got as anybody I know," said Dr. Phil Fordyce, an FSU vice-president who would become interim athletic director, as he left.

In binding times, Bridgers resisted those who would eliminate other sports to better ensure the preservation of football, ignored those who would cut back on women's athletics — instead, expanding that program into one of the nation's best as he hired Barbara Palmer to run it.

And as the football team won just one home game in his

first three years, Bridgers' decision to play all home games at night was a major factor in increased attendance. In 1974, that first season of all night games, crowds rose by 8,000 per game, and in 1975 by 3,000 more.

When a decision was made to change coaches following the 1975 season, Bridgers went out and hired fellow Birmingham native Bobby Bowden, quietly and quickly outflanking some who would have chosen others.

Just as the football team capped that phenomenal rise from 0-11 to 11-0, Bridgers said goodbye, a little more than six years after he came. He took a like job at New Mexico, a school that had just come under investigation — by the FBI, never mind the NCAA — for mail fraud and bribery in connection with basketball recruiting.

He went primarily because Frank Bridgers, head of a thriving engineering firm and his identical twin, was in Albuquerque. He went secondarily because he felt he had not received the backing at FSU he felt he should have.

It is well to know, however, that one can surely count on one hand the number of popular athletic directors in our land. The nature of the job is not conducive to widespread popularity.

And it is well to know, too, Bridgers was hardly solely responsible for the transformation of an athletic program. Many played prominent roles, but none bigger than Bridgers.

His low-key style, and a notably stubborn quality in matters he felt right, rubbed some wrong. But folks that know him well tend to be uncommonly loyal to him. As one, Texas' Darrell Royal, said, "John is the type of fellow who sneaks up on your blind side."

Before he came to FSU, Bridgers made extraordinary contributions in many places, including European combat in World War II as a field-artillery captain.

Frank, the twin, recalls both going to Auburn to try out for football scholarships. On a day that Frank had the flu, John won scholarships for both, lining up when Frank's name was called, as well as his. (In high school back in Birmingham, the Bridgers twins had played guard on either side of Vaughn Mancha at center.)

A football coach first during his army years, Bridgers was

later coach at two schools of high academic reputation, first Sewanee and then Johns Hopkins. His success at the latter caught the eye of Weeb Ewbanks, who in 1957 hired him to the Baltimore Colts, coaching offensive tackles as well as the whole defensive line.

Bridgers played a telling role in what some historians call "the greatest game ever played" — the Colts' astonishing 23-17 victory over the New York Giants in sudden death of that NFL championship on Dec. 28, 1958. His defensive line attacked an offensive line coached by Vince Lombardi, then a few years removed from becoming a legend.

"John never got the credit he deserved for his coaching role in that game," said Jack Patera, whose assignment as middle linebacker was to step up and close the gap when Gene Lipscomb called his name — a signal that the one they called "Big Daddy" was going to blitz.

Bridgers had unusual rapport with several Colts, including Lipscomb, offensive tackle Jim Parker and Raymond Berry, the phenomenal receiver who the day of the great game wore a corset on his back, contact lenses for his bad eyes, and special orthopedic shoes because one of his legs was shorter than the other.

Just as he left FSU after the big season, Bridgers departed Baltimore after a world title, attaining fame for a pass-oriented offense during 10 head-coaching years at Baylor. Once during that period he appeared at an FSU clinic, as a headliner with Vince Lombardi, at a time when Bowden was coaching FSU receivers . . . .

"Anything he told me I would believe," said John Steadman, a highly respected Baltimore sports writer, at a recent Super Bowl, "because I don't think John Bridgers knew how to lie."

CHAPTER 25

BOBBY BOWDEN:
A NICE GUY WHO WINS

Coach Bobby Bowden has won a national college football championship in the 1994 season as head football coach at Florida State University. He has had a remarkable record. In his first 19 years at Florida State, he has won 176 games, lost 47 and tied four, an average of 9.3 wins per year. In the previous 20 years of Florida State football seven coaches won a total of 132 games, which is a pretty good average of 6.6 wins per year.

Up until 1947 Florida State University was Florida State College for Women. The university became co-ed in 1947 after World War II. Bobby Bowden is the first college coach in NCAA history to win 10 games or more a season for nine consecutive years, and that streak is still alive. He also has the best bowl record of any coach in college football. He has taken the Seminoles to 13 consecutive bowls (1982–94) and has won 12 and tied one. His overall bowl record is 13-3-1 at Florida State.

In 1976 I was in my fourth year as athletic director. Florida State's football record in 1973, 1974, and 1975 was 4-29. Two football coaches had been fired, and there was a lot of pressure to bring in a coach who could get Florida State back on the winning track.

President Stan Marshall and I agreed Bobby Bowden was the

best choice for Florida State. Bobby had taken his West Virginia team to the Peach Bowl in Atlanta. West Virginia defeated North Carolina State 13-10 and ended up with a 9-3 record. We called a meeting of the Athletic Council and submitted our recommendation that we make an offer to Bobby Bowden of a five-year contract and to negotiate a salary offer.

I called Bobby in Tampa and offered him the job. He wanted to wait until he returned to Morgantown before making a decision. A couple of days later I called him in Morgantown, and he accepted our offer of a $37,500 salary plus a $2,500 expense allowance.

What were the reasons Dr. Marshall and I selected Bobby over the other candidates? First of all, I believe he really wanted the job. Bobby had been an assistant coach at Florida State. There are very few people who have lived in Tallahassee who didn't like it. Bobby was a native of Birmingham, Alabama, and liked warm weather.

At the press conference, when we introduced Bobby Bowden as the new head coach, he told the following story: "When Ann and I returned to Morgantown after the All Star game in Tampa, it was snowing and the roads were iced over. There's a steep hill on the way to our house. We couldn't get traction and the wheels were spinning on the icy road. I told Ann I would get out and push until we passed that particularly slippery spot. I was pushing as hard as I could, and my feet slipped out from under me and I fell face down on the frozen road. As I was lying there, I said, 'I'll take it, John, I'll take it.'"

That was Bobby's version of when he decided to take the Florida State head coaching job. Bobby has a very likable personality with a good sense of humor, a quick wit, and he often makes himself the butt of a story.

Bobby had been a winner in his two head coaching jobs. He had five of six winning seasons at West Virginia, with a 42-26 record. His record at Samford University in Birmingham was 31-6 in four years.

At Florida State we had recruited two quarterbacks in successive years from Leon High in Tallahassee. Both were outstanding passers but were slow and not threats as runners. Bobby said, "They were so slow that we had to take time out to get them off the field." I felt we had to have a good pass offense in order to win with the only two underclass quarterbacks we had on our squad. Bobby had coached the receivers at Florida State as an assistant, and I knew he had a good knowledge of the passing game.

On the other hand, Pat Dye coached the wishbone offense with the quarterback running the triple option of handing to the fullback, the quarterback running off tackle or pitch to the halfback running to the outside. When we interviewed Pat Dye, he said, "I don't think you can win in college football with a pass offense."

In Bowden's first four years at Florida State he went 10-2, 8-3, and 11-1 after an opening season of 5-6. Wally Woodham and Jimmy Jordan led the team during the three winning seasons with outstanding passing. In 1978 and 1979 the Seminoles won 15 consecutive games, primarily due to the passing of Woodham and Jordan. Bobby Bowden seemed to have a sixth sense in going with the quarterback with the hot hand — sometimes Woodham and on other occasions Jordan.

I felt very good about our selection of Bobby Bowden as our head football coach, but in my wildest dreams, I never expected him to do as well as he has done.

After he took over the job, we discovered some additional talents that we really had not counted on. He has exceptional talent at working with the players. He has high standards as far as the conduct of his players attending class and following team rules. However, if a player makes a slip but shows a good attitude and remorse over his mistake, Bobby gives him a second chance.

Bobby did an excellent job of selling his offense to his team. He normally had two wide receivers and ran out of an "I" formation, although he used other formations at times, such as two tight ends on short yardage and goal line.

In 1993, along with the "I" formation, he used the shotgun, which was a spread with four wide receivers, one back and the quarterback lined up next to the remaining back about five yards deep. With a very quick and good runner as he had in Charley Ward at quarterback, the offense was very effective. It was difficult for one rusher to hem up Charley Ward. And with four wide receivers spreading the secondary and linebackers, Ward normally averaged eight to ten yards every time he ran. He had the ability to avoid a rusher who appeared to have him contained. He had been a very effective point guard on the Florida State basketball team, and he could juke a rusher out of position and penetrate the defensive secondary about like he penetrated to the hoop in basketball. However, most of Florida State's yardage came on his passing.

Bobby specialized with the offense. As a former quarterback, he called most of the plays during his early years. Recently, he has turned the play calling over to the offensive coordinator, but in a close game he will still have an influence on the play calling.

Over the years he's built a reputation of coming up with unexpected and trick plays which have often worked for big gainers and made a difference of winning and losing in several games.

Coach Bowden is a lucky coach. One reason is because of the confidence he reflects to his players. In his first year at Florida State, going into the ninth game of the season with a 2-6 record, the Seminoles won the last three games with four scoring plays of over 90 yards, three of them in the closing minutes. Florida State was trailing Southern Mississippi 27 to 23 with only a couple of minutes left in the game. Jimmy Black completed a pass to Rudy Thomas, who went 95 yards for a touchdown to win 30-27. In the next game, North Texas State was leading 20-14 in the last minute. Jimmy Black threw to Kurt Unglaub, who went 91 yards for a touchdown and with the extra point won 21-20. In the final game of the season Virginia Tech had a 21-14 lead. Larry Key ran 97 yards for a touchdown to tie the score, and then in the final minute Jimmy Jordan threw a 96-yard scoring pass to Kurt Unglaub for a 28-21 victory.

In the previous 20 years of Florida State football there had never been a scoring play of 90 yards or more. The fact is, to score a touchdown of over 90 yards some luck or good fortune is involved. One of the most unlikely things in football is to be able to call a 90-yard scoring play from scrimmage. Bobby Bowden didn't do it just once, he did it four different times in three games — all of which were needed for a win.

Bowden delegates the defensive coaching to the defensive coordinator and his assistants. While Florida State has never ranked extremely high in scoring defense or the least total yards allowed except in the 1993 season, they have been a big-play defense with outstanding linebackers and defensive secondary. Interceptions, big losses, and runbacks of punts, kickoffs, and interceptions have characterized the defense.

Another area of excellence is recruiting. Florida State recruits speed on offense and defense. That's the most important reason they have so many big plays. Bowden is a masterful recruiter himself. At age 64 he has had lots of experience. He understands how important it is and will not allow himself to play golf, which is his favorite recreation, until after recruiting season is over. One policy he has is that each position coach must approve of any player recruited for the positions he coaches.

In addition to all of the above, Bobby Bowden is a teetotaler and has very strong religious convictions. There's no telling how many church congregations he has addressed from the pulpit, but it would number in the hundreds. Bobby is an excellent and entertaining speaker. He seldom uses notes and ad libs in most of his talks. He thoroughly understands the value of public relations.

Bobby Bowden may do as good a job with the print and electronic media as any coach in the country. The fact that the University of Florida has the School of Journalism and most of the Florida sportswriters graduated from that university gives Florida an advantage throughout the state. However, Bobby Bowden has done a great deal to negate that advantage. With his light-touch sense of humor, even the Gator graduates have a hard time hating him. My guess is that Bowden has won over most of the neutral fans who did not attend Florida, Florida State, or the University of Miami.

Bobby has learned not to respond to criticism unless he thinks it's justified, and then he will agree with the critic. I wish I had been that smart when I was coaching.

Often when a coach doesn't win, one of the common criticisms is that the coach is not tough enough. You hear this often when one coach is evaluating another coach. The implication is that the coach is not tough enough with his players. I personally believe that the important thing is for the coach to stick by his standards and principles rather than adopt new standards every time he is under pressure to change his operational principles. He may under certain circumstances make exceptions to general rules, but he should have good reasons for such exceptions which are understood by his football team and assistant coaches.

Bobby Bowden is not a tough-talking coach with his players or coaches, but he does have a well-thought-out system of discipline and standards. Bobby Bowden is what you might call "tender tough." He's tender on the outside but tough on the inside. He makes rare exceptions with players in disciplinary actions, but to my knowledge he has not had to make the second exception for a player.

A coach who makes the hard decisions, especially when it involves unpopular decisions with the fans or involves a long-standing friendship with an assistant coach, is the coach who is tough enough to be a winner.

There have been many successful coaches who have used fear to keep good discipline on their football squads. It's the same kind of discipline found in the military, which no one can question as being effective. However, there is generally more than one way to be successful at something. I personally believe the most important contribution a coach can give his team is to increase individual and team confidence. To be most effective it must be the kind of confidence that can survive disappointment and temporary failure. It's a hard thing to measure, but I believe Bobby Bowden has been able to add to the individual and team confidence of his players. Certainly, his record would indicate this is true.

With all his attributes Bobby Bowden is not perfect. He makes mistakes like every human being makes, but he doesn't make many big ones.

In 1993 Bobby Bowden added a national championship to his laurels after coming agonizingly close for the previous six years, when he won 10 games or more each year. He missed chances for a national championship twice, when the Seminoles missed very makeable field goals against the University of Miami in 1991 and 1992. Florida State was undefeated in 1991 until they met Miami in their 10th game and had been ranked number one for the entire season. Miami won 17-16 when a last-minute Florida State field goal went wide right. In 1992 their only loss was 19-16 to Miami and again missed a late field goal wide right. The Seminoles were ranked number one until the Miami loss and ended up number two in the AP Poll. In 1987 Florida State also ended up second with the only loss being to Miami 26-25.

In 1993 Florida State was ranked number one until a 10th game loss to Notre Dame in South Bend 20-13. Notre Dame took over the number-one spot, but lost the following week in an upset loss to Boston College 42-41 in South Bend. Boston College was ranked seventh and the loss dropped Notre Dame to fourth in the AP Poll. Nebraska was undefeated and untied and received the number-one ranking. Florida State, who won their last two games, was ranked number two.

On the basis of a coalition vote of the Coaches/USA Today Poll and the AP Sports Writers Poll, Nebraska and Florida State were selected to play for the national championship in the Orange Bowl. Nebraska had suffered losses in previous Orange Bowl games and were determined to overcome their past disappointments with a victory over Florida State in the Orange Bowl. The game was one which was not decided until the very last second. Nebraska led almost throughout the first half and had a 7-6 lead at halftime. Florida State rallied in the third quarter to take a 15-7 lead. In the fourth quarter Nebraska kicked a field goal to narrow the margin to 15-10. Then, in the last three minutes of the fourth quarter, Nebraska began a drive which ended in a touchdown to gain a 16-15 lead. Nebraska's try for a two-point conversion failed.

There was a minute and 20 seconds left on the clock when Nebraska kicked off. Charley Ward, the Florida State quarterback who won the Heisman Award, led the Florida State drive which was aided by a 15-yard penalty to Nebraska for a victory celebration after taking the lead on their touchdown, and another 15-yard penalty on an out-of-bounds hit on a Florida State pass reception. The drive ended up inside the Nebraska 10-yard-line with a Florida State field goal to give Florida State an 18-16 lead with 20 seconds left in the game.

Coach Bobby Bowden's description of the last few seconds, as aired on *The Tonight Show*, reveals the ebb and flow of his emotions in the last few seconds of the game:

> When Nebraska completed the last pass, I was looking at the clock and I saw it wind down to 4 seconds, 3, 2, 1 and zero and now we've gotten that national championship. About that time the players dumped the large container of ice water over my head. I started walking across the field about half frozen and soaking wet to find Tom Osborne. When I got to the other side of the field, I couldn't find him. I finally saw him in the middle of the field, and he said the game wasn't over as the officials had put one second back on the clock. I noticed the officials were marking the ball at the 34-yard-line, which would have been a 51-yard field goal. I thought, that's o.k. because they don't have anyone who can kick a field goal that far. But then I saw the officials move the ball to our 28-yard-line, which was well within the range of their field goal kicker. I became very depressed. I thought, "We will never win a national championship." It ap-

peared the game was over, but here Nebraska was getting ready to kick a 45-yard field goal. The ball snapped and the holder placed it down, but the kicker pulled his field goal attempt to the left. I decided the "wide left" is a lot better than "wide right."

It was a game where both teams *refused* to lose. How many games have been played where both teams scored to take the lead in the last 90 seconds? With 20 seconds left, Nebraska moved the ball to the Florida State 28-yard-line, and with one second left and an opportunity for a third score within 90 seconds and a victory, but a missed field goal from a very makeable distance kept them from winning. In 42 years as a coach and athletic director, I've never seen a stronger finish by both teams without a single play which covered more than 30 yards nor a single turnover.

One writer wrote that neither team deserved to win the college football national championship. I disagree strongly. I thought *both* teams deserved to win a national championship!

Tom Osborne, the Nebraska coach, like Bobby Bowden, is one of the finest gentlemen in the coaching profession and is highly respected by his peers. Tom did an outstanding job in getting his team prepared for a magnificent effort.

Ever since Dr. Stan Marshall, the Florida State University president, and I hired Bobby Bowden in 1976, Bobby has expressed appreciation for giving him the opportunity to coach at Florida State University. Just recently, in a letter to me, Bobby Bowden wrote, "How can I ever says thanks to you for hiring me at Florida State University? You know any time you move and take a new job, you are never sure you are doing the right thing. The reason I came to Florida State was because of you. Many men claim they were the reason I came to Tallahassee, but there was only one man — that man was John Bridgers."

Bobby Bowden is one of the greatest coaches who has ever coached the game of football. I am especially proud that I had a hand in bringing him to Florida State University. He is a genuinely nice guy who has won more than any active coach other than Joe Paterno of Penn State, who is also a nice guy.

In May 1994, a newspaper story revealed that at least seven (maybe more) Florida State players had been victimized by unauthorized sports agents by accepting gifts of merchandise and cash.

Two of the unauthorized sports agents were from Las Vegas, Nevada. With the assistance of a Tallahassee resident, who was a former assistant high school coach, they befriended several Florida State players. The players were offered illegal gifts such as shoes, jackets, and other merchandise from a Tallahassee sporting goods store during the 1993 football season. All of this was done without the knowledge of Coach Bobby Bowden or the staff. It was the first time in Coach Bowden's eighteen years at Florida State that Florida State players had been accused of accepting cash and gifts in violation of NCAA rules.

At this time it is not known just what action will be taken by the NCAA. Most of those receiving gifts were seniors, but there were two or more underclassmen included in the group. It is anticipated that players with additional eligibility will lose their scholarships and be ruled ineligible for future participation in intercollegiate athletics.

The lesson to be learned is that athletes must be suspicious of strangers offering gifts of merchandise and cash. Nothing good can come from accepting gifts from either strangers or friends.

If coaches on the Florida State staff, fans or alumni had been involved in any way, it would be highly likely that Florida State would be put on probation by the NCAA. Time will tell what kind of penalty, if any, will be assessed by the NCAA.

The only positive thing to come out of the story is that Charley Ward, the Florida State All-American quarterback and Heisman Trophy winner, refused to talk or meet with the Las Vegas con men. It was stated in *Sports Illustrated* that the unauthorized agents' main objective was to involve Charley Ward.

It is sad and unfortunate that Coach Bobby Bowden, his coaches, Florida State University, and its fans have to be embarrassed and saddened after many years of building a reputation for winning with a clean football program and after a year the Seminoles won a national championship.

However, the 23–17 Sugar Bowl victory over the University of Florida on January 2, 1995, did a great deal to diminish the hurt of the illegal shopping spree by a few of the Florida State players. I believe coaches and players learned valuable lessons from the shopping incident and were able to come together for a 10-1-1 record in 1994 and continued to be ranked among the top four teams in college football for the eighth consecutive year.

CHAPTER 26

1980–87

THE UNIVERSITY OF NEW MEXICO:
SOME SURPRISING PROGRESS AND
DISAPPOINTING DECISIONS

I came to the University of New Mexico in December of 1979 full of hope and enthusiasm. After 30 years I was going to live in the same town as my twin brother, Frank. My wife, Frances, stayed in Tallahassee while we decided what we would do with our home there. We had built a nice home on the golf course, and we both hated to leave it.

I moved in with my twin brother, Frank, and his wife, Jean. We had a press conference the day after I arrived. I really don't remember many of the details of the first press conference except that I came away with a negative reaction from the questions and the attitude of the media.

Over the first couple of months I was pictured as a tough, demanding person who managed by use of fear and intimidation. That's really not my nature. I've always enjoyed a relaxed and easygoing relationship with coaches and fellow administrators. My image in the Albuquerque papers was "my way or the highway." One of the writers who helped establish the false impression of my being such a stern and harsh leader really felt he was being favorable and supportive of me by writing in such a fashion.

The first day I went to work at New Mexico was December 5,

1979. While I was adjusting to my new surroundings, the FBI came into the building and confiscated the records of the basketball team. The FBI had tapped the telephone of a known gambler in Albuquerque. Norm Ellenberger, the New Mexico basketball coach, was visiting in the gambler's home.

The FBI taped a conversation between Ellenberger and his chief recruiter and assistant coach, Manny Goldstein, who was a native of New York City. In the conversation Goldstein told Ellenberger he had gotten a basketball prospect a junior college degree. He had bribed one of the officials at the junior college to add 16 credit hours to the prospect's transcript. At the time a junior college player needed a degree from a junior college to be able to be eligible the first year he enrolled at a senior college. Otherwise, without a degree he would have to be in residence for a full year before he was eligible to play.

Manny Goldstein was immediately suspended and was fired a short time later. Norm Ellenberger was removed as basketball coach and placed under suspension. Norm's other full-time assistant was named interim head basketball coach. After two weeks of headline stories on the front page and sports pages, Norm Ellenberger was fired by Dr. William E. "Bud" Davis, president of the university, for "willful and grossly incompetent conduct." New Mexico was now without a football and basketball coach.

When I took the job, I knew there were problems with the basketball team, but I had no idea they were that serious.

I liked "Bud" Davis, the New Mexico president, very much. While serving as alumni director at the University of Colorado, he was named interim head football coach in 1962 when Sonny Grandelius, the head coach, was fired for breaking NCAA rules. Bud Davis was very personable, an excellent leader and administrator. In his younger years he was a football player at the University of Colorado and had coached high school football after graduating. After receiving his Ph.D., he later became president of Idaho State, where he served several years before becoming president at the University of New Mexico.

At New Mexico he inherited Lavon McDonald as athletic director and Norm Ellenberger as head basketball coach. Dr. Davis fired McDonald as athletic director in November of 1979. Ellenberger was a very successful basketball coach measured by the number of wins and losses. Ellenberger also had strong support from at least two of the five regents of the University of New Mexico.

After a thorough investigation, it was revealed that Ellenberger was guilty of arranging phony credits for basketball players to get them admitted to the university. He also had arranged for illegal benefits to the players. The basketball scandal which resulted in his firing was one of the most publicized athletic scandals in history.

I've never worked for a president who worked harder or cooperated more to get to the bottom of a critical problem than Dr. Bud Davis did. Ellenberger had won two Western Athletic Conference basketball championships and was an extremely popular man in Albuquerque. Despite the revelations about his violations of NCAA and institutional rules, he still had very strong support in the community. A number of people wanted to blame President Davis more than Ellenberger. Believe me, a president doesn't know the daily activities of a basketball coach. There are more demands on a college president than any employee of a university. He must trust his athletic director to keep him informed of any misconduct or unethical and illegal practices of a coach.

President Davis had heard reports of possible rules violations and called Ellenberger and McDonald in to talk to them, but both stated emphatically that they were not guilty of violating NCAA rules.

Through the investigation initiated by President Davis, seven basketball players were ruled ineligible for the 1979-80 season. It was found that all had received credit for courses they had never taken. The UNM basketball team ended up with one starter left, and he had a record of being an untrustworthy individual although a very gifted basketball player.

I met with all athletic department employees and told them we were going to run an honest program and conform to NCAA and University of New Mexico rules. I put it as strongly as I knew how.

In addition to not having a football coach or a basketball coach, our wrestling coach and the assistant athletic director resigned. Later our track and cross-country coach was dismissed.

I decided I would personally locate and hire a football, basketball, and wrestling coach. Later in the spring, after we lost our track coach, I would hire a track coach. Another important position we filled was that of assistant athletic director for athletic advisement.

I thought it best to play a small role in the selection of the athletic academic adviser. We named a blue ribbon committee consisting of the director of admissions, the chief academic officer of the university, and some of the most prominent and outstanding faculty members. We wanted to make certain the mistakes of our athletes having false credits being admitted to the university would never happen again.

Dr. Tom Brennan of Syracuse University was hired, and he was an excellent choice. He was intelligent, energetic, innovative, and did an excellent job of organizing our academic advisement. Any athlete in trouble academically could get immediate and competent tutors to help him over the hump. Tom had held a similar position at Syracuse University. As time went by, he took on many additional duties. His organization of academic advisement became a model for many such offices at major institutions around the country.

About a week before Christmas I met with President Davis, and we decided our most pressing need was to hire a football coach. At best we would miss the month of December as far as recruiting was concerned. It was very important to have a full staff hired and recruiting in January. I requested of President Davis that I be allowed to go on the road and interview three or four candidates where they lived. I told President Davis that by the end of the following week I would have a recommendation for a head football coach and a head basketball coach.

I wanted to hire a coach with successful head coaching experience in football and basketball if possible. I had three candidates in mind for football. One was Bill Mallory, former head football coach at the University of Colorado. He had a good record despite the fact he had been fired at Colorado. Bill was a strong person and a very sound football coach. He is now head coach at Indiana University, where he has been for several years and has done a good job.

The second was Joe Morrison of the University of Chattanooga. Joe had played for 14 years with the New York Giants as a running back. He was an outstanding pass receiver and an excellent all-around football player. As head coach at Chattanooga he had won three Southern Conference championships at the Division I-AA level, which was one level below Division I-A, the top level in college football. He had a good staff, and I thought he might be able to bring some of them with him as assistant coaches.

The third coach I seriously considered was John Mackovic, who at that time completed a very successful season as head coach at Wake Forest University. A coach has to be good to win at Wake Forest. Of the three he was the least interested and would not be available until sometime after January 1 due to a bowl game in which Wake Forest was a participant. Mackovic is now head coach at the University of Texas and also has been head coach for the University of Illinois and the Kansas City Chiefs, an NFL team.

I also interviewed an assistant football coach with the Houston Oilers, but he did not have any head coaching experience.

I called Joe Morrison and invited him to come to New Mexico for a visit. He and his wife flew out to Albuquerque. His wife, J. V., was a beautiful, striking blonde who was Miss Tennessee in the Miss America contest. Dr. Davis was impressed with Joe Morrison and J. V., and we announced him as our head football coach. It proved to be a good choice.

The next task was to hire a basketball coach. A year before I left Florida State, Hugh Durham, who had been head basketball coach at Florida State for almost 20 years, took a job as head coach at the University of Georgia. Hugh was a great coach and had taken Florida State to the finals of the NCAA championships in 1972, where he lost a close game to UCLA, the perennial national champions in the eighties under Coach John Wooden. One of the finalists for the Florida State head basketball coach position was Joe Williams, who was head coach at Furman University and had coached at Jacksonville University when they played in the finals of the NCAA tournament. Arlis Gilmore was their outstanding player. The other finalist was Gary Colson. Gary had been a successful college coach for years at Valdosta State in Valdosta, Georgia, and at Pepperdine University near Los Angeles. We decided on Joe Williams, as he had more name recognition in the northern part of Florida.

In the meantime Gary had resigned as head coach of Pepperdine and wanted to see if he could be happy as a representative of the Converse Shoe Company. The college basketball season had already been under way for a month. I felt it would be difficult, if not impossible, to get a successful college head coach to resign his position after the season had started to take a job at New Mexico, a school which had made headlines for the past three weeks for having one of the worst college basketball scandals ever.

I called Gary to find out if he would be interested. He had missed coaching and was eager to get back into college basketball. I invited him to meet with President Davis and me, and subsequently Gary was offered the head coaching job.

Gary Colson did a superb job of getting New Mexico back as a contender for the Western Athletic Conference Championship with a winning program, and perhaps more important he did it honestly with a program of good players, who were good citizens and conscientious students. The grade point average of the basketball team had the highest academic average of any men's sports team within four years after Colson took the coaching reins.

We hired Bill Dotson as head wrestling coach. Bill was Division I NCAA wrestling champion in his weight class as a senior at Northern Iowa. He also was the Division II champion in which Northern Iowa competed. However, a champion in Division II is eligible to enter the Division I championship tournament, which Bill did and won again.

Dotson is an excellent coach who knows wrestling. Unfortunately, the New Mexico wrestling budget has been the poorest financed sport of all New Mexico sports, but despite lack of sufficient financial support he has had some excellent teams and outstanding individual wrestlers.

In the latter part of the spring I hired Del Hessel as track and cross-country coach. He was truly dedicated to track, was very knowledgeable, and was an excellent recruiter. The track program grew in stature until the Lobo track team was an annual contender for the Western Athletic Conference Championship. The cross-country team was equally competitive.

Del was fired in 1991 upon the recommendation of Linda Estes, the former women's athletic director who had been placed in charge of all men's and women's non-revenue sports. Estes had a dislike for Del Hessel as long as I can remember. When I was athletic director, she charged Del with paying from university funds the transportation, room and board of an athlete who was ineligible to compete in a California track meet.

Dr. Leon Griffin, faculty athletic representative for the university and acting athletic director when I took the job in December of 1979, thoroughly investigated the charges and could find no evidence that the athlete's expenses were paid by university funds. Dr.

Griffin has been one of the top leaders and professors in the Department of Physical Education at the University of New Mexico and is highly respected on the campus.

Del Hessel was fired for violation of NCAA rules. He had problems interpreting some of the rules, but some of them are so vague a rocket scientist might have trouble giving a clear interpretation. From conversation with Del and others, I believe the charges were magnified. Most of the charges stemmed from a Nigerian athlete he recruited. Baylor University and Kansas State charged that his transcript was fraudulent. Later it was determined that his transcript was not fraudulent but admissible. The athlete won the 400-meter dash the following spring in the conference championships. He also had better than a 3.5 academic average his freshman year at New Mexico.

After Hessel was fired, the men's track team became a non-contender in the WAC track championships. It's hard for me to believe that Hessel intentionally violated NCAA rules. I can believe he misinterpreted them.

Another excellent coach I hired two years later was David Gaetz, who had been the best player on the New Mexico tennis team for three years and graduated with a degree in electrical engineering. David was an excellent student and could have had a successful career in engineering, but he wanted to coach tennis. Through his efforts the tennis team improved from a non-contender to a second-place finish in the Western Athletic Conference. After I announced that I would retire in June of 1987, David applied for the coaching job at the University of Minnesota. He won the Big Ten Championship in his first year there.

One of the primary reasons I left Florida State was I did not believe that the Seminole Boosters, the fundraising organization, was under institutional control. I found it to be even less true with the Lobo Club, the athletic fundraising organization at New Mexico. I asked Bud Davis before I took the job at New Mexico if he would help me get the Lobo Club under the control of the university. He said he would, but that was before the basketball scandal surfaced. With the situation which existed with basketball, Dr. Davis was fighting for his survival.

The executive director of the Lobo Club resigned shortly after I went to New Mexico. Johnny Jones, a wealthy road contractor who was the most influential person in the Lobo Club, used his power and influence to hire a new executive director without so much as consulting me or anyone else with the university, to my knowledge. The man he hired was George McCarty. George had previously been athletic director at the University of Texas at El Paso and the University of Wyoming. McCarty had been fired at the University of Wyoming and had applied for the athletic director's job at New Mexico. He was hired as executive director of the Lobo Club after I had accepted the job. George did not believe the Athletic Department should use funds raised by the Lobo Club in the athletic budget. He thought that the monies should only be used as supplemental funds for the athletic program. The only reason I can think he should come to that conclusion was the State of Wyoming provided funding for the entire athletic budget at Wyoming, so the contributed funds by the Cowboy Club members were used to defray unexpected expenses for entertainment and other unbudgeted expenses. As a result of George McCarty's beliefs, he really never gave a high priority to raising funds for the athletic program.

With a total of 23 sports and with only $900,000 of state appropriations of a $4,700,000 budget, we urgently needed contributed funds to be used in our operating budget to pay for scholarships and other expenses. We needed additional funds to compete with institutions in our conference and on our schedule. The cost of major college athletics began to increase rapidly in the sixties and seventies, and has continued to multiply until the present time. In the sixties and seventies athletic budgets ran $4–10 million. Now it's not uncommon to see athletic budgets at $15– 20 million.

I really don't have any reliable statistics on the size of athletic budgets, but my guess is there are very few teams competitive now with budgets of less than $8–10 million in the top echelon of Division I-A football. Teams just competing in Division I basketball can get by on a much smaller budget. The size of the athletic budget is certainly not the most important factor in success, but there is a point an institution cannot be competitive without a budget somewhat comparative with the competition.

Because we wanted to raise our level of competition at New Mexico, we would have to increase contributions to the Lobo Club. I spent a large segment of my time in fundraising. We set a goal of 40 contributions of $5,000 or more to Lobo athletics for my first full year as athletic director in 1980-81. I visited each donor personally and made the request for a $5,000 contribution. We were able to reach 36, which brought $180,000. When I retired in 1987 some of the same donors were still making $5,000 annual contributions. In addition we had a large number of donors giving from $500 to $2,500. I personally raised over $3 million in pledges and cash, but not all in Lobo Club contributions. Pledges of $500,000 for the new track plus $1,200,000 in pledges for the expansion of the stadium (which were canceled by President May), plus repeat contributions to the Lobo Club, sponsorship for televised football games, and sponsorships of men's football and basketball coaches' TV shows were included in funds I raised.

I was able to get car dealers in Albuquerque to provide over 40 cars for the personal use of our coaches and administrators. It started back in the late sixties and early seventies that universities would provide coaches and administrators with the use of a new automobile. At that time the salaries were too low for most coaches at the majority of institutions to purchase two cars. The coach could leave the family car for a spouse and use the courtesy car for his or her transportation.

I spent a good deal of time working on a home and home football schedule. When I retired we had completed our schedules through the year 2001. I had scheduled 40 games other than conference games — 20 games were scheduled in Albuquerque and 20 games on the road.

We scheduled home and home games with Arizona, Tennessee, Arkansas, University of Oregon, University of Houston, Rice University, Texas Christian, Baylor University, Tulsa University, Texas Tech, Memphis State University, and Fresno State. I left New Mexico with the best schedules in history, and half were home games. Since that time changes have been made by subsequent athletic directors, resulting in more games on the road than at home and the cancellation of other games.

One of the best ways in my opinion to increase revenue is to play good football teams and traditional rivals at home and away. Unless a team has established a tradition of selling home game season tickets, playing a couple of patsies in two of the five or six home games does not encourage fans to buy season tickets. Large season ticket sales improve fundraising by putting a premium on the best seating locations, which can require contributions for options on those best seats.

One of the vital needs at the University of New Mexico is improvement of the football stadium. The present facility was built in 1960, and except for a pressbox which includes 648 mezzanine chairback priority seats, there have been no improvements in the stadium which have added to the appeal or to the convenience of the spectators. The cost of the pressbox added in 1976 was $2.1 million. President Davis combined the bonded indebtedness to that of other bonds for university improvements, and thus eliminated annual payments by the Athletic Department to retire the bonds.

The design of the stadium is poor. The seats are situated at too flat an angle, which interferes with vision, and seat rows are in straight lines parallel to the playing field rather than on a concave curve so that spectators are seated facing slightly toward the center of the field. Restrooms and concession stands are inconveniently located about 40 yards beyond the end zone. The exception is that there are restrooms on the upper level of the west stands, which serve spectators between the 30-yard-lines in the upper level of the stands. The capacity of the stadium is 30,646.

The stadium was built with an eight-lane track around the playing field. That put the front row of seats 65 feet from the sideline. Players' benches, with coaches and players standing, blocks the vision in the lower rows.

The track deteriorated until it was almost unusable. We planned to put the track on the east side of the east stands. The dirt berm would provide the foundation for over 5,000 seats for the track. I made an appointment with President Perovich and told him that I would raise $500,000 in private donations if the university would provide another $500,000 of the projected million-dollar cost. Actually, I raised a little more than $500,000 in pledges, most of which were $25,000 pledges payable over a five-year period. The running track, as well as runways for the jumps and takeoff areas, have a polyurethane surface in a garnet color, the same as the university's school color. It is one of the finest tracks in the nation.

Moving the track gave us an opportunity to improve our football stadium. Working with one of the best architects in the history of the state of New Mexico, we came up with a plan to lower the field nine feet and add 10 rows of chairback seats on the east and west stands, along with 10 rows of bench seats in the end zones. We planned a concourse under the sideline seats, with a stairwell at each aisle leading to it. The concourse would contain restrooms and concession stands.

The project would add a total of about 4,000 seats. The demand for chairback then available in the basketball arena and in the press-box mezzanine for football indicated the popularity of chairback seating. End zone seats would be discounted seating for fans of high school age or under and family plan seating.

We had a tried and true plan to solicit the purchase of five-year options on the chairbacks on the sidelines at $500 per seat between the 25-yard-lines and a $250 option on seats from the 25-yard-line to the goal line. If all options were sold, that's a potential revenue of $3,759,000 over a five-year period. The estimated cost was $2 million.

Adding the 4,000 seats would make better seats of all the seats in the stadium, especially the lower row of seats. The first row would have an eye level of a spectator sitting in a seat about eight feet above the field. The players' benches would be close to the stadium wall, and spectators would see over them to the playing field. The end zone seats would make the stadium look like a college football stadium. It would in effect bring all the spectators closer to the field of action, which is a characteristic of all stadiums which are considered the best in college football and for all sports for that matter.

I had one big problem. I could not get approval from President May or the regents. When I first told President May about our plans, his reply was, "I don't see how anybody can oppose that."

Many avid football fans believe they could be a great athletic director and look for an opportunity to express their opinions about any subject which might arise in athletics. At any rate, Dr. Jerry May changed his mind completely and would not support my stadium plan nor would any of the regents of the university. I'm sure the regents and the president heard many amateur opinions expressed on the expansion of the football stadiums. Probably the most frequent one, "Wait until they sell all the tickets for the seats they now have before expanding."

The truth is that there has never been a major college team in the country who expanded who did not significantly increase their ticket sales, regardless of how many games they won or lost. It wouldn't have cost the university a dime and would have provided

$700,000 to $800,000 in revenue for the football program annually for an infinite time. The income would come from the annual sale of the options on the chairback seating — the same as the annual contribution for chairback seating in the basketball arena and chairback seating in the football pressbox.

Without any support from the president or the regents, I personally received in cash or pledges $1.2 million of the $2 million estimated cost of our stadium expansion. The president told me to forget the project and turn the money back to the donors.

As of 1993 there still has been no expansion of the football stadium or improvements except to replace some of the wooden benches with aluminum benches. It is my understanding the university has a plan to just add end zone seats, to bring the capacity to about 45,000. Construction costs are much higher when seats are built from the ground level upwards rather than lowering the field and using the ground as support for the seats. The projected cost is 10 to 15 times greater to build the end zone seating without lowering the field, and nothing would be done to improve the present seating.

It is very difficult to understand the thinking of New Mexico as far as the athletic program is concerned. In the non-revenue sports of golf, tennis, track and field, and gymnastics, the University of New Mexico facilities will rank in the top five percent of those facilities at institutions in the Division I-A levels. Swimming also has an excellent facility for swimming and diving. The facilities for soccer, wrestling, and baseball are average although baseball has some use, particularly in the early spring, of the Albuquerque Sports Stadium, which is one of the best minor league baseball parks in the country and incidentally was designed by Max Flatow, our architect for the stadium improvements.

The facilities for track, tennis, and gymnastics were built while I was athletic director. I never heard a word of criticism about the university spending money on those facilities, although the total spent (except what I raised in private pledges for the track) came from university funds and none from Athletic Department funds. Yet when we announced at a press conference our plan to add 4,000 seats to the football stadium, the sports pages of both newspapers replied with negative articles. There were editorials opposing the expansion and letters to the editor criticizing our plans, although it involved no expenditure of university funds. It would be totally financed through private funding.

Since the football stadium was built in 1960, there have been only 10 years of the 33 years the stadium has been in existence that the attendance averaged over 20,000 per game. In only five years has there been a 20,000 average from 1971 through 1993. In four of the first six years of the stadium's existence, the average was over 20,000, with the all-time record in 1962 (23,730 average). The population of the Albuquerque metro area has approximately doubled since 1960.

I believe it's very important at the Division I-A level for football to pay its own way. At the great majority of schools in the Division I-A level, football is the major revenue producer. That's not true at New Mexico. You hear that Albuquerque is just not a football town, but I'm not sure any city with a football facility comparable to the University of New Mexico Stadium would be considered a football town.

The only two head football coaches at New Mexico with winning records since World War II have been Marv Levy, the present coach of the Buffalo Bills with a 14-6 record, and Joe Morrison, with an 18-15 record in three years.

The Joe Morrison Years

Joe Morrison looked like a football player. He had a strong face and body. Joe was a quiet person, not given to much conversation although he had a good sense of humor and people liked him. He commanded respect among the players, partially because he had been an outstanding performer himself. He delegated most of the coaching to assistant coaches. His judgment in selecting assistants was very good. Even though he didn't talk much, there was no question as to who was in charge.

I don't ever remember seeing him when he was not in full control of himself. He never showed much emotion.

In Joe Morrison's first game as head coach in 1980, the Lobos stunned Brigham Young, the defending Western Athletic Conference champions, 25-21 in Albuquerque. Brad Wright, the New Mexico quarterback, had a good day and led the Lobos on a couple of long scoring drives. The highlight of the game was the gambling, blitzing defense of the Lobos, which sacked Jim McMahon, the Brigham Young quarterback, nine times. However, Jim McMahon came back after the New Mexico game to win 11 straight victories, including a holiday bowl victory over SMU with the remarkable feat of scoring three touchdowns in the last two minutes to win 46-45. McMahon went on to pro football fame with the Chicago Bears, Philadelphia Eagles, and in 1993 with the Minnesota Vikings.

Brad Wright, the New Mexico quarterback, was injured in the Nevada–Las Vegas game and then lost their last three games of the season for a 4-7 record in 1980. Joe Morrison repeated with a record of 4-7-1 in 1981. Six of the seven losses were by 10 points or less.

In 1982 the Lobos won the most games in a single season in their history, as David Osborn at quarterback and Johnny Jackson at linebacker led New Mexico to 10 wins and a single loss to Brigham Young. The Lobos won the first three games by two touchdowns or more. The most impressive was a 14-0 victory over Texas Tech, which was only the third time New Mexico had beaten Texas Tech in 25 games between the two teams. The fourth victory in 1982 was a wild, high-scoring game as the Lobos beat Air Force in Colorado Springs 49-37.

The game that followed was for the Western Athletic Conference Championship, and Brigham Young won 40-12. The game was played in Albuquerque and drew the largest home crowd in the history of New Mexico football (29,761). We had sold over 30,000 tickets for the scheduled night game, but ABC selected the game for regional television and changed the starting time to an afternoon game. President Perovich ruled we had to reimburse fans for tickets already sold due to the change in starting time. In my 42 years as athletic director and football coach, it was the only time I've ever heard of reimbursing tickets due to a change in starting time of the game.

The game was very close until the third quarter, when we suffered some very costly penalties and turnovers.

New Mexico won their last six games for a 10-1-0 record. However, the bowls gave us a cold shoulder. Average home attendance of 23,336 was the second highest in New Mexico history, but it didn't impress the selection committees for the bowl games.

Joe Morrison was very disappointed not to receive a bowl bid, as were all of us. When the University of South Carolina invited him to visit Columbia for consideration of their head coaching position, I knew Joe would be impressed with their facilities. He accepted the job with over three times the salary and financial benefits he received at New Mexico.

The 1982 season was the last winning football season New Mexico had in football until 1993, when the Lobos had a 6-5 record.

Coach Joe Lee Dunn's Turn as Head Coach

Joe Morrison's defensive coordinator, Joe Lee Dunn, was a very popular figure in Albuquerque. Many fans thought he was more responsible for the Lobos' great 10-1 season than Joe Morrison. I had been impressed with his ability to judge talent in a game film. I always felt it was difficult to judge recruiting prospects in film because it is hard to judge speed in a film. Our offensive coordinator, Jerry Sadler, had done an outstanding job also, and a number of people thought he deserved consideration for the head coaching position.

I recommended Joe Lee Dunn for the head coaching job. I was hoping he could keep some of the coaches on our staff from leaving for South Carolina. Only one coach chose to stay in New Mexico, and that was Stan Quintana, who had been an outstanding quarterback for the Lobos from 1963 to 1965.

Overall, Coach Dunn did not select an impressive staff. Most of the coaches he hired had not coached at the major college level.

Joe Lee visited Joe Morrison at South Carolina shortly after accepting the head coaching position. He would never again be happy with the facilities we had at New Mexico after seeing the 72,000-seat stadium with most impressive dressing rooms, weight training room, and athletic dormitory. I think Joe Lee blamed me for the lack of facilities, but he didn't know how little influence I had in trying to improve our football facilities.

Joe Lee won his first game impressively, beating Utah 17-7 in Albuquerque, but lost six of the next eight games. He won the last three games to end up the season with a 6-6 record. In 1984 he won his first four games but then lost the next eight. In 1985 he won one of the first eight games and ended up 3-8. Joe Lee's final year was 1986. He lost his first five games, broke even with the next six games, and finished with an excellent win over Memphis State at Memphis for a 4-8 record.

During the latter part of the football season, President Farer was out of the country. I thought we needed to consider a change in the head football coaching position. I drove to Santa Fe and met with Jerry Apodaca, a regent, whose son played on the team. As I recall, Apodaco expressed no strong feelings one way or the other. Joe Lee's record was 17-30-1 for four years.

I decided not to take any action to make a change. A few days later Joe Lee resigned and accepted a job at South Carolina under Joe Morrison as defensive coordinator.

I really thought Joe Lee had the ability to do a better job than he did as head coach. He never really had an overall good staff. However, Ben Griffin, his offensive coordinator, did an extraordinary job in 1985 with his "run and shoot" offense. Joe Lee fell short in recruiting. The overall talent took a big drop in the four years he was head coach. In the following year, 1987, the Lobos were 0-11 under Mike Shepherd.

I would have to say one of my biggest mistakes at New Mexico was hiring Joe Lee Dunn as head coach. Joe Lee was one of the few head coaches I hired in any sport with whom I did not have a good personal relationship. He took the attitude that I was not trying to help him have a successful tenure. Actually, there was nothing more I could do because of the general attitude of the university administration toward football, and the lack of revenue produced by football.

Since Joe Lee left New Mexico in 1987, our relationship has been much more pleasant. I believe he realizes that he made some mistakes and that I really wasn't able to do more than I did to support the football program.

Joe Lee is presently defensive coordinator at the University of Mississippi, where he did an outstanding job in 1992. His defense was a big factor in a winning season and a victory in the Liberty Bowl. In 1993 Ole Miss finished near the top in NCAA defensive statistics in Division I-A competition.

Gary Colson — Basketball Coach

Gary Colson did an outstanding job in two distinct areas:

1. He brought Lobo basketball back from the depths to be a strong contender for the Western Athletic Conference Championship.

2. He built the program with honesty and full compliance with NCAA rules and with players who were good citizens and good students.

In 1979-80 the New Mexico basketball team was coached by Charles Harrison. He was appointed interim coach when Norm Ellenberger was suspended for violations of NCAA rules. Gary Colson was hired in late December, but it was agreed to allow Harrison to finish the season as coach. Charlie did an admirable job and gained respect from the fans, as the Lobos were 6-22 after having seven varsity players, including four starters, ruled ineligible for receiving phony credits on their transcript before entering the university.

Colson's first year was 1980-81, and the team showed much improvement with an 11-15 record and a 6-10 conference record. In 1981-82 the Lobos were 14-14 and 7-9 in the conference. One of the highlights was defeating Utah 85-71 and Brigham Young 67-65 in the final two games of the season.

In 1983-84 Gary coached the Lobos to a 24-11 season and 10-6 in the conference. They defeated Brigham Young in the conference tournament before losing to UTEP in the semifinals 44-38. In 1986-87 Colson won the most games a New Mexico team has ever won in a single season, with a 25-10 record. They missed an invitation to the NCAA Tournament by losing to Wyoming 64-62 in the finals of the Western Athletic Conference Tournament. New Mexico had beaten Wyoming 92-89 the week before the conference tournament. New Mexico also beat Brigham Young two of three games that year. Wyoming and Brigham Young received NCAA bids, but New Mexico was left out again.

I retired as athletic director in June 1987. Gary Colson had a clause in his contract that his contract would be automatically extended one year unless he was notified he would not get an extension by April 1. John Koenig became athletic director at New Mexico on July 1, 1987. Shortly afterwards he notified Colson that his contract would not be extended, which left him with two years on his contract going into the 1987-88 basketball season rather than three years.

John Koenig told me that President Jerry May and the women's athletic director, Linda Estes, were strongly opposed to Gary continuing as basketball coach.

Dr. Jerry May knew as little about college athletics as any college president I ever worked for, and I worked for 13 college presidents. I believe whatever opinion he had about Colson as a basketball coach came from basketball fans who never accepted Colson when he succeeded Norm Ellenberger. I also believe there were some regents, along with Linda Estes, who were very critical of Colson to President May.

I recall being at a reception before a conference meeting in San Diego. Western Athletic Conference Commissioner Dr. Joe Kearney and several athletic directors were commenting on what a good job they thought Gary Colson was doing as New Mexico's basketball coach. Dr. Jerry May joined the conversation. He was the only person to say anything uncomplimentary about Gary Colson. I figured then Gary was in trouble.

Jim Brandenberg was head basketball coach at Wyoming and later at San Diego State. I remember him telling me what an excellent coach he thought Gary Colson was. He said, "In the last minutes before the half of a game when Gary's team was trailing, he always came up with something special to put points on the board."

In 1987-88, the year after I retired, New Mexico won 22 games and Gary Colson was fired. With 47 victories in 1986-87 and 1987-88, it was the most games a New Mexico team ever won over a two-year period. In addition he swept both New Mexico State and UTEP, the two traditional rivals, in home and away games in 87-88.

Gary Colson had taken a team that was totally decimated by the basketball scandal. In the first couple of years he had a hard time getting into a recruit's home much less recruiting him. He gradually built a team that was strongly competitive in the Western Athletic Conference. The players he recruited were good students, good citizens, and 70% received their degree. Colson was able to take players with less than outstanding ability and use their talent in such a way that they were able to sustain a winning record. Except for Luc Longley, a 7'0 center from Australia, none of the New Mexico players stayed with an NBA professional team long enough to get more than a cup of coffee.

Some of his players who played extremely well were Phil Smith, Kevin Scarborough, Rob Robbins, Darrell McGee, and Kelly Graves at guards; Hunter Green, Allen Dolensky, and Mike Winters at forwards; and Luc Longley, Rob Loeffel, and Johnny Brown at center.

In my opinion, there was no way the University of New Mexico could justify firing Gary Colson. His teams never finished lower than eighth in Division I college basketball attendance. One of the reasons given for firing Colson was that they wanted to hire a coach that could take the basketball team to a higher level.

Dave Bliss was hired to succeed Gary Colson. Dave Bliss is a good man and a good coach. He's had a good record as a basketball coach, but no better than Gary Colson did in his last three or four years, except he did get a couple of bids to the NCAA Championship Tournament. Gary Colson's teams deserved a couple of NCAA bids also. I would guess that Dave Bliss' salary and financial package is at least double that of Gary Colson.

CHAPTER 27

1983–87

THE UNIVERSITY OF NEW MEXICO:

A RECIPE FOR FAILURE

Most of my experiences at every institution where I've worked have been very positive, although in athletics there are always ups and downs. The two places where I worked and left with memories that are not good are the Pittsburgh Steelers and the University of New Mexico. I was only at Pittsburgh one year and we had a bad team. It was Chuck Noll's first year as a head coach. He's recognized as one of the greatest coaches in the history of professional football. I certainly give him credit for his football knowledge, but, frankly, I did not enjoy working with him. He lacked the thoughtfulness and empathy toward other human beings that I observed in many men. For example, he once said, "Never trust a football player."

At the University of New Mexico I was met with skepticism, distrust, and suspicion. I was treated more like an untrustworthy individual rather than as a person who has spent a lifetime establishing a reputation for honesty and complete integrity.

I would like to write more good things about the University of New Mexico. There were many good friends who provided encouragement and financial assistance to the university. I had some excellent coaches and good people on our athletic staff, and I'll always look upon almost every single one as a genuine friend. But I feel obligated to write about some unpleasant experiences with persons in high positions at the university. The treatment I received was unjustified, and to this day I'm not sure at all what I did to merit such unfair treatment.

Below are six experiences I had with a group of persons or individual persons which made it very difficult for me to be successful or for the university athletic program to experience success.

1. *The Manufactured Deficit of 1983-84 by the Financial Administrators of the University* — I came to the university in December of 1979, just as one of the most publicized scandals in college basketball began to unfold. I found as the fiscal year came to an end, on June 30, 1980, that the athletic expenditures were balanced by some year-end adjustments to revenue and expenditures. That was my first experience with an operation of that kind. However, it changed rapidly in 1980-81, and the athletic budget at the University of New Mexico soon became perhaps the most publicized budget in intercollegiate athletic history.

The crisis came in 1984-85, two years after the best football season New Mexico had in their modern football history. Coach Joe Morrison had led his team to a 10-1-0 season.

Along about early April of 1984, Hal Donovan, our assistant athletic director for finance, and I were going over our financial records, and we were stunned to discover we were looking at a sizable deficit for the 1983-84 fiscal year. The Accounting Department kept all records and gave us a monthly report which was sometimes 30 to 60 days behind the actual expenditures and incoming revenues. We had no computers. Hal Donovan worked on budget reports the old-fashioned way, with a pencil on a spreadsheet.

I immediately called President Tom Farer and told him what we were facing. After consultation with the financial administrators, Hal Donovan and me, and possibly with other administrators in the university, President Farer had a press conference and announced the possibility of an athletic budget deficit of about $800,000. The final records of the Athletic Department showed a deficit of $782,918.

President Farer told me to take total responsibility for the deficit and placed me on probation as athletic director. It certainly didn't help my image for my picture to be in newspapers throughout the country with a caption that I had been placed on probation for the $800,000 deficit. I felt certain that our athletic operations had done nothing to justify such a deficit. However, I didn't have any facts to go on. In the television interview I accepted responsibility for the deficit.

Joe Goldberg, a UNM law professor, was assistant to President Farer. He tried to convince me to resign as athletic director. I refused to do so.

After our budget year ended on June 30, 1984, and we received the final figures for the fiscal year from the Accounting Department, I began to make comparisons of our income and expenses in previous years of 1980-81 through 1982-83. I soon discovered that $416,649 had been added to our expenses by the accounting office that the Athletic Department had absolutely nothing to do with. There was also a $283,761 reduction in revenue from two sources, the elimination of $98,899 for faculty and staff season football and basketball tickets by the Accounting Department and a 58.3% reduction (or $184,862) in unrestricted Lobo Club contributions to the Athletic Department for 1983-84. The total of the increase in expenses and the decrease in income added up to $700,710 of the $782,918 deficit, or about 90%. In addition, there was also a 67% (or $140,312) increase in medical expenses, which seemed highly unreasonable. The most shocking increase came in the cost of football scholarships, from $195,705 in 1980-81 to $449,210 in 1984-85. Except for a $200 allowance for books, which I believe remained constant during that period, athletic scholarships consisted of room, board and tuition. We reduced the number of scholarships for each year to the same number as 1980-81 for comparative purposes, and the increase was 63% (or $123,337) more than the university increase for room, board and tuition.

If we eliminated the expenses added by the Accounting Department and the decrease in income by the Accounting Department and the Lobo Club, the Athletic Department profit would have been $574,944 for the five years.

I believe this injustice was due to Carroll Lee, the comptroller (chief accounting officer), Jim Wiegmann, the budget director (who along with Carroll Lee increased utilities and overhead expense by $70,000 after our profit with a 10-1 football season in 1982), and Robert Schulte, director of food and housing. Another change President Farer made was to fire our assistant athletic director of finance, Hal Donovan. Hal Donovan had nothing to do with our deficit. He was given a very demanding job with no tools to work with. They sent an accountant from the Accounting Department, and he took over Hal Donovan's financial duties. He was given a computer and other up-to-date equipment, plus additional personnel.

The Accounting Department became the watchdog for our financial operation. That was like appointing the fox to guard the hen house.

An amazing thing happened to football and basketball scholarships. In the next two years, 1985-86 and 1986-87, the increase in football scholarships and basketball scholarships was less than the university increase in room, board and tuition. Remember, in the previous five years football scholarships had increased 63% more than university room, board and tuition.

Another interesting experience happened. I was meeting with Jerry Apodaca, one of the regents. When we finished our business he invited me to attend a meeting with him and the other regents with Carroll Lee, the comptroller. I soon found out the meeting was for the purpose of gaining information which could lead to my firing as athletic director.

Carroll Lee passed out a lengthy paper which was very critical of me but contained little or no real substance. He did not plan on my being there, but after handing a copy to everyone, he felt he could not avoid giving me a copy.

After the meeting I called Carroll and asked him why he would write a paper like that. He said, "I was told to, John." He wouldn't say who told him to do it.

Among other equally ridiculous charges, Carroll criticized me for getting cars from the automobile dealers for our coaches and administrators. To the best of my knowledge every major university in the country furnished courtesy cars to their coaches and administrators. He suggested I could have raised a lot more money if I had solicited the car dealers for cash rather than courtesy cars. He also incorrectly accused me of spending over $3,000 of university funds for an Athletic Department party at my home to welcome coaches and staff members at the beginning of the academic year, and for another party for Golden Lobo Club members ($5,000 or more donors). We did use university funds (Athletic Department) for the

Golden Lobo Club party which was held on campus. However, I always spend my own personal funds for any entertaining I do personally, whether it is for soliciting funds from a prospective donor or entertaining in my own home. I learned long ago how quick people are to criticize a person for spending too much money on entertainment, especially those in university accounting offices.

I immediately wrote a letter to the president and all the regents answering all the criticisms Carroll Lee made in his paper. I also sent a copy to Carroll Lee. I never heard another word about the matter.

Below is an itemized list of the expenditures and reduced revenue for 1983-84 which were initiated by Carroll Lee, Jim Wiegmann, and Robert Schulte.

Increase in Expenses and Decrease in Income
Through Budget Director, Comptroller's Office,
Housing and Food Services and Lobo Club in 1984-85 Only

Decrease in Income

1. Reduced income by not paying 1/2 cost of faculty and staff season tickets to football and basketball games. (1984-85 was the only year in which I was athletic director that 1/2 the cost of season football and basketball tickets for faculty and staff was not paid by the university.) $98,899
2. Lobo Club net contributions to Athletic Department of unrestricted contributions decreased from $316,928 in 1982-83 to $132,066 in 1984-85. $184,862

    Total Decrease in Income   **$283,761**

Increase in Expenses

1. Added utilities and overhead expenses $ 70,000
2. Added expense for overcharge of football scholarships (Corrections for same number of scholarships 1980-81 thru 1984-85) $123,337
3. Added expense for overcharge of basketball scholarships (Corrections for same number of scholarships 1980-81 thru 1984-85) $ 15,536
4. Added expense for no allowance of tuition waivers for 1984-85 (estimated) $160,000

5. Added expense for outstanding medical bills for
   student athletes after team doctors and Presbyterian
   Hospital had pledged to contribute services for all
   bills not paid by insurance   <u>$ 57,776</u>

     Total Expense Added   **$416,649**

     Total Decrease in Income and Increase in Expense   <u>**$700,410**</u>

I was very shocked at the increase in expenses. The increase in utilities and overhead expense was not revealed to me until the fiscal year was about half completed. As far as the $160,000 for not allowing the Athletic Department to take advantage of tuition waivers, I had been told more than once that we would receive tuition waivers if we needed them. There was a state law which permitted the state institutions in New Mexico to take tuition waivers for athletic scholarships, but we were not allowed them while I was athletic director.

The reduction in Lobo Club contributions of $184,862 was another surprise. The Lobo Club kept their own records and I was not privileged to those until they gave us a copy of their year-end financial statements. I had continued raising funds for the Lobo Club and was not aware there was a significant reduction in funds contributed. I am still not sure there was a large reduction. It's the first time to my knowledge that university financial administrators deliberately created a large deficit in order to discredit the athletic director of a university.

2. *University of New Mexico Regent Calvin Horn* — Calvin Horn was a very wealthy man. He was a leader in the First Baptist Church in Albuquerque, New Mexico, and was on the University of New Mexico Board of Regents. It was surprising but true that he was a close friend of UNM's former basketball coach, Norm Ellenberger.

After President "Bud" Davis fired Norm Ellenberger, Calvin Horn became very critical of President Davis. In fact, he made things so uncomfortable for President Davis that he resigned to take a job with the State of Oregon. A lot of people blamed President Davis for Ellenberger's rules violations, although there was never a shred of evidence that Bud Davis knew anything about the rules violations of Norm Ellenberger other than the fact that Ellenberger and

Football Scholarships Costs

1980-81 to 1984-85 Compared to UNM Increase in Room, Board and Tuition

Academic Year	Football WAC Eligibility and Scholarship List	% of Increase From 1980-81 For Each Succeeding Year	Football Scholarship Expense Per Fiscal Year	Football Scholarship Cost Reduced To 1980-81 Number of Scholarships	% of Increase From 1980-81
1980–81	68	—	195,705	—	—
1981–82	78	14.6	248,870	212,535	8.6
1982–83	78	14.6	322,763	275,640	40.8
1983–84	80	17.7	384,116	316,127	61.5
1984–85	78	14.6	449,210	383,625	96.0
Total Increase	10	14.6	253,505	187,920	96.0
*University of New Mexico's (UNM) Increase from 80–81 to 84–85 for Room, Board and Tuition				64,583	33.0
Addt'l Athletic Department Costs over UNM Increases from 80–81 thru 84–85 Football Scholarships for Same Number of Scholarships				123,337	63.0
Average Increase of Football Scholarship Costs Over UNM Room, Board and Tuition Increases Per Year				30,834	15.75

*Source: Dr. Richard Cady, Institutional Research, University of New Mexico — Based on 80% Out-of-State Tuition and 20% In-State

Athletic Director Lavon McDonald were quoted as saying he knew what was going on. Yet when President Davis called Ellenberger and Lavon McDonald in for a meeting and asked about possible rules violations, both gave their word that there had been no violations on their part.

Calvin Horn became one of my sharpest critics and of the Athletic Department. When I negotiated my contract, I asked for a $5,000 annual expense allowance to be advanced to me for otherwise unreimbursable expenses. This was primarily for entertainment expenses, since state laws were very restrictive on entertainment and guest meal expenses. I was responsible for reporting my expenses through my income tax return rather than through university channels. I had a similar arrangement at Florida State. Such expense funds were available to the head football coach and head basketball coach. Calvin Horn found out about the expense money, and he was quoted in the *Albuquerque Tribune* as saying, "It appears the athletic director, basketball coach and football coach have voted themselves a raise."

The effect of the story with the administration was to add the expense allowance to our salaries. They began immediately to deduct social security and withholding taxes on the amount of the expense allowance.

Later Calvin Horn began a strong campaign for the regents to place a limit on the athletic budget. There were a number of articles in the newspapers giving the reasons he felt there should be a ceiling on our athletic budget. Horn wanted to set a limit of $4 million. We had prepared our budget for a revenue and expense of $4.5 million. Calvin Horn had convinced some of the regents that a budget limit was the proper thing to do.

I really don't know for certain, but I believe President Perovich convinced the regents to reverse their decision, and setting specific budget limits wasn't their responsibility. President Perovich approved our requested budget of $4.5 million. That was the year our football team went 10-1. Our revenue went up to $4,735,000 for a $192,000 profit.

I made an appointment with Regent Horn and asked, "Why is it you have been so hard on me and the Athletic Department?"

Calvin replied, "You said Norm Ellenberger sold the university down the river. That poor man has suffered enough, and you don't need to criticize him further."

Calvin Horn's priority was to punish and make things as uncomfortable as possible for President Davis, who fired Ellenberger, and for me, who had the responsibility to see that the athletic program was run honestly and according to the NCAA rules.

In addition to NCAA rules violations, Ellenberger was convicted by a jury in state district court on 21 of 22 counts of fraud and making false public vouchers. However, the judge deferred sentence for a year and at the end of the year all counts were dropped.

Ellenberger's primary defense was that he just did what all college basketball coaches did. It's the same statement almost all coaches make when they are convicted of violating NCAA rules and regulations. At the same time I was trying to convince the people of Albuquerque and people throughout the nation that a coach does not have to cheat to compete and win.

Even if it were true, it wouldn't do any good for me to say, "Ellenberger sold the university down the river." All it did was further alienate Ellenberger's friends. He still had a lot of them in Albuquerque.

During my seven and a half years at New Mexico, I had four presidents. At least two, President Davis and President Farer, received a lot of pressure to resign. The other two, President John Perovich and President Jerry May, had relatively short terms. The presidency of the University of New Mexico is a very difficult job to keep. I believe one of the reasons is that through the years the regents haven't given the presidents the support they deserve as the chief executive officers of the university.

President Bud Davis gave me the most cooperation and had the most confidence in my judgment. Tom Farer liked athletics and I believe he changed his mind about my being at fault for the budget deficit. (Read what he wrote in a letter to the editor of the *Albuquerque Journal* at the end of this chapter.) I really don't think John Perovich really wanted to be president. Jerry May didn't have the background or experience in athletics. He paid less attention to my opinions than any of the four presidents.

3. *The Local Print Media* — The total negative attitude and constant criticisms of the sports print media in Albuquerque kept the general public as a whole from having any confidence or hope in those responsible for intercollegiate athletics. The two chief critics

were Dennis Latta, who was sports editor of the *Albuquerque Journal* for most of the years I was in Albuquerque, but later was relieved of that responsibility, and Richard Stevens, principal sports columnist of the *Albuquerque Tribune* and in some years assigned as the sports reporter for football or basketball games.

Latta always searched hard for something to criticize, whether it was a decision by the athletic director or a coach's decision on strategy in a game. In my early years at the University of New Mexico, he wrote a series of articles criticizing our budget expenditures. He really had no informed opinions of what he wrote about. For example, one of the things he criticized was our travel expenses. We were in the Western Athletic Conference and our schedules in football and basketball covered the largest geographical area of any conference in the country. When you add in the non-conference games, our travel ranged from as far west as Hawaii and California to as far east as Florida, Tennessee, or Texas, depending on the year and the sport.

In administrative travel to NCAA conventions, College Football Association meetings, and Western Athletic Conference meetings, the distances were equally as long, and the meetings were normally held in resort areas where expenses were not necessarily economical.

We were desperately trying to improve our competitive level, particularly in football and basketball after the basketball scandal surfaced in 1979-80. Regardless of how honest and clean an athletic program is, it doesn't impress the fans unless the teams are competitive and win their share of games. It was necessary for us to increase expenses in both football and basketball. Our non-revenue sports for the most part had a tradition of being competitive, and we tried to maintain that high level of competition.

Dennis Latta was particularly critical of Gary Colson. In fact, he wrote a column advocating that Colson should be fired. Latta made big stories out of things which were rather inconsequential, such as the headline story on Gary Colson's son being issued books on loan from the Athletic Department.

Richard Stevens was nasty in his criticisms. He liked to belittle New Mexico schedules in football and basketball. In football, when we played New Mexico State or University of Texas at El Paso in Albuquerque, he wrote columns expressing the opinion their teams were so poor that fans shouldn't waste their time going to see them play. He was particularly critical of me as athletic director. He ridiculed me and second guessed decisions. He was also very critical of Gary Colson. He pictured himself as a real expert in basketball fundamentals and strategy.

Richard Stevens suggested more than once that I was able to raise money through intimidation. Believe me, you don't raise money in contributions by intimidating the contributor. A donor may cancel his contribution at any time he pleases. There is never a contract to make a contribution, even if there is a signed pledge.

The only time I ever recall Richard Stevens writing anything complimentary about me was when I retired. He did say I showed a lot of determination and persistence in trying to get the football stadium expanded. His positive comments came too late to be of any help.

Both Richard Stevens and Dennis Latta spent time with Linda Estes, the women's athletic director. I believe that Linda Estes was the source of some of their criticisms. Adam Teicher, a sportswriter of the *Tribune* and now in Kansas City, said Linda gave information to him that discredited me, other coaches, and sports programs.

Richard Stevens really didn't need much help to write critical columns and articles. He is one of the great "poison pen" writers of all time.

Over the years there have been few college athletic programs which have done well that didn't have strong support from their local media. Some football programs which come to mind with excellent local media support are Arizona State, Florida State, Louisiana State, University of Arkansas, University of Tennessee, University of Alabama, and Auburn University. I'm sure there are many others.

4. *Linda Estes, Women's Athletic Director* — In all my years in athletics I've never known nor heard of anyone who was as disruptive and disloyal as Linda Estes, our women's athletic director. She was appointed to head the women's program when Title IX came into effect in the early seventies. She constantly demanded higher funding for women's athletics. That didn't bother me, as that's what you would expect an athletic director to do. She didn't stop at that, however. She was always critical of men's football and the money which was spent on football. She talked down football to the sports

writers, to the administration, and to anyone who would listen to her.

Linda didn't like Gary Colson, our basketball coach. She took a very active role in seeing that Gary was fired. Linda also had a dislike for Del Hessel, our track coach. After I left, she was able to get him fired by accusing him of breaking NCAA rules and regulations.

Some funding for our athletic program came from state appropriations and student fees. The formula I used was to divide these funds equally among all sports.

Since women's basketball was the most popular spectator sport for women, we gave an additional allotment to basketball. We also divided unrestricted contributions among all sports, although not equally but on the percentage of cost of each sport to the total operating budgets of all sports. On that basis men's football and basketball received the larger share of unrestricted contributions.

In my first full year, women's athletics received an increase of over $100,000, and by their fifth year, 1984-85, their expenditures *were more than doubled the 1979-80 budget,* which was the year before I became athletic director. According to Athletic Department financial records, women's athletics spent $1,044,589 in the 1984-85 budget year.

"Designated contributed funds" increased a particular sports budget by the amount of the designated contributions. Men's non-revenue sports raised almost $200,000 more than women's sports in designated contributions.

Two of the administrators of women's athletics told me to never expect Linda Estes to say a kind word about me. I believe she worked very hard to undermine me among the faculty and administration at the university. She told everyone who would listen what a horrible job I had done administering the athletic budget and blamed our deficit on my mismanagement.

For her disloyalty to me, Gary Colson, Del Hessel, the football program, Hal Donovan, Tom Brennan, who headed our academic advisement program, and to others in the men's athletic program, she received a promotion after I left and was placed in charge of all sports except men's football and basketball.

I'll relate one incident which happened about two years before I retired.

I was playing golf one afternoon with a couple of our scholarship donors. I received an emergency call from my secretary. She said that Dennis Latta of the *Albuquerque Journal* was going to release a derogatory story on Gary Colson, our basketball coach. I was told that while auditing the books which were lent to athletes on scholarship, a book ticket was found that had been signed by Gary Colson's son. Someone had given Dennis Latta a copy of the book ticket. The person doing the audit was a former employee in the book store but had retired and was working as a volunteer with the Women's Athletic Department. She was not a person who would have any reason to know Dennis Latta, the sports editor of the *Albuquerque Journal*. I assumed she gave a copy of the ticket to Linda Estes, and that Linda had given it to Dennis Latta.

I called Gary Colson and Gary said that he had asked his secretary if she thought it would be okay if his son borrowed books from the Athletic Department. His secretary said, "Sure, that's okay."

I then called Dennis Latta. He admitted having the book slip and had written a story for the next morning's paper. He wouldn't admit that Linda gave him the book slip, but he would not deny she gave it to him. If Linda had not given him the slip, I believe he would have stated emphatically that she didn't give it to him.

In the next morning's paper there was a headline story about Gary's son getting Athletic Department's books on loan for the semester. It covered the whole width of the top of the first sports page with a picture of the book slip. I went to the basketball office the first thing the next morning and told Gary to write a check for the books, which he did. I turned it over to our accountant. It was a dumb thing for Gary to do, but in his defense he had coached 10 years at Pepperdine University in California, a private institution, and I knew from experience that employees with faculty or staff status at private institutions receive free tuition for their spouses and children and many benefits which are completely taboo in a public or state university.

I called Linda Estes and told her I wanted to see her. I asked her if she gave Dennis Latta the book slip. She would not admit she did, but she didn't deny it. I still felt sure she did. I told her in very strong terms it was not her duty to report to the press a mistake or alleged wrong doing of a person in the Athletic Department, and I expected her to show loyalty to me and other employees in the Athletic Department. She stormed out of my office as mad as she could be. After that incident our relationship worsened. Linda Estes really didn't believe she should answer to anyone in the Athletic Department.

I asked one of our presidents if I could fire her. He said, "No, you can't do that." At least two of the regents were very close friends with Linda.

5. *The Lobo Club* — The Athletic Department's fundraising organization was not under institutional control. The Lobo Club had been in existence for many years before I came to the University of New Mexico. The membership as a whole never really felt any strong urgency to raise funds for the Athletic Department. However, I believe that has changed for the better in the past few years (although the expense to raise money for the athletic contributions far exceeds what is expected of a charitable organization). The 1989-90 financial statement prepared by one of the Big Eight accounting firms showed unrestricted contributions at $775,000 and the expense for fundraising was $380,000, or 49% of the unrestricted funds raised. That's entirely too high.

In the past the Lobo Club has selected executive directors without any input from the Athletic Department or the university. The time is long past due for the Lobo Club and the Athletic Department to work together as a team and coordinate their efforts so that the maximum dollars may be turned over to build a truly excellent athletic program.

6. *The Athletic Council* — The Athletic Council at New Mexico has been primarily an organization with adversarial relationship with the Athletic Department. From my experience with the Athletic Council they have adopted a role to question athletic operations and to find fault with the department. At the other five universities where I've worked, the Athletic Council felt their purpose was to support the athletic program and find ways they might be helpful.

At Florida State, when we had a budget crisis in 1973-74, Dick Baker, who was chairman of the Athletic Council, worked with me and our business manager for about 20 hours one weekend to make every possible cut we could possibly make in each sports budget and administrative budget without crippling a sport to the extent that it could not compete and have a successful season.

The members of the New Mexico Athletic Council are appointed by the Faculty Senate. As a result, the members of the council were not necessarily sympathetic with college athletics. Some had their own agenda of how an athletic department should be run.

At the great majority of institutions the president of the university appoints faculty members who have an interest in athletics and who wish to contribute to a program of excellence.

I remember an Athletic Council meeting at New Mexico in early December in the middle 1980s. The council was discussing a basketball game which had been scheduled with our in-state rival, New Mexico State University, during the quiet period of final exams. The council asked for a vote to cancel the game. All tickets had been sold and we were assured of a crowd of over 17,000. Without the vote of our Alumni Council representative the game would have been canceled or at least voted by the Athletic Council to be canceled.

There were some good members on the Athletic Council who were interested in helping New Mexico have a good and honest athletic program, but the good ones were outnumbered by those with special interests which for the most part were not in the best interest of an excellent athletic program at New Mexico. In some cases we had members who had no interest in New Mexico athletics.

I've written about six different personalities or factors which contributed to the failure of the University of New Mexico to achieve the success that may have been possible. In each case it was the problem of the person or group of persons following their own agenda or personal interest with the goal of getting even with or discrediting those who didn't share the same viewpoint they did. There was no unified or coordinated effort on the part of these persons to work toward a common goal of developing an excellent athletic program in which the people of New Mexico could take pride. Such an approach by persons who can affect decisions is a recipe for failure.

There were many people who sincerely felt we were supporting too many sports. We probably were, but I didn't want to eliminate any of our sports programs. Every sport had a strong constituency. I felt it was much more important to get football on a basis that it could produce more revenue than was needed for football. That's exactly what Brigham Young did, and they have been the dominant institution in the Western Athletic Conference for 10 to 15 years. The year after I left, President May eliminated four sports — men's baseball and wrestling and women's basketball and swimming. The outcry was so great that all four sports were reinstated.

There is absolutely no question in my mind if the University of New Mexico had followed my plan to lower the football field nine feet and build 10 rows of seats on the sideline and end zone with the sideline seats chairback seats, they would have added $800,000 to $900,000 of revenue to football annually. The revenue would have come from $500 options on chairback seats inside the 25-yard-line and $250 options on chairback seats from the 25-yard-line to the goal line plus the price of the tickets. The tickets would be sold to the option holders, whose priority continued as long as they made the required contribution, and to the general public on the seats where the options were not sold for the current season only. Anyone purchasing an option the following year would have priority on the seats that had not been sold to option holders. The added revenue to the football program would have freed revenue for other sports or needs.

The present administration wants to keep the football field with an extra 65 feet on each sideline so that the soccer team can use the field. Unfortunately, they will never see the day when soccer will be a revenue sport in America as some believe.

I believe the university has made progress in recent years to work toward a coordinated plan. I sincerely hope they are able in the future to realize the potential the university has in intercollegiate athletics and in other areas.

Following is a letter that former President Tom Farer wrote the *Albuquerque Journal* after he resigned as president of the university. I personally liked President Farer and felt his actions against me after the $800,000 deficit were influenced by others. President Farer was never really given an opportunity to establish himself as president of the University of New Mexico. Patience has never been a virtue of the university, as far as presidents are concerned.

Despite the problems which kept the university from having a unified and well-coordinated athletic program, the university ranked second in composite performance of all men's sports to Brigham Young for the last five years I was athletic director. However, football was a disappointment except for the outstanding team in 1982. Football is still the key for a truly successful program that can really challenge Brigham Young.

Bridgers Restored UNM's Integrity

Since, in the course of my presidency of the University of New Mexico, I found it necessary temporarily to take financial control of the Athletic Department out of the director's hands, many readers may be surprised to learn that of all the administrators in various areas of higher education I have met over the past 25 years, there are few of whom I feel as much respect and affection as I do for John Bridgers.

Because he is a man of great integrity, he restored both the image and the reality of integrity to the UNM Athletic Department after the demoralizing Lobogate scandal. Because he combines a fine practical intelligence with an extraordinary capacity for work, he brought that athletic program from an over-all record at the bottom of the Western Athletic Conference to a position just below Brigham Young's. Because he is a man with a great sense of fairness, he honored the spirit as well as the letter of the commitment to gender equality, pumping money into women's athletics so that it would rise along with the men's program.

John labored under serious handicaps not of his making. One was the legacy of Lobogate. Another legacy was an athletic program that had been allowed by his predecessors to swell out of proportion to available resources earmarked for athletics. And there were other burdens he had to drag around while struggling with all his impressive dedication and capacity to build and maintain a program that could still express the aspiration to excellence.

John proved that the university cannot have a competitive 24-sport program at the Division 1A level, without running a deficit, unless the community is willing to increase support. If a man of his ability and commitment could not lick the deficit, no one could.

The harsh financial controls I imposed were a stopgap, a

way of holding the line pending decisions about the future of the program, decisions bound to provoke opposition from boosters of various sports, decisions that could not be made until UNM had a board of regents willing to back the university's administrators.

Albuquerque is fortunate that John has decided to remain here, where he has so many friends. I am proud to count myself among them.

Tom J. Farer
Albuquerque

Epilogue: Evidence of
What's Right with Football

In this treatise, I have given in-depth sketches of players I have personally coached at the professional, major college, and small college level. All of these individuals are convincing examples that football players at all levels cannot only be successful as participants in football, but for the most part at the same time possess the qualities of leadership, compete in the classroom, and in later years pursue successful careers in whatever career they choose. Their own testimony gives a great deal of credit to their success from the challenge, inspiration, and confidence they received from participating in football at the high school and college level — and the most gifted at the professional level.

Except for the fact that present-day football players are bigger, stronger, and faster due to the emphasis on weight training and the fact that through better nutrition and more attention to good health habits people are taller and larger than a generation ago, the sport of football has changed very little. There are more minority participants, which is as it should be. There is more emphasis on the passing game in college and professional football. However, the fundamentals have not changed. The basic blocking and tackling techniques, pass coverages, and defensive line play have changed

344

very little. When attending games or even when watching on television, I can recognize the pass defense coverages which were used
when I was a coach, as well as the same pass patterns and running
plays.

Human nature does not change either, and the same qualities
that made great players in the past are present in today's athletes.
Probably the most inaccurate statement I hear about coaches who
are going through a bad time is, "The game has passed him by." In
the first place, very few head coaches at the Division I-A level call
their offensive or defensive plays. They normally have a young
coach as offensive or defensive coordinator calling the offensive
plays or the defensive schemes or formations. It may well be that the
coordinator is not using the imagination and tactics which are available to him and to all coaches, or probably more often he does not
have the same quality of players as does the opposing team.

In addition to anecdotes about the players I've coached at all
levels of college football and in professional football, I've gathered
some quotes by some of the greatest leaders our country has known:
presidents, military leaders, college presidents, a justice of the U.S.
Supreme Court, famous authors, a poet, and a college football player
who was awarded an NCAA postgraduate scholarship.

President Gerald R. Ford: "We must be physically and mentally fit
because the times demand that we not only compete but that we
excel, and we must do it with enthusiasm, the enthusiasm found
most prominently in the field of sport."

President John F. Kennedy: "I sometimes wonder whether those of
us who love football appreciate its great lessons: that dedication,
discipline and teamwork are necessary for success. We take it for
granted that the players will spare no sacrifice to become alert,
strong and skilled — that they will give their best on the field. That
is as it should be, and we must never expect less, but I am extremely
anxious that its implication not be lost on us."

Admiral James Ingram: "Looking back over the years, the results
of football training are most convincing. I know of no athletic competition that develops more useful traits of character or essential
physical prowess. For example: the subordination of the individual

to team play, development of initiative, leadership and the value of persistence and physical fitness, the self-determination that inspires 'the will to win' against any odds — and along with it all, the building of real character and true sportsmanship."

General Douglas McArthur: "The game has become the symbol of our best qualities —courage, staminated efficiency. Many believe in these days of doubt and indecision that through this sport we can best keep alive the spirit of reality and enterprise which has made us great. Upon the fields of friendly strife are sown the seeds that, upon other fields, on other days, will bear the fruit of victory."

General George C. Marshall: (Chief of staff in World War II instructing an aide) "I want an officer for a secret and dangerous mission. I want a West Point football player."

Governor Lee S. Dreyfus: (Former college president) "There's no program in any school system that does for the issues of *racial equality* what athletics does. It teaches you to judge a human being on his competence and his performance."

Dr. Thaddeus Seymour: (Former president of Wabash College) "The generation gap cannot be closed in the classroom. It is outside, particularly in athletics, where the hard questions are asked, where a student gains the experience that will test his capacity to function as a citizen. The tremendous demands on endurance and the capacity of a competition to dig into his personal resources in a degree of willingness to sacrifice and give of the things that make for self-discipline — it is on this quality that our society must depend if it is to survive."

Dr. Henry C. Link: (Author of *Return to Religion*) "Instruction on the American playing field for a time filled up a vacuum created by lack of leadership in religion. Many lessons in self-control, sacrifice, teamwork, idealism, yes — in morality — were learned, taught by the high school, preparatory school *and college coaches*. There never has been anything like this phenomenon, and it reaches its fullest expression in *football* — a game which has set in some measure and competitive pattern of this nation."

Archibald MacLeish: (Pulitzer Prize Winner in Poetry) "I think I learned more on the two Yale football teams I played on than I have before or since about certain very fundamental and important matters. Without more attention to things of the mind and spirit, there can be no human understanding; and that, without such understanding, the technological information which man has gathered is meaningless."

Dr. Norman Vincent Peale: "Jesus always followed what most interested the people. He talked about the lessons found in everyday life. You can be sure he would find many lessons in American sports. He taught all the qualities that make for good sports: discipline, courage, health, cleanliness, mental awareness and the rest."

Supreme Court Justice Byron White: "Native ability plus formal education may be an inadequate formula to produce excellence we so urgently require. We need those mysterious and elusive qualities of courage, determination, presence of mind, self-control and concentration on a given task."

Thomas C. Lawhorne, Jr.: (on receiving an NCAA postgraduate scholarship) "Football may provide us some of our most valuable education — knowing what it is to be knocked down, but to get up; to hurt and keep on running; or have to bow your neck on third and one in the fourth quarter and the score is tied. These are the things that may help one become a better teacher, lawyer, doctor, citizen, father, husband and — MAN!"

I wrote previously that the 1963 Baylor football team was probably the best college team I coached. We won six Southwest Conference games, the most ever won by a Baylor team prior to 1963. Our only loss was to the University of Texas, national champions in the Associated Press and Coaches Poll. The game was not decided until the final seconds, when a Don Trull pass to Lawrence Elkins appeared to be a certain touchdown. But Duke Carlisle, their quarterback and safety, plucked the ball from Elkins' hands on a magnificent play at the goal line to preserve their 7-0 lead. Texas went on to defeat Navy, led by Roger Staubach, and the number-two team in the Associated Press Poll 28-6 in the Cotton Bowl.

In 1983 Baylor was again invited to the Bluebonnet Bowl. We had a reunion of the players who had defeated LSU 14-7 in the 1963 Bluebonnet Bowl game. I was very impressed with the successes of the Baylor players on the 1963 squad who came to the reunion. Of the 53 players listed in the Bluebonnet Bowl program on the travel squad, 51 (or 96.2%) received a BA or BS degree from Baylor. We counted 19 players who received advanced degrees. There may have been more. Among the graduate degrees, there were five lawyers, four dentists, and four medical doctors. There was one Fulbright Scholar who received a Ph.D. (Mickey Kennedy), one who received a theological degree and was a Baptist minister, two who were certified public accountants, and four who coached and received master's degrees.

From a football standpoint Don Trull and Lawrence Elkins were All-American, and each played about five years in professional football. Bobby Maples, our center, played 14 years, and Dalton Hoffman and James Ingram had brief careers with the Houston Oilers.

Tommy Turner, assistant to the vice-chancellor, and Susan Koehler, from the Registrar's Office, helped confirm the graduation and graduate degree records. There was a minimum of 35.9% of the travel squad who received graduate degrees. While I don't have statistics for the other nine years I coached at Baylor, I believe 1963 was typical of the remainder of the Baylor squads I coached. I also believe that there probably have been many major college teams over the years that can match or exceed the educational achievements of the 1963 Baylor team. However, in the past 20 years I doubt if many Division I-A colleges and universities can match the educational achievements of the 1963 Baylor squad.

Realistically, coaches are primarily judged by their won-lost record, but if all the other success factors of the players I coached are added, I believe I had a very successful coaching career. I would have liked to have done better by the scoreboard, but I did my best and don't believe I have any reason to apologize for my record.

The other success factors other than won-lost record are as follows:

1. Percentage of scholarship football players graduating with a BA or BS degree.

2. Grade-point average of football players on scholarship.

3. Percentage of football players receiving a graduate degree.

4. The kind of citizens the football players become after graduation. This would include their contribution to their community, their church, the kind of parents they become, and their

integrity. This category is difficult if not impossible to measure accurately, and I doubt if anyone has ever tried to measure it for a particular graduating class of football players. But it is of great importance.

The factors above are very important in the life of football players and to most coaches, but the only way a coach can keep his job in Division I-A football is to win football games. Presidents and faculty representatives may give lip service to the four factors above, but winning games easily surpasses the other success factors.

Our football staff encouraged high academic standards in every possible way we could think of. A football player could major in any academic curriculum available at Baylor. We awarded academic-athletic scholarships to our best students, which included students with a B-minus average or above. We publicized their achievements in our football game programs and in annual meetings with scholarship donors. We insisted on regular class attendance. We limited practice on the field to two hours or less and never had a night meeting with the players when school was in session during the 10 years I was head football coach. If we were playing an out-of-town game, we might have a meeting on Friday night before the game.

One of the criticisms you often hear about college athletics is that the athletes (basketball and football players) make the university millions of dollars but get no monetary reward for their efforts except a scholarship. The truth is that less than 10% of the schools in Division I-A football and Division I basketball make a profit, and none of the schools in Division I-AA, Division II, and Division III make a profit from their athletic programs. All with few exceptions struggle to make revenues equal expenditures.

The schools in major conferences such as the Big Ten, Southeastern, Pacific 10, Southwest Conference, and Atlantic Coast share their television, bowl game, and postseason revenues with all schools in their conference, and the NCAA College Championship in Division I basketball television revenue is shared with the NCAA to pay for their administrative expenses. On the basis of shared revenue, most schools in those conferences are able to break even financially. A few make a profit, which is used as a reserve for lean years. The thing one needs to realize is that excess football and basketball revenues in most cases pay the expenses for athletic administration and anywhere from 14 to 24 or more men's and women's sports programs which produce little or no revenue.

The same critics feel that football and basketball revenues should be used to pay the football and basketball players. Where would the pay come from if their Division I basketball program or the Division I-A football program failed to produce a profit for the athletic department? Believe me, that happens to far more schools than schools where a profit is produced. What about the Division I and Division I-A schools which operate at a loss about 50% of the time? Do you pay the players only when the team makes money? How do you justify paying basketball and football players but not paying world-class athletes in track and field, tennis, swimming, and numerous other sports which do not produce revenue? What kind of price tag do you put on a college education? Over a lifetime a college education is worth many times the actual dollars paid for a college education.

I was athletic director at Baylor University, Florida State University, and University of New Mexico for 24 years. I estimate there were two years of ten years we made a profit of any significance at Baylor, two years of seven at Florida State, and one year of seven at the University of New Mexico. Only at New Mexico did basketball pay its way, and the profit in basketball was not nearly as much as most sportswriters and fans thought it was. Generating a profit of any significance four years out of 24 years is not very impressive. During the 24 years we basically broke even, but we really worked to generate revenue.

Even at Florida State since I left, the bowl games put them over the hump as far as making a profit was concerned, according to Florida State administrators I've talked to. Their expenditures on their intercollegiate athletic program have increased more than four-fold since I left. There are probably not five schools in the nation which can match their combined successes in football and basketball.

The fact is that the profits made by colleges and universities through their athletic programs are greatly exaggerated.

There is no question but that some college football coaches break the rules and are creative in getting devout fans and alumni to provide monetary and other illegal benefits to players. However, their numbers are *decreasing rapidly*. There will probably never be a time when there will be no cheating or breaking of the rules. Football is a game where the big winner gets most of the glory, recognition, and monetary rewards. It's very competitive, and there are many good players to recruit and many highly qualified coaches. The odds are there will always be a coach who will look for an edge even though there is much more emphasis on conforming to the rules. Such a coach is willing to risk his reputation and the integrity of the institution he represents.

There are times when cheating hurts a football coach more than it helps. A coach risks losing the respect and confidence of a number of his own players, especially those who have good character and high standards. A coach may make a mistake in judgment and provide a player who turns out to be not nearly as good a player as the coach thinks he will be. I remember a player in my class at Auburn who was receiving extra benefits. He turned out to be a poor football player, and most of the squad knew he was getting extra benefits. The player cheated in his schoolwork and cheated in his business after he left college. I liked him, but I didn't respect him. The players who do produce and are not getting extra benefits are turned off when they learn a person who turned out to be a failure in many aspects of his life was getting substantial illegal benefits.

Then there is always the chance that a coach will be caught cheating. The resultant investigation and daily media stories can greatly harm a coach's reputation. One almost universal response of a coach when he gets caught is, "Everybody cheats." Newspapers and other media will give full coverage to such statements. I strongly believe that is one of the primary reasons football fans, alumni, and sportswriters believe there is a great deal more cheating than actually occurs.

In addition to coaches who get caught saying "everybody cheats," athletes who receive extra benefits will make statements which condemn other institutions for offering similar excessive benefits. Thorough investigations reveal that their statements condemning other institutions are most often not true.

Read what longtime leaders in the NCAA say about the trend as far as colleges and universities living by NCAA rules and regulations.

David Caywood, the assistant executive director for communications of the NCAA, has been employed by the NCAA for 20 years. He is highly respected throughout the country for his honesty, his efficiency, and his straightforward approach to his duties and responsibilities as an officer of the NCAA. Here is his response to the progress made in compliance with NCAA rules and regulations by member institutions in the past 20 years: "The NCAA enforcement program has made significant progress over the past 20 years. Investigative techniques obviously have improved, but most of the progress is the result of the desire of the membership to demand integrity in college athletics. The enforcement program continues to be refined to meet the goal of the membership to ensure a level playing field for everyone. It is not uncommon for institutions to self-report violations or participate in the investigations of another institution. I firmly believe there are fewer intentional rules violations in college athletics now than ever before."

The factual information available is overwhelming in favor of more integrity and a marked improvement among Division I-A institutions in complying with NCAA rules and regulations. It's not something you will read about in the newspaper because the modern trend is for sportswriters to condemn college football as being very corrupt. Certainly, not all and perhaps not even the majority of sportswriters believe that college football is corrupt. The other advocates of corruption in college are coaches and athletes who have been found guilty of violating NCAA rules and regulations versus coaches and administrators who have been in college athletics for many years and believe in the integrity of college athletics on the basis of their own experience and the experiences of the many athletes they coached. To name a few such coaches are Darrell Royal of the University of Texas, Bobby Bowden of Florida State University, Frank Broyles of Arkansas, Paul Dietzel of LSU, Army and South Carolina, Charles McClendon of LSU, Grant Taeff of Baylor and now athletic director, Lavell Edwards of Brigham Young, Bill Walsh of Stanford University, Eddie Robinson of Grambling State University, among many others. Some of the athletic directors in Division I-A football whom I commend for integrity are Mike Lude of the University of Washington and presently Auburn University, Dr. Gary Cummingham, Fresno State University, Dr. Glenn Tuckett of Brigham Young University, Dr. Cedric Dempsey, University of Arizona, Tom Butters of Duke University, Vince Dooley, University of Georgia, Homer Rice of Georgia Tech, Doug Weaver of Michigan State, and Dr. Joe Kearney, commissioner of the Western

Athletic Conference and former athletic director of the University of Washington, Michigan State, and Arizona State.

A sports fan has the choice to believe known violators of NCAA rules and sportswriters who do their best to create scandals for the reading public, or believe men who have many years of experience in coaching and administrative roles in college athletics and whose reputations for integrity are above reproach.

I took actions to help insure that our coaches in all sports understood very explicitly that they were expected to know and abide by the rules and regulations of the NCAA. The NCAA required an annual NCAA rules review to be conducted by the CEO of each member institution or his designated representative, which is normally the athletic director. All coaches and all administrative personnel in the Athletic Department were required to certify in writing they had reviewed the NCAA rules. There are a great many rules, and they are not what you would call "light reading." If a coach was out of town and had a legitimate reason not to attend this review, we scheduled a make-up session. We assigned different coaches or administrative persons the responsibility to review specific sessions in the original and make-up sessions. The meeting lasted from three to four hours.

I started off the meeting by telling everyone it was their responsibility to know the rules and abide by them. They didn't have to agree whether a rule was a good rule or bad rule. It was their job to follow the rules.

I also told them that any violation of a major nature would result in my recommendation that the person violating the rules would be fired for cause. If they didn't believe me, I asked them to just test me and I would demonstrate I meant what I said. An employee fired for cause has no right regardless of his contract, and his employment ceases immediately. That's exactly what I told our coaches and administrative staff, and none of them ever tested me.

I also strongly urged them to ask questions if there was any doubt whatsoever that they might violate a rule. If a coach or administrator could not get a satisfactory answer within our staff, then we would make a long distance call to the NCAA office or in some cases to the conference office.

One time at Florida State I heard from a reliable source that a member of our football staff or members of the staff had made an illegal offer to a football player from Miami who ended up signing with an out-of-state university. I did not know what specific coach or coaches made the offer, but I called the entire coaching staff for a meeting. While the illegal benefit was offered, it was never made. I spoke very strongly to all the football coaches that we would not tolerate such tactics, and that I would recommend any coach involved in arranging illegal benefits to be fired. The head coach whom I believe knew about the proposed offer stood up and said, "John is right. I apologize to him that we even considered such an offer. I pledge to him and to all of you we will operate an honest program."

I don't know whether any illegal offers were ever made by that football staff again. I hope not and have no reason to believe that any additional such offers were made. None of that staff is presently at Florida State.

I believe that Coach Bobby Bowden and his staff have proven you can recruit excellent football players within the rules. In the last 11 bowl games Florida State has played, they have won 10 games and tied one with Georgia Tech. Florida State has the best bowl record of any Division I-A institution in the nation who have appeared in more than six bowl games.

Some other practices followed by many schools to discourage rules violations are as follows:

1. Put in writing in the coach's employment contract that if there is a major violation of rules, the coach will be dismissed and his contract is null and void (or similar language).
2. Many schools have a full-time compliance officer. It is his duty to see that each sport is in compliance regarding scholarship aid and NCAA rules reviews by players and coaches, and to make certain the university is conforming to all institutional, conference, and NCAA rules for eligibility in regular season as well as postseason participation.

After thirty-seven years of coaching and serving as an athletic director, it is my opinion that far too many college presidents and university administrators are not aware of the importance that alumni, prospective students, college students, and the general public place on having a good athletic program. Realizing this importance to such a large constituency of a university, a college president gives himself a better chance to enhance the educational programs of a university. A high percentage of financial benefactors to a university initially become interested in the university's athletic program.

Coaches and players should look upon the period players are in college and attending classes as a time of preparation for what comes after their undergraduate college years. The players can learn a great deal from their classes, but some of the most valuable lessons can be learned from their participation in football. The players can develop their skills in football, but as amateur players under NCAA rules they cannot expect to be paid according to their achievements. The same is true for every other sport sponsored by a college athletic program.

Their reward is in the satisfaction, friendships, achievements, and lifetime memories of their participation. In a relatively few cases, there is the opportunity to be rewarded financially in professional sports after their college sports participation has been completed.

For those who cannot wait for the financial rewards or cannot be content with the non-cash rewards, there is the great risk of disgrace, humiliation, and the prospect of losing more than they have gained during those difficult years of attending classes and tiring practices on the football field while in the process of acquiring knowledge, experience, and confidence to enable them to overcome handicaps and difficulties.

There have been many disciplined players who have earned and saved sufficient funds from summer and vacation jobs during the Christmas and spring holidays to meet their minimum needs not provided by their families or their scholarships. Among those included are players who received no financial assistance from their parents or other relatives.

A football scholarship in Division I-A football will take care of food, lodging, books and supplies, tuition and fees during the school year. For those who do not receive a scholarship or only a partial scholarship, they must get a part-time job. Dick Watts, one of my Johns Hopkins players, worked in a service station from 7:00 P.M. to 1:00 A.M. every night during the four years or more he attended Johns Hopkins, and yet competed successfully as a lacrosse player and football player, in addition to earning his degree.

In closing, I would like to summarize some of the things that are right and good about football at all levels of play — high school, college, and professional.

Football creates lifetime memories, and the good memories tend to outlast the bad. The game teaches lessons of sportsmanship, hard work, sacrifice, to keep trying regardless of the odds, of teamwork and what is possible through the human spirit. It stresses the importance of a strong body and excellent physical condition. Football can increase self-confidence and the added confidence can open up new vistas in one's life, such as education, leadership, and achievements in other areas unrelated to football. Through such organizations as the Fellowship of Christian Athletes, many football players have developed a more meaningful spiritual life. Football provides heroes to young people and role models that are lifetime inspirations. Participation results in great friendships and strong loyalties to teams, fellow teammates, and coaches. You can't find many former high school football players who do not believe their high school football coach wasn't one of the most influential persons in their life. Besides football's advantage to players, millions of people are entertained by the sport as football has become the most popular spectator sport for the American public.

Sure there are failures along the way and mistakes are made. But the good far outweighs the bad and the right far exceeds the wrong.

John Bridgers, author. Received Gilman Award at Johns Hopkins 1956–57, an annual award to a faculty member for outstanding contribution to student life. Elected to Baylor University Sports Hall of Fame after 10 years as Baylor athletic director and head football coach. Elected to Florida State University Sports Hall of Fame after seven years as athletic director, and named to National Association of Collegiate Directors of Athletics Hall of Fame after serving seven and one-half years as athletic director at the University of New Mexico.

Burt Reynolds — well-known actor who played football at Florida State University as a halfback — receives awards from mayor of Tallahassee at halftime of Florida State football game. At far left Dr. Steve McClellon, vice-president at Florida State, and far right John Bridgers. Others in picture were members of Burt Reynolds' traveling party.

Above: Coach Bobby Bowden head football coach, Florida State University, 1976 to present (1994). Only college coach to win 10 or more games for eight consecutive years. In the past eight years Florida State has ranked in top four teams in the nation with a No. 1 ranking and national championship in 1993. FSU has averaged 9.3 wins per year in Bowden's 19 years as head coach at Florida State. His bowl record in the past 13 years at Florida State is 12–1–0. He has the most bowl wins of any head coach in history of football — 16.

Below: Coach Joe Morrison head coach University of New Mexico 1980–1982. He had 10–1 season with New Mexico in 1982, the only season in New Mexico's history to win 10 games. While head coach at University of South Carolina for six years 1983–1988 he went to three bowl games before dying of a heart attack in early 1989. Morrison played 14 years with the New York Giants and stood out as a ball carrier and pass receiver.

Top: John Unitas — QB (6'1, 190), Baltimore Colts, 1956–1972. Named by *Pro Football News* as the "Best Ever" QB in tie with Otto Graham and Joe Montana. Led Baltimore Colts to World Championships in 1958 and 1959 and Baltimore to the best record of any professional team in the sixties.

Bottom: Gino Marchetti (6'4, 250), defensive end, Baltimore Colts, 1953–1964. Rated by many as "Best Defensive End Ever." His quickness, speed and technique made it almost impossible for one blocker to keep him from getting to the quarterback. Played football at University of San Francisco after serving as combat infantryman in World War II.

Top photo: Raymond Berry (6'2, 182), Baltimore Colts 1955–67. Played football at SMU 1953–1955 and was late draft choice by Baltimore in 1955. When he retired he had caught more passes (631) for more yardage (9,275) than any receiver in history of NFL. May have best hands of any receiver in professional football. Caught 68 touchdown passes; his average games played per year was a little less than 12 (11.8). If he had played 16 games per year, which is the regular season schedule now in NFL, his records might still stand.
Bottom left and right: Vick Costellos (5'11, 175), guard, Auburn University 1940-42. Captain of 1942 Auburn team that upset number-one ranked University of Georgia, which defeated California in Rose Bowl and ended up as number one. Vick Costellos was one of the finest leaders on and off the football field that I've ever known.

Above: Lawrence Elkins, Baylor's All-American pass receiver in 1963–1964 is shown going high for a pass reception between three SMU defenders in a 1964 game against SMU in Dallas. The Bears overcame a 10–0 SMU lead to win 16–13. Elkins scored the last 8 points on a TD catch from Southall and then Southall threw to Elkins for the 2-pointer.

Bottom: Jim Parker (6'3, 275), offensive tackle and guard, 1957–1970. Rated as best offensive lineman in history of NFL by many. Outstanding pass blocker and run blocker. All-American at Ohio State. From his rookie year as first-round draft choice until he retired, Parker was outstanding.

Above: Lawrence Elkins — Baylor wide receiver (1962–63–64). Consensus All-American at Baylor in 1963 and 1964. Broke All-Time NCAA record for pass receptions in 1963 with 70 in 10 games; caught seven in Bluebonnet Bowl victory over LSU in 1963. Caught 144 passes in three years of eligibility. Inducted into College Football Hall of Fame in 1994.

Below: Don Trull — Baylor QB in 1961–62–63. Led nation in pass completions in 1962 with 125 completions and in 1963 with 174 completions, becoming first passer to lead the nation in pass completions for two consecutive years since Davey O'Brien of TCU in 1936 and 1937. Trull led nation in touchdown production in 1963 with 10 touchdowns running and 12 touchdown passes. He was All-Southwest Conference in 1963 and made All-American mention on several All-American selections, although Roger Staubach was the consensus selection at QB in 1963.

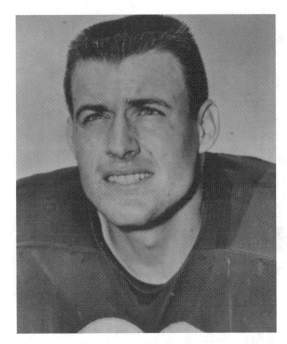

Left: Ronnie Bull (6'0), Baylor halfback and fullback, 1959 through 1961. Best all around back in author's 10 years at Baylor. All-Southwest Conference and All-American. No. 1 draft choice by Chicago Bears; NFL Rookie of Year with Chicago Bears in 1960 as offensive back.

Below: John Bridgers, author (with projector) with Colt defensive line reviewing an opponent's film in 1958. Left to right, Gino Marchetti, defensive end; Art Donovan, defensive tackle; Ordell Braase, defensive end; Ray Krouse, defensive tackle; Don Joyce, defensive end; and Eugene "Big Daddy" Lipscomb, defensive tackle.

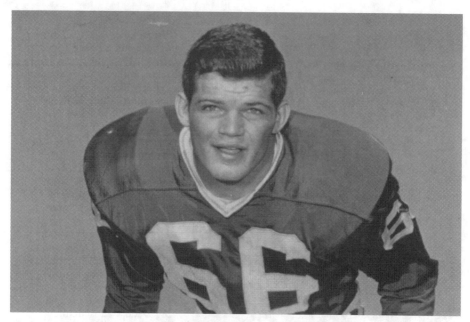

Upper: Herb Adkins — Baylor (1959-60-61). Played offensive and defensive guard, 3-year starter, All-Southwest Conference in 1961. More than held his own against much larger players (190 pounds). One of best competitors I've ever coached.
Lower: Mike Bourland — Baylor offensive guard (6'0, 197). All-Southwest Conference offensive guard for 1965, outstanding leader and excellent pass blocker. Co-captain of 1965 Baylor team.

Above: Tommy Smith (5'11, 175). Very disciplined pass receiver with great hands at Baylor. Did not have outstanding speed but ran excellent patterns and could catch almost any pass he could touch. In 1966 tied all-time record set by Lawrence Elkins of 12 catches in a single game with 12 catches against SMU in 1966. Named outstanding South Lineman in 1966 Blue-Gray All-Star Game when he was the game's leader in passes caught. Received master's in computer science after majoring in mathematics at Baylor. Now a property tax consultant in San Antonio.

Below: Greg Pipes (6'0, 235), Baylor 1965–1967 defensive tackle, had more ingredients for a great college defensive lineman than any I coached at Baylor — size, quickness, speed, strength, and spirit. All-Southwest Conference, 1st Team All-American on the American Football Coaches Association All-American team in 1967. All-Pro in Canadian Pro League. Received law degree from Baylor Law School; assistant attorney general in Fort Worth.

Above: Vaughan Mancha, University of Alabama center and linebacker (6'1½, 235). Four-year starter at Alabama 1944 through 1947; played in Rose Bowl and two Sugar Bowls. High school teammate of author at Ramsay High School, Birmingham. Voted to All-Time Sugar Bowl Team, Alabama Sports Hall of Fame, National Collegiate Football Hall of Fame, and Alabama's All-Century Team. 1st Team All-American.

Below: *Left:* Larry Littman (5'11, 175), center at Johns Hopkins 1956–58. Did not play high school football but started at center in 1956 as a sophomore with only previous experience on freshman football team in 1955. Played 60 minutes in last seven games of season. Owns manufacturing plant in Connecticut. *Right:* Frank Frenda (5'8, 180), guard, was a sophomore in 1956 and probably played more than any nonstarter. Became excellent lineman and started in 1957 and 1958.

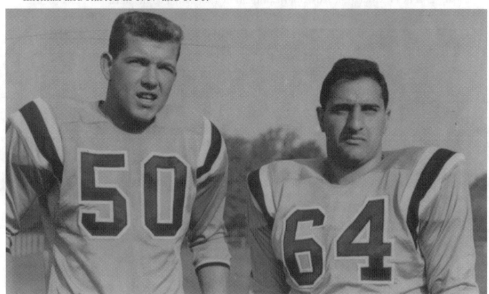

Ronnie Rogers (5'7, 185), Baylor University guard 1959–60–61. Extremely quick and strong. Consistently outplayed linemen opposite him with 15- to 65-pound weight advantage. Now an oral surgeon in Garland, Texas.

Dick Watts (5'11, 175), Johns Hopkins fullback and linebacker 1953 and 1954. Was a 22-year-old sophomore in 1953, married with a child, punter and leader of the team. Showed great determination to stay in school and earn his degree. Fulfilled his ambition to be a coach; coaching for 40 years (1955–1994).

Ordell Braase (6'4, 240), Baltimore Colts defensive end. Played 12 years in the NFL at right defensive end opposite Gino Marchetti at defensive left end. Selected to play in Pro Bowl games in 1966 and 1967 and was two-term president of the NFL Players Association.

Don Gallagher (6'2, 190), center and linebacker with Johns Hopkins University in 1954–55–56. A knee injury in the pre-season of 1956 prevented him from playing his senior year. Best linebacker in author's years at Johns Hopkins.

Kenneth McGraw, co-captain, Johns Hopkins 1956, 3-year starter at tackle, Little All-American, Williamson Rating System. First Team, 2nd Team Associated Press Little All-American. Played every second of every game — offense, defense, and special teams. Primary positions offensive and defensive tackle but filled in at center and linebacker when Don Gallagher, the other Hopkins co-captain, received a season-ending injury in a pre-season scrimmage. Honor graduate and received master's degree from Harvard Business School.

James Ingram (6'1, 185), wide receiver, Baylor, 1961–1963. Excellent hands and ran precise patterns. Clutch receiver — caught winning touchdowns in last few minutes in 1961 as we nosed out Pittsburgh 16–13; against Texas Tech caught two TD passes in last 6 minutes to give Baylor 21–17 victory and two TD catches against LSU in fourth quarter to edge LSU 14–7 in 1963 Bluebonnet Bowl game.

Above: Reed Bell (5'9, 180). Sewanee fullback 1946–47–48. 2nd team Little All-American Associated Press in 1948. Co-captain of Sewanee in 1948. Excellent linebacker, blocker, and strong runner. Phi Beta Kappa and became an M.D. specializing in pediatrics. His vision and leadership led to an outstanding children's hospital in Pensacola, Florida, his hometown.

Below: Bob Snell (6'1, 200). Sewanee tackle 1946 through 1949. Was a 4-year starter and captain of Sewanee team in 1949. Had physical attributes to play at higher level — excellent strength and speed. Attended School of Theology and served 39 years as Episcopal minister.

Above: Jim Elam (6'1, 195), Sewanee tackle 1950–51–52. Came as freshman in 1949 and became starting tackle in 1950, 1951, and 1952. Was captain in 1952 and was selected on *Look*'s Little All-American Team. Top student, named to Phi Beta Kappa at Sewanee. John Bridgers was line coach in 1950 and 1951.

Right: Bill Austin (5'11, 195), guard, Sewanee. Explosive sprinter and weight man on track team. Graduated magna cum laude from Sewanee and received academic scholarship for graduate study at Harvard. Set record for most points scored in Track and Field at Sewanee. Outstanding lineman in football. Now owns a successful insurance business in Jacksonville, FL.

Above: Milt Holstein (5'5, 155). Starting guard at Johns Hopkins University for three years (1956–57–58). Was co-captain at Hopkins in 1958. Despite lack of size was a consistent and determined performer who was inspirational to his teammates and coaches.

Right: Charles Lindsay (5'11, 175), Sewanee center and linebacker. Three-year starter, captain of Sewanee team in 1953. Phi Beta Kappa, awarded Danford Graduate Fellowship, Fulbright Scholar at University of Paris, France, Sullivan Award as outstanding senior graduate at Sewanee. Now professor of mathematics at Coe College in Iowa. Received Ph.D. in mathematics at Vanderbilt University.

Jim Ed Mulkin (5'5, 139), Sewanee halfback in 1948 through 1951. Quick, deceptive runner, outstanding on punt and kickoff returns. 1st team Little All-American in 1951; Phi Beta Kappa; captain of 1951 Sewanee team.

Mickey Kennedy (6'0), Baylor guard and defensive tackle. Transferred from offensive guard to defensive tackle in last four games of senior year (1964) averaging 14 tackles a game. Had remarkable instinct to make tackle. Graduated with 3.91 average, (4.0 point grading system)highest average of any male graduate at Baylor in class of 1965 (Salutatorian). Has Ph.D. and heads History Department at Winthrop University in South Carolina.

 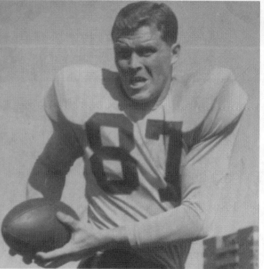

Top photo: Seniors on Johns Hopkins Mason-Dixon Conference championship team. Front row from left to right: Jerry Carr, blocking back; Ken McGraw, left tackle; Don Gallagher, co-captain and center; and John Bridgers, head coach. Back row, Clark Tankersley, guard; Don Macaulay, right tackle; John Ustach, tackle; Ben Civiletti, right end; Sam Wright, right guard; and Bob Edwards, left end.

Bottom left: Ernie Bates (6'0, 175), fullback, Johns Hopkins 1956–57. Scored winning TD when Johns Hopkins defeated Western Maryland 7–0 in our final game in 1956 to cinch the Mason-Dixon Conference Championship. First black player to play football at Johns Hopkins. Became a brain surgeon in San Francisco.

Bottom right: Benjamin R. Civiletti (6'1, 187), end, Johns Hopkins 1954–56. Was outstanding defensively. Blocked punt and was able to pick up ball and run for a touchdown for first score against Western Maryland in 1955, which led to a 33–0 win. After graduation from law school later served as U.S. attorney general under President Jimmy Carter. Now an outstanding attorney in Baltimore.

INDEX

Sonny, 137-138, 139
Tom, 220
William E. "Bud," 292, 308-309,
   310, 312, 313, 316, 331, 333, 334
D-Day invasion, 7
Defee, Richard, 162, 168, 169, 170, 172
Defensive Player of the Year, 93
Delta Sigma Pi, 13
Dempsey, Cedric, 352
Denard, Richard, 189
Denver Broncos, 118, 134, 137, 144,
   145, 159
Desert Storm, 224
Detroit Lions, 91-92, 99, 103, 109, 118
Dickinson, 52, 58, 67, 68, 70
Dietzel, Paul, 138, 153, 268, 269-272,
   282, 352
Disneyland, 139
Doak Campbell Stadium, 40, 293
Dogins, Littrell, 29
Dolensky, Allen, 324
Donovan, Arthur, 54, 80, 83, 89, 106,
   107, 131
   Hal, 327, 329, 337
Dooley, Vince, 352
Dotson, Bill, 312
Drexel Tech, 68
Dreyfus, Lee S., 346
Driver, Charley, 135
drop back passing game, 82, 98, 123,
   147, 173-182, 276
Dublin, Texas, 196
Duke University, 271
Dunn, Joe Lee, 321-322
Dupre, L. G., 89, 132
Durbin, Charley, 285
Durham, Hugh, 292, 311
Dye, Pat, 290, 299-300

E
Eagle defense, 242
Earl Blaik Fellowship, 222
East-West All-Star game, 228, 233
Edwards, Bob, 55, 57, 65-66
   Lavell, 82-83, 352
   Roy, 269
eight-man front, 207-209
84th Field Artillery Battalion, 2
Eisenhart, Jack, 168

Eisenhower, Dwight, 53
   Milton, 53
Elam, Jim, 37-38
Elgin High School, 252
Elkins, Lawrence, 115, 146, 149, 150,
   159, 160, 161, 162, 163, 172, 215,
   220, 221, 223-230, 247, 263-264,
   347, 348
Ellenberger, Norm, 308-309, 323, 324,
   331, 333-334
Ellisor, Don, 189
Elway, John, 124
Enforcement Summary, viii
Epilepsy Association, 223
Erwin, Jim, 139
Escambia County Medical Society, 33
Estes, Linda, 312, 323-324, 336-339
Evans, Jim, 137, 139, 241
Ewbank, Weeb, 25, 26, 78-81, 95, 96,
   98, 99, 102, 107, 108, 122, 124,
   126, 127, 129-130, 133, 210, 297

F
Farer, Tom, 321-322, 327, 329, 334,
   341-343
Fayetteville, Tennessee, 45
FBI, 296, 308
Fellowship of Christian Athletes, 118,
   167, 223, 245-246, 254, 258, 280,
   356
Ferguson, Bill, 163
Fewster, Wilson, 54, 71
Ficca, Dan, 241
Fidelity Union Life Insurance
   Company, 193
5th Cavalry Regiment, 29
1st Cavalry Division, 28
Fitzgerald, Joe, 119
Flatow, Max, 318
Florence, Alabama, 29
Florida Flambeau, 285-286
Florida Pediatric Society, 33
Florida State, 27, 36, 40, 42, 43, 166,
   173, 182, 187, 188, 205, 255, 257,
   271, 272, 273, 274, 275, 282-306,
   311, 313, 336, 339, 350, 354
Florida State Athletic Hall of Fame,
   293, 295
Florida State College for Women, 298
Flynn, Alvin, 189, 190